College Organization and Professional Development

A thought-provoking textbook written for Higher Education and Student Affairs Masters and PhD programs, *College Organization and Professional Development* focuses on the framing of critical issues in organizational practice, the gaps between moral beliefs and actions, and improving equity within organizations. This breakthrough text seeks to revolutionize how we understand ethical practice. It can be used as a text in Organization, Leadership, and Professional Practice courses seeking to integrate moral leadership and reflective practice. Unlike the majority of Organization textbooks currently available, which lack a social-contextual understanding of moral issues and social justice, this text encourages the use of action research to inform and support change in professional practice.

Readers will find the pedagogical exercises useful for reflecting on goals, examining practices, and testing new intervention methods. Reflective assignments are suggested for readers to help them engage in a process of reflective analysis of professional practice.

This book can also be used in graduate programs across professional fields including Educational Administration and Business. Practicing professionals and academics who wish to reflect on the gaps between their moral values and their actions in work situations will find this text informative and useful. The chapters include fundamental and insightful guidance for reflection on the topics raised and discussed.

Edward P. St. John is Algo D. Henderson Collegiate Professor of Education at the University of Michigan's Center for the Study of Higher and Postsecondary Education.

College Organization and Professional Development

Integrating Moral Reasoning and Reflective Practice

Edward P. St. John

Algo D. Henderson Collegiate Professor,
Center for the Study of Higher and
Postsecondary Education,
University of Michigan

Routledge
Taylor & Francis Group

NEW YORK AND LONDON

First published 2009
by Routledge
270 Madison Ave, New York, NY 10016

Simultaneously published in the UK
by Routledge
2 Park Square, Milton Park, Abingdon, Oxon OX14 4RN

Routledge is an imprint of the Taylor & Francis Group, an informa business

© 2009 Taylor & Francis

Typeset in Minion by Swales & Willis Ltd, Exeter, Devon
Printed and bound in the United States of America on acid-free paper by
Edwards Brothers, Inc.

Library of Congress Cataloging-in-Publication Data
St. John , Edward P.
College organization and professional development : integrating moral reasoning
and reflective practice / by Edward P. St. John
    p. cm.
  Includes bibliographical references and index.
  1. College administrators—Professional ethics.   2. Universities and colleges—
Moral and ethical aspects.   3. Universities and colleges—Administration.
  I. Title.
  LB2341.S74 2009
  378.1′01—dc22
                                                        2008039577

ISBN10: 0–415–99211–7 (hbk)
ISBN10: 0–415–99212–5 (pbk)
ISBN10: 0–203–88166–4 (ebk)

ISBN13: 978–0–415–99211–4 (hbk)
ISBN13: 978–0–415–99212–1 (pbk)
ISBN13: 978–0–203–88166–8 (ebk)

CONTENTS

TEXT BOXES, FIGURES, AND TABLES

Text Boxes

Figures

Tables

gap is essential in democratic societies, given the reliance on professional expertise. I encourage professors to engage in the redesign of their education programs to integrate and emphasize methods to reduce this gap. This moral responsibility has been integral to professional education since its origins, as the legend of Socrates conveys in such a compelling way. The purposes of *College Organization and Professional Development* are to stimulate an informed dialogue about moral reasoning in the professions and encourage the redesign of graduate education in ways that move ethics and moral reasoning to the forefront. However, it may be even more important for senior professionals to ponder their roles within their organizations than it is for professors to redesign their educational programs. The core chapters of this book encourage introspection by providing guidance for reflection as part of framing questions and searching for solutions. Practitioners who read this text and engage in introspection about the questions raised should have a better basis for developing their own interventions within their communities of practice. As the questioning embedded in the legend of Socrates reminds us, we all bear responsibility for integrating our reason and values into our actions.

The primary topic of this book—moral reasoning in professional practice—has long been central to academe. From the Dark Ages through the early Enlightenment, academe was largely dominated by religion-centric moral reasoning. As Charles Taylor documents in *A Secular Age*, the transition from religion-centric education in the sixteenth century to contemporary modernism was a gradual process. By the late nineteenth century the academy had made the transition to modern science and secular functionalist reasoning. While there was a tension between religion and science, there was a general consensus about social and economic progress that held up in the discourse within democratic societies through most of the twentieth century.

In my view, the gulf between religion and academic thought has now become seriously problematic. In this global period of economic development, the notions of markets and individual rights have prevailed over social justice. Democratic societies have failed to define a common set of basic standards of human capabilities that should be extended to all, although fortunately Martha Nussbaum has encouraged us to do so. The fracture between the economic reasoning of globalization and the social good necessary to sustain the globe and achieve justice within our human societies requires reconciliation so that just practitioners can learn from experience when their actions fall short of their values. On the one hand, when people divorce their faith and moral beliefs from their education and their daily work it is easy to act in ways that create a gap between espoused values and action. On the other hand, subjugating moral judgment to faith is even more problematic. In this book, I argue that we need to create discursive space for introspection on values—religious and secular—when we encounter problematic situations in practice. Academics need this space in their discourses on their educational programs. More practitioners in all professions also need discursive space when critical problems arise (i.e. the recurrent issues that cause the gap between our shared values and the courses of action we follow). Creating such discursive space may add to the ambiguity, at least initially, but open exchange provides means of reducing the gap by creating the space to discuss underlying issues. Since the process of inner reconciliation has persevered and has been conveyed within our faith traditions, we should not ignore this preserved knowledge and wisdom in an attempt to redesign and create new forms of action in troubling situations for professional practice.

The most widely referenced theory of moral development—Lawrence Kohlberg's developmental model—does not work well as a framework for professional education. His theory of moral development is situated in Jean Piaget's theory of childhood development, but uses moral philosophy as a basis for the higher stages. This creates two problems for professional education. By the time people enter college as young adults they have reached a level of maturity that extends beyond the utility of the theory. Most college students have attained Kohlberg's Stage 3 or Stage 4—what he refers to as conventional moral reasoning. Indeed, they have already matured through the underlying development sequences of childhood. Kohlberg's postconventional stages are situated in moral philosophy, with Stage 5 situated in institutional reasoning (e.g. religion) and Stage 6 framed by universal values (e.g. enlightenment). While both enlightenment- and faith-based values are important sources for reflection in problematic situations, the philosophies themselves do not provide the basis for situated action. Rather, it is reflection on the meaning of the message and the implications of values that provide the insights to help us solve problems. There is usually a great deal of moral ambiguity in problematic social situations, so it is important to ponder consequences of actions from different vantages.

To work through the situated nature of moral problems in practice, I turned to the fields of action science (especially the works of Chris Argyris and Donald Schön) and critical theory (especially Jurgen Habermas). Argyris and Schön introduce a way of thinking about gaps between theory and action that can be applied to values in action situations. Habermas, in his critiques of Kohlberg's theory, reveals the importance of retaining distinctions between preconventional moral reasoning (i.e. acting in ways that are problematic), conventional reasoning in action (i.e. acting in ways consonant with rules of practice and ethical codes), and postconventional moral reasoning in action (i.e. publicly pondering why problems exist in the first place and envisioning new solutions to test). This way of framing moral reasoning in action is extremely helpful in attempts to redesign professional education in order to achieve an integration of moral reasoning.

A related problem is that while childhood development is not central to moral reasoning in professional education, we still need some sort of developmental lens. In this book, I use Karl Jung's theory of individuation as a basis for rethinking maturation in adulthood, as I did in *Action, Reflection, and Social Justice: Integrating Moral Reasoning into Professional Development*. Not only has Jung's notion of midlife transition been central to most theories of adult life phases (e.g. early adulthood, midlife transition, and late career), but it captures the inner and outer aspects of change during adulthood. His notions give us a framework for thinking about individuation, even though his work is legitimately vulnerable to criticism from the Judaic moral frame. In this book, I further decouple the idea of maturation during adulthood from the practice of moral reasoning, as a way through the puzzling aspects of Jung's theory. Both young people and senior citizens can act in nefarious or moral ways, follow organizational rules (e.g. policies, regulations, and ethical codes) as they understand them, or engage in discourse about whether the rules address critical challenges that emerge. Maturation is integral to professional development and expertise, but moral reasoning is not entirely dependent on age. Jung tended to divorce inner development from social responsibility during adulthood; this is a fracture of logic and values that we can no longer tolerate if we are to find ways of reconciling action with justice in troubling situations. The moral and Gayle Lazard were among the students at the University of New Orleans who challenged me by asking thoughtful questions and trying out new approaches to practice. Students at Indiana University who were great to work with on these topics include Kimberly Kline, Glenda Musoba, Eric Love, Debra Gentry, Stacey Jacob, and Pauline Reynolds.

Finally and not least, a very special thank you to Phyllis Kreger Stillman, the technical editor with whom I have worked closely throughout the process of writing this book. My editorial skills are far from perfect. I have appreciated Phyllis's patience on this and other writing projects.

INTRODUCTION

Although ethical and moral problems abound in the practice of all professions, from sexual misconduct of clergy (Revell, 2006) to providing misinformation on weapons of mass destruction before the Gulf War (McClellan, 2008), the role of moral reasoning in the daily lives of professionals receives too little attention. The actions of professionals (e.g. doctors, lawyers, teachers, consultants, and professors) manifest the moral ethos of democratic societies. The codes of ethics for the professions frequently emphasize service to the poor (e.g. pro bono work in law, the Hippocratic Oath in medicine, etc.), yet social justice seldom prevails within contemporary global society. The failure to integrate moral reasoning into professional action as common practice harks back to the failure of professional education to address the challenge.

Social inequality and injustice are not new. The emphasis on public charity, common in public life in the nineteenth century, although commendable was inadequate relative to the severe injustices of the period (Katz, 2001). Professional education in fields other than the education of teachers and clergy emerged in the late nineteenth century (Thelin, 2004) and most professions adopted concepts of charity as core values. The social progressive movement gained momentum in the early twentieth century with regulation of railroads and other progressive reforms. Early social welfare programs emerged in response to the Great Depression of the 1930s and as part of the War on Poverty in the 1960s, but this commitment waned by century's end. Inequality grew once again as a consequence of decline in social programs. For example, college enroll-ment rates among high school graduates were nearly equal, proportionally, for African-Americans, Whites, and Hispanics in the 1970s, a period when educational programs promoted equal opportunity. The subsequent decline in educational opportunity and social welfare hastened the growth of inequality once again in the late twentieth century.

It is time for reflection on social responsibility within professions and to reconsider how moral reasoning can be integrated into professional practice through reform in the education of professionals and interventions in communities of practice. Regardless of the reasons for growing inequalities and injustices in Western civilization—whether due to changes in political ideologies (Huber & Stephens, 2001) or to economics (B. M. Friedman, 2005) as have been variously argued—professionals of all types are increasingly confronted by inequality. Professionals can either overlook these problems by engaging in business as usual or place a greater emphasis on addressing critical social challenges they encounter. Such choices are made tacitly and routinely every day by professionals in every line of practice.

Differences in values often complicate efforts to address inequalities in accessing education and health care, for example. Differences in values likewise complicate efforts by professionals in other fields to address critical social challenges. The legally mandated remedies to racial inequality resulting from decades of litigation (e.g. *Brown v. Board of Education*, 1954) did not resolve racial inequality: Schools were more segregated in the late 1990s than in the early 1950s (Orfield & Eaton, 1997).[1] At present, radically different notions of the "public good"—the definitions of fairness in education and employment—are held by liberals and social conservatives (Pasque, 2007). While it is easy to attribute such divisiveness to modern times, such tensions are hardly new. Antagonisms over beliefs and values of reformers have been evident since the emergence of enlightened thought which accompanied the development of democracies in the late eighteenth and early twentieth centuries (B. M. Friedman, 2005; Habermas, 2003). The progressive values of the period were in conflict with the then dominant religious traditions in which education was situated at the time (Thelin, 2004).[2]

Part of the problem is that action frequently falls short of espoused beliefs. Both faith traditions and enlightenment values emphasize social justice, so there is consonance on central values even though there is not consensus on many social issues. Since the values related to social justice are evident on both sides of secular and religious divisions, focusing on reducing the gap between values and action offers one piece of the puzzle regardless of the stances people take on these grand issues. The core values of charity and justice for the poor are evident in Judaism, Christianity, and Islam (Heft, 2004), just as they are in social democratic thought (Habermas, 2003; Nussbaum, 2004; Rawls, 2001). The tensions between faith and secular principles of social justice—along with conflicts between and within faith traditions—are poor excuses for the failures of teachers, doctors, lawyers, consultants, and other professionals to integrate an emphasis on social values and moral reasoning into their daily practices.

There are swings between the dominance of religious evangelism and egalitarianism in the public sphere (Fogel, 2000; Taylor, 2007), but such episodes in the public discourse and in legislation should not deter professionals from acting with care and justice. The fact that actions often fall short of the espoused values within professional organizations should not be overlooked in the midst of ideological, faith-based, and political conflicts. Finding ways to remedy this core problem—the gaps between beliefs and actions—remains critical in daily interactions between professionals and their clients (e.g. doctors and patients, teachers and students, lawyers and litigants). Since most professionals work and serve clients as practitioners within organizations (e.g. doctors in medical practices, professors in universities, engineers within firms, and so forth), it is also important to consider the role of organizations in promoting social justice and perpetuating inequalities.

REDUCING THE GAP BETWEEN ACTIONS AND BELIEFS

The primary aim of this book is to address the challenge of integrating moral reasoning into professional education and the professions. It is written as a text for aspiring professionals and can be used as an integral part of graduate courses on organizations, leadership, ethics, and moral reasoning. It can also be used by practicing professionals— women and men at different stages in their careers—as a guide for reflecting on gaps between their moral values and their actions in work situations. The reflective case studies included in this volume can be used for both purposes. The chapters include guidance for reflection on the topics raised and discussed.

This book further develops and extends methods of teaching and intervention originally developed and tested in *Action, Reflection, and Social Justice: Integrating Moral Reasoning into Professional Development* (St. John, 2009). This recent book used action inquiry to build new understandings by:

- rethinking Argyris and Schön's theory of professional effectiveness (1974, 1996) based on teaching experiments using their methods;
- adapting Karl Jung's theory of individuation during adulthood (1968, 1971, 1984) based on analyses of graduate students' reflective essays on leadership development;
- using Habermas's (1985, 1987, 1991) theory of communicative action as a lens for studying interventions in elementary schools that use an inquiry-based reform model to support teachers;
- reconceptualizing Kohlberg's (1981, 1984) theory of moral development based on introspections of critics of the theory (partially reviewed above) and an interpretive analysis of the Synoptic Gospels (Matthew, Mark, and Luke);[3]
- formulating a set of reconstructed understandings of action inquiry and further testing these notions in interventions within collaborating colleges and universities.

The five new understandings provide the points of departure for this book. My focus on moral reasoning in adulthood provides a basis for addressing the critical social challenges[4] in professional practice. The understandings reached from this set of inquiries focus on reconciling the tension between the application of professional expertise and introspection on critical social challenges that emerge as part of a practice.

First, "individual professionals—not their professors or interventionists—are responsible for the moral centering of their own actions" (St. John, 2009, p. 17). Students, along with new, mid-career, and mature professionals bear the responsibility for their own actions. Learning about this core aspect of moral responsibility represents a critical challenge for all professionals and should be an integral part of professional education as well as interventions by professionals.

Professors whose teaching helps prepare beginning professionals bear a responsibility to their students for encouraging them to center their judgments in moral reasoning, rather than to merely rely on and follow the rules—the knowledge, skills, and methods—of their professions. Placing professional rules above moral reasoning within professional education sets the stage for, and even tacitly validates, behaviors among professionals that perpetuate moral and ecological problems and social injustice. It is important to value both moral reasoning and the rules of the profession, rather than letting one dominate the other.

Using this approach, the moral and professional obligations of interventionists—external consultants who facilitate organizational change—in challenging professional situations shift from recommending and rationalizing solutions to encouraging and enabling client groups to learn for themselves how to address organizational challenges. This moves professional action from prescriptive instrumental strategies (i.e. setting out steps to be followed) to communicative action (i.e. encouraging moral reasoning that promotes the *social good*[5] as a part of practice).

Second, "moral development in adulthood involves centering one's self in the ethics of both justice and care. Professionals of all types bear responsibility for their own moral development as professionals—a lifelong task" (St. John, 2009, p. 18). Justice in the professions is often objectified as a set of ethical standards. This form of reasoning deemphasizes the social good, especially in relation to fair and socially just practice, in favor of a specified set of rules of practice. Based on my experience with action studies in professional education and interventions in educational organizations, I concluded these rational concepts must be balanced with care. My argument is that professionals should reflect on and discuss the moral consequences of their practices, including the ways the rules—the assumptions, knowledge, and methods that comprise expert knowledge and skills—of their professions should be interpreted in critical situations. Graduate school in the disciplines[6] and other forms of professional education should enable students to build an understanding of the ways their own value traditions, whether based on faith or social justice, relate to their professions and their practice as professionals. I argue for balancing justice and care in making professional judgments.

Third, "there are gaps between the espoused theories of practice held by most professionals and their actions as practitioners. Learning how to engage in practices that reduce these gaps is crucial to professional development and moral consciousness" (St. John, 2009, p. 19). Argyris and Schön (1974) provide an approach to this problem. Their theory of professional effectiveness distinguishes espoused theories of action from theories in use. They argue that the gap is universally evident: Most people demonstrate a pattern of rationalizing, but that pattern can be overcome through intervention, action science (Argyris, 1993), or reflective practice (Schön, 1987). In my experience with graduate education and educational interventions, along with my own introspections on faith, I frequently find gaps between beliefs and action: They seem to be part of human nature (St. John, 2009). Not only do rationalization processes run the risk of dividing truth from practice (Habermas, 2003), but the resolution of gaps between espoused beliefs and action involves inner personal growth, a process often referred to as *individuation*. Habermas (1996) recognizes the roles of introspection and religion in this process, but he places religion in a subordinate role to theory: "As long as no better words for what religion can say are found in the medium of rational discourse, it will even coexist abstemiously with the former, neither supporting nor combating it" (p. 145).

My argument is that, when confronted by morally problematic situations, we can use reason and values (i.e. critical and spiritual reflection) to ponder why the problems exist in the first place. The religious traditions and moral philosophy provide bases for introspection on just and caring practice, and are part of the process of reducing gaps between espoused (or rationalized) notions and the truth of action (what really happens). Both the religious traditions and the principles of care and justice can be treated as sources of introspection about critical social situations rather than as rigid rules of practice that can end up undermining reason and denying care.

Fourth, "human development through adulthood creates opportunities for professional growth and potential for conscious action, especially if the inherent sequence of learning about self and practice is realized and acted upon" (St. John, 2009, p. 20). There are distinctions among the primary tasks of professionals across periods in the professional development process: beginning professionals focus on mastery of the knowledge and skills of their profession (i.e. learning the rules); mid-career professionals often strive for excellence in practice while also building and supporting a practice that could involve other professionals (i.e. taking on managerial responsibilities); and late-career professionals are more likely to shift their focus to the meaning of work, mentoring, and the well-being of professional organizations and the communities they serve. This cycle corresponds with the maturation process during adulthood, or individuation.

Whether professionals stay on one narrow career path, shift careers, or come to their professions in midlife, the life cycle can play a role in building understanding of problematic situations and possible methods of resolving them. The individual's stage in adult life and her understanding of her profession—acquired through experience—are sources of unique insights into practice and the imagination of the possible. Across her life cycle, these insights and the ability to speak of justice and care can change and mature. The understandings discovered in this inner process of development, especially the ability to voice insights and understandings of replicating patterns, are essential to organizational development in professional communities.

Professional organizations are frequently experienced by professionals as communities of practitioners who work in groups (e.g. departments, committees, teams, workgroups, etc.) to solve problems. The insights and discoveries that come through the processes of engagement in teamwork, along with the maturation of individuals and their ability to illuminate patterns of injustice, provide a diversity of insights and voices that can pinpoint underlying causes of problems that emerge in practice, as well as be a source of inspiration and imagination to resolve these problems in new ways. Using action inquiry as a method can bring these inner human resources into the problem solving process, but method (i.e. another set of rules) does not replace the need for reflection, introspection, insight, imagination, and communication. The steps in action inquiry provide a guide to assist with the process, acting as another set of methods for practice.

Fifth, postconventional moral reasoning involves critical and spiritual reflection on morally problematic situations, along with testing strategies that might transform these situations. Sharing insights into the source of problems is necessary, but it is not a sufficient method for resolving critical problems. Moral learning involves building understanding within communities of practice about the way patterns of practice can cause injustice within the community and for the constituents being served, and methods of intervening to resolve these challenges. For individuals, the ability to engage in and foster these processes may coincide with the professional development cycle and maturation during adulthood.

For beginning professionals, the underlying causes of problems are not always visible or foremost in their minds. Their focus is usually on learning the rules of the profession, rather than reflecting on underlying problematic patterns in relation to their own actions. Early in a career, these problems within a practice may be hard to see or understand, even if the profession focuses on revolving social problems. Counselors, ministers, and interventionists of all types must learn about their professions through experience, testing assumptions formed in graduate education as they refine their practice. Like other professionals, they face the plights of discovering and building understanding of how their own actions and rationalizations contribute to, or even cause, critical social problems. As individuals mature, they may find such insights easier to discover, particularly if they have focused on such matters through their careers. That said, beginning professionals who feel called to their work based on inner ideals are often the most acutely aware of injustices (especially in fields related to client services). However, they may not understand the recurrent cycles of ordinary problem resolution within practice. Beginning professionals should be encouraged to voice their concerns, while their experienced colleagues should provide insights into pathways toward their resolution. Thus, the moral learning process in organizations involves both new and experienced practitioners addressing critical social challenges within communities of practice.

Diversity of peoples, religions, and voices complicates efforts to maintain just practices. Even if people intend to practice in ways consistent with the ethical codes of their professions—and unfortunately this is not always the case—gaps develop between intent and action. If, as it seems, it is a common tendency for people to overlook problems to which they contribute, then creating an open dialogue about the causes of critical social challenges within professional organizations is a recurrent challenge. Without interventions by internal practitioners or external interventionists, problematic patterns cause injustices to fester and replicate. Postconventional moral reasoning in professional practice involves engaging in efforts to illuminate and resolve these recurrent problems; such are processes that foster moral learning.

ORGANIZATIONS AND PROFESSIONAL PRACTICE

A secondary aim of this book is to provide a context for understanding the relationships between professional action and the strategic orientation of organizations that engage in professional service (e.g. education, research, healing, designing, building, etc.). Professionals work within their communities of practice as subunits of larger organizations. Very often sole practitioners (e.g. lawyers, doctors, counselors, etc.) build skills within a professional organization as early career professionals and/or provide services to organizations as well as to individuals. Thus, a focus on organizations helps build an understanding of the context of professional development and reflective practice. It also permits the exploration of organizational responses to critical social issues—ranging from the development of ethical standards to the transformation of organizations as they address new legal standards from legislation, voter initiatives, or court decisions—as an integral part of the context of reflective practice and moral reasoning.

Viewing organizations in their social contexts—the perspective provided by the sociology of organizations—is an appropriate vantage point for starting the task of building an understanding of the role of organizations in relation to professional development. Sociologists who crafted the base theories of organization and society, from Max Weber to Talcott Parsons, viewed organizations from within, and as influenced by, society and social evolution.[7] Weber (1948) observed the early formation of bureaucratic organizations and, interestingly, pointed out both the advances in rationalization of society made by this form of organization and the problems with such rationalizations. For example, while he coined the term *bureaucracy*, Weber noted the limitations of the organizational form. Ironically, most modern organizational theorists overlook Weber's critical analyses, instead coupling their critiques of bureaucratic organization with critiques of Weber (e.g. Bolman & Deal, 1996). Since professionals work in rule-bound organizations that are—at least in part—bureaucratic, we should not overlook these roots.

Parsons (1960) developed theories of organization and society that are still influential today. He considered the experiences of people within societies and organizations (the *lifeworld*). He viewed these in relation to the structure of society (the *systemic*) as an aspect of organization. Centrally controlled strategies can have a substantial influence on professional practice (Gumport, 2000). For example, college faculties have been referred to as *managed professionals* (Rhoades, 1998). My argument is that this concept of organization and practice overlooks the way professions can adapt based on an introspective understanding of structures and the unintended consequences of their own actions.

While the idea of lifeworld may at first seem abstract, it is related to concepts of experience and culture that seem more familiar. Within the functionalist tradition of organizational studies and social theory, life experience is typically viewed as an artifact of, or as dependent on, the system (Habermas, 1987). In the simplest form, this could imply that actions follow plans. However, the cultural lives and social norms in organizations are, in my view, more complex than is assumed in this functionalist view. This book uses Jurgen Habermas's (1987) distinction between the system and lifeworld. He treats them as different aspects of the same phenomena, which means that our experiences in organizations are related to the system and its structure, but one does not determine the other. Further, the way we might experience a requirement, rule, or ethical codes within an organization may be different than intended, due to the various ways different people interpret and act.

Habermas derives his reconstructions of lifeworld and system, at least in part, from the sociology of Talcott Parsons. Habermas's reconstruction reads as follows: "The mature Parsons reinterpreted the structural components of the lifeworld—culture, society, personality—as action systems constituting environments for one another" (1987, p. 153). Habermas departs from the functionalist tradition of social thought as constructed by Parsons, and carried forward by many other social scientists. Similar to Parsons, Habermas distinguished human systems (i.e. formal organizations and their subsystems) from the lifeworld (i.e. the experience of human interaction within and around organizations), but he also criticized Parsons's implicit assumption that the lifeworld is subordinate to the system. Habermas distinguished the two—the system and lifeworld—as different and related, but argues that experience should not be subordinate to the system.

The distinction between the system and social aspects of professional practice is too seldom made in organizational analyses of higher education (e.g. Gumport, 2000) or business administration (e.g. Cameron & Lavine, 2006). For example, in spite of their extensive amount of work and focus on the communicative aspect of human action, Argyris and Schön (1974, 1996) did not sufficiently distinguish between the system itself and the communicative processes on which they focus. (In Part II, I focus on the links among system control, professional reflection, and action within organizations.)

This book builds on Habermas's concepts of strategic and communicative action as a basis for examining professional learning about practice and interventions within organizations as related processes. In the chapters examining organization theory in relation to professional action (see Part II), five organizational contexts (i.e. stages of organization development) are differentiated: instrumental; closed strategic; open strategic; communicative; and transformational (see Table 0.1). These stages distinguish the strategic orientation of the organization as a whole (i.e. its mission and strategic initiatives), and the norms of professional practice in communities of practice within organizations. My hypotheses about the alignment of norms in communities of practice with the strategic orientation of organizations follow:

- Organizations that take an instrumental approach to mission and strategy would be most compatible with norms of practice that focus on the rules, or on working around the rules.
- Organizations that centrally initiate reforms that attempt to manage change centrally would be most compatible with communities of practice that align their practices with those centrally selected initiatives.
- Organizations that maintain openness to initiatives taken by groups within while pursuing central aims would be compatible with groups of professionals that adapt practices to address critical issues while also pursuing centrally defined initiatives and practices.
- Organizations that maintain a communicative orientation would create discursive space for evidence of injustices and for interventions addressing them.
- There is also a possibility of transformational practice within organizations (and communities of practice within them) that emphasize balancing concerns about justice (e.g. reducing inequalities and moving toward environmental sustainability) with choices, aims, and strategy, thus encouraging and enabling internal communities of practice to maintain this balance.

These intermediate hypotheses were generated from the analysis of case studies of professional learning and organizational practices (St. John, 2009), some of which are presented in this book and are explored further in Part II. Since this book was written as a text with cases rather than as a new set of research studies testing a new theory, these hypotheses are appropriately stated as intermediate because they have yet to be fully tested. Further study of action research and other forms of intervention are needed to further test these new conceptual frames of organizational change and transformation.

Readers are encouraged to test these hypotheses through action experiments in organizations and graduate education, and suggest strategies for this purpose. Practitioners should not assume that congruence of practice with organizational forms implies rigid alignment of form of practice and organizational strategic orientations. As noted earlier, learning new modes of practice occurs over time and across the course of a career. As some of the cases discussed in Part II illustrate, communities of practice can develop different norms than their organization and, thus, function in ways that are inconsistent with or change central practices. For example, a case study of a team of professionals in a statewide community college system (see Chapter 7) illustrates it is possible to use an open-strategic approach to change within an organization that has an

Table 0.1 Intermediate Hypotheses About Alignment of Strategic Orientations of Organizations with Norms and Practices within Communities of Practice

Frame	Instrumental	Closed-Strategic	Open-Strategic	Communicative	Transformational
Organization					
Strategic Orientation	Implement mission	Adapt strategies to address new challenges	Openness to adaptations of strategic initiatives	Encourage new initiatives from within	Emphasize response to critical social issues as integral to aims[2]
System Relation to Lifeworld	System dominance of lifeworld largely unquestioned; value placed on making the system work	Strategic initiatives may address critical issues arising from lifeworld	Discursive openness creates room to adapt strategic initiatives via critical issues in lifeworld	Dialectic between system and lifeworld views of experience; change possible	Balance adaptations to address critical issues with systemic strategies; emphasize equity and justice
Communities of Practice					
Norms within Communities of Practice	Play by the rules and/or work around rules to fix problems	Align strategies with organizational initiatives	Adapt practice to address new challenges	Craft practice to reduce social injustice[1]	Balance expert practice with care and justice
Congruent Practice	Learn and practice accruing to the rules of the profession	Try out new strategies within centrally controlled practice	Engage in open critical reflection-on-practice and in evidence-based reforms	Interventions that highlight critical issues and test alternative practices	Design and test methodologies to facilitate change within communities of practice

1 According to theoretical arguments (see Part I), this might also include "crafting practices to improve environmental sustainability." However, since the cases examined in this book (see Part II) do not explicitly address this question, this notion is conjecture and does not merit distinction as an evidence-based hypothesis.

2 "Aims" refers to collective intentions or goals within the organization (e.g. mission or strategic initiative). This emphasis may also include "response to environmental issues" related to organizational practices, but this is still conjecture.

instrumental orientation (i.e. making local adaptations in an organization that was heavily regulated centrally).

Colleges and universities are the types of organizations explicitly considered in this book for several reasons. Professional education occurs within universities and several professors are involved in the case studies. Professionals of all types have experienced higher education, creating a common base of understanding. As a professor in the field of higher education, many of my interventions, including the ones studied in this book, have taken place within colleges and universities, giving me a set of interventions to study in depth. While the case studies of professional learning situations and organizational changes considered in Part II are mostly situated in colleges and universities, the lessons learned can be adapted to other settings.

Colleges and universities have frequently been studied using social theory as a lens. For example, late in his career Parsons completed studies of higher education (Platt & Parsons, 1970). In addition, most researchers who study colleges and universities as organizations focus on organizations within their social contexts (Altbach, Berdahl, & Gumport, 2005; Gumport, 2008). This lens is also used to study curriculum (Bastedo, 2006) and graduate education (Gumport, 2006). Thus, rebuilding understanding of the distinction between lifeworld and system is vital to the study of colleges just as it is to the study of other types of organizations in twenty-first century societies. It is appropriate to situate the organizational analysis within the sociology of organizations, at least as a point of departure, but I encourage readers to also consider the primary aims of this book as they read it. The primary aims are to build a better understanding of moral reasoning in action and to describe how transformations of practices contribute to an increase in social justice.

ABOUT THIS BOOK

Part I considers the foundations for moral reasoning in practice and rethinking organizational chance through action inquiry. Chapter 1 focuses on professional responsibility for socially just action, examining the moral challenges facing professionals situated in a historical context of education for the professions. Chapter 2 reconsiders common foundations for moral reasoning, such as philosophy and religious traditions, and encourages readers to reflect on their personal beliefs as a starting point for their own moral development throughout their careers. Chapter 3 explores the relationship between professional knowledge, moral reasoning in practice, and adult development, focusing on ways of framing and knowing with respect to professional practice. It introduces logical *frames*[8] of action that can inform efforts to engage in moral learning and professional development. This chapter encourages introspection on inner sources of inspiration and belief that guide action and imagination of pathways and choices that lay ahead in a career. Finally, Chapter 4 presents methods of assessment and action inquiry that can be used in efforts to inform and transform practice in professional settings. (Case studies of organization change initiatives are used in Part II to illustrate multiple roles of action inquiry within organizations.) In combination, these chapters emphasize four ways of framing critical social challenges: critical (Chapter 1); interpretive (Chapter 2); social (Chapter 3); and technological framing (Chapter 4).

The five chapters in Part II focus on frames of professional development as both patterns of reasoning and developmental pathways. While it can be argued that moral reasoning develops through maturation, it is also evident that most, if not all, professionals engage in different forms of discourse as part of their practice. Thus, they are provided the opportunity to test new approaches to moral reasoning. People face moral challenges whether or not they demonstrate a mature framing of problems. Studies on college-age students consistently find that some students respond to surveys indicating postconventional moral reasoning, at least at an espoused level (Pascarella & Terenzini, 2005). However, actions based on moral logic (i.e. integrating moral reasoning into action) represent a different maturation challenge—one that can only be faced in practice. Part II introduces five forms of reflection on action that can be practiced by individuals and groups within professional communities. While I think the frames-of-mind approach is crucial to moral learning, I also consider the development of these skills as it evolves over the adult life cycle.

There is an underlying sequence of skill development in acquisition of actionable knowledge about moral reasoning as a learning process. Even though moral beliefs and values do not necessarily correspond with age, the skills used in postconventional moral reasoning in action situations (i.e. initiating and engaging in discourse on problematic issues and trying out methods for resolving them) build on prior experiences in action situations and engagement in discourse. The tensions between maturation and skill development on the one hand, and between values and ideals on the other, are complex and too little understood in practical ways. Part II views the five forms of action as both sequential stages of skill development and as frames of mind learned in part through engagement in discourse. The forms are:

- instrumental action, which focuses on the application of knowledge and skills and is considered a process of building expertise (Chapter 5);
- closed-strategic action, which is an adaptation of method and practice aimed at improving individual practice that considers the artistry of practice (Chapter 6);
- open-strategic action, which involves collaboration in and facilitation of processes that engage practitioners in action aimed at realizing the missions of their organizations and is considered professional effectiveness (Chapter 7);
- communicative action, which involves collective efforts to engage diverse groups and include clients in understanding why problems persist, and transforms collective practices to face *critical social challenges* (Chapter 8); and
- transformational action, which is viewed as experimenting with methods to facilitate communicative action and critical social change within and across communities of practice (Chapter 9).

One view of practice presented in the chapters on each form of reasoning assumes a sequential process of skill development, recognizing that one type of skill can build on another. However, it is also possible to gain experience with skills out of sequence, especially when exposed to open discourse, which can be a catalyst of personal development. Therefore, another view of the forms of action focuses on framing assumptions used by practitioners and emphasizes engagement in multiple forms of reasoning (i.e. trying out different frames). Developing the ability to be situational—to use different forms of reasoning in different settings—provides a method for communities of professionals to create dynamic organizations that support professional development across the career cycle, from beginning professionals to late-career professionals, within communities of practice.

In Chapter 4 a change strategy used in technical support for colleges and universities in Indiana is introduced as a method of integrating action and research in support of educational improvement. The Indiana Project on Academic Success (IPAS) supported change projects in Indiana colleges and universities during a three-year period. Qualitative research on change processes within colleges and universities included in the IPAS project (St. John, 2009; St. John & Wilkerson, 2006) is reexamined in relation to the organizational frames discussed in Part II. The chapters in Part II focus on case studies of college organizations for illustrative purposes.

This two-level approach to theory and practice—using reflective seminars for practitioners along with reform processes in organizations using action inquiry—provides an integrated perspective on professional development and organizational change in higher education that has broader implications: a window on strategies and methods for integrating an emphasis on moral reasoning and reflective practice into graduate education across fields. As with any new theory of practice, more testing and adaptation will be needed to refine workable approaches to the strategies of instruction and intervention proposed in this book. Adaptation of these methods should be encouraged within the practice of teaching and intervention to provide a path of actionable inquiry rather than a strict script for action.

Parts I and II include reflective assignments for readers who would like to engage in that type of learning process. These assignments are derived from experiences with teaching leadership courses and with interventions in schools, colleges, corporations, and government agencies. If readers complete these assignments, they can engage in a process of reflective analysis of their own professional practices. For students in collegiate programs in professional fields, these assignments can be completed as part of their courses. Other readers who are interested in engaging in reflective practice are encouraged to complete the assignments, possibly as part of a personal journal. Discussions with other practitioners engaged in rethinking their practices are encouraged as an important part of the learning process.

Finally, Part III focuses on the challenges of building communities of practice that support critical social change and environmental consciousness. I conclude by redefining moral consciousness in relation to social and environmental challenges facing the current generation of professionals, discussing the development and transformation of organizations to promote social justice, and discussing the use of action inquiry as a means of integrating professional knowledge with moral consciousness in efforts to intervene in professional organizations and engage in social change.

A NOTE TO READERS

College Organization and Professional Development: Integrating Moral Reasoning and Reflective Practice articulates a new framework for moral reasoning in action, professional development, and organizational development. It can be used as a guide for individual practitioners seeking the opportunity to reflect on their own practice. Since it articulates a developmental, skill-building sequence of problem framing and solving, it can also be useful to experienced practitioners entering a period of personal introspection, as well as to aspiring professionals planning for a career.

The professional case statements in Part II are adapted from leadership courses and interventions within colleges and universities. They can be used for discussion and analysis in courses on leadership, organization, and governance in education, as well as in courses on student affairs, leadership, and organizational management. While the cases state events from leadership courses that pertain to a range of professions, including counseling, medicine, and technology transfer, this text would need to be supplemented by field-specific books when used in courses, especially in fields not directly related to the content of cases. The organizational case studies in Part II emphasize higher education. Other types of case studies should be used to supplement this text if it is used for courses in other fields. It has long been argued that field-specific content is critical to teaching reflection in action (Schön, 1987), and the same is true with respect to teaching moral reasoning and ethics. I strongly encourage faculty members in engineering, medicine, nursing, and other fields to engage in teaching experiments, using this book along with texts specifically related to organization and ethical practices in their professions.

Finally, the overall intent of this book is to encourage reflection on the critical social circumstances that pervade professional action. Not only are the moral aspects of practice discussed too little within professional communities, but there are too few conversations between professionals and their clients about problems in practice. In fact, when recurrent problems are uncovered, rules and procedures of practice are often formulated to regulate responses. Their unintended effect can be to further silence discourse. Forming rules of practice too early in a process of change—or defining rules that are too narrow in terms of acceptable responses or practitioner discretion—can limit the strategies professionals can use to address challenging circumstances. The problem is paradoxical. Reflection of critical social circumstances that defy simple application of rules is a necessary part of moral reasoning in practice; at the same time, failure to adhere to ethical guidelines is the source of most serious problems in practice and service to society. The ability of professionals to handle these paradoxes in their practice is crucial to civility and justice.

Part I

Moral Reasoning in the Professions

1

PROFESSIONAL RESPONSIBILITY

Professionals provide vital services to society. Teachers educate citizens, clergy minister to the spirit of individuals and communities, doctors and nurses promote health, engineers design structures and systems that enable modern society to function, lawyers protect the rights of citizens, government officials provide public services, and so forth. The moral codes of most professions focus on service, individual rights, and social responsibility, while the content of professional education focuses on technical knowledge and skills. The social responsibility of professional practice is often overlooked in professional education courses. Before considering strategies for integrating moral reasoning and civic responsibility into professional education and interventions, it is important to ponder two questions:

- Why focus on moral reasoning within professional practice?
- Do well-known conceptions of moral consciousness provide an adequate basis for addressing critical social problems in practice?

WHY FOCUS ON MORAL REASONING?

Professions lay claim to specific domains of knowledge and skills essential for social justice and economic development, and professionals make tacit use of their expertise, acquired through education and experience, in their daily practices. Knowledge and skills are the focus of professional education because expert judgment is central to practice. The traditional professions of medicine, law, clergy, business, engineering, teaching, and government service are now supplemented by a wide range of professional services including counseling, social work, consulting, and technical support services of all types. Much of the work of government, including a substantial share of this country's war efforts, is contracted to private firms. Thus, these new professionals, the employees of these firms, have the same public obligations as civil servants. This topic is largely overlooked in the literature on public integrity (Dobel, 1999). Unfortunately, the core values of public service are too seldom acted upon by civil

3

servants and are rarely even discussed within private contracting organizations. Divorcing the content of professional knowledge from moral reasoning adds to the critical social problems in work settings and society: the gaps between espoused beliefs about the social good and the daily actions of responsible people in modern societies.

Globalization of corporations and technology not only adds to competition among corporations, but also to similarities in products and professional services across societies and cultures (T. L. Friedman, 2005; Stiglitz, 2002), making it possible to provide professional services from halfway around the globe. Legal, engineering, computer, and other professional services can be contracted out, along with manufacturing. Unfortunately, this transition has been accompanied by an increase in inequality of access to these services and to education in the US (St. John, 2006). This is also the case internationally, especially during periods of economic stagnation (B. M. Friedman, 2005). As economies improve, services expand and improve for those who can pay; since the poor usually cannot afford to pay, inequalities can increase. In American higher education for example, college enrollment rates increased in the 1980s while the gap in enrollment opportunity increased across racial groups (St. John, 2003). Citizens of countries engaged in the global economy have more opportunity for health services and education than citizens in countries that are not so engaged (i.e. underdeveloped countries). However, the competitive forces can create inequalities within globally-engaged countries. Inequalities can be by-products of global competition for employment and educated employees, along with efforts to cut taxes. Indeed, there are growing inequalities in access to education, technology, and services within developed societies. These inequalities are compounded for immigrants who lack legal citizenship.

This changing context for professional action is appropriately understood in relation to the role of professionals within society, the struggles of people to gain access to professions as a means of upward mobility, and the complexity of changing professional education in ways that provide the skills that enable practitioners to address the injustices they face as a part of their practices. These issues merit consideration in relation to the problem of moral reasoning within professional practice, along with the ways professional education can be changed to integrate an emphasis on moral reasoning.

Understanding the Professions

Moral reasoning is important to the professions in part because of the conflicts over entry into the professions. The professions are defined by social, educational, and practical boundaries that distinguish the work of the practitioners across fields. In traditional professions, these boundaries are well defined and commonly understood in society as a whole, as well as within communities of practice, while in emerging professions these boundaries are not as well understood. Professionals have a privileged status in society. They receive greater monetary compensation for their services than most others in the workforce. They also have potential for personal satisfaction from social contributions made as part of their work—a form of reward and actualization that probably would not have been possible without their education.

Access to the professions is regulated through admission into professional education. Professional education provides a means for low-income children to gain access to a better quality of life, and for wealthy children to maintain their social and economic status. Claims by various groups about fairness of college access are central to the public discourse about equal treatment. Those who seek to maintain their status make different arguments about admission and access to professional education than those who seek to improve opportunities across generations. It is little wonder that affirmative action became a hot political issue in the late twentieth century.

Before tackling the educational aspect of this problem, it is important to examine the social aspect. The social dimensions of professions are twofold: (1) professions are integral to the social hierarchies of modern societies; (2) the professions vary with respect to the extent of tradition and social status. Both of these social aspects of professional life merit reflection by professionals, aspiring professionals, and ordinary people seeking access to services.

Professions and Social Mobility

Moral reasoning is important within the professions because of the social status of professionals. The social hierarchy among the professions is deeply embedded in social theory, and social life reflects and illustrates these theories. For decades social attainment theories have posited a stratification of types of work. Higher status professions (i.e. law, medicine, and engineering) were at the top; middle class professions (i.e. education, clergy, and business)[9] held the upper middle positions; technical and service positions, along with skilled laborers, were in the lower middle positions; and unskilled laborers, along with clerical and service workers, were at the bottom (Blau & Duncan, 1967). This hierarchy was aligned with the social class structure. It was generally thought that education, specialization, and achievement (i.e. grades and test scores), along with parental income and occupational status, were the determinants of professional status (Alexander & Eckland, 1978). This social theory was compatible with the economic theories of the mid-twentieth century, including human capital theory (Becker, 1964), which argued that people made rational choices about the economic and personal benefits of their investment in education. This type of social and economic logic functioned as an invisible hand guiding generations of Americans who struggled to achieve the American dream, to provide their children with opportunities to rise in social class, and to have a "better life."

During periods of sustained economic development it is possible that larger numbers of individuals can move up in social class—a pattern evident in the progressive century from the late 1800s through the 1970s. Through expansion of educational opportunity, more people gain access to undergraduate education, and possibly even graduate and professional programs. This was certainly the case in the US and most developed democracies during the post-World War II period. In the US, student financial aid for returning veterans, a form of grant aid known as the G.I. Bill, improved access to professional employment for vast numbers of returning veterans. However, economic stagnation can influence societies to decrease investments in expanding access to educational opportunity (B. M. Friedman, 2005).

In the US, rising college prices and declining public investment in need-based grant aid contributed to a widening opportunity gap after 1980—a gap that only narrowed slightly during the economic boom of the late 1990s (Ehrenberg, 2002; St. John, 2003, 2006). Specifically, African-American and Hispanic high school graduates enrolled in college at about the same rate as white high school graduates in the mid-1970s, but a substantial gap has been opened and maintained since. In spite of extensive government efforts to improve schools, inequalities of access to quality high school programs remain a barrier to college for students from low-income families. Students with equal preparation and achievement from families with differing incomes do not have equal opportunities to go to college—especially four-year colleges—if states do not provide sufficient financial support for prepared, low-income students who lack the ability to supplement federal grants and loans. This structural view of access to education and the professions—the argument that finances can reduce or remove barriers for students who lack family resources to enroll in college (B. M. Friedman, 2005; St. John, 2006)—may be overly optimistic because it overlooks the reproductive role of social class.

Bourdieu's (1977, 1990) concepts of *cultural capital* and *habitus* illuminate how social and cultural forces can undermine the concept of cross-class uplift embedded in social attainment and human capital theory. He argued that cultural capital is to education what dollars are to economic capital. Across generations, families that lack cultural capital also lack the prior experiences and habitual patterns necessary to attain an education. According to this theory, families replicate social class, reproducing cultural capital through habitual family patterns, or habitus, conveyed throughout the community. Viewed through this lens, schools can be a conservatory for reproduced social class (Bourdieu, 1974, 1977), reinforcing class differentiation through the grouping of children by achievement indicators and social interaction skills in elementary schools, and tracking in middle and high schools (Connell, 2007; Wells & Serna, 2007). Habitus as a social force in families and schools plays an apparently strong role in high schools (McDonough, 1997) at a time when students are making decisions about preparing for college. Social forces that reproduce class and culture can undermine structural efforts to improve access and equalize opportunity for equally prepared students.

The processes of networking and outreach, mechanisms that enable social capital formation, can potentially overcome these social and cultural barriers to college access (Tierney & Venegas, 2007). There is evidence that networking and outreach encourage people to excel in high school and college (Allen, Harris, Dinwiddie, & Griffin, 2008; Hurtado, Saenz, & Dar, 2008). Mentoring plays a crucial role in education and professional development. Indeed, sponsorship of youth and outreach to people across groups are important social forces in providing an expanding opportunity for education and access to professional occupations.

In addition, social and cultural forces play a role in gaining access to health care and other professions. For example, Edmund Gordon (1999), a noted social scientist, based his arguments about social justice in education on observations of the medical practice of an African-American doctor who lived the calling of social justice, providing care for all in need. The social outreach and community-building values of the African tradition of education were important forces in expanding educational opportunity in the early and mid-twentieth century (Siddle Walker, 1996), but there appears to be a decline in this type of outreach, and community support is not widely practiced in urban education in the post-desegregation period (St. John & Cadray, 2004).

Summary

While there continue to be debates about the role and efficacy of structural remedies (i.e. education policies and financial aid) and of cultural capital formation as co-explanations for inequality, it is clear that (1) the professions and social class are intertwined, as structural and life aspects of social inequality and (2) access to education and professional preparation is a gateway to the professions. The structural factors that play a major role in access include family background (e.g. parent's education, occupation, and income) and need-based financial aid for low- and middle-income students. Other social forces, including outreach and engagement, play roles in expanding opportunities, providing students can afford to pay for higher education (Trent & St. John, 2008). Arguments about the roles of social and cultural forces and whether there are persistent patterns of class reproduction remain issues open to interpretation. The ways people theorize the problem of inequality makes a difference in how they interpret the data. However, the fact is that inequality matters, whether one adheres to structural or cultural arguments about opportunity and access.

Social Processes within Professions

Moral reasoning is also important because of critical social issues facing professionals within their communities of practice. Forces that regulate access to professions include testing and achievement, the individual's aspirations and self-selection, the supply of educational opportunity, and the demand for professionals (e.g. employment opportunities). High grades in critical subjects and scoring high on entry tests are necessary to gain entry to high status fields like engineering and medicine. In addition, individual interests, and some argue personality type (Smart, Feldman, & Ethington, 2000), play a major role in career choice. Since the supply of educational opportunity in higher education is lower than demand, not all qualified students gain entry. In hard economic times, finances are more likely to constrain access than during periods of economic growth—not only because of academic constraints, but also because of attitudes and competition for employment (B. M. Friedman, 2005). The excess demand for quality education is one of the core sources of unequal opportunity. Creating and maintaining just and fair standards for entry—using criteria that are based on merit appropriately measured rather than on family resources—remain complex, contested issues that are not well understood.

Arguments about *affirmative action*—as race-based policies and practices that influence the entry of students into elite colleges—capture much more public attention than the inability of prepared, low-income students to pay for college. Prepared low-income students with average achievement face lower net costs (i.e. amount to be paid after aid) after enrolling in college than middle-income students with similar achievement and preparation. However, the low-income students are less able to pay the remaining net cost given their family income.

Inequality of ability to pay is difficult for middle-income families to understand because they often focus on differences in costs and debt, but fail to consider whether others can even pay their way with loans. The amount left to pay after aid is a much higher share of family income for students from low-income families than for their peers in the economic middle class. The inequality of net price as a percent of disposable income has not received sufficient attention even though the burden of educational costs—including the complicating role of student debt—troubles most college students and their parents. Middle-income students graduate with high debt, as do students from low-income families. However, low-income students often have to take out unsubsidized loans (Hartle, Simmons, & Timmons, 2005), which can mean they will have to work during college to pay off loans that come due. Excessive work reduces time to study and engage academically; loss of this quality time reduces the formation of cultural capital and the chances of academic success in college. This fate seldom afflicts the more affluent.

This economic inequality of opportunity and the resulting economic and racial inequalities of college enrollment rates are far more problematic for social progress and economic development than the racial differences of enrollment rates in elite colleges attributable to affirmative action, but that racial inequality is unjust. Affirmative action may have become a means of maintaining social status for middle-income people of color in addition to being a viable means of promoting cross-generation uplift. This is complicated not only because all middle-income families have some advantage over poor families, but second-generation college students have advantages compared to first-generation college students. Second- and third-generation students of color may be children of the middle class enrolled in high-quality suburban schools. If students with these advantages benefit substantially from affirmative action, then there may be feelings of resentment among their middle-class peers who do not have those advantages. Given the disparities in schools between low-income and other communities, enrolling in suburban schools is one of the few ways middle-class minorities *have* available to ensure their children will gain access to the advanced courses they need to prepare for college.

The fact that children who are second- or third-generation college students can benefit from affirmative action further enables social class maintenance across generations. In this context, when there are minority students from middle class families of color who meet admission qualifications, elite universities frequently overlook low-income students from segregated high schools who have not had access to advanced courses in their high schools. In these circumstances affirmative action can actually reinforce class differences within racial groups. Legacy admission (i.e. admitting students because their parents are alumni) also circumvents fairness in general college admissions. It is another process which favors students from privileged backgrounds, but it less frequently receives much attention or critique.

The reactionary critiques of affirmative action have often prevailed over concerns about social justice, a development that is abundantly evident across the US (Chang, Altbach, & Lomotey, 2006). The core problem of economic injustice has lingered as public attention focuses on measures of merit (i.e. use of merit versus race as admissions criteria). There is also a legacy of racial injustice that is not easily erased by means testing and need-based aid. However, we should not overlook the near equality of enrollment opportunity across races in the mid-1970s, a period when student aid was directed toward low-income students (St. John, 2003). Methods for measuring merit matter and deserve attention as an integral part of admission, but fairness in admission practices can result in unequal access among the equally qualified, whether or not race-conscious selection is used. The difficulties low-income students have in paying for college are no less a barrier to racial and economic equality than race-conscious admission.

Most people who make it into professional education and attain elite status as a professional have worked hard to gain entry into, study for, and complete degree programs. As a result, they have "earned" their status. Many have great amounts of debt to pay off after graduation, which means they will have to work hard to pay for their education even after they begin work. Yet many who do not get into or make it through professional programs have a sense of injustice because they too have worked hard, but they may have been denied access because of finances rather than achievement (Advisory Committee on Student Financial Assistance, 2001, 2002). Some who do not make it have, in fact, worked at least as hard and achieved more academically than those who do make it, but their futures are constrained by forces they cannot influence. The deep psychological residue of these inequalities resides beneath the surface in the consciousness of most professionals and their clients. These unspoken injustices are part of the social context of professional practice.

Social inequality is further complicated by the social status among the professions, including the extent of self-regulation and the high cost to taxpayers of providing elite professional education in public universities. High-status professions with long traditions, like law and medicine, have strong self-regulatory bodies. The American Bar Association (ABA), the American Medical Association (AMA), and the American Association of University Professors (AAUP)[10] play important roles in setting standards for entry and/or progress within these high-status professions. Some professions also require college graduates to pass entry tests. Testing for nursing, which is a middle-class profession (Slaughter, 1993), takes place after two- or four-year degrees. In contrast, bar exams for legal practice, which is an elite profession, are usually completed after graduate education.

Some professional programs have high costs for state taxpayers as well as for students. As a result, the education of sufficient numbers of medical doctors, who are highly paid professionals, and veterinarians, who are moderately paid professionals, is an elusive goal. The US imports large numbers of medical doctors from countries that educate them at a lower cost (e.g. India), providing their citizens opportunity for upward economic mobility through migration. Access to elite professional fields like medicine is more difficult to realize than middle-class fields like education and business. Programs that can be provided by lower-cost public undergraduate institutions are more widely accessible.

Yet the earnings in some middle-class professions, like education, are rarely sufficient to pay off debt from student loans, so some low- and middle-income students choose other fields with higher potential earnings. The movement toward privatization of education, especially increases in the students' share of education costs, has made it possible for governments to expand the supply of educational opportunities at a lower level of taxation and public spending per student. Enrollment rates increased in the 1990s, evidencing the expanded opportunity for those who can pay (Priest & St. John, 2006). However, expansion of expensive, high quality professional education programs is usually slow and access is severely limited. There is excess demand for high quality programs and growing access to moderate quality programs.

Almost any college can afford to offer teacher education and business programs, so most students have the opportunity to study in these fields if they have the desire and have achieved an appropriate standard of preparation in high school—and if they can afford the costs of attending college. For those who make it through the filter of preparatory education and can pay the direct net costs of college (i.e. tuition and other costs after aid), it takes will and fortitude to do the academic work required in professional education. It takes low-income students much more time to attain degrees because their high net cost makes work necessary. This condition does not hamper the middle-class majority who can borrow enough to pay the net costs of attending college (Perna, Cooper, & Li, 2007).

Newly emerging fields, like the professional services industry, lack much of this history and tradition. With the privatization of government services, larger amounts of government work, including the operation of social programs and fighting foreign wars, have been contracted to private firms. In addition, larger numbers of direct client services are contracted by public agencies in the US and other developed nations to firms in India and China (T. L. Friedman, 2005). The privatization of public services and contracting of services to individual constants or service providers in other countries have changed the nature of professional work in many instances, further complicating efforts to equalize employment opportunity and access to services. Professional services are not regulated in the same way as the traditional professions, partly because they lack associations that have a long history of self-regulation (e.g. AMA, ABA, and AAUP).

These newer forms of professional work are regulated by the standards and procedures set up by contracting firms, as well as by the negotiated contracts and legal interpretations of these contractual relationships. The pressure to realize a profit may prevail over fairness in these organizations, creating complicated moral problems for practitioners. Many professionals who work in service industries are independent contractors responsible for their own health care, while others enjoy some of the same privileges as partners in law firms, medical practices, and other elite professional organizations. These inequalities can be savage within private organizations that provide professional services. The future challenges of navigating professional pathways through this labyrinth of employment choices are not always visible for students who seek professional opportunity.

Summary

Access to the professions and equity within them are extraordinarily complicated critical social issues. There are many barriers to access and great inequalities of opportunity even for those who are fortunate enough to attain an advanced professional education. Those who overcome these barriers usually have put substantial effort into earning their success. Often they feel their hard work has earned them the privilege of a better life. Indeed, people who persevere through undergraduate and professional education do earn their way, but not all who were prepared had the opportunity to gain this access. These tensions about access to professions, along with social inequalities within the professions, complicate social life and community interaction in society as a whole. Professionals play vital social and economic roles in supporting the activities of communities, developing structures and technologies that support citizens and communities, and ensuring access to basic education and health care.

There is also reason to consider access to education and health care as rights of global citizenship, or human rights. Economic forces of globalization influence patterns of migration from one country to another, but legal rights do not always follow. One of the tragedies of globalization has been the creation of a new class of citizenship within most countries: those who labor but who lack the legal rights to citizenship. Educators, health care providers, lawyers, clergy, and other professionals often share obligations of service to all as a result of their ethical and moral codes, but such questions of rights are too frequently overlooked in professional education. The implications for taxation and taxpayer costs should not obfuscate the issue of rights. The costs for taxpayers of providing education and health care should be considered along with the human rights of global citizens.

Education and Expertise

Efforts to integrate a focus on moral reasoning into professional education are further complicated by the diversity of educational programs. Not only are there different standards of entry across professions, but the content and pedagogical methods of professional education vary across and within fields. Knowledge and skills develop over time as part of a career; learning does not stop when degrees are attained. Professional education should prepare aspiring professionals for future learning as an integral part of their development. The extent of expertise professionals actually acquire varies substantially depending on their background (including parents' income, education, and profession),[11] ability, achievement in education (i.e. how well they did in school)[12], and professional experience. Graduate programs—through both the content delivered and pedagogies used—provide basic education and contribute to the skills of beginning professionals. For individual professionals, however, expertise is built throughout a career. Professionals both specialize in their education and gain additional knowledge and skills through subsequent experience.

Professionals are considered experts by virtue of their role in society and the education that prepared them for their careers. Most people demonstrate tacit trust in expert judgments about the education of their children, health care, legal decisions and defense, and many other professional services. Without this trust, society could not function; anarchy would prevail. The expertise of professionals is built on research and practice in the professions rather than on moral judgment. The weak link between moral education and professional education has implications for social justice. Do all individuals have access to the education and health care they need for themselves and to support their families? Are services and support provided differentially based on factors such as race or financial means? Do legal and pre-legal citizens have choices about the types of services they receive? Not only are these policy issues for education, health care, and legal aid, but they are also moral issues relating directly to the methods used to educate and support professionals and their development.

The knowledge and skills emphasized within professional education vary substantially across professions. The curricula in engineering, education, medicine, law, and other professional fields are organized to include *core content*, which is defined as courses professional schools require in order to provide a common foundation for students entering the profession. Core courses vary somewhat across graduate schools within fields because schools aim to provide distinctive and high quality programs. Professors usually have well formed ideas about the content foundations of their fields, and how such content should be taught. In fact, discussions about core content are ongoing and important issues among faculties in professional schools as they think through their own market niches (i.e. the types of students they want to attract and the types of graduates for which they want to be known). In some instances, program design may be influenced by local factors. For example, in some business programs with a local appeal and student draw, the core might be tailored to local corporations. State agencies can set content standards for programs in education, nursing, and other fields with public licensure.

Elite programs compete nationally for students, and their graduates usually go into national labor markets. Highly competitive professional schools in business, medicine, and other fields may have distinct pedagogical methods. For example, Harvard Business School is well known for the case method (i.e. using case studies as a basis for discussion and analysis). These patterns of curriculum organization are critical to the core teaching functions of universities. In the advanced courses within the curriculum in graduate programs, professors assume their students will have some shared background. Specialization courses depend on a common background in and understanding of the profession (i.e. the foundational rules need to be understood as a basis for advanced course work).

Students' choices about courses, professors, and specializations play important roles in the professional education of the students who make it through the access barriers and have the opportunity to make these choices. Professional schools, which are similar to academic programs within core disciplines,[13] have specialization courses. In law schools students can choose specializations by selecting advanced courses in contracts, corporate, criminal, tax, civil rights, or international law, for example, as part of their graduate programs. Law students usually take a common curriculum during the first year, but take specialized courses in their second and third years of law school. Students may choose to apply to a specific law school because of an interest in a specialty not generally available, like maritime law. In medical schools the specializations are chosen after completing the MD in another round of selection based on achievement in courses in the medical program, supply of and demand for specialists, and other factors. In engineering, undergraduates make choices about specializations, such as chemical, civil, electrical, as part of the process of applying for admission.

Students who complete undergraduate degrees in professional programs in education, nursing, and engineering may face further choices among specializations in graduate school if they decide to go further into the education process. For example, as part of the certificate achieved during undergraduate education or as part of a special program after college, teachers choose an education level (elementary, middle, or secondary school) as well as a content area if they plan to be secondary teachers (i.e. science, history, math, etc.).[14] Master's and doctoral degrees in education provide further specialization in education administration, higher education, counseling, and so forth. In graduate programs in law and business, students can enter after receiving an education in core disciplines and choose specialties without prior courses in the field.[15]

Professors organize and purvey content, and encourage skill development using a wide range of methods. While the lecture method is widely criticized, it remains a common, perhaps even necessary, mode of content delivery in colleges and universities. Yet methods of instruction vary substantially, even in large courses. The case method is used as a prominent mode of instruction in most law schools and some business schools. Law schools emphasis the Socratic method of questioning to build logical and argumentative skills in analysis of case law, while business and policy schools emphasize problem analysis, often using empirical methods to analyze problems in case studies. Clinics with supervised interactions with patients or clients are used in many fields, but especially in nursing and other health sciences. Undergraduate programs provide and encourage work experiences, service learning, and other methods of engagement which enable students to reflect on and make more informed choices about curriculum. In addition, computer technology is increasingly used in all content delivery in both on- and off-campus programs. Computers, telecommunications, web-based technologies, and electronic storage of information are now integral to teaching, just as these technologies are integral to practice in the professions. This great diversity of methods also expands the array of learning modes students are exposed to and becomes part of their repertoire of experience even before they enter the labor market.

Further complicating this process of learning basic knowledge, students have many and varied learning styles which influence the ways they learn in undergraduate and graduate classrooms.[16] They also bring individual characteristics into the work environment after they finish their education. In fact, there is substantial evidence that personality characteristics draw students to different fields of study and to different aligned career paths (Smart, 1985, 1988, 1989). As people discover their interests, they are drawn to different but often related topics. Research strongly suggests that students who achieve congruity between interests and education are more satisfied (Smart, Feldman, & Ethnington, 2000).

The development of expertise—during professional education and subsequent practice as professionals—involves learning, applying, internalizing, and adapting a set of rules that guide professional action. Facilitating and enabling the processes of learning and applying rules (i.e. advanced concepts and methods in math, science, legal analysis, etc.) is integral to undergraduate and graduate education, including professional education. Given the great diversity of professional education pathways and teaching methods, there is limited commonality in education across professions.

The most successful attempt to develop methods of instruction in professional reasoning across professions was undertaken by Chris Argyris and Donald Schön. Their theory of professional effectiveness (Argyris & Schön, 1974, 1978, 1996), along with subsequent development of action science (Argyris, 1993; Argyris, Putnam, & Smith, 1985) and reflective practice (Schön, 1983, 1987), provided methods of integrating a pedagogy pertaining to building an understanding of habitual action and the roles of professional education and organizational intervention in changing practice. In their book, *Theory in Practice: Increasing Professional Effectiveness*, Argyris and Schön (1974) not only addressed the ways professionals learned the rules in practice, but they also introduced and tested a methodology for intervening to improve organizational and professional "effectiveness."

Argyris and Schön's body of collaborative work (Argyris & Schön, 1974, 1978, 1996) remains important in theorizing professional education and intervention. However, their work lacks an emphasis on individuation of professionals (i.e. integration of professional and adult development) and the critical social understandings crucial to integrating an emphasis on moral reasoning and social justice into professional practice, both of which are central to this book's reconstructed theory and method.

Summary: Why Focus on Moral Reasoning?

The professions—both traditional and emerging—provide the social and educational means of organizing expert knowledge. Social status, earnings, and other social and economic privileges are gained through acquiring professional education and employment. Entry to the professions is regulated through selection processes administered by colleges and universities. Students' backgrounds and their prior education play substantial roles in selection, but not all students have an equal opportunity to gain preparatory education. Inequalities in elementary and secondary schools, along with limitations in the ability of some families to pay for collegiate and professional education, constrain opportunities for low-income and minority students who have the aspirations and ability (Carter, 2001; Hearn, 2001; St. John, 2006). The social context for education—the privileges gained through and the inequalities in opportunity for entry—complicate the roles of professionals.

Professional work takes place within communities that have great inequalities of access to services, unfairness of treatment of people within the communities of practice, and inequalities of the services provided (at least with respect to access to and potential benefits from professional services). Not all citizens have equal access to health care, education, and legal and other services. While the fiduciary and social roles of professionals may shield some of them from seeing these inequalities, these social injustices are embedded in the fabric of society. The ways in which professionals deal with social equity in provision of services to and within their communities of practice are major forces in creating fairness or injustice in the daily lives for all citizens. This critical social aspect of professional practice—the ways inequalities are addressed within work settings and in the provision of services—is vitally important and merits consideration by aspiring, beginning, and experienced professionals as part of their professional development, but is frequently overlooked in professional education.

Professional education is organized by major areas of specialized content. There are common core subjects within engineering, law, education, and other professions, but there are also many opportunities to specialize within professional fields, and gain content and experiential expertise. There are also great variations in methods of instruction within and across professional programs. However, moral reasoning has not been a common area of content in professional education. Theory and research on professional reasoning by Argyris and Schön (1974, 1978) provide a starting point for considering the challenges of integrating moral reasoning into professional education, but a more explicit focus in moral reasoning is needed than was evident in their foundational works.

ARE THERE COMMON FOUNDATIONS FOR MORAL EDUCATION?

The field of moral education has been largely limited to a minor field of specialization within elementary and secondary education and, to a more limited extent, in higher education. The Association for Moral Education (AME) is concerned primarily with Kohlberg's (1981) theory of moral development, a conceptualization that has not been adequate for professional education; even though the theory is widely referenced, it does not fit well with the diversity of value traditions. Kohlberg's theory has been adapted for practical use with respect to faith-based reasoning (Fowler, 1981; Small, 2007), gender inequality (Gilligan, 1982), and race-based values and experiences (Snarey & Siddle Walker, 2004). A review of the theory and its critics and adaptations illustrates the need for an alternative perspective on moral learning in the professions.

Kohlberg's Theory

Kohlberg proposed a six-stage theory of moral reasoning—two each at the preconventional level, conventional level, and the postconventional level, plus a transitional level between conventional and postconventional moral reasoning. Descriptions of the six stages follow (abstracted from Kohlberg, 1981, 409–412).

Level A: preconventional level

- Stage 1: the stage of punishment and obedience. Right is literal obedience to rules and authority, avoiding punishment, and not doing physical harm.
- Stage 2: the stage of individual instrumental purpose and exchange. Right is serving one's own and others's needs, and making deals in terms of concrete exchange.

Level B: conventional level

- Stage 3: the state of mutual interpersonal expectations, relationships, and conformity. Right is playing a good (nice) role, being concerned about other people and their feelings, keeping loyalty and trust with parents, and being motivated to follow rules and expectations.
- Stage 4: the stage of social system and conscious maintenance. Right is doing one's duty in society, upholding order, and maintaining the welfare of society.

Level B/C: postconventional level (but not yet principled)

At Stage 4.5, choice is personal and subjective. It is based on emotions; conscious is seen as arbitrary and relative, as are ideas such as "duty" and "morally right."

Level C: postconventional level

- Stage 5: the stage of prior rights and social contracts and utility. Right is upholding the basic rights, values, and legal contracts of a society, even when they are in conflict with concrete rules and laws of the group.
- Stage 6: this stage assumes guidance by universal principles that all humanity should follow.

The first four stages were based on Piaget's (1971) theory of cognitive development in childhood, and Kohlberg used moral philosophy (1981) and other psychological theories (1984) as the basis for the advanced stages. The first three stages have a strong basis in psychological theory of childhood development, while stages five and six launch into philosophical conjecture.

At the preconventional level, Kohlberg proposed obedience associated with fear of punishment as Stage 1, and instrumental purpose and exchange as Stage 2. Both of these stages are thought to be related to the early learning of moral standards and behaviors. However, it is also possible that adults who espouse conventional or postconventional moral values can act in ways that abuse power, either through asymmetry of authority or quid pro quo (Habermas, 1990).

Not only are critical social problems of exclusion a preconventional dimension of moral ambiguity, they are also practices that defy the standards of the professions. One only needs to recall the problems from the demise of the Enron Corporation and Andersen Consulting,[17] or the G. W. Bush Administration's manipulation of information on Iraq (McClellan, 2008) to understand the problems with power in professional practice. Such incidents of misconduct, deception, and misuse of power are common, but usually on a smaller scale. Too frequently, professionals exert power to influence decisions that represent their own self-interest. The accumulation of small, incremental decisions, often made without consideration of the moral dimensions of small problems, can lead to big problems becoming crises in practice. Inquiry into the ways normal action results in malpractice and unethical behavior is crucial. Preconventional moral reasoning is not just a problem of early childhood; it is a crucial problem in professional education and practice.

Kohlberg's two conventional stages are mutual exchange, relationships, and conformity (Stage 3), and social system and conscious maintenance (Stage 4). These stages are associated with learning behaviors related to social (Stage 3) and legal norms (Stage 4). As children mature, they begin to function in the adult world as moral agents, expected to act within social expectations and the law. These concepts have been widely studied in childhood development (Piaget, 1971) and the study of college students (Pascarella & Terenzini, 2005).

Within professional practice, the common standards of practice (i.e. the ethical codes and standards that guide practice) evolve over time. For example, while sexual harassment is now routinely considered outside the accepted boundaries of professional practice, involved relationships within communities of professional practice, including professors dating students (Rosovsky, 1990), remain complicated issues. Building an understanding of the ways moral problems are articulated and understood, and how standards change is another important, and long overlooked, problem with professional codes.

Kohlberg describes two stages of postconventional moral development: prior rights based on the social contract (Stage 5), a view compatible with faith-centered moral judgment; and universal ethical principles (Stage 6). These two stages present a number of problems with respect to professional practice and justice in the adult world. There were several critical reconstructions of Kohlberg's theory, mostly provided by his advancement of enlightenment values of universal justice over other forms of advanced moral thought at the highest stage. Three compelling adaptations of the theory include those of Fowler (1981), Gilligan (1982), and Siddle Walker and Snarey (2004). Fowler proposed stages of faith, a view that was centered in Christian logic related to Kohlberg's stages and a perspective that has been adapted to examine multiple religious frames (Small, 2007). Gilligan criticized the justice-centered frame as being male-centric and proposed stages of care that paralleled the stages of moral reasoning. Siddle Walker and Snarey reconstructed the stages of justice and care to be more compatible with the African-American tradition.

These reconstructions illustrate the problem with centering the stages of moral reasoning within a single vantage point among the most enlightened assumptions. Habermas's (1990) reconstruction provides a basis for rethinking moral reasoning in relation to action. He views the preconventional as related to asymmetry of power and quid pro quo; the conventional as centric to justice as such; and the postconventional as related to an understanding of how moral problems emerge in the first place. This reconstruction provides a basis for rethinking professional action (St. John, 2009):

- At the preconventional level, it is possible to engage in immoral action through the abuse of power (a consequence of asymmetry of power) or doing and returning favors (quid pro quo)—two forms of action that can plague professional practice and undermine efforts to promote fairness and social justice.
- At the conventional level, developing laws, rules, and regulations provides a means of resolving ambiguity.
- At the postconventional level, it is possible to initiate action that focuses on under-

standing the reasons for unfairness and injustice, as well as to envision steps that can be taken to resolve these problems.

Focusing on practical discursive issues and behaviors within daily practice is essential to a transition in the understanding of moral reasoning and the consciousness of professionals. My argument is that the focus of moral education for professionals must be expanded beyond topics related to moral issues and ethical codes (i.e. how people ought to act in situations) to include building an understanding of moral reasoning in action, including the ways professionals think about morally problematic situations in practice and reconstruct strategies used to address these challenges. An introduction to moral codes and standards provides an important foundation, but it is not sufficient. To be useful in practice it is necessary for action theories to focus on the central mission of practice—"getting the job done"—but to do so in ways that are fair and just for colleagues within the community of practice as well as for clients and the society served by professionals.

Facing Critical Social Challenges

The very nature of professional expertise—its presumed claims about truth and objectivity—can undermine efforts to understand and address moral challenges when they emerge in practice. In *Truth and Justification*, Habermas (2003) further illuminates underlying problems associated with moral reasoning in professional practice. Habermas argues that "presumed truths" are frequently treated as valid in action situations, but the step of testing hypotheses about that validity is often overlooked in action situations. This limitation of expertise causes moral problems that compound if ignored. Habermas argues a focus on moral learning, along with a focus on reasoning and action, are necessary to finding ways to solve these complex problems.

The Limitations of Expertise

The problematic nature of truth claims is inherent in professional action: "*Beliefs* are implicitly held to be true in success controlled action and truth claims implicitly made in communicative action correspond to the presupposition of an objective world of things that are dealt with and judged" (emphasis added, Habermas, 2003, p. 39). Presumed truths, or beliefs, are central to professional judgment (i.e. strategic action) and collective attempts to build shared understandings of problems (i.e. communicative action). But even when common understandings about practice build through social interactions among professionals, there is an inherent risk that these assumptions might not be true, especially for groups not represented in the conversation:

> This transcending relation (i.e. between assumptions and truth) guarantees the difference between truth and rational acceptability, but puts the participants in discourses in a paradoxical position. On the one hand, they are able to vindicate controversial truth claims only thanks to the convincing power of good reason. On the other hand, even the best reasons are under the proviso of fallibility so that precisely at the point where the truth and falsity of propositions is the only issue, the gap between rational acceptability and truth cannot be bridged (Habermas, 2003, p. 40).

The power of professionals to convince non-experts and use rationalizations to objectify facts in ways that disguise truth is not a trivial matter with respect to fairness and justice in practice and access to services. Medical doctors frequently misdiagnose health problems. Their use of expert knowledge narrows the range of possible problems, but in some cases the actual health problem turns out to be different than presumed to be true.[18] For example, an orthopedic doctor might diagnose a knee problem as arthritis and fail to test for more serious problems—a pattern of behavior reinforced by efforts to reduce health care costs. In addition, the rules of insurance companies can be manipulated to deny care even when problems are diagnosed correctly. Michael Moore's film *Sicko* illustrates these problems, giving visual images to the fears of many. Lawyers use legal arguments and claims of legal justification to support their clients, but may misrepresent the facts of the case as they make justifications or rationalizations for their clients.

Even when multiple experts collaborate to build shared understandings of problems, they cannot know the future conditions about which they speculate. Collaboration and open communication do not guarantee truth or justice. For example, it was not possible to know whether the World Trade Center could withstand plane crashes, like those on September 11, 2001, until the event happened. The collapse of the Minneapolis, Minnesota bridge over the Mississippi River in August 2007, despite repeated inspections, also illustrates the limitations of expert judgment. Likewise, when educators successfully implement an educational program in one setting and researchers document this success contrasted with a control site, using an experimental research design, it does not mean the same method will work in all settings. Replicating a practice, even one thought to be a *best practice*, does not a guarantee the practice will work in all the circumstances.

While Habermas argues communicative action "fosters individuation and social integration at the same time" (2003, p. 81), he recognizes that this idealized form of action does not overcome the problem of false truth claims. He argues that even communicative action aimed at testing truth claims can fall subject to this challenge: "Finally, the orientation toward truth in the critical testing of conditional claims to validity mobilizes stands still another kind of idealization" (p. 100). One reason is that claims about objectivity acquired in the development of expertise can hold a misunderstanding of truth and evidence. "The presupposed objectivity of the world is too deeply entwined with the intersubjectivity of reaching an understanding about something in the world that we cannot transcend this connection and the linguistically disclosed horizon of our intersubjectively shattered lifeworld" (p. 100).

Expertise without moral reasoning, inclusive of both self-critique and collective efforts to understand critical social problems, is particularly vulnerable to intersubjective bias used to justify immoral action. There are many examples of this problem. For decades, research on smoking was funded and communicated by the tobacco industry, propagating a myth that science had not connected smoking to cancer.[19] Many research universities were engaged in this regime of misinformation. The rationales used to shut down attempts to reform health care in the 1990s, which were well documented in *Sicko* (Moore, 2007), illustrate the role fear and deception by the AMA and the insurance industry played in building an unfair system of access to medical services in this country.

Consider also the example of educational research. In the past three decades, education reform in the US has been promoted on research that emphasizes correlations between math courses completed in high school and subsequent educational attainment (Becker, 2004; Heller, 2004) without even considering how education policies and public funding for student aid influence access to advanced math or college attainment. There was a well-established pattern of using these correlation statistics to justify a specific course of policy (i.e. emphasizing alignment of curriculum and standards) while overlooking how policies actually influence outcomes (St. John, 2006).

In 1983, *A Nation at Risk* (U.S. Department of Education) was published citing a consensus among experts that there was a continuing problem with providing access to quality education to some youth. Since that time, arguments that standards matter and money does not (Finn, 1990) have prevailed in the minds of many policy makers, even though research has contradicted this argument (Daun-Barrett, 2008; St. John, 1994, 2006). Public policies were implemented based on these original collective judgments even as the US lost ground, compared to other countries, in high school graduation rates and college access (i.e. the percentages of students who graduated high school and went on to college). A rationale evolved that objectified the problem, leading to the perpetuation of failing policies, such as *No Child Left Behind,* that were based on seriously problematic research.[20]

The role that educational policies enacted over 35 years based on this excellence rationale played in the decline of American education still has not been seriously evaluated. Instead, the dominant beliefs regarding education reform focus on efficacy standards and accountability over funding and process-oriented school improvements. A logic similar to the so-called "excellence movement," with critiques of education based on this false information coupled with the failure of this course of policy action, continues. Recent reports by the National Governors Association (Conklin & Curran, 2005) and the Commission on the Skills of the American Workforce (2007) advance this problematic logic.

The problematic nature of education policies was too seldom questioned by those who promoted these reform agendas, initiated after the publication of *A Nation at Risk.* They failed to reflect on the underlying assumptions about whether the strategies fit the problems they were intended to address (St. John, 2003, 2006). Such self-reinforcing discourse destroys the hopes of millions of parents seeking better lives for their children. The failure of analysts to reflect is a serious problem in education, as it has been in health (e.g. smoking) and other areas of policy discourse.

The alternative approach of encouraging the professional development of educators in schools merits consideration, especially if it is coupled with an increased emphasis on improving high school curricula. Rationalizing the facts in ways that support the interests of professionals over the *social good*[21] and fairness is a critical issue. The problem is not just a matter of government policy; it is also and especially a problem of practice. Replicating patterns of deception and obfuscation are deeply embedded in professional reasoning. The misuse of expertise too often becomes common practice. Professional development with an explicit emphasis on moral learning as a part of problem solving—the integration of scientific knowledge with a basic orientation toward the pursuit of truth in practice and social justice—provides an alternative to overemphasizing expert judgment and advocating rationales based on political ideologies.

A Focus on Moral Learning

Habermas (2003) proposes moral learning is necessary to overcome rationalization in ways that obfuscate the true underlying causes of everyday problems. He argues it is necessary "to bring out the *constructive meaning* or morality in another way" (emphasis in original, p.105). He explains that

> We can represent moral learning processes as an intelligent expansion and reciprocal interpenetration of social worlds that in a given case of conflict do not yet sufficiently overlap. The disputing parties learn to *include* one another in a world they construct together so as to be able to judge and consensually resolve controversial action in light of matching standards of evaluation (emphasis in original, p 105).

Using this logic, it should be possible to bring the excluded voices into the process of reform to correct the problem. For example, in health care the problem of misdiagnosis is related to communication (i.e. a shared understanding of the problem between doctor and patient) as well as to acquisition of expertise. This is complicated by the fact that doctors and patients have very different standards of evaluation. The problem of education reform is also complex because it requires understanding the voices of teachers struggling to implement reforms, along with parents and children trying to cope with them, not just the perpetual critiques of experts aligned with policy makers who advocate for the policies being used.

However, the process of communicating about problems with those affected by implemented solutions can be undermined by the rules of a profession. In their educations, experts learn both analytic methods (e.g. mathematical manipulations, diagnostic procedures, etc.) along with methods of consultation. These rules can bind the free will of the professional to a code of practice. Habermas (2003) provides the following commentary on the role of rules in expert judgments:

- Rules "bind" the will in such a way that acting subjects seek to avoid possible rule violations; following a rule means refraining from "acting against" the role.
- If someone is following a rule, she can make mistakes and is subject to being criticized for making mistakes; unlike knowing how to follow a rule in practice, judging whether a given form of behavior is correct requires an explicit knowledge of rules.
- Someone who is following a rule must in principle be able to justify her actions to a critic; hence the virtual division of labor between the role and knowledge of a critic and the practitioner is part of the concept of rule-following itself.
- Therefore, no one can follow a rule solipsistically, on her own; the practical mastery of a rule signifies the ability to take part in a social, habituated practice; as soon as subjects reflexively ascertain their intuitive knowledge in order to justify themselves to one another, they are already engaged in this practice (p. 123).

The rules that form the codes of practice can make independent moral action difficult. Rules of practice often have an overly simplistic binary coding of right and wrong. Referring back to the example of educational research, groups of researchers and policy makers may agree on method and even advocate a policy, but if they fail to consider the consequences, their notions of scientific truth and rightness of policy may become a source of, rather than a solution to, problems with education. Decisions by individuals or small groups to resist these rules by changing or not implementing them can backfire, as Habermas explains:

> The objective world can register this "resistance" only performatively by refusing to "go along with" *targeting interventions* in a world of causally interpreted sequences of events. In this way it registers an objection only in the operational sphere of instrumental action (emphasis in original, 2003, p. 154).

When a person who sees moral problems is left out of the consensus-building process within an organization, or when she realizes there are problems with implementation of mandates from above, her choices are limited.[22] For example, teachers may resist mandated curricula based on their understanding of the learning needs of students, and, if these practices result in lower test scores, those who favor standardization and accountability label these experimenters "poor teachers." On the other hand, some of the teachers labeled as the "best" (i.e. teachers with high test scores in their classrooms) may also be among those who make decisions to resist or adapt policy mandates by experimenting, but their strategies are more successful. Intervening in ways that transform these situations is extremely difficult and may not seem possible in many instances. Habermas concludes by arguing for philosophical clarification:

> I would first of all propose that we reflect on the hermeneutic situation of the human rights debate itself, as it involves participants of different cultural backgrounds. This would draw our attention to the normative content already implicit in the tacit presuppositions of any discourse aimed at reaching mutual understanding. For, irrespective of cultural background, all the participants intuitively know full well that a consensus based on insight is not possible if the relations between the participants in communication are not symmetrical—that is, shared willingness to look at one's own traditions through the eyes of a stranger, to learn from one another, and so on.
>
> Second, I believe it would be useful to reflect on the notion of "intersubjective rights" used in the conception of human rights . . .
>
> Third and finally, it would be important to clarify the different grammatical role played by ought-sentences and by value statements, as well as those played by normative and evaluative expressions in general (2003, pp. 291–292).

Creating opportunities to test assumptions about actionable situations is crucial, especially when there are critical social problems overlooked by policies and commonly held assumptions. Habermas concludes this point:

> Here, it is all the more helpful to remember that an agreement on binding norms (ensuring reciprocal rights and duties) does not require the mutual appreciations for one another's culture achievements and life styles, but instead depends solely on acknowledging that every person is of equal value (2003, p. 292).

Basic Challenges

While these underlying problems of social justice are not the only moral dilemmas that confront professionals as they apply the knowledge of their professions, they are nonetheless critical. Failure to broaden the discourse of practice beyond the community of experts undermines a common aim across the professions: to serve society. Unless they pursue this among the aims of their practice, professionals run the risk of undermining the collective social good. While the social good, like the truth itself, is an illusive concept, there are two critical issues facing practitioners across professions: (1) to seek truth in critical social situations, rather than rely on beliefs and past practices rationalized based on the rules of the profession; and (2) to engage communities affected by practice in discourse to seek inclusive understandings of problematic situations.

CONCLUSIONS

The social context for professional action is complex, and the challenges faced by professionals are many and substantial. There is a compelling need for more well trained and caring practitioners who are concerned about social justice. While the history of professional education in law, education, ministry, and government service predate the movement toward social democracy, the professions and professional education have evolved. More specifically, professional schools became part of university education in the late nineteenth and early twentieth centuries, a period during which service and private charity were thought to be the primary means of promoting social justice. The ethos of public service is integral to the codes of ethics of the traditional professions. The newer professions emerged during a period of history when government took responsibility for extending opportunity. However, for nearly three decades there has been a shift in the ethics of public service, an area in which the responsibility of paying for services such as higher education, social services, and health care has increasingly shifted from taxpayers to consumers. Too often people are treated as clients in a privatized society rather than as citizens deserving an equal opportunity for essential services, including education, health care, and legal services.

In summary, this chapter has examined critical problems in the social context of professional action in modern societies. Several understandings emerge from this review:

- There are critical social problems with access to professions as well as in professional practice. Specifically, there are persisting and growing inequalities in access to professional education in both middle-class and elite professions. These include inequality of opportunities to prepare for college (a critical concern in undergraduate professional education) and access to four-year colleges (a critical issue in preparation for elite professions provided through graduate education). Also, there are inequalities of access to services in health care, education, business, law, and other professions. These inequalities of access limit actualization of basic human rights.
- There are two underlying critical challenges within practice for professionals of all types: (1) to seek truth in critical social situations, rather than rely on beliefs and past practices rationalized based on the rules of the profession; and (2) to engage

communities affected by practice in discourse to seek inclusive understandings of problematic situations.
- There are technical as well as social aspects of moral reasoning in professional practice. The presumptions of truth made in the application of technical *rules of professions* are not always true. While there is little reason to doubt that the methods and practices which comprise foundations of the professions were created based on common understandings (see Chapter 2), there is always the possibility that they are not correct or that they do not apply in intended ways.
- Periodically reflecting on the reasons for choosing a professional career is encouraged.

REFLECTIVE EXERCISE

It is appropriate to situate one's career choice, as a personal vocation, within a personal understanding of life goals. The reflective exercise (see Text Box 1.1) can be the first step in creating a personal journal. Some may be most comfortable journaling in private, perhaps keeping a personal paper and pencil journal, others may want to keep their journals in electronic form, and still others may be comfortable with public exchanges as a form of journaling (e.g. posting reflections on social network web pages).[23] Regardless of the method of recording reflection, engaging in the process of reflection is an integral part of personal professional development.

Text Box 1.1 Reflective Exercise: Reflection on Life and Professional Goals

Reflect on the following questions:
- What are the aims that guide your personal decisions about a career?
- What are your educational and professional goals?
- What do you want to accomplish and contribute as part of your career?
- Are there educational and social inequalities that concern you as you consider your career goals? If so, what are they?
- What are the gaps between your life aims, understanding of critical social challenges, and your current actions?

Write a reflective statement about your goals as a professional. Consider how your professional goals relate to your personal goals in life, and how your plans for education and professional development (i.e. ongoing education after graduation) can help you achieve your goals.

2

SOCIAL JUSTICE

Everyone has a way of framing issues of care and justice, formed through experiences in their families, communities, and educational institutions. The frames people hold are complex and difficult for them to articulate, perhaps even to understand, because their frames are formed through experience with formal and informal learning, including cultural experiences. One aspect of these personal frames is what a person thinks they value, or their beliefs. Most people can quickly respond to questions about beliefs, but their responses may be guarded in a social setting because of their feelings about what others may expect to hear. Actions often differ substantially from beliefs, not just because of the ways people filter what they say through social expectations, but also because values in action (i.e. the ways actions communicate values) often really do differ from their beliefs. To understand values in action, it is important to consider the role of faith traditions along with socially constructed reasoning about values.

To understand the notion of frames as they relate to espoused values and actions and with respect to shared life contexts people experience, it is appropriate to start by examining the concepts of social justice and individual development that are embedded in our religious and philosophical traditions. This chapter examines concepts of social justice and human development emphasized in the major religious traditions along with the generally accepted moral philosophies that underlie democratic systems of government. Since modern nation states had their origins in an earlier period when the rights to govern were attributed to higher powers and modern notions of human rights were derived from faith-based reasoning (Taylor, 2007), it is important to start an exploration of the values that underlie reasoning with an examination of these traditions. Democratic reasoning about social justice provides a contemporary lens for viewing human rights, but it is appropriately understood as being historically situated. This review provides a basis for encouraging readers to think about their own value traditions—the frames of references they use to judge what is fair, just, and caring. An awareness of personal values is needed before stepping forward into the process of examining one's own actions in relation to one's values, and whether there are gaps that merit attention.

THE FAITH TRADITIONS AND SOCIAL JUSTICE

Frequently, the conflict between religion and secularism in higher education, including professional education, is viewed in relation to the Christian tradition (Marsden, 1994; Taylor, 2007; Thelin, 2004). According to this view, the framing of knowledge that dominated in academe, as in society at large, was situated within religious traditions before the secular views of science and technology emerged and became dominate in higher education. This type of historical analysis leads to lamenting the loss of faith as the central value in moral reasoning about life and society, as well as in academic and political framing of social problems. For example, Charles Taylor (2007) provides a compelling analysis of how the evolution of deist views[24] on human rights espoused by English intellectual and political elites in the seventeenth century set the frame for the claims to the rights of citizens among American revolutionaries—the founding fathers—in the eighteenth century, leading to the Bill of Rights.[25] While this historical understanding can inform contemporary social justice, it creates a Christian centrism of values that limits debate about the role of religious values in relation to social justice within an increasingly global society.

An alternative to centering a discussion of values in the Christian tradition is to consider the role of social justice and of human development across faith traditions. Religions have provided foundations for the formation of social organizations and for enabling individuals to develop morally and consciously within their societies. Given the diversity of peoples in twenty-first century global communities, it is important to consider perspectives on social justice from the vantages of the Hindu, Buddhist, Jewish, Christian, and Islamic traditions. These religions not only have long histories, but they are also still widely practiced.[26] Most urban communities in the US and other democratic societies have people in at least two or three of these traditions, if not all of them.

There are several reasons for starting with a comparative vantage of faith traditions. One reason is that professionals frequently interact with peers and clients who have frames of justice and moral reasoning influenced by their respective diverse faith traditions. Therefore, an examination of core commonalities and differences across faith traditions, especially with respect to the ways of viewing fairness and justice, provides a starting point. Given my focus on professional action and social justice, my review of the five faith traditions focuses on two dimensions of the faith traditions: (1) the *social aspect* and its focus on community and equality within the tradition; and (2) the *developmental aspect*, and its image of development of the individual. The developmental aspect is important because it is the promise of a better life in the times ahead—in the after life, the next life, or on this earth—that is at the core of the faith traditions, framing what it is people strive for through faith.

Hindu Tradition

Modern mystics in the West brought Eastern consciousness into public awareness (Cox, 1977; Ouspensky, 1971). However, in order to see what this tradition contributes to an understanding of social justice in action it is important to turn to the roots of the Western understanding of Hinduism, the ancient faith tradition of the Indian subcontinent and the oldest of the major religions. Hinduism refers to both cultural traditions on the Indian subcontinent and also to methods of reaching consciousness situated in those traditions. We should ponder the consequences of abstracting methods of attaining consciousness from their social contexts.

While the English had long been in India, the English-speaking world was introduced to Hinduism through the talks and writings of Swami Vivekananda in the late nineteenth century. The original preface of the eight volumes (dated in 1907) characterizing these collected works declares that "As an authoritative pronouncement of Hinduism in all of its phases, these writings and speeches are beyond value" (Vivekananda, 1989, p. v). The goal of this tradition, as introduced to Westerners at the time, was inner consciousness: "You must remember that freedom of the soul is the goal of all Yogas, and each one equally leads to the same result" (p. 55). He describes the path of the Yoga as being "to where Buddha got largely by meditation or Christ by prayer" (p. 55). He describes this state as liberation: "Liberation means freedom—freedom from the bondage of good, as well as from the bondage of evil" (p. 55). Vivekananda described a form of consciousness welcoming to people of all faiths, as a state of being that related to development:

> This attainment does not depend on any dogma, or doctrine, or belief. Whether one is Christian, Jew, or Gentile, it does not matter. Are you unselfish? That is the question. If you are, you will be perfect without reading a single religious book, without going to a single church or temple (p. 93).

While this statement of justice (unselfishness) and consciousness (liberation and freedom) may seem egalitarian and accessible to all, there are limits embedded in the beliefs, customs, and social orders underlying the faith. Vivekananda (1989) argued that "Absolute equality, that which means a perfect balance of all the struggling forces in all of the planes, can never be in this world" (p. 114) because "We come into the world with unequal endowments; we come as greater men or lesser men, and there is no getting away from that pre-natally determined condition" (p. 114). The Hindu notions of conscious are deeply intertwined with the caste system and the notion of rebirth.

It is possible in the Hindu tradition for the individual to reach a state of being one with God; however, this right is constrained at birth. The noted psychologist, Eric Erickson (1969), described this lottery at birth as

> What we would ascribe to the beginnings of the life cycle the Hindu view projects into previous lives which determines the coordinates of a person's rebirth . . . He may emerge, then, in the caste of the Brahmans and learn to be literate . . . or among the Sudras to toil in the sweat of his brow. Or, indeed, he may miss all of these honored occupations and go through life doomed to touch what others will avoid and, therefore, be untouchable himself. But the Untouchable, too, has unlimited chances ahead of him (pp. 35–36).

For centuries the Hindu way had valued customs, respect for authority, and changes for betterment through rebirth, rather than providing a chance for salvation, or liberation, for all in this life. By the early twentieth century, it was not only the Westerners who understood this social structure as unequal, but also the revolutionaries in India. Erikson (1969) quoted Nehru (from the translation of a 1956 publication), the political father of the country of India, regarding the dilemmas of Hindu Law:

Hindu law itself is largely custom, and customs change and grow. The elasticity of the Hindu law disappeared under the British and gave place to rigid legal codes drawn up after consultation with the most orthodox people. Thus the growth of Hindu society, slow as it was, was stopped. The Muslims resented the new conditions even more and retired into their shells (p. 272).[27]

The political, nonviolent revolution in India, brought about in large part by Mahatma Gandhi's life story is, of course, of global importance in the struggle for justice. In 1934, Gandhi observed:

I believe in the fundamental truth of all great religions of the world. I believe that they are all God-given, and I believe that they are all necessary to the people to whom these religions were revealed. And I believe that, if we could all of us read the scriptures of different faiths from the standpoint of the followers of those faiths, we would find that at the bottom they were all one and were all helpful to one and another (Gandhi, 2002, p. 78).

The revolutionary consciousness demonstrated by Gandhi had an influence on the emergence of functional democracy. The values of equality have long been an aim in India, but overcoming inequality has been a struggle. Basic literacy remained a goal for many groups well into the twentieth century (Sen, 1999). More recently, India has made efforts to expand educational and employment opportunities to Untouchables, but not without resistance by people of the upper castes. Thus, while one could argue that the country of India was founded with a vision of overcoming the constraints of customs in the Hindu tradition that contributed to injustice, the struggle toward equality continues in this context.

In addition, there has been a migration of Hindus from the Indian subcontinent to regions across the world. As the population has migrated, low caste people and women have had greater opportunities. New challenges have emerged for the migrants: "The presence of Hinduism as a religion along side others requires Hindus to think about and articulate what is important to them in ways that can be understood by outsiders" (Knott, 1998, p. 108). Thus, the religion, which is comprised of many traditions fostered by many and diverse gurus, faces challenges to transform as it modernizes, at the same time as India's culture is being transformed by rapid economic change.

The struggle to confront and transform injustice is a seemingly unending challenge. Gandhi's Saygraha, or truth in action, was a method he developed in South Africa and applied in his home nation of India. I think of this type of reflection on truth as *critical spiritual reflection*, a form of introspection that is crucial to confronting injustices in action. Like Gandhi, Martin Luther King, Jr. (1967) reflected critically on the human condition within his own faith rationale as he moved toward nonviolent social action as a means of overcoming injustice in the American South in the 1960s. These contributions to a collective understanding of justice are traceable from Gandhi's early works in South Africa to the nonviolence in the pursuit of independence in India, and from the desegregation movement in the US to the eventual end of apartheid in South Africa.

Buddhist Tradition

The Buddhist tradition began with Buddha, a Hindu prince who attained status as "the teacher without equal" (Wangyal, 1995, p. 3). Unlike Hinduism, which views enlightenment as attainable by a only few, and only after many lives, Buddha provided an image of the development of the individual that is based on compassion, and therefore potentially attainable for anyone. While there are different Buddhist traditions, I discuss the Tibetan tradition.

Within the Tibetan tradition, there are three levels toward attainment of enlightenment and the qualities of the Buddha. At the lowest, or initial, level one sees "one's own misery" and seeks happiness by taking "refuge in the Buddha from faith in his qualifications" (Wangyal, 1995, p. 11). One finds happiness through following the teachings and practicing virtue. At the middle level, one sees the nature of suffering and "being afraid of this pervasive suffering, one takes refuge in Buddha and seeks the happiness of *nirvana.* The person begins the practice of the three principles—exceptional moral practice, exceptional meditation, and exceptional wisdom" (emphasis in original, p. 11). Finally, at the highest level "one sees the misery of all sentient beings and seeks to attain the perfect enlightenment of Buddhahood for the sake of all beings" (p. 11). Individuals who reach this level "unselfishly seek only to help others" (p. 11).

The Buddhist tradition carries forward a belief in past lives from Hinduism, but contends that all individuals have a chance of reaching the highest levels of consciousness. Wangyal (1995) attributes this transition in the tradition to Buddha's encouragement of his most advanced followers to go out and teach, rather than to freely choose death as a means of seeking a higher state of consciousness. Regardless of the reason for the transition in logic about who can attain enlightenment, the Buddhist tradition can be considered liberating—especially compared to the assumptions of the early Hindu tradition—and accessible.

The current Dalai Lama (Bstan-ʿdzin rgya, mtsho, 2007) recognizes the freedom to choose pathways toward consciousness. He expresses great respect for the Jewish, Christian, Islamic, and Hindu traditions. His writing helps clarify the focus on consciousness and past lives within the Buddhist tradition. The Dalai Lama describes functions of consciousness as attaining clarity and knowing:

> *Clarity* here refers to clear arising of appearances to consciousness. It does not make any difference whether or not this perception corresponds to the nature of things. A particular appearance arises to consciousness, along with awareness of its aspects or features. Now that appearance is always valid and direct. That is what is meant by *clear*—the fact that this appearance is reflected *clearly.* Once this appearance has been made clear, there is a "knowing" or awareness that apprehends that appearance, among its various aspects (emphasis in original, p. 43).

In his discussion of past lives, the Dalai Lama recognizes that there is neither scientific proof nor disproof (Bstan-ʿdzin rgya, mtsho, 2007), and he encourages the scientific study of consciousness (Bstan-ʿdzin rgya, mtsho, 2005). He also argues that understanding the concept of past lives is part of the pathway to consciousness:

> However, if there are past and future lives, it is only the virtuous habitual tendencies we create now within our mind stream that will be of any benefit to us in

the future, because it is the stream of consciousness that continues. Anything connected with us on the level of our physical body, no matter how helpful it might be in this lifetime, will not be of benefit to us in the future. This much is clear (2007, p. 134).

Before the invasion by the Chinese, Tibet was a nation state that combined Buddhism and governance. With his escape from Tibet, the Dalai Lama has reflected on the global value of the tradition as a force in liberating consciousness. Indeed, he has taken his teachings to a global scale. Perhaps this development will enable a new synergy between science, consciousness, justice for all, and caring for the health of the planet, a vision evident in his ministry (Bstan-ʿdzin rgya, mtsho, 2005). Buddhism, unlike the other faith traditions, does not have a history of being linked to war, nor is it tightly linked to the governance of nation states, with the exception of Tibet. There are nations with mostly Buddhist populations, but the authority to govern is linked to religion in the same ways it has been for nations with tight links to Christian, Islamic, and Jewish traditions.

Jewish Tradition

Judaism is the oldest of the three major monotheistic religions (Hinduism and Buddhism are not monotheistic). Historically, the tribes of Israel were enslaved in Egypt, then gained their freedom, and finally wandered the deserts of the Middle East before settling in the land known as Israel. Moses, the leader of the liberation, was a prophet who spoke with God. The Ten Commandments conveyed through Moses provide a framework for legal morality.[28] By the early twentieth century, the Jewish people were dispersed through Europe, the Middle East, and other parts of the globe. At that time, Palestine had been an Islamic state for centuries. The Crusades and World War I did not change the dominance of Islam in this region.[29] The Holocaust—the mass extermination of Jews, Gypsies, and others (gays, dissidents, etc.) by Germans and other Europeans during World War II—influenced changes in the theological landscape of the Middle East.

The return to Israel has long been yearned for by modern Jews in the US and Europe because many of the core beliefs of the faith originated in that region. A critical portion of the history of the Jewish people took place in Israel, a region occupied by Rome before the emergence of Christianity. The laws of the Jewish people emphasized cleanliness, and the Temple was a place in which only the clean could worship. The Jewish laws governing cleanliness, preparation of food, and social interactions had their basis in both early concepts of public health and religion. After World War II, the United Nations intervened and created the modern nation state of Israel. Both conservative and secular Jews were alienated by the Holocaust, and immigrated back to Israel after World War II. However, the practice of the faith was spread across the globe among the Jewish people.

The image of the developed person in the Jewish tradition is a moral person who ponders the will of God for self and community. There are many images of moral leadership within the tradition. Most of the images captured in the Hebrew Bible are of people caught between the forces of war and peace, good and evil. The moral person emerges from the struggle. While the Hebrew Bible describes a bloody history, the Jewish tradition was transformed after the Babylonian destruction of the first Jerusalem Temple, and bloody massacres were quieted through a rabbinic consensus:

As a result of this rabbinic consensus in combination with the *realpolitik* of Jewish history, Judaism remained a quietist religious civilization from the end of the second century onward for nearly two thousand years. Judaism has a consistent record. The rabbis' exegetical management of scripture succeeded in keeping divinely sanctioned war out of the repertoire of rabbinic Judaism aside from the realm of fantasy (Firestone, 2004, p. 80).

In fact, the concept of moral responsibility is very deeply held in the Jewish tradition. Introspection of decisions made is integral to the practice of the faith:

> There always remains a possibility of error. There is always the option of retreat from responsibility. Judaism recognizes that human error and human judgment may render a wrong decision. It nevertheless requires that humans take responsibility to struggle with difficult issues and be accountable for the results of human action (Firsestone, 2004, p. 85).

This deep sense of moral responsibility requires introspection and inner reconciliation. To hold a self-image as a moral person in this tradition requires reconciling past errors within current practice.

Social justice has also had a long tradition within the Jewish tradition. There is evidence of an early emphasis on social welfare for low-income peoples within urban communities among Jews for centuries before the emergence of democratic states (Walzer, 1983). Greenberg (2004) argues that the test for those in the Jewish faith is to see others in the image of God. In fact, it is this leap of faith that determines the deep commitment to community and humanity within the Jewish tradition, a complex process that is not easy for the non-Jew to understand:

> Experiencing others' equality and uniqueness elicits the desire to protect them. If one truly internalizes the value of equality, then one understands the other has the right to justice and not to be discriminated against even if the other has less money, less access to legal representation, or is somehow outside the official pale. Recognition of equality triggers the sense of the right to a fair share—not to be hungry, not to be poor, not to be oppressed. Similarly, if one recognizes the dimension of uniqueness as an intellectual construct, but one out of emotional response to the uniqueness of a person, then this encounter summons up the sense of obligation to offer what special help this person needs when he or she is sick, or handicapped, or middle class. If the other has a particular yearning for an unmet need, then one wants to help fill the need (Greenberg, 2004, p. 86).

The obligation to social justice is as deeply embedded in the faith tradition, as realized through the largely oral tradition of the practice of the Jewish faith. The challenge is to see people of other faiths—including Christian and Muslim—as the image of God: "The task of this generation is to ally with the new communication trends to incorporate others in all their status as images of God into the positive central religious categories as creatures worthy of love and help" (Greenberg, 2004, p. 99). Rather than arguing for communities with the same values, Greenberg argues for a new form of religious pluralism:

Therefore, I would offer a religious criterion that all faiths that show the ability to instill these values (of viewing the human as infinitely valuable, equal, and unique) in their adherents, all that teaches believers to honor these dignities—and therefore show their creeds' capability to raise humans in the image of God—should be judged as valid. All of a religion's additional teachings or specific truths about divine and human should be treated as strengths and weaknesses; however, the need to correct weaknesses cannot invalidate a religion's right to exist. This is a commitment that the Abrahamic faith should make—not only to each other, but also to other major religions that do not fit the conventional model (2004, p. 108).

This reconstruction of the image of community points in a direction that is needed, given the deep global conflicts about religion. Smoothing over differences by creating communal notions of justice has not proven workable. The gaps between actions and beliefs—with respect to war and peace and to preserving and abusing the planet—have become far too serious to move ahead without beliefs, values, actions, and discourse across belief traditions, inclusive of nonbelievers (recognizing nonbelief as a tradition of belief).

Christian Tradition

Christianity had its origins in Israel during the Roman occupation. Jesus was a roaming rabbi of the people who preached an interpretation of Jewish law that was socially just. His interpretation required a caring attitude toward people of the Jewish tradition, as well as those who lived outside the tradition and were foreign to it, and used faith in God as a measure of the value of women and men, rather than the practice of the law per se. After Jesus died, his followers continued to preach and practice the emergent faith, both among Jews and across the empire. Eventually the empire adopted the faith, and became the Holy Roman Empire. When the Empire split, two versions of the Christian religion emerged: the eastern portion became known as Orthodox and the western portion as Catholic. During the subsequent centuries of religious and political upheaval—the period now known as the Reformation—various Protestant sects broke off from the Catholic tradition. In the early twenty-first century there are many competing Christian traditions and no single theology. In this context, it may be important to reflect on the gospels rather than to discern a single contemporary doctrine.

To build understanding of the underlying social and human values of the faith, we can look back at the records of Jesus's life history as documented in the Synoptic Gospels (i.e. Matthew, Mark, and Luke).[30] The Synoptic Gospels[31] of the Bible tell the story of Jesus, a carpenter who became a rabbi and teacher. The historical Jesus lived in a revolutionary period (Spong, 1997). There were ragtag groups of Jews called Pharisees, who openly rebelled against Roman domination. There was a yearning for a political messiah among the population, and the Pharisees were more sympathetic to this aim, possibly even to the rebellions. There was an inherent tension between the Pharisees, who were the social progressives of the period (Armstrong, 1993), and the Scribes, who kept the religious laws in compliance with the Temple priests. Jesus preached as a roving rabbi of the faith, but with a new vision of God's kingdom. He had to contend with the prospect that people would project their yearning for a political messiah on to him. At the same time, he had to speak and answer questions in public settings in ways that were consonant with the laws kept by the Scribes. Because of threats to free speech, much

lifetime], was not instituted in the final form until the Farewell Pilgrimage of 632" (p. 62).

The pillars communicate both the images of development of the individual and the community. The developed individual is devout and prayerful. More than members of the other faiths, the Muslim has an obligation to act on Allah's will. The public prayer and the emphasis on charity created a strong sense of social cohesion and community among Arabs followers in the first millennium, well before formal government systems of social welfare. Compared to the other faith traditions, Islam is more highly protective of the virtues of women. It should also be noted that, at the time, Mohammad had a socially progressive attitude toward the rights of women, but over time Islam has become more conservative—especially compared to the evolving rights of women in the other faith traditions.

Within the Islamic tradition there is sill a strong alignment between the nation state and the faith tradition (Khadduri, 1966), a factor that complicates international discourse about human rights (Rawls, 1999). Within democratic states with diverse peoples and faiths, a major challenge is to retain an atmosphere that supports the core beliefs within a coherent community life. The newest of the monotheistic religions, Islam was developed within a multireligious life context, which provides a foundation for thinking about this contemporary problem. Early in his career, Mohammad lived, worked, and meditated in Mecca, a multireligious community at the time (Osman, 2006). This diversity of experience is reflected in the Qur'an:

Sure, the Qur'an criticizes some Jews and Christians, but it does the same with some Muslims as well. It is the Muslim moral responsibility not to take advantage of the critique of others in the Holy Qur'an in order to cover the Muslims' own shortcomings. If nothing else, because the Qur'an, as the word of God, is almost unique in appreciating the goodness of people of other religions . . . the Muslims have a duty to carry out the spirit of tolerance in the midst of religious pluralism (Ceric, 2004, p. 45).

In fact, contemporary Muslim scholars draw a parallel between this history of Islam in a multifaith community (as it was in Mohammad's lifetime) with the current tensions facing Muslims in modern democratic states. For example, Ghada Osman (2006) compares the seventh-century Mecca with the life of Muslims in the US:

Despite the obvious differences between the two communities, an examination of the social circumstances of each reveals deep similarity. At a time when Muslims in the United States are attempting to regenerate the core of their identity and their place in society, a look back at the early community provides some thought-provoking motifs and lessons (p. 191).

This sort of analysis, drawing from the history of the faith tradition to understand the present, offers an avenue for building understanding within and across faith communities. Certainly the identity of oneself as a person of faith is crucial to practice of faith and the discovery of the meaning of the principles of social justice within the faith traditions.

Comparison of Traditions

All five of the major faith traditions have images of the developed person as mature and moral (see Table 2.1). They all emphasize the practice of faith as a means of building moral consciousness and social responsibility. They also promote images of just communities that include caring for the poor and recognizing suffering. They also provide a means of reflecting on multifaith communities as a part of their historical practices. There are, of course, differences in the extent to which the different traditions emphasize social justice, but the foundations for a multireligious pluralism are evident within the traditions.

The challenge, in my view, is to value both faith-centered and enlightenment-based forms of moral reasoning, but to avoid letting one dominate over the other. Indeed, balancing reason and faith may be critical. Claiming the primacy of one form of morality over the other, after all, is part of the problem. Rather than insisting on one faith tradition over another, pushing enlightened logic as superior to faith, or arguing for a religious pluralism, I argue that our challenge is to find inner space to care about justice—be it centered in faith, theories of justice, or some combination—that gives us individual capacity to act morally in diverse communities. Individual introspection—accompanied by collective reflection among adults about how their experiences with faith and reason inform their values—provides a possible way to create public space for justice. An understanding of moral philosophy is needed to take this step.

MODERN MORAL PHILOSOPHY

In addition to recurrent wars, there were great inequalities in medieval societies. Most nation states were governed by monarchs who claimed a divine right to rule. In the seventeenth century, scholars began to address inequalities and speak to human rights,

Table 2.1 Social and Developmental Aspects of Hindu, Buddhist, Jewish, Christian, and Muslim Faith Traditions

Tradition	Social Aspect	Developmental Aspect
Hindu	Strong emphasis on tradition and social customs; caste system; originally views equality as impossible.	Focus on the consciousness of the individual; fate (and social caste) set at birth; unlimited life opportunities.
Buddhist	Emphasis on understanding the suffering of all as a step toward consciousness and caring for all.	Focus on consciousness of the individual, recognizes the potential of all for development.
Jewish	Sense of obligation to the other as equal; provide for the welfare of others.	Moral responsibility for individual decisions requires introspection, discernment, and reconciliation.
Christian	Social gospel of care and justice for all, including people of different faiths.	Doing the will of God; consciousness of the image of God within (Holy Spirit); being like Jesus.
Muslim	Emphasis on community prayer and charity for the poor (within the faith community).	Belief in God; private as well as public practice of prayer; acting on the will of Allah (as communicated in the Qur'an).

which were initially framed as given by God to humankind (Taylor, 2007). The American and French revolutions were influenced by these arguments. Democratic forms of government emerged, but social and economic progressivism did not begin on a mass scale until the late nineteenth century. For nearly a century, there were improvements in the economies of nation states and, especially after World War II, massive investments in education and social welfare.

In the late twentieth century there was a global decline in equality as democratic governments backed off their investments in social welfare. There was little disagreement about the swing away from progressive policies, but there were arguments about whether the causes were ideological shifts (Harvey, 2005; Huber & Stephens, 2001), religious fervor (Fogel, 2000), or economic stagnation (B. M. Friedman, 2005). The concept of modernity preceded the development of social democratic forms of government and the century of economic progress that started in the late nineteenth century. This background is critical to understanding the images of social justice and individual development that prevail in modern societies.

The Problem of Faith in the Modern Period

There are serious problems that must be overcome to realize the potential for just and caring communities respectful of differences across faith traditions. The challenges are formidable, as depicted by Fr. James Heft in the introduction to his book *Beyond Violence: Religious Sources of Social Transformation in Judaism, Christianity, and Islam*:

> Especially since the religious wars of the sixteenth and seventeenth centuries, many people in Europe have linked religion with violence. Bloody conflicts between Catholics and Protestants, and then between Protestants and other Protestants, lasted for decades. Once the leaders of the Enlightenment added to the horrors of these religious wars the memories of the Crusades, and especially the Inquisition, they concluded that if religion were excluded as a force from public life, violence could be minimized. They believed that once "privatized," religion would no longer be a source of violence. The public sphere would then be governed, they assumed, by people who followed the light of their own reason, even people who followed no faith. In fact, some Enlightenment thinkers claimed that people without any religious faith would be more reasonable than those whose passions were fueled and judgments shaped by religion (Heft, 2004, p. 1).

Of course, history has shown that World Wars I and II and the Cold War were waged by countries with secular governments. And now the world is nearly engaged in a new global war being waged by people making both secular and religious claims about justice. Framed by the West (i.e the US and its allies) as a "War on Terror," many of these individual conflicts seem to replicate old patterns of religious conflict.

There are extreme tensions among faith traditions, especially among the Islamic, Jewish, and Christian traditions. Heft's critique alludes to the history of conflict between Catholics and Protestants and across Protestant sects, a tension socially evident in U.S. and European history (Taylor, 2007), as well as in the history of war. The tensions are evident in the history of education as well: In the US Protestant schools became free public schools, whereas many Catholics continue to pay for a private education (Thelin, 2004; Reese, 2005). The privatization of Catholic education in the US is literal (i.e. religious education is ineligible for government support), as it is for a growing number of Christian families in fundamentalist Protestant denominations. However, the Christian faiths are not alone in this severe tension within the faith tradition. The tensions in historic Shiite and Sunni traditions (Ruthven, 2000) have become evident globally, and wars in the Middle East rage on across generations. These tensions play out in wars between nations, and discrimination within nation states. Thus, having multi-faith communities and nation states requires reconciliation of differences within and across faith traditions.

The history of the Crusades, mentioned in Heft's critique of Enlightenment reasoning in the governance of states, is eerily reminiscent of the recent multinational conflicts often characterized as the "War on Terror." The return of Jews to Israel after World War II as a people wronged by European governments created a fury in the Middle East. Once contained to conflicts between Israel and its Muslim neighbors, there is now global conflict. Terrorist cells are waging a global Islamic Jihad, which is the Muslim version of the Crusades (Khadduri, 1969). The U.S. war on Iraq, rationalized by the 9/11 terrorist attacks in New York City, may be even more egregious than the Crusades and, at the very least, is reminiscent of them. However, these wars seem to be about protection of theocracy rather than the imposition of faith.

In this context, the idea that communities can live with religious pluralism is appealing. The historic images from which we can envision a future are compelling: Mahatma Gandhi's nonviolence and truth in action; the Buddhist image of enlightenment based on an understanding of suffering and the discovery of caring for and teaching others; the Jewish ideal of seeing the image of God in others; Jesus's emphasis on acting with care and love for the other; and the lived multifaith community evident in the Islamic tradition. These images let us know alternatives are possible and have even been realized for moments in time. However, although religious pluralism and multi-faith communities may provide a starting point for creating caring communities of people, they are insufficient if they are not balanced with an emphasis on justice.

The destructive forces of racism and sexual discrimination are not resolved by reliance of multifaith traditions alone. A demonstrated lack of tolerance of people with gay, lesbian, and transgender identities is prominent among many who clamor about religious values. This is illustrative of the contemporary problem, as is the history of rationalizing racism based on misinterpretations of faith. For example, lynching African-Americans in the American South in the twentieth century was rationalized with images of Christianity by the Ku Klux Klan. Secular reason and systems of justice are necessary even within communities that base action on faith. To untangle this problem, we need to reconsider what modernity created and what it gave to society, including a new moral philosophy.

Modernity Reconsidered

In *The Secular Age*, Charles Taylor (2007) examines the transition from faith-centric governance of nation states in the sixteenth century, through the French and American revolutions in the eighteenth century, to the dominance of scientific reasoning by the end of the nineteenth century. He describes the transition in moral terminology, arguing that the way people imagined their society changed in the late seventeenth century:

The picture of society is that of individuals who come together to form a political entity, against a preexisting moral background, and with ends in view. The moral background is one of natural rights; these people already have certain moral obligations to each other. The ends sought are certain common benefits, of which security is the most important (p. 159).

Taylor argues that in the Middle Ages, the lack of economic change created an environment in which most people, including religious leaders, viewed the ideal as not of this life. With the beginnings of economic growth it was possible to envision a better life on earth. In this context, he argues, it was possible to imagine a progressive society in which humans had rights not currently recognized by their government. In addition to this new image, three other forces reshaped the "objectified reality" commonly held: "They are respectively: (1) the 'economy', (2) the public sphere, and (3) the practices and outlook of democratic self rule" (Taylor, 2007, p. 176).

First, the concept of an economy influenced changes in the image of society (Taylor, 1987–1988, 2007). In the economic realm, Adam Smith's argument about the "invisible hand" and social progress helped create new images of society

drawn from his *The Theory of Moral Sentiments*, where Smith argues that Nature has made us admire rank and fortune, because social order is more secure if it rests on the respect of visible distinctions, rather than on the less visible qualities of virtue and wisdom (Taylor, 2007, p. 177).

Rather than focusing on the exchange of services alone, this new imagery coined the "foundational model" of "what we have come to call an economy" (p. 177). These understandings were reflected in the philosophical works of Locke and others who argued about human rights. The change in economics and social imagery were also accompanied by a new attitude toward science and technology:

The shift in the nature of "science" is also connected to the change I noted . . . The invisible-hand guided "economy" is one such aspect; but other aspects of social life, or culture, or demography will later be singled out for scientific treatment (p. 183).

Second, the concepts of a "civil society" and a "public sphere" also gained common acceptance. In building this portion of his argument, Taylor relies on Habermas's arguments about the changes in the social sphere that took place in coffee shops, bars, and other spaces where people could discuss revolutionary ideas and ideals: "The public sphere is the locus of a discussion potentially engaging everyone (although in the eighteenth century the claim was only to involve an 'enlightened' minority) in which the society can come to a common mind about important matters" (Taylor, 1987, p. 188). This public space created room to discuss the role of the Church and the state. In America, it stimulated discussion on the role of taxation relative to political representation, an issue central to the argument for the revolution. Taylor argues that is was through discourse in this public space that "secularity" emerged as a concept in the common space (p. 192).

Political transformation followed the emergence of this discursive process within the public sphere. In the American context, this transformation was hastened within the religious communities engaged in creating a new image of social life:

The first puritan churches formed around the idea of a "Covenant" provide examples of this. A new ecclesiastical structure flowed from a theological innovation; and this becomes part of the story of political change, because civil structures themselves were influenced in certain American colonies by the ways churches were governed, as with the Connecticut Congregationalism, where only the "converted" enjoyed full citizenship (Taylor, 2007, p. 197).

The basic concepts of modernity had taken shape by the late eighteenth century: "The colonists started by asserting the traditional 'rights of Englishmen' against an arrogant and insensitive imperial government" (Taylor, 2007, p. 197). This backwards-looking argument about legitimacy—the argument that they were denied their rights as Englishmen—formed the logic for revolutionary mobilization. However, the diversity of governing relationships within the states, partly an artifact of the diverse ways the public space of religious governance was constructed, gave rise to the federalist notions: "The new government had to have its own base of legitimacy in a 'peoples of the United States' " (p. 198).

Theories of Justice

Images of society also influence the discourse on social justice, which is evolving in the United States and other Western democracies. John Rawls's *Theory of Justice* (1971) is widely heralded as a generally accepted statement of principles of justice for modern, democratic societies (Habermas, 2003; Nussbaum, 1999, 2000; Taylor, 2007). Below I review Rawls's original argument, consider some of the criticisms of his concepts, and explore Nussbaum's arguments about basic liberties and social justice for women.

Rawls's Original Position

Rawls (1971) identifies two principles that help frame the role of justice in public policy: One principle focuses on equal treatment, the other on equity of opportunity. While there have been substantial developments in theory and research since Rawls wrote this seminal work, it nonetheless provides a starting point for reconsidering the role of government in promoting postsecondary opportunity. Both of Rawls's principles merit reconsideration.

The first principle is that "Each person is to have an equal right to the most extensive total system of equal basic liberties compatible with a similar system of liberty for all" (Rawls, 1971, p. 302). This principle argues for equal treatment for all. Expanding the opportunity for access to postsecondary education relates directly to this concept, assuming a similar system of liberty for all. Rawls suggested the "first priority rule":

> The principles of justice are ranked in lexical order and therefore liberty can be restricted only for the sake of liberty. There are two cases: (a) a less extensive liberty must strengthen the total system of liberty shared by all; (b) a less than equal liberty must be acceptable to those with lesser liberty (p. 302).

Thus, while Rawls argued that the first principle is the first priority, given his lexical order, he recognized that unequal liberty presented a problem. He suggested two criteria for judging whether there is an equal basis for liberty, both of which relate to the absence of impediments to equal opportunity. First, Rawls argued that the system of "natural liberty" implies that "careers were open to all, based on their talents" (Rawls, 1971, p. 72). If all college applicants had the same opportunities before they attended college, then the equal application of a single set of admissions criteria would be consonant with this assumption and would provide a means of rationing access, or opportunity, to attend higher quality universities.

Rawls also acknowledged that natural liberty assumes the existence of a "free market economy." He recognized that the notion of free markets assumed "that all have at least the same legal rights of access to all advantaged social positions" (Rawls, 1971, p. 72). This assumption has a different meaning for postsecondary education, which has not been accessible to all, than it does for K–12 education, which is compulsory. In K–12 education, much of the current education policy debate centers on equal access to quality education. One strand of reform emphasizes improving the quality of troubled schools (i.e. educational standards and testing), an approach that seems to argue for equalizing the supply of opportunity.

The second principle is that

> Social and economic inequalities are to be arranged so that they are both: (a) of the greatest benefit to the least advantaged, consistent with the just savings principle, and (b) attached to offices and positions of fair equality of opportunity (Rawls 1971, p. 302).

Before considering the second principle for postsecondary education, we must examine what Rawls means by the "just savings principle." Rawls framed this concept within the notion of cross-generation responsibility. He argued that capital was and should be passed on from one generation to the next. He defined the just savings principle as follows: "The just savings principle can be regarded as an understanding between generations to carry their fair share of the burden of realizing and preserving a just society" (1971, p. 289). This principle provides Rawls's rationale for public investment in education:

> Each generation must not only preserve the gains of culture and civilization, and maintain intact those just institutions that have been established, but it must also put aside in each period of time a suitable amount of real capital accumulation. This savings may take various forms from net investment in machinery and other means of production to investment in learning and education. Assuming for the moment that a just savings principle is available, which tells us how great investment should be, the level of social minimum is determined. Suppose for simplicity that the minimum is adjusted by transfers paid for by proportional expenditure (or income) taxes. In this case raising the minimum entails increasing the portion by which consumption (or income) is taxed (p. 285).

Thus, Rawls's second principle of justice rests on the notion that cross-generation investment, generated through taxation, is essential for maintaining a just social system. This means that the second principle of justice rests on an assumption that taxpayers are willing to pay for an educational system that provides equal opportunity.

Rawls's Critics

Perhaps the best known of Rawls's critics is Michael Walzer, author of *Spheres of Justice: A Defense of Pluralism and Equality* (1983). Some of the specific criticisms in this text merit consideration, especially as they apply to the aim of redefining the public interest in and finance of education. Walzer's critique focuses primarily on the difference principle. He argues as follows:

> It is possible to set limits to the new conversion patterns, to recognize but constrain the monopoly power of the talented. I think this to be the purpose of John Rawls's difference principle, according to which inequalities are justified only if they are designed to bring, and actually do bring, the greatest possible benefit to the least advantaged social class. More specifically, the difference principle is a constraint imposed on talented men and women, once the monopoly of wealth has been broken. It works this way: imagine a surgeon who claims more than his equal share of wealth on the basis of the skills he has learned and the certificates he has won in the harsh competitive struggles of college and medical school. We will grant the claim, if, and only if, granting it is beneficial in the stipulated ways. At the same time, we will act to limit and regulate the sale of surgery—that is, the direct conversion of surgical skill into wealth (pp. 14–15).

This can be considered a conservative criticism of the equity principle which assumes talents are constrained by just practice. This type of argument is not unlike the argument against affirmative action, including arguments by Ward Connerly (2000), the primary advocate of ballot initiatives in California and Michigan outlawing affirmative action. Walzer and Connerly assume a base of just practice has already been attained. Walzer argues that the difference principle imposes constraints on talented people when wealth is no longer a factor. This assumption of a just basis (the breakdown of injustice due to wealth or poverty) within democratic societies is questionable, however.

Other critics of Rawls argue that he assumes too much, that society is far from equal. Consider, for example, Alejandro's (1998) critique of the problems with Rawls's theory in respect to the conditions of unequal liberty:

> The worth of fair equal opportunity is unequal (my hypothesis). All citizens are entitled to education (formal character of the principle of *fair equality of opportunity* [FEO]). But it does not follow that the quality of education will be the same for all persons. All citizens are entitled to medical care (formal character of the FEO principle). It does not follow that the quality of medical care will be the same for all citizens. All citizens are entitled to legal representation before a court of justice (formal character of the EFO principal). But the quality of that legal service is unequal. And so on (emphasis added, p. 163).

This more radical criticism is based on the notion that fair equality of opportunity is not fully dealt with in Rawls's theory. Alejandro's criticism further exposes the problem with the assumption that a state of equality has been reached, an assumption made by Walzer (1983) and Connerly (2000). In my own attempts to apply Rawls's principles to education policy (St. John, 2003, 2006), I have not assumed equal status already exists, but instead treated equality as an ideal seldom reached in any domain of society. The assumption that inequality is not only possible, but it is present and growing, is seriously problematic.

Justice in Perspective

While the concepts that underlie theories of social justice are rooted in the Judaic and Christian tradition and have general acceptance in Western democracies, there is not a consensus of what human rights are, or should be, or whether we can assume social equity in the US. Alejandro's critique of Rawls illustrates a problem with the assumption that modern societies are just (i.e. whether there is a precondition of equal basic rights). To address this issue we need to consider the limits of technological and social progress. In doing so, it is also important to consider notions of individual development in Western society.

Images of Individual Development

While moral philosophy has given extensive treatment to issues of justice, the concept of development of the individual as a mature adult has been in the domain of psychology. Sigmund Freud developed concepts of the human psyche (e.g. the ego, id, superego, conscious, unconscious, etc.), and his work, to some extent, continues to provide the foundations for modern thought on mental health and correcting problems in the psyche. Jung departed from his mentor as he explored psychological health in adulthood. He developed a theory of individuation that illuminated the role of midlife transitions and the pursuit of deeper meaning in the second half of life. This part of Jung's theory has been central to theories of adulthood. While Jung's work and career became controversial in the late twentieth century, it merits reconsideration since it is the root of most theories of adulthood (Levinson, 1978; Sheehy, 1977).

Jung's Theory

Carl Jung's theory of adult development focused on the process of individuation and the role of archetypes in attaining a more integrated sense of self. In *The Archetypes and the Collective Unconscious* (1968), an edited collection of papers published originally in the 1930s, Jung defines the individuation process as:

> Finally, there is any amount of literary and historical evidence to prove that in the case of these archetypes we are dealing with normal types of fantasy that occur partially everywhere and not with the monstrous products of insanity. The pathological element does not lie in the existence of ideas, but in the dissociation of consciousness that can no longer control the unconscious. In all cases of dissociation it is therefore necessary to integrate the unconscious into consciousness. This is a synthetic process which I have termed the individuation process (pp. 39–40).

Jung defines individuation not as a process of insanity, which was the dominant basis of psychology during this period, but as a process of integrating the conscious and the unconscious. The mechanism, or the discovery process, through which a healthy individual comes to integrate the unconscious is the experience of archetypes. Jung defines the archetype:

From the unconscious there emanates determining influences which, independently of tradition, guarantee in every individual a similarity and even a sameness of experience, and also of the way it is represented imaginatively. One of the main proofs of this is the most universal parallelism between mythology motifs, which on account of their quality as primordial images, I have called archetypes (1968, p. 58).

Jung used a critical review of historical and mythological literature, enhanced by a review of individual cases from his clinical work, to build an understanding of the archetypes. Jung describes the role of several transformative archetypes—the child, the wise old man, the mother—in the individuation process. Later in his career, Jung critiqued Western religion, focusing on the consequences of ignoring the dark side and casting the devil out of the trinity construct:

The devil is the aping shadow of God . . . He is "Lord of this world," in whose shadow man was born, fatally tainted with the original sin brought about by the devil. Christ, according to the Gnostic view, cast off the shadow he was born with and remained without sin (1984, p. 73).

Not only did Jung not shy away from religion, he took a more radical position on human growth and development than most religious scholars. While the Christian and Catholic intellectual tradition focuses on becoming like Jesus, it generally does not accept the view that Jesus was preaching about inner knowledge, which is a perspective advanced by scholars exploring the Gnostic tradition (Hoeller, 1989; Pagels, 1981).

Jung's Critics

The late career stage in Jung's work is by far the most controversial. Kaufmann (1992), a noted philosopher, severely criticizes two aspects of this set of works. First, Kaufmann argues that Jung's writing posited that Aryan unconscious was of "higher" potential than "the Jewish" (p. 292). His critique reveals that we cannot and should not side step issues of religious consciousness as we address professional competence. The problem for Jung was that he tried to maintain neutrality while serving as head of the German Psychological Association during the Nazi period. His theory may not be as problematic as his actions. Second, Kaufmann argues that Jung's concept of the archetypes "explains nothing" (p. 252). In particular, Kaufmann is exceedingly critical of Jung's arguments about the inner dialogue with God. Kaufmann's criticism of the lack of social responsibility in Jung's work merits serious consideration in this chapter, given my aim of testing some of Jung's concepts in the domain of professional practice. From my perspective, Jung's argument about neutrality was naive. However, his insights on consciousness in adulthood should not be discarded without rethinking his arguments about maturation during adulthood.

If we focus exclusively on the inner aspects of the journey without addressing the moral issues of abuse of power and social responsibility, we can easily fail to engage the critical challenges of our day, just as Jung did. If rationalized in this way, as an argument for inner transformation over personal engagement in social issues, Jung's work was easily misused.[33] Jung may have deceived himself with assumptions of

being used at an excessive rate and the quality of the environment was being destroyed in the process. The book, written by an international team of scholars, warned of an impending crisis:

> *The Limits of Growth* (LTG) reported that global ecological constraints (related to the resource use and emissions) would have significant effects on global developments in the twenty-first century. LTG warned that humanity might have to divert much capital and manpower to battle these constraints—possibly so much that the average quality of life would decline sometime in the twenty-first century. Our book did not specify exactly what resource scarcity or what emission type might end growth by requiring more capital than was available—simply because such detailed predictions can not be made on a scientific basis in the huge and complex population-economy-environment system that constitutes our world (Meadows, Randers, & Meadows, 2004, p. x).

The thirtieth anniversary update presented an even more troubled prediction for the world's future (Meadows, Randers, & Meadows, 2004). It argues there are too many boats fishing the seas and too many chemical plants producing chlorides depleting ozone. These are patterns of "overshooting" that are depleting resources and destroying air quality and, thus, accelerating global warming. The consequence of inaction is now well known, thanks to Al Gore's *An Inconvenient Truth* (David, Bender, & Burns, 2006), the movie that awoke the masses to the problems of melting ice caps, rising waters, and decreased capacity to feed the world population. After running numerous simulations, Meadows, Randers, and Meadows once again argue that new forms of human action are needed:

> The global challenge can be simply stated: To reach sustainability, humanity must increase the consumption levels of the world's poor, while at the same time reducing humanity's total ecological footprint. There must be technological advance, and personal change, and longer planning horizons. There must be greater respect, caring, and sharing across political boundaries (p. xv).

The link to improving the conditions for the poor is profound. The authors' plea for a change in practice is inexorably related to the general argument of this book: There is a need for new forms of professional practice that care and respect people and the global environment, along with conscious moral reasoning and action aimed at resolving critical challenges. In this case, the argument is that care, personal choice, and sharing are necessary to change global patterns of resource overuse and environmental decline. Indeed, the authors are arguing for a new image of human action in a global community.

These arguments form the very core of the debate about the clash between human values centered in faith versus scientific knowledge. More than two decades ago, Jonas Salk (1983), the inventor of the polio vaccine, in *Anatomy of Reality: Merging of Intuition and Reason*, reflected on the evolution of humanity and raised questions about our capacity to change patterns of growth. He argued that at any point in time and in any human endeavor, it was possible to continue to make progress, plateau, or decline. He argued that seeing the possibility for decline required a shift in perspectives. Regarding the role of the human mind in evolution, Salk argues:

Evolution is a process of changing relationships. It is a process in which new relationships emerge and older relationships terminate. In the process of mutation and selection, chance plays a role. This applies to society and to human systems as it does to biological systems (p. 54).

Salk argues that the abilities to see error, predict consequences, and correct action are forms of intuition that, when integrated with reasoning, are critical to adaptation for individuals, organizations, and society: "Success is increased by thinking ahead (feed-forward) so as to provide the basis on which to make the best choice" (1983, p. 55). He goes on to argue that "The capacity to predict, to anticipate consequences, is one of the most important capacities of the human mind" (p. 115). Linking this capacity to the human role in evolution, he speculates that "The ability of the mind to function in this way must have been selected in the course of evolution" (p. 115). From this perspective, the appeal by Meadows, Randers, and Meadows for changes in human action and attitudes toward the poor could be construed as a form of critical thinking about the environmental future in relation to the human condition, a form of environmental consciousness.

Rethinking Links Between Faith and Science

The lingering split between science and faith is troubling because, on the one hand, those who deny faith and spiritual values may be more likely to disregard concerns about the future of the planet and social inequality in favor of a modernist Social Darwinism. On the other hand, fundamentalists may adhere to literal interpretations of religious texts that deny evolution (Ruthven, 2007). It is, after all, evolutionary sciences and modern biology that provide the foundations for environmentalism. Fortunately, there are spiritually aware people of science and scientifically aware people of faith who are reflecting critically on these problems.

Francis C. Collins, head of the Human Genome Project, has written about his own reconciliation of faith and science in *The Language of God: A Scientist Presents Evidence for Belief* (2006). As a person of faith, he reflects on the place of God within a world view that accepts the overwhelming evidence of evolution. He raises an important question:

Now that we have laid out the argument for the plausibility of God, on the one hand, and the scientific evidence data about the origins of the universe and life on our plant, on the other, can we find a happy and harmonious synthesis? (p. 142).

Reflecting on the history of Galileo and the Church, which took more than three centuries to resolve within the Catholic hierarchy, and on the history of discord between evolutionary theory and religion, he observes: "Unfortunately, in many ways the controversy between evolution and faith is proving to be much more difficult than an argument about whether the earth goes around" (p. 158). After reviewing arguments that science should trump faith and vice versa—that faith should trump science or that a reconstructed creationism is appropriate—Collins argues for harmony between faith and scientific logic:

It is time to call a truce in the escalating war between science and spirit. The war was never really necessary. Like so many earthly wars, this one has been initiated and intensified by extremists on both sides, sounding alarms that predict eminent ruin unless the other side is vanquished . . . So let us together seek the solid ground of an intellectually and spiritually satisfying synthesis of all great truths (pp. 233–234).

The reintegration of science and faith is not a foreign concept to many practitioners of faith tradition. In the book *The Universe in a Single Atom: The Convergence of Science and Spirituality*, the Dalai Lama (Bstan-ʿdzin rgya, mtsho, 2005) also argues for a deeper integration of science and spirituality. His arguments about Darwin's theory recognize the value of the theory:

On the whole, I think the Darwinian theory of evolution, at least with the additional insights of modern genetics, gives us a fairly coherent account of the evolution of human life on earth. At the same time, I believe that Karma can have a central role in understanding the origination of what Buddhism calls "sentience," through the media of energy and consciousness (p. 111).

Like Collins, the Dalai Lama notes the importance of altruism: "I feel that the inability or unwillingness fully to engage in the questions of altruism is perhaps the most important drawback of Darwinian evolutionary theory, at least in its popular version" (p. 114). He questions why modern biology focuses on competition and aggression rather than cooperation and altruism. In Collins's view, humankind's evidence of altruism was viewed as an emphasis on faith, while for the Dalai Lama the lack of this emphasis is a limitation of science.

Learning to Live within Limits

From the late nineteenth century through the late twentieth century, a model of technological and economic development prevailed in the US and other developed nations, an enterprise that produced waste that is now transforming the globe, indicating that the ways we have lived are no longer sustainable. At the same time that there is growing recognition among scientists and *global citizens*[34] of this new pattern of decline, many nations are in the early stages of economic growth. The globalization of corporations has accelerated environmental decline and global warming because they transcend the boundaries of government, and global solutions have yet to be realized.

Learning to live within the limits of the planet's resources will continue to be a major challenge for decades if not centuries. It represents a major transition from a collective ethos of growth reliant on technology to one of sustainability. A central question is: How can our collective values, including the values of altruism and social justice, be illuminated in ways that allow us to live within the constraints of the globe? This question underlies the reflections of scientists and religious leaders. Part of the answer may be to reemphasize human values as integral to action, a major consideration in this book.

Social and Educational Inequality

The environmental decline may be the most critical issue facing all of humankind, but it is not the only sign of a reversal of progress. While environmentalists may emphasize humanism, altruism, and faith traditions as foundations for rethinking our relationship to the globe we share as peoples, the decline in social equality also illustrates the end of progressivism in the way it was once known. We may have to organize government and human services in different ways than have been evident in the past century if we are to have fair, just, and democratic societies on an overtaxed planet.

Growth in Inequality

The challenges in social equality will probably only become greater if we cannot muster the will and resources to reverse the pattern of environmental decline. Social scientists and economists have addressed the growing inequalities in the US, Europe, and Asia in recent decades (Harvey, 2005; Huber & Stephens, 2001; Sen, 1999). One compelling and revealing treatment of the problem is by Benjamin Freidman in the *Moral Consequences of Economic Growth* (2005). His book examines the growth of inequality globally. He traces the history of economic growth in relation to equality, finding a tight link. However, he finds a problem: "The prospects of achieving economic growth are now in question in much of the core European countries" (p. 401). He indicates there have been problems for two decades, going on to describe troubling conditions in Asia and South America. Regarding the conditions in the US, he observes that "America too is at an economic crossroads. As we have seen, living standards for the majority of citizens grew little from the early 1970s to the early 1990s and along the way inequality widened significantly" (p. 401). After a brief boom, growth halted and inequality began to grow once again in the early 2000s.

In my research on college access, I have frequently pointed to the inequality of opportunity for students from groups with low socio-economic status—more prevalent among Hispanics and African-Americans than whites—to enroll in college in the US (see Figure 2.1). A substantial enrollment gap opened after the maximum Pell Grant award for individuals failed to keep pace with rising college costs.[35] This gap persisted through the 1980s, 1990s, and into the 2000s. Compared to whites, the differential was 7.7 percentage points for African-Americans and 11.7 percentage points for Hispanics in 1990. These differentials had narrowed only slightly by 2000 (to 4.8 and 7.9 percentage points, respectively) and have not improved this century. In sum, there has been a slight reduction in the gap since 1985 (the period of the most severe inequality), but the equality of the mid-1970s has not been restored.

In the US, the federal Pell Grant program played a crucial role in equalizing educational opportunity from 1973 until 1978, when financial aid for middle-income students became a priority. Pell Grants rapidly declined in their purchasing power after they were fully implemented, as is evident in Figure 2.2. In 1975, the maximum Pell Grant award actually exceeded the average tuition in public colleges. However, the half-cost provisions limited the maximum award to half of the total cost of attendance, so many public college students did not get these high awards. As the purchasing power of Pell Grants decreased, these cost provisions were dropped from the Pell Grant program.

A comparison of Figures 2.1 and 2.2 illustrates that the growth of the Pell Grant funding gap (see Figure 2.2) corresponds directly with the growth in differential enrollment rates for minorities compared to whites (see Figure 2.1), especially for Hispanic high school graduates (the lowest income minority in the US). The decline in the purchasing power of Pell Grants explains most of the increase in the funding gap during this period which, in turn, appears to be linked to inequality. The reforms in

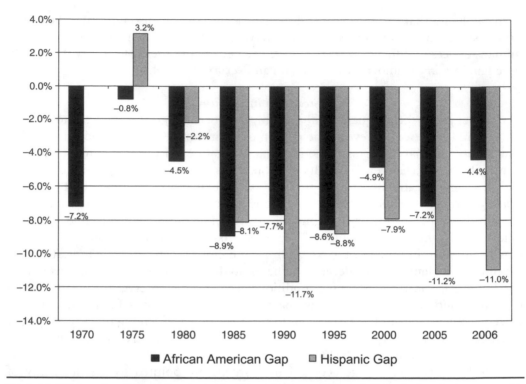

Figure 2.1 Difference in college enrollment rates for African-American and Hispanic high school graduates compared to White high school graduates

Source: Data from NCES Digest of Education Statistics 2007, Table 195.

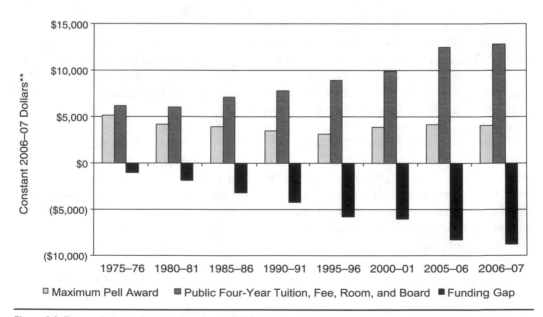

Figure 2.2 The gap between the actual maximum Pell Grant Award and university attendance costs

Source: Data from College Board: *Trends in College Pricing 2005*, Table 4a; *Trends in College Pricing 2007*, Table 4b; *Trends in Student Aid 2005*, Table 8a; *Trends in Student Aid 2007*, Table 8b.

** Dollar amounts adjusted to July 2006–June 2007 (CPI-U)

K–12 education and the growth of encouragement programs, the policies thought to be linked to access, simply are not viable explanations for the rise in inequality (St. John, 2003, 2006). As is evident from the review of other policies below, state and institutional financing strategies also contributed modestly to the increased inequality.

In his discussion of steps that should be taken to reduce inequality, B. M. Freidman (2005) focuses on the central role of education in overcoming the problem of inequality:

> Getting more young people to go to college—and among those who do, getting more to finish—presents a different set of issues [than intervention in early child-hood care, another source of inequality]. High school students from middle-income families often find it a struggle to go to the best institutions willing to accept them. Students from lower-income families find it difficult to go to any college at all without a scholarship (p. 424).

B. M. Friedman points to the tax cuts in the US as having accelerated inequality and as being a force that handicapped the government's ability to respond to these new conditions. He also argues that a substantial expansion in student aid, especially in federal Pell Grants (the largest federal need-based grant program in the US) is a necessary step in reducing inequality and accelerating economic growth.

My argument has been that growth in inequality of educational opportunity and the failure of the majority to vote for taxes to promote cross-generational uplift and equalize opportunity are symbolic of a major shift away from social and economic progressivism in the US (St. John & Parsons, 2004), a pattern that appears to be global (Henry, Lingard, Rizvi, & Taylor, 2001). In fact, a so-called "Washington Consensus" has emerged around policies promoting increased tuition, coupled with the use of loans, as a means of expanding opportunity in higher education across the globe (Stiglitz, 2002). The privatized, market-driven approach to higher education (Priest & St. John, 2006), along with the privatization of health care and other public services (Huber & Stephens, 2001), is part of a well established pattern.

The appropriate question, given the global shift toward marketing mechanisms in education and public services, may not be "Shall we return to a more heavily subsidized system?" but instead "How can we reduce inequality within the privatized global economic system?" Multinational corporations wield power derived from their ability to move jobs and funds across national boundaries, a freedom that drives government policy more often than government policies (in the form of regulations) drive corporate actions. At the start of the progressive period, government regulation of business (e.g. railroads, public utilities, and other necessary services) was central to the acceleration of social and economic development in the US and Western Europe. Now, as corporations expand beyond national boundaries, they make decisions about business strategies that have global economic consequences. In this context, regulation of social services and equitable distribution of resources may require new responses. Policies that equalize opportunity are necessary, but it is also important to rethink human rights in this shared global community.

Human Capabilities

While John Rawls focused on rights within developed democratic nations in *A Theory of Justice*, Martha Nussbaum tackles the problem of injustice in developing societies. Her basic criticism is: "In short, the Rawlsian approach does not probe deeply enough to show us how resources do or do not go to work in making peoples able to function" (1998, p. 34). In her analysis of social justice for women, she defines education as a right: "Nothing is more important to women's life chance than education. With literacy, a woman may choose her options and to some larger extent shape her future" (p. 100).

Nussbaum offers a broader perspective, arguing that we must also consider investment in *human capabilities*, taking into account an understanding of public finance informed by the human capabilities position and given the inequalities in access to the new standards of basic education. Rather than accepting conservative rationales about human capital, a more compassionate perspective is needed. Nussbaum (2001) addresses this type of moral challenge in policy:

> The insights of the compassionate imagination may be embroiled in laws and institutions at many different levels and in many different ways. As with Rawls's imagining of the human need for primary goods in the Original Position [1971], they may be involved in the construction of the basic structure of society and choice of its most basic distributional principles. They may also be involved in legislation at a more concrete level: in the creation of tax code and a welfare system, in the creation of levels of offense and punishment in criminal law, in democratic deliberation about human inequality at many different levels . . . (2001, p. 103).

Nussbaum posits a comprehensive list of basic rights for women, establishing a minimum standard of justice that could be applied in developing countries. She identifies a full range of human rights, from health care to opportunities to care for and raise children, to education. While there may be disagreement about specific rights, including the right to choose abortion, the idea that a minimum threshold of rights is needed is compelling. In my own view, this human capabilities perspective has implications for all nations that strive to value the rights of all people, including developed countries like the US.

The capabilities approach, however, is not defined just by basic literacy, but by what it takes to function in society with full economic citizenship.[36] Consider Nussbaum's analysis of the education of women in Jerusalem:

> And one must ask, well, what is being taught when girls are taught. In the ultraorthodox communities of Jerusalem, all children attending state-supported schools are permitted to follow a curriculum that contains absolutely no information about world history or about the life of the world outside (just as at home television and radio are entirely forbidden). They do learn modern math and science but women are carefully shielded from any image of a woman's proper role that is not that of the ultraorthodox community. They will not be in a position to choose their own way of life as the result of their very own reflection (1998, p. 101).

Raising the standard of basic education to a level that enables citizens to function in society is relevant to the debate about school reform in the US (St. John, 2006). Applied to the US, it is apparent that the standard for the basic level of high school education is in a period of redefinition. Through most of the twentieth century, a general high school education was expected for economic citizenship and wellbeing, and attendance of both elementary and secondary education was compulsory. In the middle of the twentieth century, comprehensive high schools emerged as the primary strategy for high school education. Small high school districts consolidated so they could afford to offer three types of curriculum: general, vocational, and college preparatory. In this old model, high school graduation was the general or basic standard. There was a history of local control of schools and community board standards for high school graduation, and there was substantial variation in the number of courses of different types required for graduation.

The new emphasis on improving high school preparation raises the standard for a basic high school education to the level equivalent to college preparation. While this new standard is widely advocated (Adelman, 2004; NCES, 1997, 2001; Pathways to College Network, 2004), there is a great deal of variability in the rate of implementation of the new standard across states in the US. One aspect of the problem facing the US is that not all high schools have advanced courses available to all students. The analyses illustrated that the positive effects of the new policies were not evident for minority students, probably because minority-serving schools lacked the financial and/or human resources to offer quality preparatory curriculum. The inequality of the opportunity to research the emerging standard of academic preparation is reflected in the gaps in test scores, college enrollment rates, and postsecondary attainment rates. This unequal situation is made worse by college admission standards that use test scores (e.g. SAT and ACT). There is a relatively tight link between advanced high school courses and achievement on SAT tests, controlling for background and other achievement indicators (St. John, Musoba, & Chung, 2004). Thus, the use of standardized test scores in college admissions, without adjusting for high school contexts—especially whether students had the opportunity to take advanced courses—adds to the inequality in access in the US.

High schools located in towns and suburbs benefited very substantially from the formation of comprehensive high schools where communities had the will and resources to fund advanced courses and provide supplementary courses in music, drama, and other options. Urban school districts often maintained open access to vocational and regular high schools, while rationalizing access to preparatory high schools with entrance examinations. Urban communities that did not follow the comprehensive model for public high schools have had the greatest difficulties adjusting to the new educational requirements. Another aspect of the problem relates to the apparent relationship between the new standards for basic education (e.g. higher requirements, higher test scores, etc.) and high school graduation rates. The implementation of these policies in the 1990s was associated with reductions in high school graduation rates. In the US, we must recognize that the capacity to implement quality instruction in advanced topics is dependent upon instruction relevant to the learning styles of high school students offered by teachers with content knowledge. A small portion of high school math teachers have a sufficient understanding of calculus to competently teach this topic. The challenge of improving the quality of instruction in high schools to meet the new standards is enormous.

Thus, the transition to college preparation as the standard for basic education poses enormous problems for K–12 education systems in most states. Other nations, too, have had limited college preparatory curriculum in the past. For example, high schools in many European countries schools are usually divided into vocational high schools and preparatory high schools. Whether the teachers and programs are at separate schools sites or at the same sites, the problems of transition are largely similar. In fact, it is possible that American high schools have some advantages in making the transition because most high schools have at least some college preparatory courses even if they do not have all of the advanced courses now considered necessary.

The problems associated with providing access for all students to basic education that meets contemporary college preparation standards are so difficult because current systems often provide access to this quality of education only to a select group. The will to invest in ways that would transform the system are constrained both by limitations in public finance and public willingness to use tax dollars to address the problems (St. John, 2006), as well as and to the ethos of the society and the professionals who service global citizens (in this case, the teachers). The issues—the willingness to provide tax support and the predisposition toward actually caring for all, rather than merely espousing that value—are critical in not only education but also health care, legal aid, access to technology, and a plethora of other issues in contemporary societies.

Post-Progressive Stance

The notion that a progressively better state of affairs will evolve is now likely false. Indeed, new forms of action are needed to achieve equality and global sustainability. This assumption was not only implicit in enlightenment reasoning, but has been a driving force through human civilization. The early religions established the notion of a better future life. In Hinduism and Buddhism it is felt that if you lived justly in this life, you will have higher status in the next life. In Christianity, too, there is a belief of a better existence after a life lived well in the after life. Using technological advancement to change production, coupled with enlightened thought about human rights as a basis for reorganization and the role of government, the basic precepts of modernity and the enlightenment are no longer sufficient supports for a naive belief in progress. Of course, the fact that material goods continue to be produced at an accelerated rate seems to verify the notion of progress. However, there are three compelling reasons to question these progressive assumptions: (1) The rate of increase in production of goods has been accompanied by increases in pollution, growth of the human population, decline of other species, and global warming; (2) There is a growing inequality in opportunities for health care and education, especially in the US, undermining the notion of progress for all; and (3) The decline in global resources and increasing public resistance to taxation combine to decrease the capacity of governments to address environmental and social challenges.

These conditions suggest that regression of the human condition could be inevitable unless there are radical changes in the role of government (i.e. in the willingness to tax and use tax dollars to address these critical challenges) and fundamental changes in the social ethos, including the willingness of professionals of all types to engage in critical reflection of their actions and to reorient to addressing critical challenges in their daily practice. Regardless of the direction public policy takes with respect to taxation and the role of government, there is a need to ponder the role of professionals in the current post-progressive period.

At the very least, there is little doubt there is also the possibility of a continued regression in social equity and environmental conditions. Faced by the potential regressive conditions—at a minimum, a short-term continuation of environmental conditions and inequality of opportunity seems inevitable—holding a progressive frame seems naive or deceptive. If we apply Jonas Salk's notion of imagination to our current condition, we must engage in imagining action on new progressive practice. This is not just a matter of policy change, it also requires fundamental changes in perceptions, attitudes, and practices. This represents a formidable challenge for aspiring and experienced professionals.

CONCLUSIONS

The environmental decline and growth in social inequality since the late 1970s give reasons to rethink the assumption of inevitable progress toward a better state of society, a common presupposition during the transition from religious to secular societies that took place in the nineteenth and twentieth centuries. The transitions from monarchies to democratic forms of government and from agrarian to postindustrial societies evolved in parallel. This transition was also accompanied by a shift in the role of faith in governance. In the US in particular, the emergence of democratic governance occurred within a multifaith state, including multiple Protestant sects. However, intolerance of faith differences persists in the US along with intolerance of racial, ethnic, and transgender differences.

My argument is that the social aspects of injustice and intolerance impede efforts to reconstruct governance in ways that promote both social justice and environmental sustainability. Nationally, a bipartisan reconstruction of policy that will provide means for improving access to education, health services, and other services that promote human capabilities is needed. Whether or not inequalities of access are resolved, there will continue to be a compelling need for ongoing action within the professional organizations that provide education, health, legal, and other professional services. Social injustice and environment decline are artifacts of human values in action, not just public policy.

For aspiring and practicing professionals in the twenty-first century, it is important to consider how values of social justice and human development form the assumptions of professionals about their professions and practice. Issues of human rights are complex. Even when they are legally mandated, people interpret them through their own values. They may use their beliefs to rationalize working around the rules, creating new injustices based on rationales that espouse beliefs. Practitioners may even use the new rules (i.e. the requirements that services be provided) in ways that differ from the intent as a means of forcing their values on others.

In summary, this chapter has examined diverse foundations for collective reasoning about social justice and human development, the interpretive frames often used to reason about social problems in modern societies. Several understandings emerge from this chapter:

- The major faith traditions value social justice and human development. The early concepts of nation states were closely aligned with different faith traditions. While most modern nations, east and west, have transitioned to secular governments, the faith traditions remain central to the moral reasoning of most global citizens in most societies. Increasingly, practitioners across professions work within multifaith communities, requiring introspection on values and beliefs across faith traditions.

- Modern concepts of justice emphasize basic rights while images of human development emphasize well-being and the realization of human potential. The human capabilities perspective provides a lens for integrating thought about professional practice relative to providing access to services related to human rights, and opportunities for human development.
- A post-progressive stance, the assumption that progress is not inevitable, is necessary to build an understanding of the ways current trajectories of policy and practice undermine human rights and deny opportunities for development, the core human capability of just and caring societies. Two critical issues merit reflection across professions: (1) growing inequalities in access to quality education, health care, and other human services since the late 1970s create a context of regress rather than progress; and (2) failure to recognize the links between declining global resources and the daily practice of professionals and lived lives of all global citizens contributes to the context of environmental regress.

REFLECTIVE EXERCISE

Questions facing practitioners across the professions include: (1) How do your beliefs relate to the professional challenges you face now and expect to face in the future? and (2) How do your daily choices about courses of professional actions relate to the underlying issues of social equality and environmental stability? Pondering the second question does not mean that each choice changes the trajectories of the human condition or the environment. Rather the question recognizes that our own actions are part of the course of human events, the ethos of humanity that is vital to the quality of life for all (see Text Box 2.1).

Text Box 2.1 Reflective Exercise: Values and Beliefs Guiding Your Personal and Professional Choices

Reflect on the following questions:

- What beliefs about social justice and the potential for human development guide your actions?
- How do your beliefs about social justice and human development inform your goals and plans? (Consider your statement from the reflective exercise in Chapter 1.)
- How do your actions align with your beliefs about social justice and human development?
- How do you know when your actions are inconsistent with your beliefs?
- What issues related to social justice and personal development concern you as you think about moving ahead educationally and professionally?
- What are the gaps between your life aims and your current actions and understandings of these challenges?

Write a reflective statement based on your reflections. Consider how your professional goals relate to your personal goals in life and to your beliefs about social justice and the human potential.

3

PROFESSIONAL DEVELOPMENT

An emphasis on moral judgment should be integral to professional education but it should not be treated as dominate of, or determining, professional action; rather, moral judgment is exercised as part of professional choices. To achieve this integration, we need an understanding of professional action that is inclusive of moral judgment. It is widely argued that people act from a frame of mind, an argument often made in the literature on moral philosophy (Taylor, 2007; Habermas, 1985, 1987). This argument provides a way of viewing technical and moral aspects of judgment in action situations. Whether or not the moral aspect is explicitly considered as part of professional education, moral judgment is nonetheless integral to the daily choices professionals make. Ignoring the moral aspect of decisions poses risks for professionals, their clients, and society.

When professionals allow the technical or procedural aspects—what we can think of as the rules of the profession—to dominate over situated judgment, they ignore the moral aspect of reasoning in action situations. In most of the daily decisions professionals make, they rely on their expertise—the combination of knowledge and analysis that is used in action situations. To be integral to action, moral reasoning must be viewed as part of expert judgment. Therefore, the moral aspect of professional expertise should be viewed as part of the framing of problems, an approach that guides integrating the two aspects of action. This chapter examines the problem of integrating the technical and moral aspects of professional reasoning from the vantage of technical expertise in relation to the implicit role of moral judgment.

EXPERT JUDGMENT

Expertise within a field of endeavor has been the central foundation of professional knowledge for more than a century. This reconstruction of professional knowledge in relation to moral reasoning starts with an examination of the relationship between technical expertise and moral reasoning. Next, the role of "professional effectiveness" as originally conceptualized by Argyris and Schön (1974) is reviewed, relative to the task of developing a contemporary understanding of frames of professional judgment in action situations. Then the role of the critical social context for professional action is considered to recontextualize professional action. Finally, with that background, a retheorized sequence of professional frames is presented.

Technical Expertise and Social Justice

While there is a body of literature that considers the personality types associated with different professions and academic fields (Smart, Feldman, & Ethington, 2000), the orientation toward moral reasoning cannot be differentiated by personality type. Instead, the mode of reasoning must be considered, so a different set of schema needs to be used to differentiate the ways in which moral reasoning is viewed in professional action. The two dimensions of a new typology (see Table 3.1) are the orientation toward issues of justice and the field orientation toward basic and applied fields.

The meaning of justice, including the ways justice and care are understood, can vary across professions. The orientation toward justice can be differentiated into four frames:

- *Critical*, which focuses on injustice as a problem (Chapter 1);
- *Interpretive*, which focuses primarily on the meaning, experience, and understanding of justice and injustice (Chapter 2);
- *Social*, which focuses primarily on social interactions as a means of practice and may include an emphasis on caring for others (Chapter 3);
- *Technical-Scientific*, which focuses primarily on technical and scientific subjects, and can have an explicit emphasis on environmental preservation (Chapter 4).

Table 3.1 Typology of Applied Professional and Basic Fields by Emphasis on Interpretive, Social, and Technical-Scientific Expertise

Type	Critical	Interpretive	Social	Technical-Scientific
Orientation toward Justice	Justice as advocacy	Justice focuses on interpretation and experience	Justice focuses on social interaction and/or caring for others	Justice as analytical, technical and scientific
Applied Professions (Examples)	• Lawyer • Politician • Advocate • Political Analyst	• Journalist • Lawyer (human rights) • Musician • Artist	• School Teaching • Counseling • Ministry (practice) • Nursing • Counselor	• Engineering (most specializations) • Management • Chemist • Medical Doctor
Basic Fields of Study	• Political Science • Law • Policy Studies • Economics	• Languages • Literature • History • Arts and Music • Philosophy • Religion and Theology (study)	• Social Sciences (e.g. Sociology, Anthropology, and Political Science) • Psychology • Education • Seminary	• Basic Sciences (e.g Chemistry, Physics, and Biology) • Engineering • Information Science • Environmental Sciences

The subject matter of fields varies substantially across professions, as well as the orientation toward justice and care, similar to the concept of organizational frames.[37] Critical aspects of justice are important across areas of professional practice, as argued in Chapter 1. Many professionals practice primarily as social actors who apply their expertise in group projects or in service to clients who have an agenda. Professions with an advocacy orientation include law and politics.

Consistent with the view taken in Chapter 2, interpretive fields rely on the traditional methods of interpreting issues of justice, which may be based on literature, arts, writing, or history. In these fields, the argument often focuses on interpretation and the content knowledge has to due with texts (i.e. literature, music, forms of media, etc.). Proof within interpretive fields tends to focus on meaning. For example, Chapter 2 considered how meanings of social justice varied across religious traditions and how definitions changed during the modern period. Taylor (2007) argues that most people are not fully aware of the value frames they use because they are historically and discursively situational. My argument in Chapter 2 was that each individual is responsible for defining how their values influence their framing of moral issues (i.e. the frame from which they interpret what is right, fair, and just).

Social interaction within communities of practice (e.g. teams working on projects, teachers in schools, and groups of practitioners organized as primary work units, like faculty in an academic department or engineers in a division of a firm) is the primary focus in this chapter. In this section I focus on two aspects of social practice: (1) the orientation toward effectiveness and/or justice; and (2) the critical social context of action. Both of these aspects of social interaction are important in understanding the moral frames of action.

Within the technical-scientific fields, methods of proof are more analytical and scientific. Many fields are oriented toward technical and scientific evidence as the primary focus, but evidence is important in both interpretive and social orientations toward justice and care. In Chapter 4 I discuss methods of integrating analytic methods (e.g. methods of classroom, qualitative, and quantitative research) into interventions aimed at improving justice and care within communities of practice.

The distinction between basic and applied fields relates to the orientation of professionals toward evidence. While many of the professions focus on the application of knowledge, they build on basic research (the emphasis of academic fields) that can also be differentiated according to this schema. Whether a professional field is basic or applied depends on the context for use of evidence in action. In applied fields, the emphasis is on evidence in practice, but basic fields will have a different rigor of proof. For example, the improvement of the health of patients may be the best evidence of the effects of treatment by medical practitioners; a medical researcher uses the standards of science, usually in some form of the experimental method. Most professions have a professional degree, but applied professionals build on more basic fields of knowledge. A medical doctor would receive an MD, but a biologist working in a medical school would probably have a PhD in biology, possibly in addition to the MD. College professors tend to have PhD degrees.

The identification of fields of practice across these categories in this typology is based on my judgment about the orientation toward evidence and attitude toward justice within a range of fields, and is illustrated in Table 3.1. Some fields can be further split by their orientation toward justice. For example, we can classify theology and religion in the interpretive orientation because of their focus on interpretation of texts on religion, while seminaries and the ministry itself focus on ministering to justice. However, based on this hypothetical typology,[38] most fields have a logical alignment. For example, the social sciences focus on the study of social groups and culture, and can clearly be classified as being focused on the social aspects of justice with a basic orientation toward evidence. In contrast, engineering is both technological-scientific and applied. This typology is important primarily because the content of professional expertise varies by fields.

Professional Effectiveness

The social interactions and communications within professional practices have been extensively studied in fields like business and education. One theory in this tradition that has been considered to be universally applicable across fields is Argyris and Schön's theory of professional effectiveness (1974). It is the foundation for action science (Argyris, 1993; Argyris, Putnam, & Smith, 1985) and reflective practice (Schön, 1983, 1987). While this theory can be criticized for lacking an emphasis on critical social aspects of practice (St. John, 2002), it does provide a reasonable starting point for rethinking ways of framing action within the professions.

More than three decades ago, Argyris and Schön (1974) provided a lens for viewing theories of human action that still provides a basis for viewing expert judgment in action situations. They defined a theory of action as follows: "We have defined *theory of action* in terms of a particular situation, *S*, and a particular consequence, *C*, intended in that situation" (emphasis in original, 1974, p. 6). They also link theories of action to practice: "A *practice* is a sequence of actions undertaken by a person to serve others, who are considered clients" (emphasis in original, p. 6). They proposed two general theories of action (Model I and Model II) that provide a basis for understanding goal-directed action. Argyris and Schön acknowledged that there are many possible theories of action, but they distinguished between two generic types of theories of action (Model I and Model II). Both models are constructed as having *governing variables*, which are basic assumptions that are implicit in the practitioner's framing of most situations; *action strategies*, which are forms of behavior that emanate from governing assumptions; *consequences in the behavior world*, which are behavioral effects of the action strategies; and *consequences for learning*, which are what the individuals learn from their experience. There is also an assumed linkage to effectiveness, with Model I leading to "decreased effectiveness" (p. 68) and Model II leading to "increased long term effectiveness" (p. 87). The assumption that actions consistent with using one model (or type of theory of action) decrease effectiveness, and that actions consistent with another model increase effectiveness, was a logical extension of their prior assumption that action is intended to influence specific consequences. Therefore, I treat this last aspect of Model I and Model II[39] differently than the other aspects. The action strategies, governing variables, and their consequences provide a coherent whole that can be critically examined.

Argyris (1993) offers compelling evidence that at least certain aspects of corporate effectiveness were improved through a long-term intervention in a consulting firm. However, this intervention was undertaken within a private firm that had profitability as an overarching intent. His claim is that interventions aimed at transforming organizations from Model I to Model II may have some validity, especially if profit is a motive, as is the case in the corporate organizations they studied. However, Argyris's notion of effectiveness is bound up in a strategic view of organizations, which is of limited use in professional practices that aim to be socially just. The issue of the strategic orientation of this theory also surfaces in the student texts examined in the next section, especially as it relates to interactions between experiences as a practitioner and the values embedded in the organizations in which they work.

According to Argyris and Schön, Model I consists of four interrelated governing variables (see Table 3.2) that represent an integrated way of viewing action:

- *Define the goals and try to achieve them.*
- *Maximize winning and minimize losing.*
- *Minimize generating or expressing negative feelings.*
- *Be rational* (emphasis in original, 1974, abstracted from pp. 66–67).

These governing variables, along with their related strategies and consequences, merit examination. First, Argyris and Schön (1974) link the first governing variable ("define goals and try to achieve them") to an action strategy of designing and managing the environment unilaterally, a process enacted through persuasion and appealing to larger goals.

Second, Argyris and Schön (1974) link the governing variable of "maximize winning and minimize losing" with the action strategy of owning and controlling the task (i.e., claiming ownership and being the guardian of its definition and execution), which they claim leads to defensive interpersonal and group relationships without adding substantively to finding the solution to problems. The behavioral consequences also seem logically linked—if we experience others as defensive, it is hard for us to avoid having defensive interpersonal relations with them. The third governing variable of Model I ("minimize generating or expressing negative feelings") is logically related to the behavioral consequences of the first governing variable. Argyris and Schön argue that this variable is enacted through "unilateral protection of self"—a process that involves speaking in inferred meaning and being blind to the consequences of actions on others and the incongruities between action and behavior—which further reinforces defensive norms.

The fourth governing variable of Model I ("be rational"), seems logically linked to the second. Argyris and Schön argue that being rational is enacted through the unilateral protection of others from being hurt, a process that involves withholding information, creating rules to censor information and behavior, and holding private meetings. The consequences of this behavior, according to their line of argument, are low freedom of choice and little risk taking. If unilateral control of tasks leads to defensive interpersonal and group relations (the second governing variable), then a coping strategy might be to unilaterally protect others from being hurt. Appearing rational—or rationalizing—may be a way of avoiding overt defensiveness.

Model II has three governing variables, or assumptions, that provide the primary basis of the way of viewing action:

- Valid information,
- Free and informed choice, and
- Internal commitment to choice and constant monitoring of implementation (Argyris & Schön, 1974, p. 87).

Table 3.2 Model I Theories in Use

Governing Variables	Action Strategies	Consequences for Behavioral World	Consequences for Learning	Effectiveness
Define goals and try to achieve them	Design and manage the environment unilaterally (be persuasive, appear to have larger goals)	Seen as defensive, incongruent, competitive, controlling, fearful of being vulnerable, manipulative, withholding of feelings, and overly concerned about self and others or unconcerned about others	Self-sealing	
Maximize winning and minimize losing	Own and control the task (claim ownership of the task, be the guardian of the definition and execution of task)	Defensive interpersonal and group relationship (dependence upon action, little additivity, and little helping of others)	Single-loop learning	Decreased effectiveness
Minimize generating or expressing negative feelings	Unilaterally protect one self (speak with inferred categories accompanied by little or no directly observable behavior, be blind to impact on others and to incongruity between rhetoric and behavior, reduce incongruity by defensive actions such as blaming, stereotyping, suppressing feelings, and intellectualizing)	Defensive norms (mistrust, lack of risk-taking, conformity, external commitment, emphasis on diplomacy, power-centered competition, and rivalry)	Little testing of theories publicly; much testing of theories privately	
Be rational	Unilaterally protect others from being hurt (withhold information, create rules to censure information and behavior, hold private meetings)	Low freedom of choice, internal commitment, and risk-taking		

Source: Argyris & Schön, 1974, pp. 68–69.

The action strategies associated with these variables place an implicit emphasis on cooperation among individuals and facilitation of development (see Table 3.3). They argue the first Model II governing variable (valid information) is enacted through action strategies that "[d]*esign situations or environments where participants can be origins and can experience high personal causation* (psychological success, confirmation, and essentiality)" (emphasis in original, p. 87). The consequences of these strategies that emphasize the other's concerns are that in the behavioral world the actor will be experienced as being a facilitator, collaborator, and choice creator. Also, the consequences for learning are that hypotheses are created which can be disconfirmed.

Argyris and Schön (1974) argue that the second Model II governing variable (free and informed choice) has an associated action strategy of jointly controlling tasks, which results in minimally defensive interpersonal and group dynamics in the behavior world and *double-loop learning*. In explaining their construct of double-loop learning, Argyris and Schön (1974) claim that joint control of the design and execution of tasks creates a possibility to make explicit the situational governing assumptions, which increases the practitioners' ability to test their own framing of assumptions and thus experience a greater sense of personal causation.

The third Model II governing variable (internal commitment to the choice and constant monitoring of its implementation) is enacted through joint protection of self and bilateral protection of others. Embedded in this notion of joint control of tasks is an emphasis on the process of mutual self-protection. Argyris and Schön (1974) argue that when these behaviors are enacted, participants "speak in directly observable categories, [and] seek to reduce blindness about their own inconsistency and incongruity" (p. 87). They assume that in an open environment participants will discuss their reasoning and be interested in learning when their assumptions are not correct, or when they have not understood another's meaning or experience. Argyris and Schön argue that the behavioral consequence is that learning-oriented norms include trust, individuality, and open confrontation on difficult issues. Public testing of theories is viewed as the learning consequence.

Reframing Action Science

The limitations of Argyris and Schön's theory for understanding the role of moral reasoning in action are evident in the ways they conceptualized the role of theory. They defined theory of action as follows:

> When someone is asked how he would behave under certain circumstances, the answer he [or she] usually gives is his espoused theory of action for that situation. This is the theory of action to which he [or she] gives allegiance, and which, upon request, he [or she] communicates to others. However, the theory that actually governs his action is his theory-in-use, which may or may not be compatible with his [or her] espoused theory; furthermore, the individual may or may not be aware of the incompatibility of the two theories (1974, pp. 6–7).

The three constructs embedded in this passage—that theories of action are situated, aimed at achieving goals, and can be both espoused and actionable—merit closer scrutiny with respect to the intent of this book, which is to achieve an integrated way of viewing moral reasoning and human action.

Table 3.3 Model II Theories in Use

Governing Variables	Action Strategies	Consequences for Behavioral World	Consequences for Learning	Effectiveness
Valid information	Design situations or environments where participants can be origins and can experience high personal causation (psychological success, confirmation, and essentiality)	Actor experienced as minimally defensive (facilitator, collaborator, and choice creator)	Disconfirmable processes	
Free and informed choice	Control tasks jointly	Minimally defensive interpersonal relations and group dynamics	Effectiveness of problem solving and decision making will be great, especially for difficult problems	Increased long-run effectiveness
Internal commitment to the choice and constant monitoring of its implementation	Learning-oriented norms (trust, individuality, and open confrontation on difficult issues)	Public testing of theories		
	Bilateral protection of others			

Source: Argyris & Schön, 1974, p. 87.

First, Argyris and Schön essentially argue that theories of action are situated: that our inner internal theories of action that tell us what we will do in a specific situation are based on situated circumstances. The idea that our actions are based on theory and not just instinct or moral values is important because it is one of the premises for all professional education. The core notion of professional education in medicine, education, business, and so forth is that through education and training we can provide practitioners with knowledge and skills they can use in practice. This book broadens the concept of theories of action to include a more complete understanding of the situated circumstances of social issues. It is also necessary to broaden this framing to include both the technical and moral aspects of framing choices in action situations.

Second, for Argyris and Schön, human actions were aimed at achieving specific outcomes: Humans take action in order to achieve intended consequences in the situations they encounter. They essentially claim that action is linked to consequences, implicitly assuming all actions take strategic form—all human actions are goal-directed by their very nature—a view that ignores the possibility of considering a behavior as an effort to build understanding. In one sense their theory overcomes this limitation by distinguishing between two general types of action—closed-strategic action (Model I) and open-strategic action (Model II)—both of which emphasize goal achievement over building an understanding of problems that might alter reasoning about rules, missions, and other rubrics that delimit and define goals, and encourage rationalization. In the reworked theory of action used in this volume, I include both an instrumental frame as a step before (closed or open) strategic action and a communicative frame that focuses on building understanding of the moral aspects of problematic situations in practice.

Third, Argyris and Schön distinguish between *espoused theories* of action (ET) and *theories in use* (TIU). Their idea that professionals, or any human agents for that matter, may act differently than they say they might act—that there might be a gap between word and action—was hardly a novel notion, even three decades ago. When the notion of the gap between values and actions is linked to the construct of theory of action, we have a new window for viewing the causes and consequences of this gap. If, as Argyris and Schön argue, professional action in a given situation is undertaken with the intent of achieving a consequence, then the linkages between situations and intent are embedded in action. In this case, human action would give us a window on TIU, just as spoken intentions would give us a window on ET of action. The TIU is carried forward here because it holds up in both graduate education and organizational interventions, at least in my experience as an action researcher (St. John, 2009). Given our focus on the gap between values and action, the idea of theories of action must be broadened to include the moral dimension. Specifically, the concept of espoused beliefs must also broaden, as was evident in the discussion of social justice in Chapter 2.

Reorienting Toward Communications Action and Moral Responsibility

Two aspects of change in professional action are necessary in a post-progressive world with the potential for decline in social equity and the quality of the environment: (1) an orientation to reflective action as integral to professional practices, especially reflection on critical social and environmental challenges; and (2) reformation of professional organizations to facilitate professional development and civic responsibility. These dimensions of professional and organizational development are examined below.

Reflective Framing in Professional Practice

My recent research (St. John, 2009) identified a sequence of five frames as a basis for viewing professional knowledge and judgment in relation to their contexts: (1) an *instrumental* frame focusing on best practice; (2) a *closed-strategic frame* focusing on the development of artistry of practice; (3) an *open-strategic frame* focusing on collaborating to set goals and design strategies, including reducing the gap between espoused beliefs and action; (4) a *communicative frame* focused on identifying and addressing morally problematic situations in practice; and (5) a *transformational frame* focusing on designing and using strategies that enable organizations to integrate an emphasis on transformational changes. Inherent in this are the following transitions:

- *Learning the instrumental (basic) foundations of the profession*: New professionals focus on learning the knowledge associated with their professions and practicing basic skills. This may (and probably should) include a basic orientation to issues of justice and care. New professionals need to learn the basic skills of their professions, be it counseling, teaching, nursing, designing, or analyzing.
- *Learning to adapt practice to meet diverse client needs and build new skills*: The artistry of professional development involves adapting practice to improve the quality of service. As professionals develop their skills, they need the freedom to assess their practices and to test new approaches that might improve the quality of service. Freedom does not come without responsibility however. The process of adapting practices should be closely linked to the goal of improving service, including being more just and caring in practice.
- *Learning to engage in setting goals and in designing strategies in a community of practice*: As practitioners gain experience and success with the adaptation in their own practices, it is easier for them to engage in dialogue about the collaborative process of designing and enacting new strategies. Most people want to be responsible for their commitments, to engage collectively in setting goals, a process that differs fundamentally from giving and receiving directions (even when done in a friendly manner).
- *Learning to recognize critical, and possibly recurrent, challenges and to envision practices that address these challenges*: Challenges emerge over time in almost any setting. After being engaged in a community practice over a period of time, it is possible to approach problems in new ways. If the organizational environment supports communicative action, it may be possible to engage in collaborative processes of addressing the challenges.
- *Learning to envision and enact interventions that enable communities of practice to develop communicative skills*: While rare, most organizations need senior practitioners who care about mentoring and the design of more caring and just communities of practice (St. John, 2009, p.179).

These reconstructed stages and learning processes also provide a way of examining organizational interventions. In the study of college change presented in *Action, Reflection, and Social Justice* (St. John, 2009), I analyzed interviews with professors and administrators in five colleges and universities where there had been evidence of success using a systematic guide for action (the action inquiry process discussed in Chapter 4). Based upon comments of interviewees across the campuses, there was evidence of all of the frames (e.g. strategic and communicative) being used. Although, one type of framing logic generally predominated on each campus among teams engaged in change projects, depending in part on the organizational context for their actions.

The reconstructed sequence distinguishes forms of reasoning and learning aims associated with each of the transitions (see Table 3.4). It provides a way of viewing professional judgment as an additive learning process that applies widely to the process of learning new sets of skills and how to adapt them. The more experienced professional will be able to go through the sequence from learning a new skill set to adapting it more quickly than the beginning professional because of their experience with the learning cycle. On the other hand, it is also possible that beginning professionals will learn to acquire and adapt new skills more rapidly in organizations that are supportive of their efforts.

Table 3.4 Professional Development: Individual Praxis and Organizational Support

Transition	Individual Praxis	Organizational Support
Learning Basic Professional Skills	Focus on professional knowledge and building technical skills (may include human relations, action inquiry, and reflective practice).	Organizational environment with support for best practices, including mentoring and professional support.
Transition to Closed-Strategic Frame	Focus on testing assumptions about opportunities to innovate; engage in new projects that develop and extend skills.	Incentives for professional development within the system; encourage and support innovation and ongoing improvement.
Transition to Open-Strategic Frame	Focus on engaging with colleagues in setting goals and designing strategies; engage in action projects that test new approaches to organizational practice.	Professional development support for senior managers; encourage development of communicative skills and integration of just and caring practices into the organization.
Transition to Communicative Frame	Focus on identifying morally problematic practices that create inequities within the organization and for clients, and designing situations that encourage staff development and improve justice within the organization.	Research support for action inquiry, including quantitative and qualitative operational analyses; support evaluations of collaborative experiments that address injustices and inequalities within the system.
Transition to Transformational Frame	Focus on redesign of structures and practices that encourage justice, reduce inequalities, and empower peers; engage in processes that integrate justice and caring.	Build culture and tradition of caring and justice; integrate justice and caring into the mission; establish support structures for systemic innovations.

Source: St. John, 2009, p. 169.

Changing Professional Organizations

While the application of professional expertise in problem solving has long been considered critical to technological and social development, there has been limited theorizing about change within professional organizations to support professional development. Most organizational theory adapts theories of business organizations to professional organizations. The emphasis on strategic action and strategy planning illustrates this emphasis. For example, in the study of higher education, strategic planning has long been emphasized (Chafee, 1983; Keller, 1983) and remains the most common theoretical perspective in the study of higher education (Gumport, 2007).

However, the core mission of support for professional development, including introspection issues of equity within professional organizations, has been largely overlooked. The emphasis on professional growth requires a shift from an orientation toward strategies for goal attainment to an emphasis on building understanding (e.g. to a communicative orientation). A communicative orientation does not mean ignoring financial contingencies or matters related to efficiency, but it does call into question the preoccupation with effectiveness. The notion of organizational effectiveness implies that the aims of the organization are fixed or strategic. What if the problems facing organizations and the communities they serve defy the simplistic notion of effectiveness?

Addressing the two major critical issues within organizations—the decline in social equity and the decline in global resources—requires a reorientation of the basic precepts through a deeper integration of a moral consciousness that recognizes the central roles of social justice and sustainability. For professionals to provide services to society that foster equity and enable sustainability, it is necessary to emphasize building an understanding of these issues as they relate to professional action, rather than assuming that the pursuit of specific aims, including the emphasis on mission statements, is the predominate goal of professional organizations. To provide morally responsible service to clients and society, it is necessary to consider professional development, with an emphasis on moral reasoning, as central.

The forms of organizational support commonly associated with instrumental and strategic action (see Table 3.4), including mentoring, incentives for productivity improvement, and communications, are common within professional organizations, including universities. However, the forms of organizational support associated with communicative action that is oriented toward addressing morally problematic situations, including action inquiry and a culture emphasizing justice and care, are less common. An aim of this book is to focus on organizational developments that support integration of moral reasoning and reflective practice within professional organizations.

MORAL DIMENSION OF PROFESSIONAL ACTION

In retrospect, I realize that while the sequence of frames (see Table 3.4) provides a way of viewing how individuals frame professional action, it does not fully integrate the moral aspect. When I began this line of research I assumed that critical social action comes with maturity, but this was not always the case (St. John, 2009). Often young people hold higher ideals and are quicker to point out problems with practice than veterans of extensive practice. Indeed, research on college students indicates that most students are capable of conventional moral reasoning (Stages 3 and 4 in Kohlberg's scheme), but some students hold postconventional values when they enter college

(Pascarella & Terenzini, 1991, 2005). To address this problem we need to reconsider moral development theory in relation to the sequence of frames. Below I reconsider Kohlberg's theory of moral reasoning. I then use Habermas's critique (1990) as departure point for integrating moral reasoning into the frames.

Kohlberg's Stages Reconsidered

In Kohlberg's six-stage theory of moral judgment (see Introduction), the first two stages emphasize preconventional moral reasoning. Stage 1 focuses on punishment and obedience while Stage 2 focuses on individual purpose and exchange. Stage 1 is characterized as egocentric with the individual viewing actions in terms of consequences, including physical punishment. Stage 2 takes a concrete, individualistic perspective, using exchange as an instrumental process to resolve conflict. For children, the progression through the first two stages is closely linked to early childhood development, consistent with Piaget's research on children. There is substantial research evidence that children pass through the first two stages in sequence (Kohlberg, 1984).

The second two stages emphasize conventional notions of morality: the stage of mutual interpersonal expectations, relationships, and conformity (Stage 3); and the stage of social systems and conscience maintenance (Stage 4). Stage 3 places greater emphasis on social relationships and involves a concrete orientation to the "Golden Rule," which involves putting oneself in others' shoes (Kohlberg, 1981, p. 410). Stage 4 places more emphasis on what is right in association with doing one's duty in the social order. Individuals in this stage differentiate the societal view from the personal and focus on defined rules.

Kohlberg's (1981) advanced stages focus on postconventional moral reasoning: a stage of prior rights and social contract or utility (Stage 5); and a stage of universal ethical principles (Stage 6). In Stage 5, the individual is aware of "values and rights prior to social attachments or contracts" (p. 412). At this stage, individuals not only consider the moral and legal points of view, but also recognize how they conflict and the difficulty associated with reconciling these points of view. Stage 6 implicitly assumes that universal values focus on a moral point of view. The individual takes the position of recognizing the moral point of view, focusing on respect for individuals as ends rather than means toward an end. In stating these two stages as distinct, Kohlberg distinguishes between two types of postconventional moral reasoning. In one stage individuals situate their values within social or religious traditions or values, and in another they center these choices in universal human rights that are placed above social and religious systems.

Postconventional moral reasoning is crucial to professional education but has received too little attention because of the emphasis on conventional reasoning, including ethics, within professional education. I have three specific concerns about using Kohlberg's theory in professional education: (1) The preconventional stages are based on early childhood theory and, as a consequence, overlook some of the ways adults can engage in preconventional moral behavior; (2) The advanced stages are based on philosophical arguments about enlightenment reasoning having higher value than spiritual or faith-based reasoning, an interpretive position that has serious limitations (see Chapter 2); and (3) The developmental sequence is not compatible with the learning processes of adults and the ways they reason in action.

Revisions of the theory that address the ethics of care (Gilligan, 1982) and spirituality

(Fowler, 1981) have addressed other limitations of Kohlberg's theory, but they do not address the critical challenges facing an integration of moral reasoning into a theory of action that be used as an integral part of professional education. Kohlberg's critique and reconstruction provides a starting point for this.

Habermas's Reconstruction

In his reconstruction of Kohlberg's moral development theory, Habermas (1990) points to three broad levels of moral reasoning. Habermas's first level of moral reasoning is preconventional, consistent with Kohlberg. At this level, individuals have not internalized conventional rules and behave according to their own perceived self interest until caught and punished. Habermas argues:

> Hence, *preconventional notions of bond and loyalties* are based on the complementarity of command and obedience or on the symmetry of compensation. These two types of reciprocity represent the natural embryonic form of justice conceptions inherent in the structure of action as such (emphasis in original, 1990, p. 165).

This reconstruction not only gives us a window on reasoning processes consistent with Kohlberg's theory, but also provides a way of understanding the link between behavioral interactions and the moral aspect of experience. Habermas emphasizes power and control. Power embedded in hierarchical control (in families or formal organizations) can be abused, creating problematic situations. The mechanisms of obedience and command, and of symmetry of compensation, can reinforce the abuse of power—part of the critical social context of action. This provides a lens for viewing moral problems embedded in practice that were completely overlooked in most of the literature on moral reasoning and ethics, which tends to focus on ethics.

Also consistent with Kohlberg, Habermas carries forward a second level of moral reasoning characterized as conventional. In Habermas's reconstruction of the conventional mode of moral reasoning, the individual accepts the conventional definition of moral standards and tries to behave consistent with them. He argues that "Only at the conventional stage, however, are conceptions of justice conceived *as* conceptions of justice" (1990, p. 165). Using conventional moral reasoning, we seek system solutions to moral problems (e.g. advocated change policies to address perceived problems), but we may overlook underlying causes that foster the problems in the first place.

Habermas also reconstructs the definition of postconventional moral reasoning. Unlike Kohlberg, he recognizes the implicit shift to the ideal forms of thought and actions inherent in the transition to the postconventional mode of moral reasoning. He defines the postconventional mode of moral reasoning: "And only at the postconventional stage is truth about the world of preconventional conceptions revealed, namely that the idea of justice can be gleaned only from the idealized form of reciprocity that underlies discourse" (Habermas, 1990, p. 165). It is at this stage that one begins to untangle the reasons why changing the rules based on conventional moral arguments may not address the serious problems that confront people in the critical social context of public action.

The examples of public votes on affirmative action in states like California, Washington, and Michigan illustrate the problems within common conceptions of conventional and postconventional moral reasoning. In these states, voters who thought it was unfair to have college admissions favoring people of color voted against it. The decision to vote for these proposals and propositions represents the voters' own self interests. This form of collective action—voting to redress a perceived unfairness—is certainly compatible with conventional reasoning about justice. However, from the postconventional moral vantage, this advocacy position fails to consider why the problem exists in the first place. There were unequal schools in these states, which prevented many students from taking the advanced preparatory courses necessary to achieve high test scores. Also, there is a history of racial prejudice that created unequal school systems. Further, as discussed in Chapter 2, the three decades of education and finance reforms from the late 1970s through the late 2000s actually increased inequality rather than reducing it, adding to the serious moral problems created by the early removal of consideration of race under-representation in selection processes.

Integrating Moral Reasoning and Frames of Action

Habermas's reconstructed concepts of moral reasoning are largely independent of his frames of reasoning. Young people who are entering colleges or professional programs can hold postconventional attitudes toward care and justice, and make an effort to act in ways consonant with these beliefs as they learn new knowledge and skills related to their chosen field of study. At the other extreme, it is also possible for seasoned professionals who are oriented toward social justice to abuse power in pursuit of their aims to reform systems. Thus, the reconstructed framework (see Table 3.5) has two dimensions. The first dimension relates to the frames of professional action: instrumental, closed-strategic, open-strategic, communicative, and transformational reasoning. The second dimension contains the reconstructed levels of moral reasoning: preconventional, conventional, and postconventional.

This reconstruction is still hypothetical, based on understandings from reviews, reconstructions, and research testing reconstructed understandings (using both quantitative and qualitative methods of inquiry), coupled with an orientation toward action (St. John, 2009). The 15 statements about frames in relation to moral reasoning are hypotheses, or propositions, that are further explored in this book. The interesting problem with these particular propositions is that they are appropriately tested in action. As part of their reading of this book, I invite aspiring and experienced professionals in higher education and other fields to engage in testing these propositions for themselves, as part of their own efforts to learn about moral reasoning in action.

In addition to theorizing a new set of relationships between moral reasoning and professional reasoning in action—in a form that can potentially be tested in action—I suggest methods that can be used in the learning process, testing these new logical constructs in action, and to the extent appropriate, extending, revising, refining, and reconstructing them to fit different sorts of learning situations and professional settings (see Chapter 4). In fact, to encourage this process, I discuss how action inquiry methods have been used in my action studies of change in educational professional settings. I encourage others to engage in the pursuit of actionable knowledge.

CONCLUSIONS

This chapter has focused on the social aspects of professional practice in relation to social justice. I examined professional judgment and moral dimensions of professional

Table 3.5 Relationship Between Moral Reasoning and Professional Development

Levels of Moral Reasoning/ *Frames of Action*	Preconventional Moral Reasoning	Conventional Moral Reasoning	Postconventional Moral Reasoning
Instrumental Frames	Using rules without considering underlying problems.	Applying rules of practice consistent with ethical codes.	Using extant methods to address moral challenges.
Closed-Strategic Frames	Adapting methods to achieve ends without considering moral problems created by new practices.	Adapting methods to address challenges; attempting to reconcile ethics within rules of practice.	Adapting strategies to address moral challenges, including issues that challenge rules of practice.
Open-Strategic Frames	Collaborating on strategies that use power and persuasion to achieve aims with little regard for consequences.	Collaboratively developing goals and adapting strategies to achieve mission; reconciling strategies with ethical standards.	Collectively considering strategies for adapting mission to address client concerns, diversity, and issues of justice.
Communicative Frames	Reaching false consensus within professional groups; using beliefs to construct rationales that reinforce problems in practice; failing to consider diverse voices and dissent.	Focusing on actions consistent with ethical standards; considering ambiguities between ethical codes and organizational strategies; may emphasize resolving moral ambiguities.	Openly reconstructing rules (i.e. practices and methods) to address moral challenges; focusing on including diverse views and evidence of effects of action; willing to reconstruct theories of action.
Transformational Frames	Emphasize advocacy of agendas; revise aims rather than reflection on critical issues; overlook moral ambiguities; contest opposing views, except to advocate agenda. (Risks looping back to instrumental frame.)	Facilitating change strategies; collaborating on changing agendas of agencies; collectively constructing action strategies with allies; considering opposing views in relation to ethical standards; collective dissent/resistance.	Developing and testing action guides to enable communicative discourse on moral challenges; willing to reconstruct based on testing opposing views; reconstructing action theories based on testing assumptions.

action as distinct but interrelated aspects of the social dimension of justice in practice. Several understandings emerge from this chapter and are further developed in Part II:

- Different professions have different orientations toward social justice including: (1) a focus on examining of critical issues and engagement in their resolution (critical); (2) a focus on interpreting events and building understanding of challenges facing groups and society (interpretive); (3) a focus on developing interventions and pedagogical processes that encourage professional development and social change (social); and (4) a focus on the technical for improvement of systems to support human development, social change, and environmental sustainability (technical-scientific).

- Professional development has an underlying sequential process that involves: (1) learning new knowledge and skills (professional expertise); (2) adapting new practices through reflective practice and alignment of strategy with organizational initiatives (artistry and strategic adaptation); (3) initiating strategic changes involving open refection on adapting practices in relation to organization initiatives (professional effectiveness); and (4) creating guides to inform practitioners committed to using their knowledge and skills in organizational and social change (transformational practice).
- Professionals face moral challenges throughout their careers, including: challenges that put them at risk of breaking ethical and moral codes or abusing power to achieve personal, organizational, or social aims (preconventional moral challenges); challenges related to acting consistent with personal beliefs and values within professional settings where there may be (or appear to be) misalignment of organizational norms and moral/ethical codes (conventional moral challenges); and/or challenges related to confronting system rules (i.e. organizational constraints, laws, and moral codes) that undermine and inhibit efforts to act with justice and care, and encourage on responses that might lead to system change (postconventional moral challenges).

REFLECTIVE EXERCISE

This chapter has argued that professionals should not divorce the moral aspects of our working lives from our professional actions because our actions have moral consequences. The best way to understand this problem—the interrelationship between reasoning in action and the moral consequences of action—is to engage in reflection on our experiences. This reflective exercise (see Text Box 3.1) provides one way to begin the process of reflecting on one's own development process as a practitioner within a profession. The remaining chapters encourage and enable readers to engage in reflection on their actions, with a focus on the moral consequences of action in social settings.

Text Box 3.1 Reflective Exercise: Rethinking Reflection and Moral Reasoning
Reflect on the following questions:

- How do your professional aims relate to different ways of framing social justice (i.e. critical, interpretive, social, and/or technical-scientific frames)?
- How do you assess your own stage of professional development (i.e. building expert knowledge and skills, improving artistry and strategy, engaging in support of improving professional effectiveness in communities of practice, and/or integrating beliefs about social justice and human development)? (Consider your statement from the reflective exercise in Chapter 1.)
- When have you experienced circumstances that involved: Abuse of power? Struggles to maintain conventional moral/ethical, legal, and moral codes of

behavior? Collaborative efforts to rethink practices—organizational polices and procedures, legal codes, and so forth—that reduce moral ambiguities created by conventional reasoning?

- How does your understanding of these issues inform your plans for the future?

Write a reflective statement based on your reflections (or revise and rewrite your statements for the reflective exercises in Chapters 1 and 2). Consider how your professional goals relate to your personal goals in life and to your understanding of professional development and moral reasoning in practice.

4

ACTIONABLE KNOWLEDGE

Building knowledge that can inform action differs from research that takes an external stance to observe organizational or individual behavior and predict outcomes. Argyris, Putnam, and Smith (1985) trace the roots of actionable approaches to research on practice to Kurt Lewin (1952), their point of departure for research on organizational change. In a more basic sense, a focus on inquiry in action, an alternative form of scientific reasoning that can be integrated into practice, originates with the works of John Dewey (1927 & 1988). These research traditions provide a base for building actionable knowledge in professional organizations. Support for professional development should be tightly linked to organizational change strategies. Both aspects of building actionable knowledge merit attention as foci of purposive action within professional organizations.

Argyris and Schön (1974) made arguments about reflective practice that hold up well in action situations (St. John, 2009): (1) practitioners use theories of action—assumptions about behavioral actions and their consequences in specific situations—as integral to their professional work; and (2) practitioners often act differently than they expect, indicating their espoused theories (ET) of action differ from their theories in use (TIU).[40] Reflecting on action situations can build awareness of ET–TIU gaps, thus increasing their ability to adapt and address problematic situations. Building an organizational capacity to support *open critical reflection*, a shared orientation toward understanding and resolving critical social issues, is extremely difficult.

Adaptation to address *critical social challenges*—critical problems in the social context of organizations including internal inequities and unfairness in client services—differs from normal goal-directed practice. In critical social situations, the relationships among rules (including ethical codes), actions, and outcomes are usually not well understood, and alternative strategies for addressing these issues usually have not been previously attempted. So to address recurrent critical social problems in organizations it is necessary to assess the nature of the problems and to test new strategies for resolving them.

Chapters 1 through 3 laid out critical, interpretive, and social perspectives on moral reasoning and social justice within professional organizations and on practitioners' interactions with the clients they serve. This chapter focuses on the technical-scientific aspects of integrating moral reasoning and reflective practice into professional organizations. It has two aims: (1) to introduce a pedagogy that can foster open critical reflection about theories-in-use in organizations; and (2) to introduce an approach to action inquiry that can encourage and foster open critical reflection within organizations.

This chapter presents two frameworks later used to examine professional development and organizational change in Part II. First, the pedagogical methods for encouraging professional development are the primary focus of this book; they provide a framework and reflective exercises that enable practitioners to build skills in critical refection that integrate moral reasoning and reflective practice. This method of analysis of practical situations is applicable across professions. Second, I introduce an action inquiry model (AIM) that was used in the Indiana Project on Academic Success (IPAS). AIM focuses on change within universities as organizations. Given the complexity of using action inquiry, the specific methods necessarily vary across different types of organizations (e.g. a different version of AIM would be needed for hospitals or small businesses). The restatement of AIM below attempts to generalize across different types of organizations but further adaptation is usually warranted.

PEDAGOGY FOR REFLECTIVE PRACTICE

Pedagogical aspects of reflective practice should be encouraged, which requires support from within professional organizations. Forms of organizational support for reflective practice include:

- mentoring as a basic form of support for junior professionals within organizations;
- incentives for productivity improvement as a means of enhancing and achieving organizational aims (e.g. pay increases based on performance);[41] and
- open communication about organizational challenges and their potential solutions.

If practitioners in organizations are capable of maintaining openness regarding problematic issues and encouraging open reflection without attribution, then these common mechanisms of support can function relatively well. Maintaining openness that supports reflection on strategies used and their outcomes can overcome limitations of the strategic aspects of organizations. However, openness of this type usually proves extremely difficult to maintain even if it only occurs occasionally. In fact, the tendency toward rationalization of actions and self-protection can overcome efforts to create open discourse within organizations.

Graduate professional programs should provide opportunities for open critical reflection so that new professionals enter their organizations with an orientation toward openness and critical reflection. This does not mean that professional programs should send out graduates who are naively open and expect their organizations to change whenever they raise a problem. Rather, graduate professional education should introduce students to reflective practice and to the difficulty of enacting openness within communities of professional practice (i.e. the teams and organizational units that undertake new initiatives). In addition to encouraging reflection on the goals, assumptions, and values used to frame action (i.e. reflective exercises in prior chapters), I suggest a three-stage process of building reflective practice skills:

- Develop reflective cases statements using the methods proposed by Argyris and Schön (1974).
- Analyze and reflect on case statements using revised frames (i.e. instrumental, closed and open strategic, and communicative) and group discussions to encourage open reflection.
- Undertake interventions as action experiments in practice as a means of testing new strategies, along with analysis of and reflection on these interventions.

Using this method in a structured learning environment of workshops and/or graduate courses, it is possible to encourage *reflection on action* as a retrospective process of learning about one's own theories in use and analyze them in relation to one's personal values and beliefs, and, with experience, reflection in action. Reflection in action is a process of using conscious awareness of action situations to foster open critical reflection on critical social issues and strategies for addressing these challenges.

Case Statements as a Window on Theories of Action

Retrospective reflection on action situations fostered and encouraged by graduate course work and coaching can build the capacity for reflection in action. This method was used by Argyris and Schön (1974; Argyris, Putnam, & Smith, 1985) to build their initial theory, and by Argyris (1993) in subsequent interventions. It involves having individuals develop case statements based on their experience (see Text Box 4.1). Within

---

Text Box 4.1 Assignment for Case Statement

Describe a challenging intervention or interaction with one or more individuals that you have already experienced or expect to experience in the near future.

If you have difficulty with either of these conditions, try a hypothetical case in which you doubt your effectiveness.

Begin the description with a paragraph regarding your strategy. What were your objectives, how did you intend to achieve them, and why did you select those goals or strategies?

Write a few pages of the dialogue that actually occurred or you expected to occur. Use the below format.

On the left side of the page, write what was going on in your mind while each person in the dialogue (including yourself) was speaking.	On the right side of the page, write what each person actually said or what you expected him/her to say. Continue writing the dialogue until you believe your major points are illustrated. (The dialogue should be at least two pages long.)

Describe the underlying assumptions that you held about effective action.

Source: Argyris & Schön, 1974, p. 41.

my own lasses on leadership and reflective practice—taught at four universities over 20 years—I have found this assignment to be a workable approach to encouraging open reflection.

Usually students will complete the first case statement by recalling an incident from their memory they would like to spend some time thinking about. I encourage them not to use an incident that would cause personal embarrassment if discussed openly in class. This was an instructional method I was exposed to as a graduate student in a course with Chris Argyris. My experiences as a teacher reinforce Argyris's argument that these case statements, even when constructed from what may be unreliable recollections, provide a good window of theories of action, including both espoused beliefs and theories in use. The chapters in Part II use student case statements (with permission from the students involved) to illustrate how to work with case statements.

Engagement in conversations about the case statements enables students to learn about their own theories in use. The common tendency to rationalize action—to argue that what one has done is just and right in a situation—is so strong that it is often easier for students to gain insight into their own theory in use when they hear others reflect on the cases they have constructed. I organize small group discussions as part of class time, explaining in the syllabus that when the author's case is discussed, she can answer questions before the discussion, but should listen to the group's analysis. Each member of the group has a chance to hear their case discussed and to participate in the discussion of the other cases.

Previously, I asked students to use Models I and II to analyze case statements. However, I encourage readers to use the frames developed in Part II of this book. The advantages of using these newer frames are: (1) if students have the opportunity to consider the full sequence, they can integrate considerations of moral reasoning as part of professional action; and (2) the new sequence integrates an emphasis on moral reasoning in action. The major innovation of this book is the integration of the frames of action with forms of moral reasoning (see Table 3.5). When this framework is used to analyze case statements there will be increased opportunity to reflect on the moral aspects of action.

Reflections on Framing Assumptions

The critical aspect of building reflective practice skills using this methodology involves reflection on one's own actions in relation to replicating patterns of action. There were problems with the original statements of Models I and II: (1) they did not recognize the underlying skill development process; (2) they did not distinguish the moral aspect of action from the logic; and (3) they did not distinguish the aims of practice within professional organizations from the life experiences of professionals. Using the frames that will be articulated in Part II can help students and faculty overcome these problems.

A skill development process in reflective practice is embedded in the restructured sequence. The assumption in Model I was that practitioners were experienced professionals capable of adapting practice (i.e. setting goals and trying to achieve them). My argument, based on three decades of experience as an interventionist and professor, is that the skill sets within the reflective frames are sequential and build on each other. The reflective frames are:

- *Instrumental.* Learning about basic principles of action, based on professional knowledge, is at the core of professional judgment. Practitioners need some basic experience with the knowledge and skills of their profession before they begin to adapt those skills. This skill set precedes the general assumptions in Model I.

- *Closed strategic.* Adaptation of practice—the process of applying professional knowledge and skills in new ways—builds on the core knowledge of the profession. Unless one knows how to do something (e.g. how to use linear regression or how to give professional advice), one is more prone to error if they attempt to be creative and adapt basic procedures. This skill set is consistent with Model I.
- *Open strategic.* One needs understanding of and expertise in professional skills (i.e. minimum competencies) before they can fully engage in open discussion about how to adapt strategies to better achieve organizational goals. Normal practice involves judgments about practice, often made in collaboration with other professionals and with clients. Ability to reflect openly and to analyze the unintended consequences of one's own actions is essential to this form of social interaction. This set of skills is consistent with Model II.
- *Communicative.* With this foundation of knowledge and skills, it is possible that practitioners can openly reflect, among themselves and with their clients, on recurrent patterns of professional practice, including injustices (i.e. inequalities, human suffering, and environmental destruction). When best practices cause critical social problems, a high level of expertise is needed to uncover underlying causes, along with the ability to foster open discussion. In my view, the focus on organizational effectiveness that dominated the framing of Model II literally prevented conceptualizing this type of expert adaptation.
- *Transformational.* After gaining experience with adaptations in organizations to better address critical challenges, it is possible to propose and test new approaches to action that have the potential of building transformational capabilities. This book, along with the many studies that led to this new theory (St. John, 1994, 2003, 2006, 2009; St. John & Wilkerson, 2006), add to a base of understanding about designing new methods, as well as proposing an approach to action inquiry that encourages others to experiment with methods. Having taken this step, I recognize that new approaches can fall subject to the limitations of all types of rules and may be treated as instrumental.[42]

Human action is not independent of moral reasoning. Rather, a specific action may be moral or immoral—using or abusing power—in different situations. One can abuse power unconsciously, in which case preconventional moral action can be unintentional. This means that learning about power abuse and other forms of immoral action in practice is necessary. An unintentional transgression does not mean one should give up or cover up, but instead that one should continue learning about themselves.

Often, action situations that do not work out are covered up, rationalized by people who have become accustomed to talking their way out of problems. In this book, I encourage readers to take a new step forward. Part II provides a new approach to integrating them with the three forms of moral reasoning. Preconventional, conventional, and postconventional moral reasoning can be enacted within each frame. A group of professionals oriented toward rectifying injustices can collectively choose to abuse power, to engage in quid pro quo responses to the actions of opponents whom they consider to be unjust. It may be easy to rationalize abusing power to solve a problem, but such actions should be recognized as such, as power abuses in response to injustice. Nonviolence and Gandhi's concept of truth in action set a very high standard of practice. If communicative action aimed at solving injustice can be unjust, then all forms of reflective practice can be prone to abuse and misuse. There is also potential for power misuse in many situations. I strongly encourage readers to engage in critical reflection on their experiences with misuse of power. It is much easier to build critical rationales than it is to act with justice. Regardless of our politics, society requires and should demand that professionals act responsibly.

By assuming that the aim of professional action is to be effective within a predefined notion of organizational strategy (i.e. aligned with centrally defined aims), the common theories of professional effectiveness and reflective practice have not paid sufficient attention to the lived experiences of practitioners—particularly their experiences of injustice. Reflecting on our experiences can help us understand injustice. To see and feel injustice we must periodically step out of the cognitive mindset imposed by organizational aims. Argyris (1993) focused on top down reform, while Schön (1987) focused on artistry of practice. However, neither of them provides encouragement to question the role of central authority. Their approach tacitly accepts the notion of control as the overarching rationale of the firm. Action science advocated a top–down change strategy and was dependent on executive buy-in. The aims of the profession were tacitly accepted in schools as the artistry of practice. These are forms of hegemony, of subjecting people to the power of the rationalized ordering of things, ideas, and processes. Of course we need laws, rules, and regulations in order to define justice, just as we need organizational goals to define collective action. However, unless we see these patterns for what they are—organizational frameworks that constrain and direct action, limiting freedom of action and discretion in somewhat artificial ways—it can be difficult to discern injustice or to act with care and justice in a critical situation.

If we take Habermas's critical leap of logic (viewing life experiences and systems as different aspects of the same phenomena), we can liberate ourselves from assuming the primacy of systemic control. We can reflect on the reasons why current practice creates social, organizational, and technical problems. Critical reflection on values and beliefs within organizations and practice creates windows on rationality that transcend the uncritical predisposition toward logic of action that often predominates.

Action Experiments

When beginning practitioners (i.e. graduate students or new professionals) gain experience with reflection on practices they begin to see patterns in their own behavior and to reflect on behavioral changes that might improve outcomes. This phenomenon is central to the claims about effectiveness made by Argyris and Schön (1974). While they did not create space for critique of organizational aims in the conceptualization of their original and subsequent intervention methods, they did communicate a basic understanding of the role of interventions and action experiments. In spite of conceptual limitations with respect to the moral aspects of practice and social injustice—the issues addressed in this book—the critical role of intervention in learning new methods of action was not overlooked in these prior theories.

In my experience with teaching graduate courses on reflective practice, I find that when students write a second case statement they often focus on an intervention they undertook, describing how they designed experiments to learn more about their organizations and themselves (St. John, 2009). This is a healthy process, one that was strongly encouraged by Arygris and Schön. The chapters in Part II present cases where students engaged in experiments along with some initial dialogues. By presenting and analyzing these experiments, I am encouraging readers to think about approaches they might use to experiment in action.

The individual's skill set for reflective practice should include a focus on building a capacity to experiment in practice, a feature of both strategic and communicative action. In closed-strategic action, individuals may experiment through their own practices. To make the transition to an open-strategic frame, practitioners must build skills in open communication about problems and strategies, including collaborative action experiments. In addition, the communicative frame reorients collective action toward untangling problems with the current system and experimenting with solutions. In these later stages of collective action, teams of individuals are involved in initiatives that address critical challenges. Professional organizations that encourage this form of action may want to foster action inquiry (addressed below).

Integrating Reflective Practice

The process of developing skills in reflective practice parallels the process of acquiring expertise. Reflective skills can be learned through reading, reflection, and actions that involve trying new practices. Reflection on action situations, including the moral aspects of practice, should be encouraged in all professional organizations. In addition to mentoring, incentives, and open communications, professional organizations can actively engage in change of practice. In my view, action inquiry provides a sound approach to organizational change aimed at addressing critical social challenges within organizations.

When members of organizations have skills in open critical reflection, it is easier to engage in initiatives involving collaborative action inquiry. However, even in organizations with missions that emphasize social justice, collaborative engagement in action inquiry is often not an easy process. It involves: research on the organization and the effects of services provided to clients; analysis and reflection on research to uncover problems; collective and critical reflection of possible methods of addressing problems; and experimental actions (i.e. interventions) and evaluation. It can help if groups treat current practices as pilot tests of strategies, and use evaluation results as baselines against which to compare alternatives.

The content of changing professional organizations is field specific, but it can be classified with generic theories of organizations and professional development. Most of the content on organizations in Part II, for example, is derived from research and interventions in higher education. Examples of practitioner reflection are drawn from case statements about student affairs, financial operations, technology transfer, and medical education. This diverse array of examples illustrates the potential for more general use of different ways of framing problems. However, for the approaches to reflective practice proposed in this book to be useful in other fields, a new generation of studies will be needed in those fields.

Using scientific methods in support of change and transformation in organizations involves a radically different orientation toward practice. Collaborating between practitioners and researchers in action projects that adapt strategies to meet situated challenges has a greater chance of improving services than attempts to replicate practices tried elsewhere. The methodological standards and rigors do not differ substantially from other types of research; evaluation of pilot tests using action inquiry should have rigor when possible. The focus shifts from experiments for replication to pilot testing locally-situated strategies for addressing critical challenges. While the experimental method may have value in developing new varieties of corn and other types of crops or in designing new drugs, for example, it is an extremely problematic method with respect to human action and professional practice. Replication of interventions thought to be best practice (i.e. basic practice or a set of rules) is a foundation of professional practice, but expert action involves adaptation and artistry in practice. AIM provides a method of using scientifically sound methods, along with human understanding and critical reflection, as an integral part of organizational strategy and professional action.

INTEGRATING ACTION INQUIRY

The process of integrating research into the organizational change process is complicated. The most simplistic approach is to conceive of research as being basic, and action as the application of knowledge obtained from research. Research in support of a change process is considered applied, and is often viewed as second class by those who center their inquiries in basic research. An alternative is to view research, including basic research, as being actionable and requiring testing of claims in action. In the process of testing ideas in action, it is possible to reframe theory. In this view there can be two types of claims: (1) universally applicable (U); and (2) situated (S) in a specific context.[43]

Universal claims about actions in social settings are problematic because action is situated. For example, the notion that there are patterns of action, and these patterns can be reflected by individuals, has both a U aspect (general patterns can be identified) and an S aspect (individuals can reflect on and alter action to address problems). The argument that a particular action strategy (e.g. an intervention tried in one place, possibly as an experiment) can have similar results elsewhere (a U claim) may run into problems in practice when different people reflect on and adapt the strategy (S phenomenon).

If it is true that action is situated—and there is a great deal of evidence from across the social and biological sciences that it is—then experiments in social settings cannot possibly control for all S phenomena. The old explanation of this problem—that people respond differently when they know they are a subject of an experiment (McGregor, 1960; Bolman & Deal, 1991)—is extremely difficult to overcome in scientific methods of intervention in organizations. An alternative realization of the process is that individuals reflect in action, creating nearly infinite permeations of patterns of implementation when attempts are made to replicate practices that have appeared successful elsewhere. To borrow a practice—that is, to learn and use a best practice—may be a starting point for organizational change, but the practice of borrowing without reflection and adaptation cannot be considered good practice. In fact, without reflection on practices, including consideration of the possible effects of changes, it is unlikely that any professional learning can occur.

To create actionable knowledge (i.e. building new understandings that practitioners can use to address challenges they face in practice) is a different form of knowing than is assumed in functional and scientific reasoning oriented toward a U assumption. Actionable knowledge involves professionals in assessing challenges in the situations they face (forming new S assumptions) and testing these assumptions in action. Integrating research and action provides a means of creating actionable knowledge that is situated (S) in specific problems. Situated understanding may or may not help inform generalized understandings about the change process in organizations (U). It is crucial, however, to recognize that the new U assumptions are subject to the same limitations that befall all basic research on humans and many other species.[44] Generalizing from a situated solution to a universal practice has inherent risks. Thus, it is important to think about the problem from the researcher's vantage (integrating research into action) and from the practitioner's vantage (using research in action, or action inquiry).

Integrating Research Into Action

The process of rethinking research in action starts with the comparison of the scientific approach of hypothesis testing to a critical-empirical approach (see Table 4.1). In the scientific method it is necessary to start with a hypothesis that is usually situated in a theory. Seldom is it possible to test a whole theory, but rather to test a concept within the theory. Very often in studies of humans, researchers test assumptions about relationships between one phenomena and another, assuming the relations follows a universal pattern. For example, in research on college student persistence, the hypothesis is that integration into academic activities is related to the intent to persist (Tinto, 1987), an assumption that holds up in many, but not all, studies that test this assumption (Braxton, 2000; Braxton, Sullivan, & Johnson, 1997).

The critical-empirical method starts with the assumption that U theories provide lenses to view problems and that multiple theories should be tested to build new understandings. To use the example above, we can think about different assumptions

Table 4.1 Comparison of the Scientific Approach and Critical-Empirical Approach

Dimension	Scientific Approach	Critical-Empirical Approach
Relation to theory and prior research	Review prior research and theory to develop a hypothesis that can be tested in a well-defined research study.	Review competing theories and diverse research pertaining to the policy problem. Identify different, possibly competing claims.
Accepted methods	Quantitative studies allow for accepting or rejecting hypothesis. Experimental designs, including natural experiments, are currently favored. Large-scale data collections and secondary data analyses are also frequently used.	Use methods appropriate for testing specific claims; often stated as questions rather than hypotheses. Methods depend on the nature of the theory and claim. May involve quantitative and/or qualitative research, critical reviews of research, or action experiments.
Role of research	Research is used to confirm and verify claims. Often offered as a proof of the theory, claim, or model.	Research is used to build understanding, develop theory, and inform action. Emphasis is on actionable knowledge.
Implications and limitations	Research often used for building rationales for reform. Research tends to be self-sealing and overlooks competing views.	Research examines competing views and can be used to open conversation. Research tends to be overlooked in policy forums because of complexity.

Source: St. John, 2007, p. 69.

about integration into activities during college and persistence. The notion that integration explains the intent to persist in college (Tinto, 1987) is based on Émile Durkheim's research on suicide (1951). His research, originally conducted in the late nineteenth century, compares rates of self-termination across different religious groups in Europe. More recent theorizing by another French scholar, Pierre Bourdieu (1990), introduced the notion of cultural capital. He hypothesized that education was to cultural capital what money was to economic capital. He argued that wealth, of the lack thereof, could influence the ability to acquire education, and thus cultural capital. In a study of high-achieving, low-income students of color (St. John, 2008), I examined how perceptions of family finances and the ability to pay, along with financial aid received, influenced working with faculty during college—a form of academic integration used in research on persistence and achievement (Braxton, Sullivan, & Johnson, 1997; Pascarella & Terenzini, 2005)—as well as how the financial variables and academic integration influenced persistence.[45] The findings were that concerns about finances and financial aid influence academic integration, as measured by working with faculty, but that, controlling for these variables, academic integration was not significantly associated with college persistence (St. John, 2008). In this example, it is important to recognize that: (1) those who hold to social integration theory should consider the role of finances; (2) advocates of cultural capital theories should consider the impact of ability to pay for college in our privatizing public system of higher education; and (3) practitioners should consider the relationship between the academic expectations of students and students' financial capacity (e.g. work hours impinge on time to engage in out-of-class student activities). Hopefully this illustrates how working with multiple U theories helps us build better, more robust understandings of the academic challenges facing diverse groups—in this case, talented, low-income minorities—than does the adaptation of a single theory.

Using a critical-empirical perspective (i.e. recognizing there are competing explanations for problems) is especially important when framing problems in organizations. Some will view problems from one vantage and hold related ideas about the solution, while others may look at it differently and have other views. Creating discursive space to consider evidence from internal and external observations and prior research provides a basis for comparing competing explanations and generating new understanding of causes and possible cures. In either case, research and observational evidence can be used to test assumptions; without explicitly comparing assumptions about the causes of problems, however, several competing theories of the problem may be simultaneously held and rationalized based on the same evidence.

The scientific approach to research on human action runs the risk of being self-sealing, reinforcing universal (U) assumptions that do not fit the situated (S) problem. Continuing the example from research on college student persistence, for two decades researchers focusing on the social integration theory of persistence overlooked financial aid (Braxton, 2000; Braxton, Sullivan, & Johnson, 1997). Consequently, some of the college drop-out rate among low-income students—an artifact of the lack of financial resources to engage in academic activities—was attributed to a lack of social integration (Tinto, 1997). Practitioners who uncritically believed the assumption would continue to promote ineffective intervention methods and blame talented low-income students for their failure to engage academically, when in reality they could not take time from work for these supplemental activities.

A reconstructed understanding of the research problem derived from testing different assumptions and claims provided different lenses to view the original problem. To extend the example, we can conclude interventions that include financial aid and support for academic integration would be desirable over policies that ignore student aid (Trent & St. John, 2008). However, this solution is more complicated than the strategies typically used by academics since academics do not play a role in financial aid decisions. To remedy this type of problem, it is necessary to coordinate different offices within a university and implement coordinated interventions.

Compared to the scientific approach, there is the additional complexity of thinking from a critical empirical vantage: It requires looking across theories to build new hypotheses about a problem and conduct research in different ways, possibly encouraging groups of practitioners to redesign their programs so they can test new S assumptions about how to solve problems. This requires better collaboration between researchers and practitioners. It also requires researchers to think through two dialectical tensions:

- *Framing Assumptions: Functionalist v. Critical.* In the social sciences, arguments about functionalist and critical views of action are often stated philosophically, as beliefs. The functionalist research tradition seeks to test universal theories while critical theorists are concerned about diverse groups, often in situated circumstances. If U beliefs can be suspended long enough to derive testable S claims, it is appropriate to conceive of testing claims in action contexts.

- *Methods: Quantitative v. Qualitative.* There is also a tendency among many researchers to argue for the superiority of quantitative or qualitative methods. Very often, critical researchers adhere to qualitative methods while functionalists adhere to quantitative methods. Some traditional researchers are now advocating mixed methods (Creswell, 2003), and some quantitative researchers are addressing critical claims (Stage, 2007). These developments allow us to move closer to an integrated approach that uses diverse methods in appropriate ways to test different assumptions and build new understandings of recurrent problems. Both quantitative and qualitative methods can be used to test S assumptions on action experiments.

Using Action Inquiry

Toward the aim of using research in practice and involving practitioners, I propose AIM as a process-oriented, research-informed change that can be used by professionals in diverse organizations for: (1) assessment leading to the identification of critical challenges (e.g. challenges related to academic success for high school students who aspire to gain entry to college); (2) organization of teams to address critical challenges through initiatives designed to address the challenges; (3) engagement in the action initiative reform process to address challenges (e.g. those related to improving college access and academic success); and (4) targeted evaluation of the challenges identified and the solutions proposed and tested to refine and improve interventions (see Figure 4.1).

This statement of AIM builds on understandings reached in a multi-year project, the Indiana Project on Academic Success (IPAS) (Hossler, Ziskin, & Gross, in press; St. John & Wilkerson, 2006). Interested readers can find out more about the research base from the planning studies for IPAS (St. John & Wilkerson, 2006) and findings from

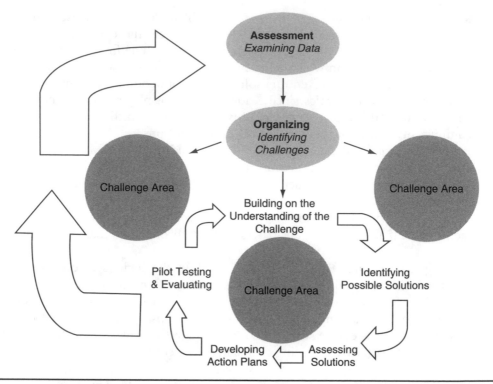

Figure 4.1 Action Inquiry Model (AIM)
Source: St. John, McKinney, & Tuttle, 2006.

assessments and interventions (Hossler, Ziskin, & Gross, in press; St. John, 2009). These supplementary readings, however, are not necessary to use this guide.

The Action Inquiry Model (AIM) is described here, briefly, as a generic approach to change that could be applied in different professional service organizations. AIM has four stages that can be integrated into ongoing strategic change efforts:

- *Stage 1: Assessment.* Analyze key organizational outcomes as a baseline assessment. In higher education this might include academic preparation, enrollment, major choice, and persistence by college students. Ideally this research would examine the factors associated with outcomes informed by either quantitative studies, qualitative studies, or both. The purpose of this process is to step back from current practice and think collectively about what the serious problems are in the organization. As a consequence of talking through assessment results at the organization level,[46] and possibly within basic organizational units, critical challenges should be identified.
- *Stage 2: Organization.* Challenges may cut across units of practice or be centered in a unit within a large organization. AIM teams, or workgroups, can consist of practitioners who are concerned about the problem and can be part of the solution. If necessary, professional release time from other responsibilities and financial resources should be dedicated for AIM teams to address challenges.
- *Stage 3: Action initiatives as reform process.* The AIM teams develop action plans

to address critical challenges, pilot test solutions, and collaborate on evaluations. The AIM project team can provide support for major organizational change initiatives.

- *Stage 4: Evaluation.* The AIM project team and other organizational leaders collaborate on the design and completion of evaluations of the interventions.

Action inquiry should be conducted by workgroups (AIM teams) organized to address challenges. Workgroups are comprised of practitioners (e.g. faculty, staff, and students in higher education) who have an interest in addressing a critical challenge of common concern. Some members of each team may have professional responsibilities in organizational units involved in addressing the challenges; others will have knowledge and skills that relate to the specific challenge area. Each of the five tasks in the action inquiry process is introduced below, with examples to illustrate the use of the methodology.

A Guide for Action Inquiry

Inquiry Task 1: Build an Understanding of the Challenge

Start by asking: Why does the challenge exist? What solutions have been tried in the past and how well did they work? What aspects of the challenge have not been adequately addressed? What aspects of the challenge require more study? Develop hypotheses (S claims) about the causes for the challenges using data to test the hypotheses. Consider the second order question: Do the explanations hold up to the evidence?

It is often assumed that once a challenge is identified it is relatively easy to find a solution. Some members of workgroups may believe they know the best solution to the challenges in the organization based on their experience or their understanding of best practices or research literature. However, consider the following alerts:

- *Beware of jumping to conclusions too soon.* If a problem is systemwide it has existed for a long time and may be resistant to commonly accepted solutions.
- *Analyze the problem.* Consider why the challenge emerged in the first place. How might action experiments inform understanding of possible causes? Do not fall into the trap of assuming universal claims (e.g. best practice solves our problem).
- *Tackle the underlying problems or causes.* Generate new solutions that are most likely to address the challenges facing your organization.
- *Allow for several attempts to try out solutions.* Before the workgroup has a well-grounded understanding of the problem, it is important to assess all possible explanations or causes. Interventions that address the real causes have the greatest chance of improving outcomes.

Inquiry Task 2: Look Internally and Externally for Solutions

Participants are encouraged to consider best practices related to the challenge, and how they might be adapted to meet local needs. With a common understanding, the team will be ready to look at the literature on best practices and related research, with an explicit focus on what practices are likely to address the challenges that appear central within the organization. Often there is extensive descriptive information available on best practices but few (or no) studies that actually test the results of these interventions (Patton et al., 2006). The team should visit other organizations with projects and initiatives that have tried out different approaches to solving the problem. It is important to consider how well these alternatives address similar challenges in the organization. As part of the process of building an understanding of the challenge, the workgroup will develop a shared understanding of the organization's history with the problem, how it has been approached in the past, and how it might be approached in the future. This stage in the inquiry process involves not only looking at what works elsewhere, but using your insiders' knowledge and shared understanding of the problem to make informed judgments about possible next steps. Replication may be a high form of praise, but given the increasing diversity in the US and other democratic societies, and the differences among peoples and across organizations, there is reason to question whether models should be transferred from one locale to another without adaptation to meet local needs.

Inquiry Task 3: Assess Possible Solutions

Based on critical reflection on the problems, team members are encouraged to consider alternatives in relation to the understanding of the problem developed in Task 1. Workgroups should identify a small set of possible solutions. When assessing solutions,[47] they should consider questions like: How will the solutions address the apparent cause of the problem? Is more data and analysis needed before choosing among alternatives? How can the solution be pilot tested? If the solution was tried, how would you know it worked? and What information would you need to collect to know how well it worked?

This analytical step of thinking critically and openly about alternative scenarios should not be skipped in the change process. Most practitioners value certain forms of action (i.e. their U assumptions) and will advocate for them, arguing that they are the best ones for the situation. They assume knowledge of best practice based on their expertise. Real life problems are seldom as simple as assumed when such advocacy statements are made. To avoid the mistakes of mindless or uncritical replication, it is necessary to reflect on questions like those above in relation both to quantitative and qualitative evidence about the local problem.

Inquiry Task 4: Develop Action Plans

Action plans should address the implementation of solutions to be pilot tested. Consider solutions that can be implemented by current staff. If there are additional costs, develop budgets for consideration internally and externally. Be cautious, however, because seeking additional funds can slow down the change process.

Action plans should include time frames for implementation and evaluation. The pilot testing of potential innovations is the core element of action research. Well designed research or active experiments can be published in journals in all fields of inquiry. Engaging faculty and professionals in the process of testing alternative solutions through action experiments can enhance the level and quality of discourse in departments and professional units. The action plan for an experiment may require review within the organization for human subjects approval if needed (e.g. in an educational setting, human subjects approval is needed if workgroup members want to publish results) and by administrative groups if additional funding is needed.

Inquiry Task 5: Implement Pilot Test and Evaluate

Workgroups should use the results of experiments as a basis for communicating about strategies for institutional improvement. The plans for action experiments should include the design of the project, methods for implementation, people responsible for activities in the implementation, and an evaluation plan.

Evaluation designs should be considered as part of action planning for pilot testing new approaches, even if only qualitative data will be used to judge how well the solutions address the challenges. Use evaluation results to refine the solution and provide feedback to workgroups and the coordinating team. Also, evaluation can be used as a basis for seeking additional funding from internal and external sources, to the extent that additional revenues are needed to fully implement the solution.

Integrating Research Into the AIM Change Processes

Evaluation has three specific functions: (1) evaluative thinking is integral to all four stages of AIM; (2) an evaluation process should be included as a step in the inquiry process; and (3) a recurrent process is needed that allows the model to turn back on itself, updating the assessment in the next iteration of the change process. Evaluation is a vital component to the success of a new project, facilitating the usability of the model in the production of actionable knowledge (Text Box 4.2 illustrates how research and evaluation fit into each stage of AIM).

Using AIM as an organization-wide strategy involves a comprehensive set of activities. Workshops and technical support should be provided to organizations that engage in comprehensive reforms of this type. Argyris and colleagues (Argyris, 1993; Argyris, Putnam & Smith, 1987; Argyris & Schön, 1974) have argued that process consultation is necessary to support comprehensive organizational reforms. Based on my experience (St. John, 2009), I agree that process reforms require external support and that the extent to which such reforms change practices is dependent on the reflective practitioners in those organizations.

Intervention methods necessarily provide guides for action that identify the steps that can be taken to address new, critical challenges. However, if guides are reduced to a list of rules or procedures to be implemented, then they are prone to being implemented instrumentally. When practitioners implement change processes in procedural ways, the chances that practice will change are minimized.

The complexity of the process relates in part to the role of the frames of action held among practitioners within the organization. It is crucial that people up and down the hierarchy have an opportunity to reflect on current practices in relation to critical challenges as they engage in inquiry about causes and possible solutions. This means that it is important to have experienced members of the team engaged in the inquiry process as they are senior members who can ask questions and share experiences. However, if this discussion only focuses on excuses for why solutions will not work, then the reflective aims will not be realized. These complexities of the relationship between framing problems and analyzing open inquiry are considered in Part II, along with exercises that can help beginning and experienced practitioners build reflective skills.

CONCLUSIONS

Professional development and change processes that engage practitioners in addressing critical challenges are related phenomena; both start with the process of reflecting on actions, including one's own actions. As people gain experience with collaboration on reform initiatives, it is possible to craft strategies that address inequalities.

Text Box 4.2 Role of Research and Evaluation in AIM

Stages	Key Tasks	Role of Research
Stage 1: Assessment	• Identify possible challenges • Collect and analyze data • Prioritize challenges • Organize work groups	• Identify critical success indicators (CSI) for challenges (outcome measures)
Stage 2: Organizing	• Coordinate budgeting to provide necessary support • Appoint AIM Scholars • Coordinate inquiry with planning and budgeting	• Identify targets of opportunity for improvement

Stage 3: Action Initiative Reform	• Engage each workgroup in a process to:
	  1. Build an understanding of the challenge
	  2. Look internally and externally for solutions
	  3. Assess possible solutions
	  4. Develop action plans
	  5. Implement pilot test and evaluate
		• Design interventions and evaluations
		• Use evaluation methods that provide information about critical success indicators

Stage 4: Evaluation	• Workgroups coordinate implementation and evaluation, providing reviews of plans, encouraging presentations to budget and planning groups, and facilitating coordination of the inquiry process with organizational planning • Coordinate evaluation support of pilot tests with other work groups as needed	• Consider implications for planning, budgeting, and practice in future years

Note: Glenda Musoba, a colleague on IPAS (e.g. Musoba, 2006), originally developed this Text Box.

This chapter has introduced a two-level framework for thinking about and practicing the integration of reflective practice and moral reasoning into action situations. The first level involves individual reflection on action situations. First I adapted a method originally developed by Chris Argyris and Donald Schön (1974), and encourage students and their professors to use this method as a learning exercise. Part II uses student case statements to illustrate the reasoning processes in action situations. Second I introduced a generic Action Inquiry Model (AIM) as a method of engaging practitioners in changing their organizations. Part II uses case vignettes from research on colleges and universities engaged in the Indiana Project for Academic Success (IPAS), a research-based, process-oriented reform initiative. Using this two-level approach, I hope to illuminate how the dominant forms of reasoning within organizations inform and shape the reasoning and applied problem solving of practitioners.

The links between reflection by professionals, including reflection on troubling situations, and engagement in systemic change initiatives is important. Engagement in collaborative initiatives provides opportunities to reflect on strategies for addressing critical challenges. Organizations that welcome change initiatives provide a means of supporting professional development. The AIM presented in this chapter provides one means for professional organizations to engage practitioners in reforms that can encourage reflection and professional development. While AIM was developed for colleges and universities, it can be adapted to other organizational settings.

REFLECTIVE EXERCISE

As a next step in their efforts to develop skills in reflective practice, I encourage readers to try developing their own case statement, using Text Box 4.1 as a guide. This can be a reconstructed conversation from memory or even a hypothetical exchange. For the purposes of the learning process encouraged in this volume, I recommend that you choose an incident that involved learning the *rules of practice*, the behavioral norms in a work setting. This may include an attempt to apply a new skill in a practical setting. The case statement should be about an incident you want to reflect on. Reflect on different framing assumptions and discuss them with others. In fact, readers are encouraged to take time out for this task before reading ahead since Part II focuses on analyses of critical incidents in professional practice. Readers will have an opportunity to engage in reflection as they move through the book.

Part II

Reflective Practice and Organizational Change

Part II provides a two-level perspective on organizations and professional practice. Building on the methods presented in Chapter 4, Chapter 5 introduces expert action as an individual process of developing knowledge and skills, and as an organizational process of control and regulation. Chapter 6 focuses on adaptation, reflection, and artistry among practitioners, and on strategic initiatives in organizations. Chapter 7 focuses on professional effectiveness and trust, including communication within communities of practice as a practitioner skill and organizational strategy. Chapter 8 considers communicative action to resolve critical challenges as forms of individual and organizational action. Finally, Chapter 9 examines transformational action initiated within communities of practice as a means of changing organizations. The underlying sequential process of knowledge and skill development is examined—from developing basic skills through initiating transformational change initiatives—at both the individual and organizational levels in these chapters.

At the level of practice, these chapters focus on how practitioners learn about professional practice and how organizational cultures influence the ways practitioners learn to frame practice. The specific aim is to build an understanding of ways graduate and professional education can be adapted to:

- encourage learning that enables practitioners to achieve their aims as professionals, as well as realize the dreams that motivated their choice of profession;
- enable reflection on assumptions, actions, and outcomes in ways that promote learning about improving practice and developing and refining skills, along with reflection on the moral aspects of practice;
- promote organizational development that enables professional development and encourages learning;
- improve services provided by professional organizations that promote justice and improve sustainability.

The organizational-level analysis focuses on discourse within organizations in relation to organizational strategy and strategic initiatives. These chapters seek to illuminate not only the strategies practitioners use to intervene when addressing critical challenges in practice, but also how organizational strategies can provide an environment for practitioners which can enable them to develop and apply interventions. Therefore, a related aim is to build an understanding of: (1) the alignment between organizational strategies and norms, and (2) the implications of this alignment for professional practice and organizational change. Specifically, the orientation toward strategy taken within organizations influences the opportunities for practitioners to reflect on and initiate changes in strategy and practice. Intermediate hypotheses about each mode of organization, generated from the analyses in these chapters, were stated in earlier chapters.

Part II uses organizational case studies and student case statements to derive lessons learned about each of the ways of framing practice in organizations. These lessons are intended to help practitioners and interventionists find their ways through complicated problems in professional practice within organizations.

5

EXPERT KNOWLEDGE AND SKILLS

Professional knowledge is learned in undergraduate and graduate programs. As part of that education, exposure to work and community settings through internships and service learning enables students to learn from experience within applied settings. These practices of teaching the content of a field and encouraging exposure to practice in the field as part of professional education assume a process of learning about professional organizations and the norms of the profession. Beginning professionals, along with their professors in higher education and mentors in professional organizations, make implicit assumptions about practice and what forms of practice and action are thought to be best practices. Application of content knowledge in action situations is an instrumental form of actionable knowledge.

This chapter focuses on learning knowledge and skills—acquiring instrumental expert knowledge—within professional fields. Knowledge and skills are the basic foundations for professional development. In this chapter the theoretical foundations of instrumental learning of expert knowledge are presented, followed by an analysis of case statements by students learning about professional practice, then a discussion of practice in organizations that emphasize instrumental action (i.e. organizations that focus on best practice without encouraging reflection, adaptation, and professional development), and finally a conclusion that focuses on organizational contexts and professional development.

BEST PRACTICES

Identifying and learning best practices is a core component of developing professional knowledge and skills. This orientation is especially evident in K–12 education, since the federal government has pushed best practices through a systematic approach to disseminating research information as part of the new emphasis on education science. A similar method is now being promoted in higher education research and by the federal government, states, and some of the foundations that support colleges and universities. This form of judgment involves applying or implementing what is hypothesized[48] (or believed) to be best practice. While best practices usually are an appropriate starting point, implementing practices, policies, and procedures should not be viewed as the sole aim of professional education. Indeed, much more emphasis on strategy and artistry—more advanced forms of practice—is needed across professional fields (see Chapter 6).

To build an understanding of how professionals learn about practice and act as professionals, it is important to examine the ways professionals frame action. This process is examined in three parts: (1) basic frames of action from research on organizations, coupled with informed speculation about the ways frames of organizational action might link to professional knowledge;[49] (2) the role of ethics and moral reasoning within professionals; and (3) the links between basic professional frames of action and moral reasoning.

Expertise Dimension: Basic Frames

There is substantial research that indicates that an early learning of the rules of a profession is linked to future success. Instrumental action starts with a process of discerning situations and applying rules (as methods and other forms of practice) that fit the problem. When decision making focuses on the application of a model or method, or when a best practice is chosen and implemented, the implicit assumption is made that the action is doing the right thing or accomplishing the desired goal. For many types of problems in practice, this assumption is appropriate for up to, perhaps, 80 percent of the cases (based on classical quality control principles).[50]

Bolman and Deal's (1991) method of viewing how professionals frame organizational problems is widely used in leadership courses in business and education. Based on their review of the extensive literature on organizations, they argue there are four basic ways individuals view problems within organizations:

- *structural*, with the central assumption that, "Organizations exist primarily to accomplish established goals" (p. 48);
- *human resource*, with the central assumption that, "Organizations exist to serve human needs (rather than the reverse)" (p. 121);
- *political*, with the central assumption that, "Organizations are *coalitions* composed of varied individuals and interest groups (for example, hierarchical levels, departments, professional groups, gender and ethnic groups)" (emphasis in original, p. 186);
- *symbolic*, with the central assumption that "What is most important about any event is *not* what happened, but *what it means*" (emphasis in original, p. 246).

While there are several assumptions associated with each of these frames, the core assumptions illustrate how different outlooks about an organization might influence the ways people view problems. Within graduate programs in educational leadership there is usually a range of basic frames represented in the classroom. Comparative framing of problems allows for a discussion of issues. However, while there is variation within fields, it is also evident from experience that social and political frames dominate among students in graduate courses on educational leadership (St. John, 2009).

Bolman and Deal (1991) argue that holding a basic frame constrains the understanding of problems in organizations. They encourage graduate students and professionals to examine problems from different vantages. They illustrate some of the ways people with different basic frames might view a range of organizational problems. They argue that the typical response to problems in the organizational frame is to focus on training people (human resources), with structural responses emphasized by those who hold the structural frame, and political responses by people within the political frame. In contrast, people with the symbolic frame are more likely to think about the meaning of a problem and how to manage the means as part of the organizational response.

Bolman and Deal also encourage students to reflect from different vantages on problematic situations. By examining problems from multiple vantages, they argue, practitioners gain not only a more complete understanding of the problem but also the types of responses that are appropriate. While this process of reflecting on problems can improve the understanding of problems and enable students to think strategically, it essentially involves encouraging reflection on basic assumptions about practice without explicit evaluation of outcomes in relation to those assumptions. Until groups within organizations reflect on evidence related to practice and the results of solutions imposed, they are not reflecting on practice.

Bolman and Deal's frames are consonant with the typology of professions used in this book and an orientation toward justice and care. They distinguish between: interpretive perspectives (What is justice?); social/political perspectives (What is just and caring action?); critical perspectives (What interventions can reduce inequality?); and technical-scientific perspectives (What are the effects of policy on equity outcomes?). With this adaptation of the typology, it is possible to suggest a natural alignment between basic frames and professions:

- Professions that are interpretive in their content, knowledge, and skills—including journalists at one extreme, with respect to implicit emphasis on values, and ministers at the other—emphasize practices that are aligned with symbolic frames.
- Professions that are social in their orientation to content, knowledge, and skills—including teaching, nursing, and business administration—emphasize human resources frames because of the content of these fields.
- Professions that have an inherent advocacy position—including lawyers, politicians, and activists—emphasize political frames.
- Professions that are technical-scientific in their orientation toward content, knowledge, and skills—including engineering, science, and medicine—emphasize analysis as problem solving or structural frames.

These hypothetical alignments are based on the content and central assumptions of Bolman and Deal's frames in relation to the frames of social justice. It is probable that many aspiring professionals are attracted to fields which are logically aligned with their intuitive frames. For example, people with analytic frames who reduce social problems to these elements may be more drawn to scientific fields. Some fields related to social science, such as financial management in business administration or economics, might also attract people with structural analytic frames (see Table 5.1).

Since the knowledge of ethical issues in scientific fields is often treated as a technical matter, it is sometimes easier for people in these fields to think about problems in technical ways. For example, scientists and medical doctors would focus on finding a vaccine for polio or AIDS (structural response). In contrast, a journalist might focus on what the AIDS epidemic means for society (symbolic response), while a teacher could

Table 5.1 Interpretive, Social, Critical, and Technical-Scientific Expertise and Orientations Toward Expertise

Type	Interpretive	Social	Critical	Technical-Scientific
Orientation toward Knowledge	Primary orientation toward justice focused on interpretation and experience	Primary orientation toward justice focused on social interaction and/or caring for others	Primary orientation toward justice is advocacy	Primary orientation toward justice is analytical, technical, and scientific
Applied Professions (Examples)	• Journalist • Artist • Minister	• Teacher • Business Manager • Nurse	• Politician • Activist • Lawyer	• Engineering • Programmer • Medical Doctor
Foundations	• Art and Literature • Interpretation • Creative Expression	• Social Sciences • Professional Services • Organization	• Political Advocacy • Public interest	• Basic Sciences • Technical Knowledge • Information
Hypothesized Primary Basic Frame(s)	• Symbolic (Meaning)	• Human Relations (Care)	• Political (Advocacy)	• Structural (Analysis)

focus on education about AIDS and sex (human resources response). An AIDS activist might engage in protest as a means of encouraging public support of research or public subsidy of medicines (political response). While this way of viewing professions over-simplifies the complexity of human responses, as do earlier notions of frames, it introduces the role of alignment of assumptions and the content of professional fields, a topic that merits further examination.

Focusing on the basic ways in which practitioners frame problems provides a starting point for how to act in a situation. Action based on false assumptions without reflection or testing of assumptions is *instrumental.* In contrast, a process of aligning strategy with conscious reflection on assumptions can be considered *strategic.* If the reflection on assumptions is shared openly and considers evidence, it might be considered *open strategic.* Such topics are addressed in later chapters.

Moral Dimension

It is appropriate to view ethics as integral to the basic knowledge of a profession. However, the literature on organizations and framing of practice is largely silent on ethics and moral reasoning. For example, Bolman and Deal (1991) examine morality and ethics within their discussion of political frames (pages 119–124), but do not discuss the topic in relation to other frames. Argyris, Putnam, and Smith (1985) discuss moral reasoning in relation to experiments (i.e. the lack of reflection in some experimental methods), but do not consider explaining it as an integral part of their theory. Most theories of organization implicitly assume moral action is a part of convention and integral to the content, knowledge, and skills of the profession. As part of the reflection on basic frames, it is important to consider ethical codes for professions. Professional education in all fields should treat ethics and moral reasoning as a basic part of the curriculum.

One of the oldest known ethical statements is the Hippocratic Oath. The original statement was clearly situated in the religion of the time by swearing an oath to the gods and goddesses. This orientation to faith reminds us of the origins of moral reasoning in higher education and the professions (see Chapter 2). Even before the monotheistic religions emerged there was an orientation toward faith in practice. It is certainly appropriate that aspiring, beginning, and experienced professionals take time to reflect on their values—whether they are situated in faith, enlightenment, or both—in relation to the ethical codes of their professions and their own practice.

The original oath values the teaching and the teacher of practice. In its current form, academic medicine is less oriented toward transmission of knowledge from one person to another than it is to learning a defined curriculum and set of methods. Respect and value of others, inclusive of instructors and patients, is critical and should be part of the code of ethics. However, in my view there is no reason to hold professors in a more revered position than others just because they teach. Care and commitment can, of course, develop between mentors and mentees in any field, but I think it is important to treat everyone who holds similar values with respect and care. I say this as a personal reflection, based on experience as well as my understanding of mentorship. It is important that mentors and guides respect the ethical codes in their relationships with students and mentees (Guggenbuhl-Craig, 1971 & 1982).

The basic orientation toward just practice is evident in the oath, as is the commitment to doing no harm. This commitment is evident in both the use of "dietary" remedies (i.e. drugs) and using of the "knife" (i.e. surgery). These principles seem sound, as does the commitment to avoid sexual relations with patients. These statements relate to the commitment to not abuse the power that comes with the role of doctor. These are important standards of practice across professions.

The original oath contains commitments related to controversial issues. When I first read the statement on Wikipedia, I was interested to see the reference to assisted suicide and abortion. I wondered about the statement's use of "abortive remedy" in the Wikipedia version, so I found the classical source, which confirmed the content. Interestingly, the issues of assisted suicide and abortion are still being debated, indicating that statements of ethics are not simple. Certainly such matters merit reflection within professions and society. (See Chapter 8 for a more extensive discussion of moral issues in the health professions.)

An examination of a modern version of the oath, written in 1964 by Louis Lasagna, illustrates how medical ethics have evolved. The modern statement departs from the original in many ways. The modern statement:

- is stated as a covenant, but is not based in faith as was the original statement;
- eliminates the commitment to the teacher, a condition that seems an appropriate update, for the reasons noted above, from my perspective as a faculty member interested in moral reasoning;
- makes an explicit statement about warmth and sympathy, using a different language than the original;
- emphasizes recognizing the limits of one's own knowledge and consulting with colleagues when needed;

- makes reference to modern diseases that are expensive to treat (e.g. cancer), and service to all regardless of income, which is a contemporary accommodation of social justice;
- is not explicit about boundaries related to abortion and assisted suicide, rather emphasizing care in these choices.

The modern statement is not as clear as the original with respect to assisted suicide and abortion. The modern statement takes the following position on life and death: "Most especially I must tread with care in matters of life and death" (Lasagna, 1964, online). This quote can be interpreted in multiple ways. From one vantage it might be interpreted as a strong argument against these practices. Yet given the capacity to extend life as a result of modern technology, care for patients may involve family choices about not using this technology. This ambiguity in the text means that it is in the hands of medical doctors to make moral judgments in their own practices. Making judgments based on "care in matters of life and death" is an essential aspect of the discretion of medical doctors (see Chapter 8). The changes in the oath from the original to the modern restatement reflect the secularization of medical ethics, a development that parallels changes in philosophy and science (see Part I).

As professionals in contemporary society, our obligations are appropriately situated in contemporary codes of practice. Employment opportunities and the ability to practice in legal and ethical ways require that this leap be made. However, when confronted by moral challenges it is also appropriate to reflect on how statements of ethics themselves have changed. Some new standards of behavior, like sexual harassment policies (Rosovsky, 1990), are more recent, having been developed in recognition of serious moral problems. However, given the controversial nature of issues related to abortion and assisted suicide, it is interesting to see how the interpretation of the oldest code of ethics has changed.

Another illustration is the statement developed by the American College Personnel Association, one of the major associations for student affairs personnel and counselors in colleges and universities. The statement has three parts: (1) a preamble that situates the statement in the profession; (2) a statement of use that focuses on individual responsibility; and (3) a statement of standards (see Text Box 5.1). The standards statement focuses on four areas: (1) Professional Responsibility and Competence; (2) Student Learning and Development; (3) Responsibility to the Institution; and (4) Responsibility to Society.

Text Box 5.1 Statement of Ethics for the American College Personnel Association (ACPA)

Preamble

ACPA—College Student Educators International is an association whose members are dedicated to enhancing the worth, dignity, potential, and uniqueness of each individual within postsecondary educational institutions and, thus, to the service of society. ACPA members are committed to contributing to the comprehensive education of students, protecting human rights, advancing knowledge of student growth and development, and promoting the effectiveness of institutional programs, services, and organizational units. As a means of supporting these commitments, members of ACPA subscribe to the following principles and standards of ethical conduct. Acceptance of membership in ACPA signifies that the member understands the provisions of this statement.

This statement is designed to address issues particularly relevant to college student affairs practice. Persons charged with duties in various functional areas of higher education are also encouraged to consult ethical standards specific to their professional responsibilities.

Use of this Statement

The principal purpose of this statement is to assist student affairs professionals (individuals who are administrators, staff, faculty, and adjunct faculty in the field of student affairs) in regulating their own behavior by sensitizing them to potential ethical problems and by providing standards useful in daily practice. Observance of ethical behavior also benefits fellow professionals and students due to the effect of modeling. Self-regulation is the most effective and preferred means of assuring ethical behavior. If, however, a professional observes conduct by a fellow professional that seems contrary to the provisions of this document, several courses of action are available. Suggestions to assist with addressing ethical concerns are included in the Appendix at the end of this document.

Ethical Foundations

No statement of ethical standards can anticipate all situations that have ethical implications. When student affairs professionals are presented with dilemmas that are not explicitly addressed herein, a number of perspectives may be used in conjunction with the four standards identified in this document to assist in making decisions and determining appropriate courses of action. These standards are: 1) Professional Responsibility and Competence; 2) Student Learning and Development; 3) Responsibility to the Institution; and 4) Responsibility to Society.

Ethical principles should guide the behaviors of professionals in everyday practice. Principles are assumed to be constant and, therefore, provide consistent guidelines for decision-making. In addition, student affairs professionals should strive to develop the virtues, or habits of behavior, that are characteristic of people in helping professions. Contextual issues must also be taken into account. Such issues include, but are not limited to, culture, temporality (issues bound by time), and phenomenology (individual perspective) and community norms. Because of the complexity of ethical conversation and dialogue, the skill of simultaneously confronting differences in perspective and respecting the rights of persons to hold different perspectives becomes essential.

Note: This statement was approved by the ACPA Executive Committee in March, 2006. http://www.myacap.org/ethics/statement/cfm Copied: November 11, 2007

Each of these standards is elaborated upon within the full statement, which is available on the Internet (see Text Box 5.1). Students who aspire to work in student affairs, along with those who already work in the field, should review these standards and reflect on them.[51] Professional responsibility is central to all fields, but as the specifics of professions vary, so do the standards. The focus on student learning and development is specific to student affairs as a field of practice and provides essential content knowledge, forming the core of expertise of student affairs professionals. Responsibility to institutions in which we work (i.e. the colleges and universities employing student affairs professionals) is important to all professionals in higher education. We are all obligated as representatives or agents of our employers. For example, within public universities we are legal agents of the state and are obligated to act accordingly. Otherwise we and/or our institutions may be legally liable. We also have obligations to society, some of which are legally constructed while others remain ambiguous.

My argument is that in the social environment of action we have an obligation to reflect on the consequences of our actions. I raise this issue because, as an employee of a university, I must reflect on my obligations in relation to my role in the university in this context. There are many compelling issues related to social contexts for action for me as a professor. Such issues include:

- maintaining a just environment in the classroom, treating all fairly and respectfully with respect to gender, race, personal orientations and values;
- maintaining appropriate relations as I guide students through advanced work;
- engaging in classroom governance in ways that promote just, fair, and caring responses to critical problems encountered in my program and other organizational units of the University of Michigan;
- orienting my research to address critical social problems, including research that informs the improvement of access, retention, and professional education.[52]

As another example of a recent statement of ethics, I encourage readers to reflect on the simple statement of bioethics advanced by Francis Collins, director of the Human Genome Project at the University of Michigan:

- *Respect autonomy*—the principle that a rational individual should be given freedom in personal decision making, without undue outside coercion.
- *Justice*—the requirement for fair, moral, and impartial treatment of all persons.
- *Beneficence*—the mandate to treat others in their best interest.
- *Nonmalficence*—"*First* do not harm" (as in the Hippocratic Oath) (Collins, 2006, pp. 243–244).

This statement includes features from the other statements reviewed above. It captures the issues of: respect of individual autonomy; fair, moral, and impartial justice; beneficence (treating people in ways consonant with their best interests, a form of caring); and of doing no harm. This simple statement captures a near universal set of standards. However, given the content and skill differences across fields, it is important that students consider field-specific standards.

The topic of ethics is not a simple one that should be skipped over when thinking about framing problems in practice. For me, the concept of the critical social problem is central to ethics. From one vantage, we need to ponder the meaning of "do no harm."

If current practice in education, health, law, and other areas of professional practice end up being more harmful to some than to others—and certainly this is a serious and pervasive problem given the very great inequalities of educational opportunity and other social inequalities—then we have an obligation to ponder how our action causes harm by maintaining this status quo. It is only after such reflection that we can begin to envision remedies.

Frames of Mind

My argument is not that moral reasoning should dominate professional reasoning and judgment. Rather, I think that it is crucial that we consider moral issues as part of professional action. There is a moral consequence of action and of nonaction. Sitting in a chair and writing—one of my own patterns of professional practice—has a consequence. Given my compulsion to write, I need to make sure I take time to work with students by reading papers and providing feedback, conduct research studies in timely ways that fulfill contractual obligations of funded research and maintain appropriate standards, and fulfill my obligations to my university. Given these other obligations and my compulsion to write, what about my family and the time I need to give them?

My point is that it is far too simple to assume that the moral aspect of action is taken care of by church, family, other professors, and other professionals. The moral is an integral aspect of action for all of us. Chapter 3 built a framework for integrating moral reasoning and frames of professional action; this chapter explores this framework further with respect to instrumental, expert reasoning.

While instrumental reasoning is widely critiqued, it is vitally important as a point of departure in professional practice; it is a personal foundation from which to build a career. In particular, it is crucial that beginning professionals reflect on conflicts between professional codes and observed practice. In my view, the basic frames of professions (e.g. Table 5.1) are essentially instrumental. As we acquire knowledge, it is natural to apply it instrumentally. Awareness of our own basic assumptions—the foundations of our personal instrumental frames—provides a departure point for learning how to voice concerns and intervene in action situations. Table 5.2 takes a step further in integrating moral reasoning in an instrumental frame of problems in practice. The key features of the instrumental frame are to apply knowledge and to build technical skills and human relations without consideration of evidence (i.e. without action inquiry). These two basic frames of action can vary along moral dimensions.

Conventional instrumental moral action involves trying to act in ways consistent with the moral and ethical standards of practice in the profession. This requires a minimum standard for professional action, but is not necessarily easy to enact. Abuse of power is central in most statements of ethical standards. If professionals treat others instrumentally, it is hard to do so without some form of power abuse. However, it is possible to comply with one's own understanding of the rules—both formal and informal—and rationalize action, making claims about practice situated in the rules and doing what was expected. While this behavior may be experienced as defensive, if it is consonant with the rules of practice and codes of ethics it is not inappropriate prima facie.

There can be a serious problem with abuse of power when supervisory action is instrumental. Many professionals inadvertently shut down questioning by clients or employees, an act that can be experienced as abusive. Such action may not intentionally be immoral, but it can be problematic. More critically, there is a strong tendency to

Table 5.2 Instrumental Behaviors in Relation to Frame of Action and Types of Moral Reasoning

Moral Reasoning/ *Frame of Action*	Preconventional	Conventional	Postconventional
Instrumental frame focus	Using rules without considering underlying problems.	Applying rules of practice consistent with ethical codes.	Using extant methods to address moral challenges.
Applying knowledge/building technical skills	• Works around problems without regard for rules • Ignores unintended consequences • Covers up for self-protection	• Practices expert knowledge and skills • Tries out practices that fit situations • Complies with rules and ethical codes	• Focuses critical, social, and environmental problems • Applies rules to solve problems or raises questions about changing rules
Human relations, attitude toward action inquiry	• Protective of self • Defensive routines • Espoused beliefs rationalize abuse	• Espoused values rationalize actions • Protective of self and others	• Empathetic • Acts on personal values/ sacrifices for others

work around problems, to justify means based on ends. Bureaucratic procedures are often experienced as problematic.

Some practitioners, based on their organizational roles, have discretion to make exceptions in critical cases, while others do not have this flexibility. If those who have discretion to deviate from rules are instrumental (i.e. they apply the rule without thought to the circumstances), then problematic situations can be made worse. For example, degree requirements (i.e. specific course requirements) can be waived by professors in some circumstances. If they are waived in all circumstances, then the value of the degree can be discounted or the trust among faculty members (i.e. the group that set the rules for academic reasons) can be threatened. But there may be legitimate circumstances for exercising discretion on a case-by-case basis. For example, a new requirement may be enacted as a guide for a profession which should be integrated into education and orientation processes. However, if an experienced professional has demonstrated he or she already possesses this knowledge or skill, there may be no reason for them to be required to take a course to learn these new rules of practice.

This basic orientation toward rules and waiving them with discretion in appropriate circumstances is central to distinguishing conventional, preconventional, and postconventional moral reasoning. The instrumental actor who is concerned about inconsistent application of discretionary rules may raise the question in a way that encourages peers or organizational superiors to reflect on the problem. Such action might be considered postconventional.

The relationship between instrumental judgment and ethics often does not receive sufficient attention in graduate professional education or other professional fields. If we do not sufficiently consider ethics as part of curriculum, we may also inadvertently skip over the roles of discretion and judgment. We may be communicating by what we do not discuss that it is acceptable to work around problems without reflection on the moral aspects of these choices.

PROFESSIONAL ACTION

Two cases illustrating the work of students' case statement assignments in graduate courses on educational leadership, reflective practice, and related topics are examined below.[53] The full case statement is presented in the first case to facilitate analysis, and an abbreviated format is used for the second. My aims in this discussion are to: (1) illustrate the applicability of the multiple frames of instrumental behavior; and (2) reflect with the reader on the implications of this framework for learning reasoning in practice.

Case Statement: Drinking With Students

This case statement was written by a student in a course of reflective practice in student affairs.[54] The case focuses on a dialogue between an intern and a supervising administrator in an office of student affairs (see Text Box 5.2). A conversation between the graduate student intern (Kate) and her supervisor (Sam), this case was written in response to an assignment to write a dialogue for a memorable situation you would like to have some time to reflect on and discuss.

Text Box 5.2 Case Statement: Drinking With Students

Context: Kate, an intern in a Student Organizations Office in a public university, had been out at a bar in the community. A fraternity president (whom she once supervised in her role in the Student Organizations Office) asked to buy her a drink. She indicated she agreed because he knew the bartender and could get it faster. She gave him the money. Kate's account of what happened was: "The drinks were ordered and my money was returned to me. As I was given the drinks, I asked my friends how they felt about the idea that a former student leader (who was of legal drinking age) technically bought the drinks. They shrugged and said 'a free beer is a free beer.' I thanked the student for the drink and I returned to my friends. I drank my beer and left as planned."

Kate's supervisor, Sam, had heard about the incident and had a talk with her at work.

Participants

Kate (K), intern in Student Organizations Office
Sam (S), supervisor in Student Organizations Office

Reflection	Dialogue
Wow, how the heck did he hear about this? I wonder what he knows. I wonder who told him and what he will say. He obviously thinks I did something wrong.	(S1) Kate, come on in and close the door behind you. Can you tell me about the situation when an undergraduate former fraternity president bought you a drink at a bar the other night?

OK, what am I going to say? I can't lie about what happened. Just stay calm, you didn't do anything wrong.

(K1) Well Sam, what you heard is true. I did find myself in a situation where a student bought me a beer.

Are you kidding me? I should take him seriously but honestly he is TOO dramatic. OK, don't jump on the defensive. Just explain to him what happened.

(S2) I am extremely disappointed in you Kate.

Maybe I'll just explain how this happened and he'll see things from my perspective.

(K2) I went out to the bar with several of my graduate student friends for one beer and then I planned to go home. The bartender got really busy, and this student claimed that he knew the bartender and that he could get our drinks faster if he ordered them. I insisted that I pay for my drinks but after the drinks were purchased, I got my money back.

So basically you're recommending that I never go out in public places where I might run into students. God forbid the students think we actually have social lives. Just because you have no social life doesn't mean that I have to live like that!

(S3) That sounds like basically the same story that I've heard from others. It is my practice that I don't socialize at establishments where undergraduates hang out. I would advise you not to find yourself in this situation again.

I still contend that I did nothing wrong. I hate that disappointed look in his eyes. I don't even think that he is listening to me.

(K3) I will certainly try not to find myself in this situation again. I have never been in this situation before. This was a seriously strange circumstance.

HA! HA! What a joke. If my other supervisory actually says something to me I will be so surprised. I've seen him drink with undergraduates before who aren't even of drinking age. Why is he being SO dramatic? I just want to get out of this bizarre conversation.

(S4) I am speaking with you personally because I have spent three years working with these students and I am frustrated that your mistake may have an effect on my relationship with some of them. I also want you to know that I have informed [your other supervisor] about this and I am sure he will handle this situation as he sees fit.

Maybe if I sound like he isn't bothering me he'll feel bad about even bringing this up.

(K4) I appreciate your speaking with me about how you feel. I am not sure though how my actions will affect your relationship with these students.

Does he honestly think that little of me? I thought I had a relatively professional relationship going. I think he is just saying these things for effect.

I think I am making a really good point here. I've collected my thoughts and I really do not think that this minor incident is not actually going to affect my credibility as a professional.

A "learning moment"? This is ridiculous. What I've learned is that I will never let myself get CAUGHT in this situation again. I am SO glad that I am leaving this place in 3 months. The only reason that I might be uncomfortable is the fact that he is being so dramatic.

Kissing up can't hurt, even though I still don't think that I did anything wrong. It is just easier at this point to say "thanks" and then get back to work

I really hope that he isn't going to hold a grudge. I am dying to ask if he is going to talk to the other staff members about this. . . . OK now he is smiling, I'm going to get out of here before this gets ugly again.

(S5) You can be certain that all of this student's friends know what happened. They are going to think you have an "in" with the people in charge.

(K5) I can see your point, but until I actually let my personal life affect my professional practice, giving these students an "in" for example, which will NEVER happen, I really don't see how this will affect our office's relationship with students.

(S6) I still think that in your position this was not a wise decision. I realize that you are still young and I just want to take advantage of this "learning moment." I am sure that this conversation was uncomfortable which shows that you may have been questioning your actions.

(K6) Thank you. I really appreciate your speaking with me and sharing your insight. I apologize if I have negatively influenced your relationship with any students. I never intended to find myself in this situation. I don't plan on this happening again. At least I didn't go back to the fraternity with him and have a few more beers (laughs).

(S7) I trust that this will not be a problem in the future. Are you going to the staff meeting? Do you know what is going on with it? I hope that it does not last too long!

Assumption: "During this conversation I definitely assumed that I would be in a less desirable situation if I told this supervisor exactly how I really feel, as though this supervisor treated me like I was one of his undergraduate students . . . I think he is jealous that his graduate students go out socially and he does not have that outlet."

Source: modified slightly from original, Kline, 2003, 128–131.

Kate's description depicts a situation in which she was bought a drink by a student in a fraternity over which she had had some supervisory authority. Within universities there are multiple ethical codes that limit freedom to take advantage of a situation. This is a situation in which Kate took a questionable position, not unlike a professor or graduate instructor taking a gift from a student that could be interpreted as a favor for a grade. Kate did not consider this an absolutely clear-cut situation and she used her discretion. Her supervisor, Sam, heard about the situation and was obviously troubled by it.

At the outset of the exchange, Kate was obviously surprised that Sam had found about the incident. Sam starts off by expressing disappointment (S2). There may have been better ways to ease into this topic, but he did express his feelings. When first confronted, Kate's response was to explain the situation and rationalize what she did (K2). Sam validates Kate's statement of the facts (S3), but tries to open a dialogue. Kate responds with a simple acknowledgement (S3), in the hope that it will end the discussion. However, Sam presses on, indicating he shared the information with another supervisor. Again, Kate verbally acknowledges the comment (K3). At this point, Sam comes to his major concern, which is a possible breakdown in the relationship built with students (S4). Kate acknowledges this (K4), after which Sam gets to his point of the potential "in" with authority (S5). Kate challenges this assumption of the "in," indicating in her response that she finds this offensive. At this point, Sam presses on to focus on learning from the situation (S6), which Kate acknowledges and then jokes about a worse impropriety (K6).

In this exchange, Kate was clearly defensive, trying to rationalize the situation, and making light of the incident when the exchange got more difficult for her. Further rationalizing in her final thoughts, she indicates she did not say how she felt about the supervisor. Her frame was social but she did not reflect on the moral aspects of the situation. We do not know from the dialogue what the supervisor was thinking or the history of his exchanges with Kate. Sam was assertive and appears to have handled the situation professionally. In a situation when there is indiscretion, as was the case here, choices need to be made about whether to confront and how to do so.

This situation illustrates a person (Sam) with conventional moral reasoning confronting a perceived problem. Sam did not openly reflect on the limitations of rules (i.e. the role of discretion), but instead assumed a rigid standard of right and wrong. In her dissertation, where this case statement was originally presented, Kim Kline's analysis of the incident was: "This situation did, however, result in a predicament where neither individual seemed truthful or open about a professional situation" (2003, p. 130). In addition to the obvious lack of open reflection, it is apparent that both people were acting instrumentally in a problematic situation.

Case Statement: International Researcher

This case involves a conversation in an Office of International Education. Fred, a staff member in the office, tried to intervene in a specific case to exercise discretion to permit a foreign visitor to stay in the country longer than initially agreed. Fred had agreed to take the researcher's case to the office director to advocate for an extension.

Fred's Reflection	Dialogue
	(F1) Fred: "About this researcher, I recommended that the extra six months would buy him some time. Is this possible, do you know?"
	(D1) Diane: "Um, Sally (other staff member) has been dealing with it, and I talked with him yesterday. Wait for Sally to return."
I didn't see any reason why it would matter.	(F2) Fred: "Wait, this guy has to leave in less than 30 days and you just can't wait for Sally. Isn't it in all of our best interests to provide him some time to find out about options, even if it means only 2 or 4 months? Why not?"
	(D2) Diane: "Look, Dr. Jones (the research professor overseeing the visitor's research) needs to know he can't bring these guys in, not pay them, and work them like slaves."

Fred raises the issue with his supervisor, Diane (F1). She tries to push the issue on another staff person to whom she assigned the case (D1). Fred persists by expressing concern and arguing for an exception (F2). At this point, Diane reveals her reason for the decision (she had problems with the professor supervising the foreign visitor's work), noting a recurrent pattern of abusing the rules (D2). Fred is not satisfied with the response, so he persists.

Fred's Reflection	Dialogue
Maybe I didn't understand the whole issue behind this decision. I sought some clarification.	(F3) Fred: "Okay. Yet aren't there other ways to do this without having to put the researcher into jeopardy?"
	(D3) Diane: "I'm sorry the researcher is caught in the middle, but maybe Dr. Jones will learn what he is doing is not right to the researcher, to the school, or to the idea of international exchange."
I wanted more information about the situation with Dr. Jones and why the director made his decision.	(F4) Fred: "Alright, but why this decision and why now?"
	(D4) Diane: "Wait for Sally."

In this part of the exchange, Fred asserts that the office had discretion (F3), but Diane returns to her defensive position that Sally has the case (D4). The attempt to intervene is deflected. In follow-up conversation, Fred has an exchange with Sally and she does not raise the case further.

This case can be viewed in multiple ways. From the vantage of social justice, the position Fred was trying to argue was that there was reason for discretion. Diane had the authority for discretion, which is why Fred persisted with her before following up with Sally, but the decision was not a good one. There was some concern about saving face, but Fred's intention was to help out in the situation. He demonstrated a critical frame of reasoning about social justice, but felt frustrated because his intervention did not result in the change for which he advocated.

Analysis

Both cases illustrate instrumental reasoning by supervisors. In the first case, there had been an indiscretion and an intervention was made under the rubric of promoting learning. In the second case, a staff member asserted discretion in a specific case. Both cases illustrate instrumental frames from the perspective of the student learning the rules at an actionable level. The cases also illustrate being corrected and treated instrumentally.

While neither of these cases presents a serious moral problem, one case illustrates potential problems with power abuse (supervisor) and failure to act according to codes of behavior (intern); the other case illustrates an attempt to intervene, based on empathy and care, and encourage a supervisor to exercise discretion. The writer of the first case was in a situation that could be considered preconventional relative to ethics in action; the writer of the second case was in a situation that could be considered postconventional because of advocating based on caring for another. We also have a window on instrumental behavior as a frame of action. In both cases, supervisors acted instrumentally in relation to the rules. In both cases, the students had the opportunity to reflect on the case and discuss the situation with students in small groups.

Both students exhibited limited learning about the rules in the behavioral world, but they had fundamentally different orientations toward those rules. Kate had been introduced to ethical codes but was comfortable playing it loose. From her telling of the story, she was in a situation where it would have been difficult to make the payment for the drinks. It was also clear that she identified more strongly with the students than with the supervisor. It is not evident whether or not a lesson was learned relative to practice consonant with ethical codes in these situations. Kate insisted, even after discussion of the case in class, that she had been treated like an undergraduate. This attitude does not show openness to reflecting on the ethics of the situation. In contrast, Fred strongly believed in the human rights of the individual researchers even though his supervisor was acting legally. He also reasserted his judgment at the end of the case, placing blame for the situation onto the university.

Fred's advocacy for the researcher was stated as a concern about an individual's right to an education. The visiting scholar had not had time to complete the degree. Diane argued the reason for this was attributable to the work expectations of the foreign student's research advisor (D2), the only comment related to a reason for not granting the discretionary extension. It appears that Diane wanted to teach the professor (the researcher's supervisor) a lesson, but it was at personal cost to the researcher who was seeking to complete a degree during a time extension. It usually is possible, although more difficult, to finish a dissertation away from campus. Thus, the decision not to allow the extension represented an educational hardship on the researcher. Conditions like granting time for degree completion are routinely, although not always, granted in discretionary decisions about time extensions in academic settings. While the researcher apparently did not have a legal right in this instance, there was a basis for considering this an educational right; even the director's comment implied that the researcher was the victim.

In retrospect, I often did not deal with the moral aspects of practice sufficiently in graduate classrooms. My analyses of these cases within the classrooms emphasized the Model I aspects of closed behavior, rationalizing, and so forth. At the time, I had not yet reconsidered the role of moral reasoning in practice, one of the central topics in this book. Given this reframing of problems in practice, I encourage readers to discuss these cases with a focus on the moral dimensions of the instrumental frame. My hope is that reflection on and discussion of cases such as these will provoke thoughtful conversations about the moral aspects of learning the rules of practice.

ORGANIZATIONAL LEARNING

The research on the Indiana Project for Academic Success (IPAS) has provided opportunities for learning about organizational changes in settings where an inquiry based model is used to guide change (St. John, 2009). As noted in Chapter 4, the project engaged campus teams in a process of examining assessment research, identifying challenges, and using action inquiry to address the challenges. The focus of the initial workshop was on inquiry, but there was plenty of opportunity for other topics. At Regional Community College (RCC), the case study summarized below, interviews by the visiting team indicated a predominantly instrumental framing of problems (as defined in this book). In the language of Bolman and Deal (1991), it could be argued that the case illustrates a structural frame, given the evident focus on outcomes and getting the job done.

Text Box 5.3 Instrumental Approach to Reform in a Regional Community College (RCC)

Some of the more compelling examples of implementation of best practices were evident in group interviews with faculty at campuses of the Regional Community College system (RCC). In interviews at one of the RCC campuses, faculty members discussed the process of setting up freshman seminars that were actually pilot tested during the first year of their IPAS project. At that meeting, there had been a lot of discussion about learning communities and the value of linking courses. When the team returned from the initial workshop, they immediately adapted schedules to try linking courses for students at their campus. One professor commented on how the small branch campus made it easier to implement a linked set of courses:

Here it is real easy because we are a small campus. I just walk down the hall and say to (names of the administrator), "Here's the classes that are linked and make sure we get enough students." and he is very supportive . . . When we know our executive dean wants it, it is easier to pull them aboard.

This comment explained how it was possible to come back from the initial training session and immediately begin to adapt practice through: (1) collaboration among faculty (i.e. verbally communicating about a new set of linked courses); and (2) having the support of the dean for quick adaptations. This type of change in practice was viewed as an important step in a rapidly developing community college facing critical challenges.

Another professor described how the linking of courses changed the learning environment. "This semester I am teaching the Writing I course and most students have the Reading I class. They are all in the same cohort and they have really formed a cohort." Thus, the rapid adaptation—changing the course linking as a response to conversations about learning communities at the first IPAS meeting—enabled faculty to try something new and, through open discourse and reflection, learn together about the value of the new practice for their students.

These professors also reflected on the ways they needed to incorporate the new practices into their ongoing activities as faculty. The professor who commented on the value of the information environment added this comment on the process: "My personal opinion is that you would need to go through IPAS more than just once or at the beginning . . . It took me a while to catch on." The other observed:

I was downloaded [teaching fewer courses] not to teach freshman seminar but to do the research part of it, develop the surveys, get them out, and do the coordination. I can't tell you all of the details, but I was pretty busy. I did not ask for a download this semester and am very much regretting it.

This comment also reflects how much time it took for faculty to jump into the process and try new ideas and projects. The campus administration had shown flexibility by providing full-time faculty the opportunity to download teaching when taking on new responsibilities, but there was still an apparent underestimation of the time requirements. Throughout the interviews comments were made about how the time required to engage in the IPAS process created a conflict with the day-to-day activities of many participants.

Source: Adapted from St. John, 2009, pp. 196–198.

At the very least, as the case study illustrates, there was a focus on central decisions at the regional level. If they had support up the line, however, the professors felt free to act. As one professor put it in an interview when discussing her efforts to bring more people into collaboration on linked courses, "When we know our executive dean wants it, it is easier to pull them aboard" (Text Box 5.3). The "linked courses" approach was a partial adaptation of the learning communities that had gained support across the Indiana network. In spite of the workshop emphasizing inquiry and avoiding jumping to solutions before the problems were understood, linking together courses so that a cohort of students could take them together was the concept a team at one of the RCC campuses left with: The campus began to implement linked courses immediately upon returning to their campuses after the meeting.

In interviews, professors expressed enthusiasm about the linked courses; they created an opportunity for professors to communicate with one another and for students to see each other in classes. The impression from interviews with professors was that they thought there had been more persistence through the term, but a full evaluation had not yet been completed. Regarding the inquiry process one professor commented, "My personal opinion is that you would need to go through IPAS more than just once or at the beginning . . . It took me a while to catch on" (Text Box 5.3). There was some recognition that they were not following the full process, but were jumping to solutions.

The community college system in Indiana was at that time adapting rapidly to an institutional change from technical college to community college status with transfer programs. The attempt to move toward implementation so quickly can be explained by the rapid pace of change and the need to expand offerings. This particular campus also had a high drop-out rate and hoped implementation of these linked courses would keep students involved. It was difficult for the interventionists to encourage campus administrators to use the research provided, although the technical support was appreciated.

When focus group interviews were conducted with students at RCC, students expressed concerns that the content was not sufficiently related across linked courses. In the Indiana Community College system, courses are defined on a statewide basis and vetted through articulation agreements. At RCC it was difficult to get approval to change course content, so no efforts were made to provide content links (e.g. themes that cut across courses). It was difficult for the professors to hear student criticisms reported to them by IPAS staff, probably because they had put a high level of effort into the reform process.

There were opportunities for RCC professors to engage in evaluative research. One professor interviewed commented,

> I was downloaded [teaching fewer courses] not to teach freshman seminar but to do the research part of it, develop the surveys, get them out, and do the coordination. I can't tell you all of the details, but I was pretty busy (Text Box 5.3).

Whether or not the engagement in research on practice promoted learning was not yet evident at the time of the interviews. It should be noted, by way of contrast, that much more learning was evident in one of the community colleges where an open-strategic frame was evident during the same time period (see Chapter 7).

The attitude practitioners hold about change influences the extent of personal learning and organizational change. In instrumental settings, the emphasis is placed on implementation as action rather than on learning as action, making adaptation more difficult. Learning to do things, like implementing a tracking scheme so students will take a common set of courses,[55] is a form of organizational change. However, the attempt to link content and create themes that encouraged learning across courses did not happen in advance of the implementation of course linking. So, other than students knowing each other better than they would have if they had not taken the same courses, the benefits of the reform are probably limited.

CONCLUSIONS

Central control is a prevalent form of practice reinforced by the new scientific approach to management and public policy. The proliferation of quasi-scientific claims about practices that work, or best practices, creates an overly simplistic mindset among professionals. While there may be basic frames of reference with respect to the ways practitioners view problems (e.g. political, human resources, structural, and symbolic), these points of view influence internal interpretation. Learning in action requires discourse, not just retrospective reflection.[56]

Organization and Practice

The cases examined in this chapter provide information for learning lessons about instrumental professional action (see Table 5.3). In instrumental organizational settings, learning is limited, as is the range of responses possible in specific situations. A limited range of best or preferred responses may be appropriate in situations in which new professionals, including interns, are engaged in implementation. However, even in these situations active learning about problems seems more meaningful than reprimands, as illustrated by the summary discussion of lessons learned in relation to evidence in the cases. Implementing designs for action thought to be best practices provides a method of rapid change, but it may not be meaningful.

When practitioners jump right to implementation without reflection on the underlying reasons for action, they limit their ability to adapt to address specific problems. The new science of defusing innovations tested in experiments—an approach being used by the U.S. Department of Education—implicitly assumes that if one practice worked better than another (i.e. the intervention compared to the control), the intervention is best practice. This type of reasoning may speed organizational responses to problems, as was the case in the RCC, but this approach is somewhat random because implementing a new rule without reflection on whether the rule fits the situation is a hit or miss proposition. Using evidence from the setting to ensure adaptation of practice to fit local problems could increase the odds of improvement.

Professional Learning in Action

The process of learning new practices by trying them out is integral to professional action. It is a beginning for learning the skills of professional knowledge. The skills of practice are tacit knowledge related to action (i.e. using the knowledge of the profession in practice). Therefore, it is important not to overlook this stage of learning when discussing professional development or engaging efforts to change organizations. When an instrumental attitude among leaders in organizations predominates, it can either prevent or expedite change, depending on the alignment of people, their alliances, and the shared rationales. There is a lack of emphasis on learning when there is an instrumental orientation toward action without reflection. This is a somewhat paradoxical situation. The appearance of change can be more readily evident when control over design and implementation is tightly regulated, but the evidence of meaningful change with respect to student learning may be more difficult to see.

Table 5.3 Lessons Learned About Alignment of Strategic Orientations of Organizations with Norms and Practices within Community Practice: Instrumental Action

Frame	Hypothesizes	Lessons Learned
Organization Strategic Orientation	Implementing mission	*Lesson 1: Replications of best practices fit instrumental framing of action in organizations.* Evidence: • Senior staff critiques of interns on behavior. • College faculty implement practice discovered at meetings.
System Relation to Lifeworld	System dominance of lifeworld largely unquestioned; value placed on making the system work	*Lesson 2: Treating practices as best or preferred, without explanation or encouragement of learning can undermine organizational aims for improvement.* Evidence: • Junior staff attempts to respond to problem that arises, but is rebuffed without explanation. • Intern shows resistance to critiques.
Communities of Practice Norms within Communities of Practice	Playing by the rules and/or working around rule to fix problems	*Lesson 3: Central control of decisions narrows range of possible professional actions.* Evidence: • The swift implementation of new practices (e.g. connected courses) is possible when administrator support is evident. • Ability to respond to problems raised by clients (e.g. visiting scholar) is reduced if administrator does not support action.
Congruent Practice	Learning and practicing according to the rules of the profession	*Lesson 4: Professional learning undermined by central control, reprimands, and uncritical implementation of best or preferred practices.* Evidence: • Intern miffed by reprimand, learns to respond as expected but does not have the opportunity to reflect openly on the situation and alternative approaches. • Junior staff member learns to resist and resent authority, rather than to reflect on alternative courses of action that promote fairness. • College loses the opportunity to adapt the strategy to fit students' needs.

Four aims were noted in the introduction to Part II. I will reflect on the content of this chapter in relation to those aims. In addition, I encourage the reader to reflect on their first case statement in relation to these aims.

Aim 1: Encourage learning that enables practitioners to achieve their aims as professionals, as well as the dreams that motivated their choice of profession. As background, in this chapter three ways of viewing basic reasoning in practice were introduced: (1) as organizational frames (structural, human resources, political, and symbolic); (2) as forms related to the foundational knowledge of professionals (critical, interpretive, social, or technical-scientific); and (3) in relation to ethical codes and moral reasoning. When considering the role of instrumental framing of action, it is important to recognize that learning the rules of action is a step in the process. It is paradoxical because it is a necessary step in learning, but trying out new ideas alone is not sufficient to build expertise. Thus, it is important for practitioners to reflect on what motivates their learning and choice of profession. Reflecting on these aims can enable students to keep an eye on whether their learning of strategies is actually enabling them to move toward their own goals. This self-awareness could encourage reflective learning (an issue addressed in Chapter 6).

Aim 2: Enable reflection on assumptions, actions, and outcomes in ways that promote learning about improving practice and developing and refining skills along with reflection on the moral aspects of practice. When beginning practitioners find themselves in instrumental situations where they are not encouraged to reflect on action, it can be difficult to adapt or try out new approaches that can lead to improved personal and organizational outcomes. The two student case statements illustrated learning about rules. In the first case study, a graduate student intern recounted an incident of being reprimanded for accepting drinks paid for by a student. This was a somewhat troubling circumstance relative to learning since the intern's supervisor was encouraging learning about ethical codes, but did not invite reflection on the issue. In the second case study, a doctoral student encouraged his administrator to exercise her discretion to extend the educational stay in the US for an international researcher. He raised the issue because of concerns about the educational rights of another. This distinction between two moral aspects of instrumental action is very important. The graduate student in the second case was acting instrumentally by expressing his ideas about exercising discretion before he had tested whether such discretion was possible in this case. Such tacit, instrumental behavior is common in professional action, but we should encourage further reflection in critical situations.

When students write case statements for courses, very often the first ones they write are descriptions of instrumental situations in which they felt they had been wronged. It can be difficult in these situations to encourage learning and reflection. In class discussions, students can practice the open testing of assumptions, a form of action that encourages reflection. Still, in some instances there is an implicit critique and a sense of hopelessness that they cannot make change until they have authority in future positions.

Aim 3: Promote organizational development that enables professional development and encourages learning. AIM, the core organizational learning concept used in IPAS, focused on promoting organizational change. The vision for the model did not encourage looking at and implementing best practices before challenges were identified. RCC leapt ahead, and indeed several administrators at these workshops had this type of action orientation. Such innovations may or may not make a difference. What is problematic in higher education is that too few interventions are evaluated (Patton et al., 2006), so there is very little learning about whether practices that are thought to be best actually work as intended.

If the instrumental frame is the base for building a culture of organizational learning—and subsequent chapters illustrate that other frames may be more conducive to organizational learning—then the case study of RCC illustrates that organizational learning is possible across all settings. Learning was evident in the comments, even though there was not full engagement at the campus level.

Only approximately one third of the campuses that agreed to participate and attend the initial IPAS meeting actually stayed with it (St. John, McKinney, & Tuttle, 2006). As we reflected on reasons why more of the campuses did not stay engaged in the process, we came up with several possibilities: (1) there was no supplemental funding for campuses, so they had to dedicate some of their own resources to the process; (2) the process required some sophistication regarding interpretation of the research; and (3) although technical assistance with the inquiry process was provided, there was not sufficient staff support for this activity. RCC probably stayed and continued to initiate reforms because the multicollege system had a very engaged service provider, and administrators from the campus were involved in collaborations with other campuses (see Chapter 8).

Aim 4: Improve services provided by professional organizations that promote justice and improve sustainability. Since the publication of *A Nation at Risk* (U.S. Department of Education, 1983), the federal government has pursued a policy of K–12 reform that emphasizes testing, alignment of curriculum with tests, and dissemination of best practices documented by experiments. After more than a quarter century of this policy, high school graduation rates have declined, there is greater inequality in college going across racial groups, and the US has fallen behind most developed countries in college-going rates (St. John, 2006). Perhaps it is time to consider the possibility that this reform strategy is an abject failure.

Why? Instrumental action within organizations, including the process of jumping to solutions without reflection on local circumstances, generally lacks the type of critical reflection necessary to adapt practice to fit local needs (a precondition illustrated by the case in this chapter). The quasi-science of education promotes uncritical implementation without reflection or an orientation toward reflective practice. There is reason to speculate that the promotion of the method of accountability in *A Call for Leadership* (U.S. Department of Education, 2006) would promote a similar quasi-academic method of change for higher education. The alternative is to encourage reflection by practitioners and use action inquiry within institutions to promote improvement in access, encourage major choice based on personal needs and interests, and enable more students to attain degrees and enter the workforce.

REFLECTIVE EXERCISE

Readers are encouraged to use the rubrics in this chapter to reflect on their case statements and personal vision statements (see Text Box 5.4). Reflection, review, and discussion of their own cases, along with reflection on the organizational contexts in which they have worked, can help them gain insight into their own ways of framing problems in practice.

Text Box 5.4 Reflective Exercise: Orientation Toward Professional Learning

A four-step reflective exercise is encouraged. If this exercise is done in class, students should take about 15 minutes to reflect on their own case (Steps 1 and 2). Small groups should have about 20 minutes to discuss each case, with the author presenting his or her own interpretation (Step 3) while listening to others.

1. Reflect on your personal vision (from the reflective exercises in Chapters 1, 2, and 3) in relation to the frame of organization. Consider your own orientation toward problem solving (i.e. structural, human resources, political, and/or symbolic) in relation to your vision statement.

2. Analyze your own case statement on learning rules of practice in your profession. (Use Table 5.3 as a guide.)

3. If you have the opportunity to discuss your case with another person or small group, ask for their feedback using evidence from the dialogue. When discussing your case, answer questions in advance of receiving feedback, but do not influence their interpretation; just listen.

4. Reflect on the feedback from others in relation to your analysis of the case. What issue should you ponder as you think about strategies for moving toward your vision?

6

STRATEGY AND ARTISTRY

Strategic thinking has become the dominant mode of professional action, just as strategic decisions have become central to planning and management in most public and private organizations. This chapter focuses on individuals' skill development and the emergence and development of strategic thinking within communities of practice. In constructing pedagogies for professional development, professors should encourage reflection as integral to action. Organizations using strategic methods aim to coordinate action and move toward a new vision. While both forms of action may be central to improvement in service by professional organizations, there is an inherent paradox: central control can undermine independent action, while shared goals can provide space for reflection and the exercise of discretion among professionals. This paradox complicates professional education as much as it does organizational adaptation.

The problem of enabling professional reflection within organizations that maintain a strategic orientation is examined in this chapter. First, I consider how these competing forces—the need to invest in improving the artistry of professionals and the pressure to reshape the directions of professional organizations as they respond to new challenges—present a problem for theory and practice. Second, I examine the case statements of students who were full-time professionals managing change initiatives in organizations that are adapting to new challenges. Third, I examine the case study of a reform initiative in a university in the midst of implementing a new strategic plan. In conclusion, I consider the role of strategic action within changing organizations and encourage readers to take this step as well.

ORGANIZATIONAL ADAPTATION AND REFLECTIVE PRACTICE

The goal of enabling professional growth through adapting organizational strategy to meet new challenges may be the optimal vehicle for change in professional organizations. However, this potential is difficult to realize if central strategic decisions and professional actions are tightly regulated and controlled. An aim of professional development should be to encourage reflective judgment in responses based on reframing the problems. Control mechanisms are integral to defining organizational strategies, both in periods of rapid change and in stable periods. The tensions between flexibility in professional learning and organizational control are evident in universities and professional schools, as well as in professional organizations where students learn their skills.

Artistry Enriching Expertise

In *Educating the Reflective Practitioner*, Donald Schön (1987)[57] examined how different types of professional education encourage and enable skills development through reflective practice. He recognizes that one view of professional competence relates to the knowledge of practice that "consists of theories and techniques derived from systematic, preferably scientific, research to the solution of the instrumental problems of practice" (p. 33). However, in his book, he argues that the alternative form of knowledge—the ability to think like a doctor, lawyer, or manager—derives from alternative sources: "On the alternative epistemology of practice suggested in this book professional artistry is understood as reflection in action, and it plays a central role in the description of professional competence" (p. 35). He continues:

> On this view, we would recognize as a limiting case the situations in which it is possible to make a routine application of existing rules and procedures to the fact of problematic situations. Beyond these situations, familiar rules, theories, and techniques are put to work in concrete instances through the intermediary of an art that consists in a limited form of reflection-in-action. And beyond these, we would recognize cases of problematic discourse around which practitioners not only follow rules of inquiry but also sometimes respond to surprising findings by inventing new rules, on the spot (p. 35).

This statement communicates a clear notion of the developmental process for professionals: learning to apply rules in problematic situations; learning to adapt by trying out new approaches through inquiry; and finally inventing new solutions in especially problematic situations. Chapter 5 considered the first step in the process (learning to apply the rules of practice), and why it is inadequate in problematic situations. With this background we can focus on the next step of developing adaptive, reflective action. This step should not be overlooked as an intermediate step toward artistry of practice that involves inventing new methods and solutions.

The reflective practicum is the method Schön (1987) recommends professional schools use to enable aspiring professionals to develop skills in reflection-in-action, based on the foundation of knowing-in-action provided by content in the professional curriculum. He argues that reflection of experience is needed, along with classroom practice, because:

- The gap between the description of designing solutions and the knowing-in-action that correspond to it must be filled by reflection-in-action.
- Designing must be grasped as a whole, by experiencing it in action.
- Designing depends on the recognition of the design qualities, which must be learned in action.
- Descriptions of designing are likely to be perceived initially as confusing, vague,

ambiguous, or incomplete; their clarification depends on dialogue in which understandings and misunderstandings are revealed through action.

- Because designing is a creative process in which a designer comes to see and do things in new ways, no prior description of it can take the place of learning by doing (p. 162).

Schön (1987) derives his argument from his review of pedagogy in music, psychiatry, counseling, and architecture. These fields have different histories of learning in practice than discipline-based education. Based on this review, he argues that reflective practica are needed to complement conventional curriculum in professional schools, providing means of integrating an emphasis on reflective practice. The design of the practicum should, he argues, consider the following criteria:

- The predicament of practitioners subject to constrictions on freedom of action in their organizational settings should be brought into the professional curriculum.
- It is more urgent than ever to develop new connections between applied science and reflection-in-action.
- There is a need to create or revitalize a phenomenology of reflection-in-action of practitioners in their organizational settings. And this phenomenology of practice must be substantively connected to traditional disciplines or risk . . . a bifurcation of the schools (p. 321).

Written more than two decades ago, this argument still resonates as highly relevant to the education of professionals, including educational leaders. For two decades I have been integrating reflective teaching methods into my courses on leadership and professional development. Along with this teaching, I have engaged in reforms using action inquiry to enable organizational adaptation in colleges (St. John, 2009). This experience has convinced me of the need for focusing on actionable knowledge and reflection-in-action. Given the increased emphasis on strategic discourse and control in organizations, these needs are greater than ever.

In the early twenty-first century, it is not sufficient to emphasize reflective practice in ancillary practicum courses within professional schools. The pace of change in most large organizations has accelerated in response to global economic forces, a decline of the environment, and growing inequalities across race and class. These conditions create a predicament in which reform of professional education is needed along with organizational responses to emergent challenges. My argument is that a greater emphasis on reflective practice and moral reasoning is needed in professional education and is an integral part of interventions in professional practice.

Organizational Strategy

At the organizational level of artistry, Cameron and Lavine (2006) propose a theory of positive organizations. Part of their argument is based on their own typology of organizational reasoning, summarized below (in relation to Bolman and Deal's frames):

- *Clan* as both internally focused within the organizations (an orientation toward individual flexibility) and a long-term orientation toward change, a collaborative oriented frame (something like the *human resources* frame).

- *Hierarchy* with an internal focus toward management, an emphasis on stability over flexibility, and a focus on incremental change; leaders are control oriented (something like the *structural* frame).
- *Market* as emphasizing stability over flexibility, focused on external positioning and valuing fast change, functioning as enablers (somewhat like the *political* frame).
- *Adhocracy* emphasizing flexibility, external positioning and new changes or innovations; leaders are oriented to visioning and creativity (something like the *symbolic* frame).

Cameron and Lavine (2006) also argue that organizations need different types of leaders, with the different leaders exhibiting different traits, to promote positive change. This position argues that innovation, adaptation, and extraordinary results occur when all forms of leadership are present. However, the authors do not necessarily argue that all people should use multiple frames, which is a position taken by Bolman and Deal (1991).

Rocky Flats was a seriously problem waste site with major human and environmental risks. After using their framework to examine the success of a company cleaning up a weapons site, Cameron and Lavine (2006) conclude:

> It is worth noting documenting the spectacular success at Rocky Flats is important mainly because these enablers and principles [derived from the four types or quadrants] may be applicable to other circumstances. The inherent interest in Rocky Flats resides in the extent to which these factors can be translated into prescriptions for leaders in other types of organizations (p. 245).

A closer reading indicates a comprehensive approach to change with enablers related to each of the frames. Cameron and Lavine (2006) argue that multiple forms of vision, control, advocacy, and collaboration are necessary for extraordinary success. These precepts may advance thinking about strategy, but they seem to stop short of openness to addressing new challenges that emerge from practitioners within organizations. Consider the following list of enablers:

- *Successful leaders create challenges and opportunities that make the current (traditional) culture appear inadequate and incapable.*
- *Extraordinary success emerges from generating collaboration among adversaries.*
- *The abundance approach[58] must be fostered among antagonists.*
- *Managers and workers must be co-located to enhance collaboration.*
- *Ensuring trust[59] trumps measurement, control, plans, and communication strategies, so maintain integrity at all costs.*
- *Positive safety risks must be provided for all at risk employees.*
- *Overcommunication and preemptive information sharing should be the norm.*
- *Use social pressure to manage resisters* (emphasis in original, Cameron and Lavine, 2006, p. 186).

These enablers focus on strong coordinating mechanisms within the collaborative environment of action. However, an overall task orientation (i.e. the aim or mission of the organization) is evident. These enablers are oriented toward moving organizations in a specified direction. The focus on quieting resisters and preemptive action indicate an orientation toward maneuvering to achieve an aim, or "extraordinary success," as the intended end. However, this image of collaboration does not include openness to addressing alternative problems that emerge, nor toward testing alternative hypotheses (a feature of the critical-empirical approach noted in Table 4.1). This distinction is important relative to the developmental perspective on framing reflection and change developed in this book. The positive organization enablers may make it possible to move more rapidly toward defined goals, but there is no reason to expect that organizations taking this approach would leave much room for openness to initiatives that might deviate from the intended course of action.

Moral Dimension

Most theories of organization and professional development sidestep critical social problems, as is the case with the exemplars discussed above. Cameron and Lavine's book (2006) provides methods that can be used to address problematic issues (their theory was derived from a study of environmental clean up, a critical environmental issue), but they do not explicitly consider how professional reasoning relates to moral reasoning. One of the intentions of this book, along with the attempt to create a new understanding of professional development and organizational change, is to explicitly address the moral aspects of professional action and organizational response and adaptation to morally challenging situations. The emergence of critical social issues requires organizational responses. As people become aware of problematic patterns, they can enact new responses, changing organizations and professional practice.

Consider the example of institutional policy on sexual harassment, which became an explicit policy in most universities during the early 1990s (Riggs, Murrell, & Cutting, 1993). Before then it was common for faculty to date students and many faculty members married former graduate students. Henry Rosovsky (1990) provided a compelling discussion of the emergence of the policy at Harvard University when he was dean. He defined the basic standard developed:

> Members of the teaching staff should be aware that any romantic involvement with a student makes them liable for formal action against them if a complaint is initiated by a student. *Even when both parties have consented to the development of such a relationship, it is the officer or instructor who, by virtue of his or her special responsibility, will be held accountable for unprofessional behavior* (emphasis in original, p. 292).

Harvard's standard is similar to those of sexual harassment policies in other professions with client relationships (Rutter, 1991). However, Rosovsky further extended the standard to unequal power relationships among faculty members: "In my opinion, these principles apply equally to relationships between tenured and non-tenured faculty members. Opportunities for abuse of power are just as common" (1990, p. 293). This second dimension of the relationship among faculty with unequal power should not be overlooked.

After Rosovsky distributed the new sexual harassment policy statement at Harvard, he received a letter from John Kenneth Galbraith, an internationally recognized economist, who pointed out that his own marriage would have been considered a boundary transgression if the policy had been in place earlier in his career (Rosovsky, 1990). In his response to Galbraith, Rosovsky indicated that the policy should be applied as a new policy when an infraction occurs rather than as a means of criticizing established relationships. This exchange illustrates the complexity of implementing a new moral, ethical, or legal standard when there has been none before.

The implementation of new policies involves deep critical reflection about power abuse, as was illustrated in the national discourse of sexual harassment during the period of implementation in academe. In *Sex in the Forbidden Zone*, Peter Rutter (1991) describes an incident that led to his interest in the study of sexual harassment in the psychiatric community. He describes his own incremental awakening to the problem as he observed a series of relationships between a medical school professor and his students and patients. Initially, Rutter was unaware there was a problem, even though the professor in question was his mentor with whom he worked closely. However, as Rutter gained evidence of the replicating pattern, he and other colleagues built the confidence to take action, initiating a process that led to the professor's dismissal.

There were also concerns raised that the new harassment policies not be implemented in ways that quieted the critical discourse necessary to raise and voice concerns within academic communities. For example, Stern (2003) warned in a *Chronicle of Higher Education* article published during this period that some campuses were writing policies that made it difficult for faculty to report a problem. If reporting had to go through the organizational structure with no one to contact outside the hierarchy, it might not be possible to raise concerns without retribution. As the policy was implemented, it was necessary for campuses to set up procedures. It was important students and younger faculty knew they had safe avenues through which to raise concerns and seek redress.

Highly skilled and artistic professionals have an increased capacity to address moral problems that arise from conflict between current practices compared to professionals using an instrumental approach. Highly skilled and artistic professionals also have greater ability to maneuver through practical problems without addressing underlying critical social challenges.[60] This creates the potential for increased moral ambiguity and increases the need to reflect on problematic situations as they emerge.

These examples, drawn from a period of institutional change, illustrate the importance of having discursive space to raise critical issues within organizations. Rules and procedures alone do not always protect people from power abuse. More critically perhaps, policy implementation is not the only time we should be concerned about discursive space. It is also necessary to have a communicative environment that provides organizational mechanisms for professionals to raise issues and initiate changes when difficult issues or problems surface. My hypothesis is that in a closed-strategic environment (i.e an organizational setting in which only issues that are consonant with the organization's strategic aims can be voiced) it is difficult to respond to critical social and critical environmental issues that emerge in practice.

Frames of Mind

With this background in mind, we can return to the task of integrating frames of action with moral reasoning. Table 6.1 depicts the hypothesized relationships between closed-strategic behaviors and preconventional, conventional, and postconventional moral reasoning. These constructs illustrate abuse of power, including nefarious action, as well as the use of advocacy in problematic situations.

Table 6.1 Closed-Strategic Behaviors in Relation to Frame of Action and Types of Moral Reasoning

Moral Reasoning/*Frames of Action*	Preconventional	Conventional	Postconventional
Closed-Strategic Frames Focus	Adapting methods to achieve ends without considering moral problems created by new practices.	Adapting methods to address challenges; attempting to reconcile ethics within rules of practice.	Adapting strategies to address moral challenges, including issues that question rules of practice.
Test assumptions about innovations; build technical skill.	• Goal directed; ends take preference over means • Maximize winning/minimize losing	• Practice situational judgments • Apply ethical codes as part of practice • Collaborate on setting situational goals	• Focus on critical social and environmental problems in interventions • Encourage others to voice concerns
Engage in projects to test new approaches.	• Manipulate emotions of others to achieve aims • Place self-interest above others	• Protect of self and others • Rationalize actions in public spaces • May be open within mentoring relationships	• Care for others, even at personal costs of time and resources • Rationalize actions based on espoused values of justice and caring

On the theme of sexual harassment we can find many examples in films from the 1970s and 1980s (a period before the sexual harassment standards were being defined).[61] The movie *Dancers* (Ross, 1987) contains a scene with competing dancers in a company talking about the tendency of the dance captain to assign the best roles to those who agree to engage in a sexual relationship with him. In *Looking for Mr. Goodbar* (Fields & Brooks, 1977), a professor and student engage in a consensual sexual relationship. The complete moral downfall of the student occurs when the professor chooses his next paramour; her decline is the subject of the rest of the film. In *The Paper Chase* (Paul, Thompson, & Bridges, 1973), a law school professor implies trouble will follow for a student who dates his daughter by ignoring the student while calling on the students around him in the classroom. Later in the film, the professor offers to give the student a prestigious assignment on a weekend when the student had planned to take a trip with the professor's daughter. In a subsequent scene, it becomes apparent that the professor had already given the assignment to a more advanced student. These fictional incidents illustrate how power can be abused in learning situations and how the emotions of others can be manipulated to achieve personal aims. The process of testing assumptions in action can occur subtly within practice, as people learn the rules of behavior that can get them ahead. Adaptive behavior (i.e. deviation from the rules and codes) can be thought of as abuse of power or nefarious action.

The forms of inappropriate action related to building new skills and testing assumptions are more pervasive and perhaps even more troubling than overt power abuse. The patterns of using power to win in decision situations are common. It is often easier to get around a problem by easing the rules than confronting authorities and trying to change the rules.

Conventional moral reasoning within the closed-strategic model also seems quite common if we reflect on practice. Professionals often make situational judgments applying their expertise. In normal practice, there often is no need to discuss strategic options; direct application of method is essential to get the job done. Normal practice within generally accepted codes is sometimes essential.

The development of skills in strategic thinking and professional artistry are steps forward in the professional development process compared to the instrumental application of rules. As people develop professional skills, they understand techniques clearly, which makes it is easier to adapt them to address critical challenges. The artistry of adapting techniques to new conditions can be facilitated by good mentoring relationships. In fact, it is important to distinguish between the quasi-private space of the mentor–mentee relationship and the open discursive space of open-strategic action within communities of practice. It is possible for mentors and their junior colleagues to confide in each other regarding developing skills by public testing of assumptions in open settings. As part of these exchanges, at least in closed-strategic organizations, mentors often communicate boundaries of acceptable action.

It is also possible within the exercise of rules to address critical social problems, as illustrated by the example of the implementation of sexual harassment policies. If problems occur and are voiced, it is possible to revise practice. The normal strategic behaviors of professionals in organizations can make it difficult to influence changes in policy or practice. This is especially the case if those who hold power are unwilling to listen to well reasoned arguments or think about evidence presented in critical incidents (an obvious limitation of closed-strategic behavior).

These hypothesized frames are intended as guides to help professionals and aspiring professionals review and reflect on action. What is new about this framing is the integration of framing of behavior with moral action.[62] Consistent with the method used in Chapter 5, the individual and organizational dimensions of closed-strategic action are considered below.

PROFESSIONAL LEARNING

Three incidents selected from student case statements developed in leadership behavior courses are presented and discussed here to illustrate the role of strategic framing. In these courses, I encouraged students to try new practices and use the case statements to reflect on what they learned from the experiments. The cases below are illustrative of learning strategic behavior. The first, a full case statement, involves a discussion among student leaders and an intervention by a student affairs administrator; the second is abstracted from a student case statement about sexual harassment in a university administrative office; the third is abstracted from a case statement by a medical school administrator initiating change related to admissions practices.

Student Event Planning

When Kim Kline was a graduate student, she brought a case to class that involved an intervention in a student planning session for a major student event at a public university (Text Box 6.1). Kim had experience as a student affairs administrator working with a student government organization. A special meeting had been called to discuss coordination of the campus-wide event with a proposal from the Black Student Union (BSU) on campus. Kim went into the meeting with concerns about the timing of the event (late on a weekend evening), thinking that it had been scheduled to dampen interest in attendance by student leaders.

Text Box 6.1 Case Statement: Student Event Planning

Context: Brit, the president of the student organization that I advise, insisted that we hold an executive board meeting at this late hour to finalize funding allocations for a major campus event. Black Student Union (a student organization) was invited by Student Government to discuss their idea of hosting a carnival. Brit made an executive decision that the only possible time for the two groups to meet was after another major event, so the meeting was scheduled for that time. (In my opinion, the meeting was called at this time in the hope that attendance would be thin . . . only one-half of the executive board attended, but all three Black Student Union [BSU] representatives were in attendance.)

Participants:
Kim (K) Student Affairs Administrator
Brit (B) President Student Organizing Committee
Annette (A) President of Black Student Union
Marie (M) Member of the Student Organizing Committee

Kim's Reflection	Dialogue
When Betty realized that Annette was one of the BSU representatives, she began to non-verbally let others know that she was in charge.	(B1) Brit: Well, Kim tells us that you have an idea for BSU and Student Government to co-sponsor a carnival. We think that it is a great idea . . . are you asking us for money? . . . or what was it that you had in mind?
	(A1) Annette: Yes, we were thinking of a carnival, and were looking into the possibility of one showcase event such as sumo-wrestling, which would cost the most. We would offset that cost by soliciting the City Fire Department and other community agencies to participate in the carnival with events such as a dunk tank, dime toss, etc. We would also ask for food donations. It would be our choice to schedule this event on the Saturday or Sunday as a way to kick off the event week while not conflicting with some other African-American sponsored events that would be scheduled during that week.

(B2) Brit: O.K. . . . we would be happy to co-sponsor this with you . . . we have so many cool ideas too! We thought that we could have this cover band, and, instead of sumo-wrestling, what about jello wrestling, and we have lots of contacts for food . . . Student Government could put a group together to decide what committees should be formed . . . what do you think?

Good point Annette

(A2) Annette: Well, before we agree to this, we thought that this carnival would be a great opportunity for our young executive to gain some experience with committee work. In the past, BSU has had other ideas for Spring functions, and other organizations have taken our idea and ran with it . . . I am not suggesting that this is your intent, but we were wondering if we could coordinate the committees and retain some autonomy over the event. Student Government could then sit on some of the committees, and we would both have a part in the success of this event.

Betty tends to be a bit controlling. Annette is ready to pounce on her!

(B3) Brit: So, you want our money, but we won't have any say in the matter . . . is that what you are trying to say?

(A3) Annette: No, am just asking for an opportunity for our e-board, the majority of whom are freshman, to gain some good experience.

I had to bite my tongue!

(B4) Brit: You had mentioned that you did not want to conflict with other African-American events . . . are you gearing this event towards African-Americans?

Kim, you need to say something . . .

(A4) Annette: Yes, I mean no, you know what I mean. . . .

(M5) But the paramedical advisors attend.

Protecting internal operations

(A4) They're only from outside colleges. No harm.

What an avoidance approach . . .

(K1) Kim: Just a suggestion, what if we got together again on Thursday night to discuss the specifics? . . . BSU could put together an estimated budget and game-plan of what they would like to do . . . Student Government could then ask any clarifying questions.

(A5) Annette: Sounds good to me . . .

(B5) Brit: Fine . . .

(K2) Kim: 7:00? (Everyone agreed, BSU left)

(B6) Brit: (to Kim and two executive board members in attendance) . . . Can you believe that crap? We can't sponsor something like that! And her attitude! Like it is our obligation to give them the money.

(K3) Kim: I don't understand . . . you seemed fine until Annette asked for some autonomy . . .

Betty is just blowing smoke . . .

(B7) Brit: I just think that it would be fun to program with them . . . they don't want anything to do with us . . . it is like they are too good . . . well, no secrets will be kept from us . . . no co-sponsorship, no money.

(K4) Kim: From what I understand, BSU has a history of being burned by other groups . . . including Student Government . . .

Thank you, someone, for speaking up!

(M1) Marie: (other board member) That sure is right . . . I think that we should support their wishes and the event . . . we just got some great publicity from working closely with BSU . . . and Student Government is supposed to be representative of all groups . . . why can't we cut them a break?

(B8) Brit: Well, this won't work, because we have to have the Board of Governors pass the funding allocations at this Tuesday's Board of Governors meeting . . .

Oh, here we go . . . I don't think that anyone has ever challenged Brit or told her that she was wrong in her whole life . . .

(K5) Kim: Brit, you already gave your word to BSU that we would meet again on Thursday . . . are you now taking that back?

(B9) Brit: BSU can't just sponsor events for Black people . . . it's not right . . . that's not the way that it works . . . I know . . . I grew up in "the hood" Black people that I was friends with worked for what they got . . . they didn't want a handout from anyone . . . You don't know Kim . . . how would you know?

(K6) Kim: Brit . . . don't get personal . . . I don't know that you want to go there in front of Amy and Liz . . .

(B10) Brit: I don't care . . . they are my friends . . . we are all friends here . . . lets get this out . . . I know that you want to say something back to me . . . just say it!

(K7) Kim: I think that you could maybe think of your role as Student Government . . . which is supposed to be inclusive . . . and your remarks did not sound inclusive . . .

(B9) Brit: Whatever Kim . . . you just don't understand like I do . . .

Did I lose control?

(K7) Kim: It is my opinion that your remarks earlier could be perceived by some as racist, and that is not a cool thing as Student Government president. They are planning a carnival, not a cultural night for African-Americans . . . how much soul food could one request for a carnival? The last time that I attended a carnival with someone who was African-American, I remember us ordering french fries with vinegar and a funnel cake for dessert . . . I don't even think that there is a soul food restaurant worth mentioning in this town!

Brit ended up calling me at 1:00 a.m. to tell me that she didn't appreciate my attitude . . . I told her that I was sleeping, and that I could talk to her after our 3:00 meeting that was scheduled for the next day.

When we met, Brit told me that Student Government had no choice but to request that funds be allocated at the Board of Governors meeting on Tuesday night . . . I convinced her (somehow) to request a $3,000.00 allocation, but to table discussion on how those funds would be spent until the next Board of Governors meeting. Brit had cooled off by then, as I had, and she thought that it was a good idea.

I felt that I went against everything that I believe in . . . that I threw student development right out the window, and actually attempted to exhibit some control over a situation that I had no business controlling . . . similar to Brit.

Source: Kim Kline, Prepared for Class Assignment

The meeting opened cordially, with the President (Brit) commenting on the reason for the meeting (B1), acknowledging that Kim had asked for the meeting with the BSU. Annette then summarized the plans for the event (A1) and Brit responded by indicating a willingness to cosponsor the event (B2). At this point in the conversation, Annette raised an issue about the control of the event. She indicated that the BSU did not want to lose control (A2). Brit responded by asking a question about control of the event (B3).

This exchange between Brit and Annette (B2 and B3) was cordial and strategic. Kim, from her reflections, empathized with the position of the BSU. The governing variable of owning and controlling the task is central to Model I reasoning in the Argyris-Schön tradition (see Chapter 3). In this case, it was a strategic conversation that became confrontational. In addition to arguments about organizational control of the event, there was an underlying question being raised about inclusivity and exclusivity. This campus had an active black minority. The exchange turned toward cultural aspects of the carnival event.

When confronted by the issue of monetary contribution, Annette responded by indicating the concern was to make sure some of the freshman in her organization could gain experience (A3). Brit did not acknowledge the concern about getting students experience, but instead focused on the issue of inclusion, asking whether this was envisioned as an event inclusive of whites (B4). Annette seemed caught off guard by the direct confrontation (A4) and responded to the question about inclusion in an ambiguous way. Kim's reflections at this point showed concern about the racial overtones. The next few comments are brief and seemingly tense. At this point, Kim intervened to encourage a rescheduling of the meeting (K1), clearly attempting to avoid conflict. The new meeting time was agreed upon.

The intervention to avoid conflict represented an attempt to maintain good relations (i.e. minimize negative feelings), a common characteristic of human relations training. An alternative intervention might have been to raise questions about the issues of control and inclusion that seemed to underlie the conflict. The process of raising difficult issues for discussion involves adaptive and reflective behaviors, an ability to abstract one's self from empathy toward one group in an exchange, and a willingness to deal with conflict. This is a difficult form of practice, especially if one empathizes with a position or group, as Kim did in this situation.

After the BSU representatives left, the conversation got more heated rather than calming down. Brit blew off steam (B6). She went on to criticize Annette for her attitude. Kim then raised what she thought was the issue (the concern about control, K2). In this part of the exchange, Kim was making an inquiry about the structural aspects of the situation. Brit's response was essentially positive about the idea of collaboration (i.e. fun to work together), but negative about relinquishing control (B7). The issues of racial inclusion and exclusion and organizational control are complex and intertwined at this point in the exchange.

Kim responded with a further probe about the issue of control (K4), carrying forward the position that autonomy for BSU had an underlying rationale (given the history of prior events). Marie, another member of the student government board, spoke up to confirm Kim's statement (M1). She also asked why they could not "cut a break" for the BSU in this instance. Brit responded that the timing was such that it would be difficult to gain approval to allocate the funding (B8), a defensive move in the exchange. Kim responded in a challenging way, indicating that Brit "gave her word" (K5). In this exchange, Kim was presenting a rationale for what she thought was right while Brit seemed to be trying to maintain control—at least we might conclude this if we follow Kim's reflection. The assumption Kim held about whether an agreement had actually been reached was not openly tested, however. That is, Kim could have asked this as a question. It is also possible there were other explanations for the reaction. For example, it is possible that the issue of who would be included in the event could have been an underlying issue that was not addressed in the exchange.

At this point, the conversation turned personal, with Brit and Kim making comments back and forth based on beliefs. It appears they were talking past each other, making points without testing for shared understanding of the problem. It seems, too, that feelings were hurt. Afterwards, there was a telephone exchange with a further expression of hurt feelings. Funds were eventually allocated for the event.

This case statement illustrates a strategic intervention by Kim, based on her personal beliefs about diversity and race. In a strategic sense, her intervention successfully achieved the intended aim, which was to encourage a fair hearing and fund the event. However, the issues of race and racism were not fully discussed. After we discussed the Model I aspects of the case—including Kim's attempt to express goals and influence events—Kim decided to pursue the topic further. Eventually she organized a classroom research study examining how social justice issues relate to reflective practice (Kline, 2007). Her initial inquiry in the class and her subsequent research help illuminate some of the ways in which we can seek to integrate discussions of critical social issues in professional practice. Her inquiry and research was a source of inspiration for this book.

Confrontation in an Administrative Office

This case of confrontation in an administrative office illustrates the complexity of implementing policies related to sexual harassment. Janet Barnes was director of an administrative office at a private university. The case she chose to reflect on is a case that had troubled her: an attempt to respond to the school's policy on sexual harassment. A female staff member told Janet she had been harassed by a computer consultant employed by the university. When she consulted with human resources about procedures for dealing with the case, Janet learned it was her responsibility to confront the male in the situation. If she failed to confront the perpetrator she would, she was told, be giving her tacit approval of the behavior. Janet was uncomfortable confronting Richard, the consultant, who had provided valuable services in the past. Janet chose to talk with him in her office.

Reflection	Dialogue
At this point, I hoped to start the discussion out on an extremely positive note. That morning, Richard had helped resolve a really sticky problem which I did not precipitate, but for which I was responsible. I did not want to "burn bridges."	(J1) "Thanks for coming back over so soon after our computer services meeting this morning. I truly appreciate the effort you put into resolving the student financial information feed to the accounts receivable. It was really a mess and I felt like I was really in the hot seal for awhile there."
I felt he was genuinely pleased the matter was resolved, and that he was aware of my appreciation toward his morning's efforts.	(R1) "Yeah, well, you really got shafted by the programmer. I'm glad we were able to divert the attention of administration to the resolution of the problem, rather than the fact that your

My discomfort with the entire situation was definitely apparent. I didn't want to be guilty of accusing anyone, or calling my own employee a liar. I also was desperately afraid of mishandling the matter, and end up with some sort of lawsuit on my hands.

entire month's bills were screwed up. So, what's going on now?"

(J2) "Richard, Martha said something to me that I feel we have to talk about. I have no desire to discuss the matter in detail. I don't feel I have that right. She states that you are making verbal sexual advances to her on the phone at work. I, personally, do not want to know if this is true or not. I have a responsibility to bring the matter up with you. If it is true, please simply stop. If it is not true, just let me know that and I'll take the issue back to Martha."

It was apparent that he was tremendously over reacting, considering that I had no administrative authority over him. This rather reinforced my thought that he might be making the calls. I also felt scared for the first time in the interaction.

(R2) "You mean after all I've done for you, you're accusing me of something like that! You're attacking my very professionalism! I will have both your jobs for this! No, better yet, I'll resign and file suit . . ."

At the outset of the meeting, Richard did not know why he had been asked to come to her office. Janet began by thanking Richard for his service (J1). Richard acknowledged that he was happy to have helped and inquired about what was up (R1). Janet raised the complaint (J2), but made no reference to university policy or her own responsibility in the situation. Due to her nervousness, she asked whether it was true, putting Richard on the spot. Richard denied the claim, exhibiting defensive behavior and self-protection (R2). In this response, Richard evoked a quid pro quo rationale when he said, ". . . after all I have done for you . . ." The confrontation became personal and got out of control. He also threatened a lawsuit. Janet tried to quiet the situation. The exchange became difficult.

Reflection	Dialogue
Because I was scared, I was trying to protect my actions and I retreat, at the same time. His constant screaming was making me angry and frightened. I felt I was genuinely losing control of the conversation.	(J3) "Please Richard, lower your voice. I am not accusing you of anything. I am simply put in a position of having to ask you about the matter. I think we are both uncomfortable with the issue. If we can clarify that it was not an issue, then you can drop the matter."

I was very firm in my knowledge that he didn't "cover" for me, but rather corrected the error, and that gave me courage.	(R3) "I'm going to call Computer Services and let them know you messed up. I covered for you, and now you've turned on me—I can't believe it!"
I wanted him out of my office. I saw no progress being made and he would display this anger and physical behavior if he did quit or report our conversation to a higher administrative authority.	(J4) "Richard, you've gotten so upset over this, that you look and behave like you are quite ill. Since you cannot control your voice and this is a professional setting, I must insist you leave now. And I genuinely apologize for my inexperience in this matter."

In response to his outburst, Janet asked Richard to lower his voice (J3). He responded by threatening to make false claims about the work situation (R3). At this point, Janet asked Richard to leave. Afterwards, she had to rely on the vice president to resolve the situation.

This exchange can be viewed in many ways. First, it represents only partial implementation of sexual harassment policy. The university had placed responsibility for resolving these conflicts in the hands of line managers who were not trained. Janet failed to voice the policy as the basis for the conversation. The confrontation was experienced as a personal attack. Richard may have been hostile and defensive, but the lack of statement about the policy made the situation more difficult. The case clearly illustrates the need to train line managers in the sexual harassment policy.

Second, this case can be viewed in the context of strategy change in the university. Viewed from this vantage, the university had implemented a sexual harassment policy and expected implementation to take place within the structure using current staff, rather than providing others in the organization trained to handle these complaints.

Third, this case can be seen as a learning opportunity for the student. Janet was able to reflect on the case, discuss it with her peers, and ponder how she might handle such a case differently in the future and to provide essential information. Certainly, this was not a desirable situation to encounter as a line manager. However, as Schön (1987) suggests, having the opportunity to reflect on the circumstances provides the chance to gain perspective and to think about alternative scenarios.

Medical School Admissions

This case involves Margaret, who was the director of multicultural affairs in a research university's medical school. She was responsible for coordinating an annual process that sought to sensitize faculty to diversity issues. Margaret decided to try out an intervention with the associated dean of her medical school. After eight years of running the Simulated Admissions Exercises (SAE) in her office, she hoped to broaden participation.[63] Based on reflection, she decided to raise the issue to the associate dean for academic affairs to whom she reported. As she discusses in the case statement, she prepared for the meeting by compiling information on the participants in prior SAE events, in hopes that she might gain approval for opening up the invitation list to the full admissions committee.

Reflection	Dialogue
(I handed him the list of participants before I sat down.) Managing the environment: I thought if I brought the issue up immediately, he wouldn't have time to think of a negative response.	(M1) I wanted to discuss with you the distribution list for announcements of the SAE. I had some suggestions for additions.
He asked without looking at the list.	(A1) Who are they?
I thought I was testing the applicability of the workshop to others.	(M2) I thought I could send the announcement to the entire faculty and student representatives.
He seemed defensive.	(A2) Why?
I thought I was sharing information, but I may have had the information to protect my right to inquire.	(M3) Well, I looked at the past attendance and noticed that the same type of people, even the same people, always attend the SAE. And I thought the objectives would be better served if we opened up the participation. Why haven't others come to the workshops?
Self-sealing	(A3) Originally, we decided to keep it among the admissions committee members.
	(M4) Why?
Self-sealing, no risk taking	(A4) Because the committee felt more comfortable discussing these issues among themselves.
	(M5) But the paramedical advisors attend.
Protecting internal operations	(A4) They're only from outside colleges. No harm.
Managing the environment by appealing to a larger goal.	(M6) Well, don't you think the faculty would benefit from the workshop? Won't some of them be Admissions committee members one day?

In the dialogue, Margaret introduced the subject (M1) and, in response to Arnold's question (A1), she pitched her idea of opening up the process to the entire committee (M2). In response to the next question of "why" (A2), she explained the data that she had provided for him, which showed that prior SAE meetings had attracted the same group (M3). Arnold responded by reasserting the reasoning behind limiting the invitations (A3), a move that was self-protective, rather than encouraging dialogue. Margaret responded (M4) by questioning this reasoning. He responded with an explanation she thought was "self-sealing," but it might also be considered defensive of past action (A4). Whether the intervention method influenced the defensiveness or there were other reasons for not opening the conversation is not clear. At this point, Margaret changed her intervention strategy.

Reflection	Dialogue
Minimizing generating negative feelings; attempts at diplomacy; also a claim to the task has been made, but the responsibility for the action (rather inaction) will be defused. (I rose from my chair.)	(A6) Yes, then they came to the workshop. That was a good point and good analysis on your part. I tell you what, I will bring the issue up with the other committee members and the dean and see what happens. Is that all right?
(I said this in the open door.) Defensive; feature of vulnerability.	(M7) I guess so, it seems like I'm dismissed.
(He reached for the phone; signaling the end of the conversation.) Attempt at minimizing negative feelings.	(A7) Oh no, if you need to talk, feel free.

Margaret appealed to a higher goal by asking Arnold's opinion on the aims of the meeting (M6). Arnold responds by noting the committee's comfort with dialogue among the group rather than exposing their logic (A6). Margaret continues to press the issue until she realizes she has been dismissed (M7). The dean ends the conversation with a claim of openness (A7) that was not consistent with his behavior during the exchange.

We can examine this conversation on two levels: first, as a dialogue involving closed-strategic behavior; and second, as a conversation about a critical social issue. On the behavioral level, it is a conversation of strategic moves, with one person (Arnold) holding the power and being dismissive as a means of closing the meeting. Arnold did not necessarily abuse power, but he did use his power to control the meeting. Nor was his behavior abusive, but in being dismissive he closed down a conversation about a critical social issue. It was a conversation within the conventional context of strategic action with both participants behaving strategically.

From Margaret's vantage, she was raising a critical social issue. While she did not make the argument, she was apparently intervening on a belief that broadening participation in the SAE could improve diversity in admissions to the medical school, but she did not voice this concern. If the discussion had been about the link between training and admission it might have opened up to discuss the underlying strategies for improving diversity. To achieve this open discussion, Margaret could have stated her notion of broadening participation as a testable hypothesis. Would such a conversation have raised issues about overcoming prejudice? Such topics are often hard to talk about. Margaret's intervention was aimed at taking an intermediate step toward improving diversity by suggesting an intervention, but she did not make her reasoning visible in the exchange.

Whether or not Margaret's strategy of opening the SAE training to more people would have made a difference in admissions was never raised as a hypothesis. In essence, Arnold indicated the committee was more comfortable with the closed environment (A3). This refusal to open the discourse to the service personnel (e.g. counselors, science teachers, etc.) who could influence the number of applications was the core issue. If the core issue had been raised and discussed, the alternative of discussing the issue in the committee might have been considered. Unfortunately, this strategy did not get presented to the committee members making the admissions decisions. Thus, the openness to diversity remained at the edges of the decision process.

Analysis

These cases illustrate the roles of reflection on practice and learning how to be adaptive. All three administrators were competent managers, but found adaptations difficult when critical social problems were involved. The first case involved advocacy based on reflection in an action situation. While Kim found herself in a difficult interpersonal situation, her intervention achieved its aim in the situation (a form of effectiveness). However, the case also revealed the great difficulty most professionals have engaging in discourse about critical social issues. In the second case, an individual was asked to intervene in a situation in which she lacked training. There was a backup process in the organization, and the problem was handled by her supervisor, the vice president, who had responsibility over all of the people involved. In the third case, the Director of Multicultural Affairs took action and, while she did not receive the outcome she wanted, the exchange was professional and she learned from it. Critical social issues are related to implementation of new policies. When incidents raised issues outside of normal practice—the inconvenient and possibly manipulative scheduling of a meeting, implied sexual harassment, and a confrontation about expanding diversity—in these cases, the pattern of response was defensive. Yet these problems are among those that graduate students and other professionals seeking career advancement are likely to confront and ponder after the fact.

While critical social issues are typically framed within the structural parameters of organizations (e.g. the development of policies on sexual harassment or affirmative action as organizational responses to challenges), the mere implementation of policies does not change the patterns of interaction that may have caused the problems in the first place. Having defined policies potentially provides a mechanism for addressing challenges, but people still must learn how to handle these problematic situations when they arise.

Integrating understanding of the moral aspect of professional behavior helps clarify the nature of these problems. The administrator (Janet) and the associate dean (Arnold) were conditioned to act in strategic patterns within a conventional mode of moral reasoning. When asked to confront abusive behavior, Janet was not prepared to present the issue properly (i.e. the reported behavior in relation to the policy). In contrast, when confronted by a critical social claim that challenged the operating practices of the admissions committee, Arnold responded defensively. Both supervisors appeared uncomfortable operating out of a conventional zone of moral reasoning in administrative practice.

These three cases illustrate the importance of discerning and reflecting on moral problems as part of administrative practice. All three interventions could have been handled more professionally: Kim could have tested her assumptions rather than acting on beliefs; Janet could have openly communicated about the reported behaviors in relation to the policy; and Margaret could have raised the issue that concerned her (i.e. the barriers to admitting qualified students of color). Having rethought these issues in the process of writing this book, I conclude that these cases are important because they reveal moral aspects of organizational practice, the very issues that have been frequently overlooked as an integral part of professional education. By presenting these cases in the context of organizational strategy, I hope to encourage discussion as part of professional education in courses using this text.

ORGANIZATIONAL ADAPTATION

As part of their restated theory of organization success, Cameron and Lavine (2006) offered a different, moral lens through which to view strategy in organizations. Their theory does not differ in fundamental ways from traditional theory that emphasizes organizational success. Indeed, their focus is on extraordinary success. They argue for adaptability and new forms of leadership within organizations seeking success (as defined by the organization). Adaptations of strategy to attain extraordinary results is crucial to commonly accepted notions of success (especially in problematic areas like the clean up of toxic waste, the subject of Cameron and Lavine's inquiry) and critical to social functioning. While I recognize that additional elements of organizational strategy are also important—including organizational capacity to enable groups within organizations to deviate from explicit aims to address critical challenges—the idea of adapting the organization and management for success is crucial. Cameron and Lavine's argument is used as a lens for examining how the Regional Technical University (RTU) responded to the IPAS.

RTU had a strategic plan that guided action strategies used by administrators and faculty members who were actively involved in governance (see Text Box 6.2). The campus had a strategic plan that provided a framework for action and provided professionals flexible space to adapt practice to address challenges related to aims specified in the strategic plan. Specifically, the supplemental instruction initiative—a program that employed successful advanced students to provide peer instruction in difficult lower division courses in math, science, and engineering—was included in the strategic plan. It had been rationalized based on the benefits for students at both levels.

The assessment process for IPAS provided research illustrating problems with retention at RTU. The university campus had a high drop-out rate during the first two years. The supplemental instruction program seemed to be targeted at a critical need for lower division students: early achievement in difficult courses. Intervention in this area could improve four-year retention as well as provide employment opportunities for returning students. As the case analysis illustrates (see Text Box 6.2), the availability of the research findings, along with the technical assistance from the new institutional research (IR) office, provided resources—what Cameron and Lavine might characterize as a new form of "abundance" of resources—to reframe the initiative.

Text Box 6.2 **Supplemental Instruction at Regional Technical University**

The Regional Technical University (RTU) had a strong, well-defined strategic plan. Supplemental Instruction (SI)—engaging experience and successful students in the instruction of younger students—was an integral part of the plan. Not only was SI emphasized as a means of educational improvement, but as a mechanism for student employment. The proponents of the initiative had been rationalized in part by the notion that campus employment improves persistence.

As part of the assessment process, the IPAS researchers had analyzed persistence at the campus before the project, a development that surprised some of staff attending the initial meeting, even though this had been communicated through prior correspondence to the campus chief executive. In an interview, the director of the supplemental instruction program described the situation at the kickoff meeting in February 2004: "They started talking to us about the different research they had done on universities and . . . different strategies for retention. I think we were probably taken aback to realize that we were being studied before we even got there." She also described how the research provided new information that had not previously been considered in the planning process:

> I think that was the first time that we started to, for me I should say, properly identify that we had such a low graduation rate. Especially in my position where I am seeing students who have struggled all along and I got to see of lot of students who actually graduate . . . No one believes that many students are making it out because we're seeing the same students trudging along and not really seeing those masses that are just falling by the way side.

Clearly the strategic planning had proceeded at the campus without good information on the high drop-out rate. Receiving evaluative information on retention of their students had enabled them to rethink their strategies.

The director also described her collaboration with the IPAS staff on alignment of the supplemental instruction with the IPAS process, a step that helped her gain more support from it:

> So when supplemental instruction became part of the strategic initiative, and some funding was going to be put behind it, you always thought someone is going to say, "Is this funding being used properly? Is it achieving its goal?" So you had to keep that information, and then, like I said to IPAS, "Are we assessing properly?"

The supplemental instruction team developed and used a new data collection system, building ongoing evaluation into their initiative. A colleague added:

> So anything IPAS needed . . . At least we were able to add it every semester [referring to the data collection] and that's a good thing for the university. And, you know it's successful, it's used by the chancellor, and it's used in our bragging pieces . . . It's very helpful.

The SI director elaborated:

> Maybe I would say, um, IPAS has helped us to look at changing our culture. We haven't had a culture of assessment. And so I see that change within the university. We are probably doing it administratively, but now we are trying to talk to faculty about that.

SI had been emphasized in the strategic planning, but the linkages between supplemental instruction and retention had not been established. It had been rationalized as a means of employing students and improving achievement.

The IPAS consultants also helped the university's new institutional research office build an evaluation program. The institutional research director commented,

> So it seems to me that IPAS is making a contribution by helping this project to further the SI effort on this campus—not just only on the campus . . . So I think IPAS made a significant contribution both in terms of this project itself and in immediate impact on [SI director] and policies she develops in her areas.

In summary, RTU used IPAS to establish links between one of their central initiatives and the need to improve student retention on campus, a critical problem that had not been well understood before they took part in the new project.

Source: Abstracted from St. John, 2009, pp. 199–201.

This case illustrates how external support can enable an organization to adapt in ways that strengthen initiatives and have the potential to improve student success. Revealing the problems with persistence and degree attainment enabled administrators to see links and recraft their arguments and strategies. This case illuminates the type of alignment of aims, strategies, and success that Cameron and Lavine identified within successful organizations.

This case also illustrates an organizational adaptation at the level of practice that was not evident in the medical school case. When the associate dean was confronted by evidence, he failed to communicate about the problem. He closed off the conversation and ended the exchange with the notion of an "open door." However, the reality of the open door was actually more evident in RTU, where there was an ability to adapt rather than just a capacity to follow a plan. Consistent with Cameron and Lavine's argument, this is illustrative of success.

Given the aim of building understanding of the ways professionals contend with morally problematic situations, recall that the three aforementioned cases pertained to critical social problems: planning for a cultural event on campus, the implementation and practice of a sexual harassment policy, and the implementation of race sensitivity in graduate school admission. The first case illustrates strategic intervention in pursuit of social aims; the second case illustrates the interpersonal defensiveness of being confronted by claims of injustice; and the third case describes organizational resistance to a diversity initiative. The defensive routines in these contexts were complex and not easily resolved by policies, information, or intervention. Thus, while creating an explicit orientation toward success may help organizations move toward defined aims, as was the case with the adaptations at RTU, this type of adaptive behavior may not be as easily realized when critical social issues are involved.

CONCLUSIONS

For nearly 30 years, strategic approaches to organizational change have been widely used in business and education (Keller, 1983; Porter, 1980). Pedagogies that encourage reflection, including the process of viewing problems through different basic frames (Bolman & Deal, 1996), provide opportunities to promote strategic thinking. Recently, strategic theories of organization have been adapted to encourage flexibility, in addition to central control of goal setting and selection of initiatives (Cameron & Lavine, 2006). These newer approaches may improve the success of strategic interventions, as has been argued, although there is limited research evidence related to this revision of strategic models.

Organizations and Professional Practice

The key distinction between strategic methods of organization and practice and instrumental approaches is the emphasis on strategy and adaptation within the central process of organizational control. The early literature on strategic planning emphasized planning (e.g. Potter, 1980), while the newer literature emphasizes adaptive, decentralized action (e.g. Cameron & Lavine, 2006). The lessons learned from these examples (see Table 6.2) are that organizations with strategic initiatives create space for adaptation by professionals (e.g. the refinement of supplemental instruction at RTU, the adaptations in the implementation of sexual harassment policies, and the efforts to modify training services provided by the minority admission program). Not all of these interventions proceeded smoothly. The completion of tasks was related to alignment with central control (e.g. RTU and administrative office cases). This close alignment is central to the nature of closed strategy. Interventions that fall outside of set parameters run a greater risk of denial (e.g. the request to change clientele for training at the medical school). If the aim of an organization is to improve successful implementation of centrally determined initiatives (a central feature of closed strategy), then there is a need for the clear definition of the intent of parameters for adaptation. This is similar to what Cameron and Lavine call "over communication and preemptive information sharing" (2006, p. 186). Information on strategy and guides for discretion would fall into this category of action.

Professional Learning

The tension between professional expertise and adaptive behavior is at the core of many of the problems that emerge in practice. Professionals learn to act quickly, applying their expertise to solve problems. Adding reflection to the process helps, as does research when it is aligned with the intent of the organization. However, individual strategic behavior, including the process of arguing for and rationalizing new strategies, can undermine collective discourse about critical social problems and the departure from the truth that occurs in habitual patterns of expert strategic action. This complexity should not be overlooked by aspiring or experienced professionals. Learning to reflect

Table 6.2 Lessons Learned About Alignment of Strategic Orientations of Organizations with Norms and Practices within Communities of Practice: Closed-Strategic Action

Frame	Hypothesizes	Lessons Learned
Organization		
Strategic Orientation	Adapting strategies to address new challenges	*Lesson 1: Emphasizing adaptive strategies increases flexibility, if it supports central initiatives.* Evidence: • Implementation of new policies improves with organizational support (e.g. sexual harassment policy). • Information does not promote change if decision makers do not support options by being advocates (e.g. medical school admissions).
System Related to Lifeworld	Strategic initiatives may address critical issues arising from lifeworld	*Lesson 2: Adapting new initiatives to align with strategic goals provides means of improving pursuit of organizational aims.* Evidence: • Program administrator of supplemental instruction integrates evaluation as means of strengthening a position of initiative within the university.
Communities of Practice		
Norms within Communities of Practice	Aligning strategies with organizational initiatives	*Lesson 3: Professionals have flexibility increased within constraints defined by organizational initiative.* Evidence: • Retention emerges as a goal for supplemental instruction at Regional Technical University as a result of involvement in IPAS. • Administrator receives organizational support after uneasy intervention.
Congruent Practice	Trying out new strategies within centrally controlled practice	*Lesson 4: Test piloting and reflecting on new approaches to practice provide opportunities to build skills, even in problematic situations.* Evidence: • All three cases illustrate opportunities for practitioner to learn from reflection on strategy.

and adapt in practice is crucial to the artistry of practice, but may not be sufficient to deal with critical issues. Before outlining another reflective assignment, I reflect on how this chapter informs us about the learning aims of Part II.

Aim 1: Encourage learning that enables practitioners to achieve their aims as professionals, as well as the dreams that motivated their choice of profession. Reflection-in-action—a set of skills that involves examining, reflecting on, and adapting practice—is critical to professional growth. Adaptation of practice, including experiments with new practices, should be encouraged, but coaching and support are crucial. Not all experiments in action will have their intended outcome. Stressful conditions, like the angst experienced by the administrator addressing a problem with sexual harassment, can create barriers to openness in problematic situations. Even well reasoned arguments can be rejected by senior officials, especially when they conflict with protected practices, as was the case with the minority services officer. These cases collectively illustrate the complexity of encouraging professional responsibility and moral reasoning.

The argument that the frame of organizational success can be broadened to create room for adaptation, a concept abstracted from Cameron and Lavine's research on successful organizations, illustrates one missing link in the organizational literature. It exposes an intermediate state between directive and instrumental organizational action and openness to critical discourse that is widely advocated but difficult to realize. If more organizations create strategic patterns of behavior with this type of openness that is inclusive of issues of justice, it might be easier for professionals to confront the problems they see and experience without fear of retribution. This form of intermediate openness to critical discourse would enable more professionals to develop the critical discursive skills so vital to justice in practice and society.

Aim 2: Enable reflection on assumptions, actions, and outcomes in ways that promote learning about improving practice and developing and refining skills, along with reflection on moral aspects of practice. The cases presented in this chapter illustrate the process of learning about how to test assumptions in action and learning from experience. It is especially important to reflect on attempts at openness that have not been entirely successful.

Reconsider the cases in this chapter. In the admission case, the office administrator intervened when called upon to do so, albeit in an imperfect way. The organization support up the line provided the necessary corrective action. Had there not been an intervention and an opportunity to reflect, this administrator may have learned to shut down in critical situations rather than reflect and learn new approaches to intervention in critical circumstances. The case of the multicultural affairs officer is more complex. She received positive feedback for the information provided even though she did not have the outcome she sought. The pace of change in organizations is complex and can be slower than desired in the moment of action. However, taking the time to reflect can enable and encourage aspiring professionals to ponder problematic situations and try alternative forms of action that enable incremental changes in attitude and action. The case of the RTU Director of Supplemental Instruction illustrates an intervention informed by research and aligned with organizational aims. It also illustrates a pattern of professional efficacy in a setting where there is collaboration to achieve organizational aims.

Openness to adaptation in organizations to make major changes in practice—from universities implementing new strategic initiatives to major corporations engaged in environmental cleanup—is vitally important to organizational success. Targeted openness to adaptation as it relates to chosen directions of an organization may not only be a critical element of organization success (Cameron & Lavine, 2006), but it may also provide means to integrate a commitment to just practice into strategically-oriented organizations.

Interventions that involve bringing new information into the discourse—as was the case with the multicultural affairs intervention and the IPAS project at RTU—can create an abundance of information that can foster and promote change. This notion of abundance as it is being developed in the literature on organization merits attention in future research on strategic change in colleges and other organizations. If scarcity of resources—including limited information on outcomes—is associated with resistance to change in some settings, then the notion of efficiency (i.e. spending less money per unit in production or per student in education) is especially problematic relative to theories of change used in market theories (especially in labor-intensive industries like education).

Aim 3: Promote organizational development that enables professional development and encourages learning. IPAS provided a process-oriented, analysis-based approach to reform in colleges and universities. It is apparent from the RTU case—as it is from other IPAS cases presented in Chapters 5 through 9—that campus team members engaged in the assessment and inquiry processes learned from the workshops. It is apparent that it is easier for faculty members and administrators to engage in change initiatives when their ideas align with university aims. Further, information provided in process-oriented change methods can facilitate this type of initiative.

This suggests a bounded openness to change initiatives is possible within organizations that have a closed-strategic frame. The critical issue is the apparent alignment of administrative initiative with the mission or strategic plan. This sorting mechanism (i.e. the alignment of initiative and perceived attitudes about outcomes) helps explain why the solution was reached in the sexual harassment case after the hostile reception at the point it was initiated. In a reverse sense, this sorting mechanism, perhaps even the resistance to opening up the process, was endorsed at the private medical college.

This closed-strategic frame of action was a prevalent form of response to IPAS among participating campuses. A Private Christian University (PCU)[64] used the evaluation support in one of its major projects and several public four-year campuses aligned evaluation support with projects underway as a method of getting started (Musboa, 2006; St. John, 2009). In these cases the evaluation support (i.e. the providing of a new resource to inform administration about the effects of reform) provided a means of opening opportunities for change. This differs from the image of freely chosen change initiatives and problem solving recommended by Argyris and Schön (1974). In fact, the action inquiry model and the IPAS process actually encourage opening up conversations about new challenges. While the research for the project identified new challenges in the state related to critical topics—especially inequality of persistence opportunities across racial groups (St. John, Carter et al., 2006)—only initiatives related to current projects were chosen as challenges at many of the campuses, in spite of evidence of other critical challenges.

However, not all of the campuses that participated in the initial project continued after the initial assessment. For the campuses that continued, the analyses provided a level and quality of research on persistence they had not previously used in their decision-making process. Not all campuses were ready to engage in a research-informed process or in a process-oriented procedure. For example, at the RCC campus discussed earlier (see Chapter 5) the research-based aspect of the reform process was overlooked in favor of new ideas thought to be best practice. Viewed from the perspective of abundance, it may seem possible that resource scarcity was a factor in this immediacy. However, at single community college (SCCC), a similarly under-resourced campus environment (see Chapter 7), there was a capacity to engage in the inquiry process and use the research to inform change initiatives. The readiness of the campuses and the limitations of staff support appear to be better explanations for variability of engagement—and campuses of all sizes lack these resources (St. John, McKinney, & Tuttle, 2006).

Aim 4: Improve services provided by professional organizations that promote justice and improve sustainability. The post-progressive stance of this book argues that social inequality and environmental decline are pervasive issues that merit attention within organizations. The case examined by Cameron and Lavine (2006) illustrated that it is possible for organizations to focus on environmental cleanup, providing they have sufficient resources. The fact that a resource-rich environment within the organization was a necessary element of the change process forewarns that correcting for decades of environmental abuse will not be easy. It may be difficult to find inexpensive or efficient means of improving the environment. Let us hope that the creativity in engineering and design disproves this hypothesis.

There is some hope for other reforms that aim to reduce inequality and improve equity in these cases. IPAS was a project aimed at assisting campuses with the process of addressing challenges in ways that improved student opportunities to gain postsecondary degrees. There were several examples of campus initiatives that made use of research and technical support to enhance change efforts, and there was evaluative evidence of effects on student outcomes (Hossler, Ziskin, & Gross, in press). It is apparent that when alignment of change initiatives and inquiry was achieved, interventions were used to improve opportunities for students. These insights into the learning side of the puzzle of reform illustrate the importance of reflection-in-action within organizations. Professional development coupled with research-informed, inquiry-based reform may provide a means of addressing critical challenges.

REFLECTIVE EXERCISE

Readers are encouraged to reflect on their own practices in relation to their aims. Readers are encouraged to think about situations (both their case statement and other situations) in terms of their own life goals (referencing their personal statement from Chapter 1). This reflective assignment is to try out an intervention-in-action to solve a problem. The situation can be at home, work, or school. Record the exchange, or a portion of it that you would like to reflect on, using the format from Text Box 4.1. To maximize learning opportunities, it might be useful to select an incident in which you tried out an intervention in practice that related to problem solving.

7

PROFESSIONAL EFFECTIVENESS

How can organizations facilitate professional development within a change process aligned with the organization's mission? This question assumes a strategic conception of organization and professional practice, a point of view widely held. It carries forward an alignment of professional action with the intent of the organization, consistent with institutional theories of organization and society. Arygris and Schön's (1978) theory of professional effectiveness carried forward this implicit system-subsuming practice, an assumption that does not differ from most theory and research on organizational strategy. However, they also stressed the importance of using valid information to inform understanding of critical problems and collaboration among practitioners on the design of interventions. These discursive practices distinguish open-strategic action from methods that rely on central control to maintain alignment of organizational aims (i.e. mission, strategies, and strategic initiatives) within actions taken by professionals in the organization.

This chapter explores this concept of professional effectiveness as a metaphor for open-strategic action. Since the concept of effectiveness implies achievement of centrally defined aims, we can consider action aimed at these ends as being oriented toward effectiveness.[65] I also focus on broadening the concept of professional effectiveness to accommodate professional action to include: (1) an understanding of strategies aimed at improving fairness and social justice; and (2) reconstructing the concept of organizational control to accommodate independent action initiated by professionals working in complex organizations. After considering the concept of *communities of practice* as groups of practitioners engaged in organizational change initiatives, I review case studies from classes on professional development and a reform initiative in a community college.

COMMUNITIES OF PRACTICE

Teams of professionals working as subunits of larger organizations are the primary force for open-strategic action. These can be basic units of practice (e.g. academic departments and small professional schools within universities, or regional offices of large firms) within large organizations. Argyris's action science focused on teamwork. His testing of the theory took place in a consulting firm (1993), a professional service organization that emphasizes teamwork among professionals working with clients. Academic units in universities and many other professional organizations (including medical practices, law firms, and so forth) have similar features (i.e. autonomous professionals working with others on a range of projects). Consistent with the methods used in this book, I consider the expertise and moral dimensions of broadening this concept to integrate an emphasis on social justice before reconsidering the role of frames.

Expertise Dimension

Professional effectiveness, as implied in the works of Argyris and Schön (1978, 1996), can be defined as the artistry of practice within complex organizations with defined missions, visions, and strategic initiatives. In my view, this form of reflective action can be distinguished from the concept of reflection-in-action, as discussed in Chapter 6, because of the emphasis on the capacity to reflect on evidence of practice in relation to implicit assumptions about strategy toward aims and redesigning practice to improve movement toward these organizational aims. To this notion, derived largely from Argyris and Schön, I think we should add the aim of addressing injustices and improving environmental sustainability as integral aspects of professional practice. The process of testing assumptions in open discourse is critical to problem solving in all types of professional organizations. My argument is that this process should integrate an emphasis on reducing inequality and environmental decline, or social justice, which is consonant with the theory of professional effectiveness if it is adapted appropriately.

Professional action is situated in individual expertise. Working within tacit knowledge and normative rules of practice in their organizations, practitioners usually learn to advocate for the practices they value and rationalize their advocacy within the language of organizational mission, a lesson evident in the prior chapter.[66] It is difficult to alter these patterns of practice without interventions led by external consultants and extraordinary leaders. It is also difficult to sustain a culture of critical reflection that promotes just practice. When extraordinary leaders leave through promotion, transfer, job change, or retirement, there is a great likelihood of a regression to more conflicted patterns of interaction if there is not a strong organizational culture supporting open discourse. In addition, environmental conditions, including the competitive positioning of organizations, are in nearly constant flux. A game theory of professional practice can predominate, requiring adaptation to normative rules of practice as means of changing and advancing within organizations. The need for constancy of change through adaptation to new circumstances is hastened by global competition in most domains of professional practice (Gilpin, 2001; Tabb, 2002).

Argyris and Schön (1978, 1996; Argyris, 1993) proposed a tight link between organizational and professional learning. They proposed and tested interventions that enabled professionals to reflect openly on assumptions about action strategies within their communities of practice and engage in interventions that could be tested with evidence. In large, complex organizations (e.g. research universities, hospital systems, and multinational professional service firms) it is difficult to maintain this culture of practice given the great diversity of locales, peoples, and types of professional expertise.

These arguments should be reconstructed to contend with the complexity of large professional organizations that do not rely on central control of practice. In reconstructing these notions, I consider the roles of both trust and evidence of outcomes.

Culture of Trust

In *Trust and the Public Good: Examining Cultural Conditions of Academic Work*, William G. Tierney (2006) outlines challenges in building collective action within organizations expected to function in service of the public good. His arguments offer a way of thinking about the problem of loose links between actions of professional communities of practice, their organizations, and the global citizens in communities and societies they serve. Tierney's concepts are situated in a rethinking of social capital theory, giving only limited attention to social inequality,[67] which is a core issue if our goal is to increase justice and sustainability within social value systems. Nevertheless, his concept of trust helps illuminate the possibility of maintaining a system with loose links between central administrative structures and the multiple professional communities of practice within complex organizations.

Tierney (2006) introduces a *grammar of trust* that includes terms such as: "repeated interaction," "dynamic process," "end" (or aim), "exchange utilizing faith," "taking risks," "ability," "rational choice," and "cultural construction" (p. 45). A language and discourse that builds understanding of these concepts seems necessary to create an open-strategic environment within large, complex organizations that rely on professional expertise, like universities. Tierney argues risk plays a central role in trust: "Whether trust is an end, or enables exchange behavior, individuals take a risk" (p. 52). He acknowledges that faith (i.e trust in God) may play a role in trust for the individual, but he also argues that trust in action also involves faith between individuals. Culture, he argues, provides the mechanism for building trust: "From this perspective, trust evolves through the ability of individuals to communicate meaning rather than rational facts" (p. 65). He uses case studies of colleges and universities to build an understanding of the culture of trust within organizations. He argues that leaders and professionals play roles in creating a culture of trust within organizations.

A recent analysis of the IPAS illustrates the central role trust played in this inquiry-based change process. As a conclusion of their review of the communication between IPAS staff and campus teams, Reynolds and Hossler (in press) observed:

> The successfully engaged teams in this study had several key, shared features that contrasted with features of teams that left the project early. Institutionally, the successfully engaged teams were empowered, had the ability to include others, and were heard when they spoke to administrators more senior than they. Perhaps due to this, the interactions between these campus teams and the members of the IPAS staff were partnerships, in which *trust and legitimacy* were established through the building of professional relationships and the engagement in dialogue about data and research (emphasis on original, page number unconfirmed).

This analysis reveals the importance of trust between interventionists (IPAS staff) and organization members (campus teams) within the change process. Interpersonal trust within and between groups engaged in reform processes is probably necessary to enable open exchange.

Tierney (2006) also uses the concept of the public good as means of understanding the fragile link between universities and society: "The idea of a public good is a deceptively simple term that individuals employ with increasing frequency but has different meanings and interpretations" (p. 176). For example, Penny Pasque's (2007) review of the public trust reveals that issues related to social inequality are largely overlooked in arguments of public and private benefits from public investment in education. In addition, given the public challenges to equity-based initiatives related to affirmative action—including Proposal 2 in Michigan—there is strong evidence that leaders in universities and voters in states can hold radically different notions of fairness as it relates to the public good.

Tierney's critique and analysis reveals that building trust is crucial, both within universities and between universities and their constituents, including global citizens living in the communities and states in which universities function. Public support is central to federal and state support of higher education. Trusting universities to make fair decisions regarding admission, conduct research in safe ways, and contribute to the economic development of their communities is a challenge for global citizens. They often fail to consider how the decline in taxpayer support for the institution and student aid increases costs for students and their families: A decline in taxpayer support increases tuition for all and decreases funding available for students with need and/or merit) (Priest & St. John, 2006). These sorts of problems with trust are not unique to higher education; there are lingering problems with the public trust of accounting firms, hospitals, politicians, and corporations of all types. Building trust within organizations so professionals can act with conscience, and between organizations and communities is a complicated ongoing challenge for all professionals.

Closing the Information Loop

Closing the loop between assumptions made about practice and the results of practice is critical in all professions if the aim is to create a form of professional citizenship and responsibility that contributes to society by building professional knowledge and using it to improve social justice and environmental sustainability. The failure to consider the link between actions taken and intended outcomes, or closing the loop between practice and knowledge of the results of action, has frequently been overlooked. In fact, the public policies that espouse this intent—including misguided accountability reform in education—have undermined this intent.

One of the most contested issues in both K–12 and higher education is related to the role and use of information within systems of control. The notion of educational accountability to government is naive. Historically, there was state and local educational control. Through the 1970s, the US held international leadership in the quality of higher education and educational attainment. In 1983, the U.S. Department of Education published *A Nation at Risk*. After a quarter century of government accountability, with increased testing, curriculum alignment, and, most recently, penalties for low scores in schools, it has become a policy that failed (Miròn & St. John, 2003). Not only has the US fallen in international rankings of college access, but high school graduation rates have faltered and inequality of educational opportunity has increased (St. John, 1997). Now, with the publication *A Test of Leadership: Changing the Future of U.S. Higher Education*, the U.S. Department of Education (2006) is promoting a similar scheme of public accountability in schools. If accountability schemes were implemented in higher education in ways similar to K–12 education, it would be a radical departure from the decentralized decision environment in state systems of higher education.

There are two serious problems with the approach to accountability used in education: (1) it fails to evaluate the effects of policy decisions or test assumptions about the links between policies and outcomes; and (2) it can de-professionalize practitioners, devaluing their efforts to reflect on problems and change practices. We should build knowledge of methods of closing the loop between professional actions and outcomes. This is a shared interest within professional organizations and between such organizations and their constituents, clients (or students), and the public, including global citizens who seek service and provide funding (through payment for service or tax subsidies[68]). There are three levels of building trust:

- *Within communities of professional practice*: The reflection on assumptions about action and outcome, as well as with the generation and review of evidence relative to outcomes of action are critical to building professional knowledge and improving the outcomes of practice and higher education.
- *Between communities of practice and their constituents*: Too frequently, unequal power predominates in relationships; clients push agendas and professionals use their expertise to make arguments. The loop of information is often closed, so actions are promoted that worsen social, educational, health, and environmental conditions. Bringing the loop of information linking actions and outcome back into the exchange between professionals and their constituents should be a priority.
- *Between organizations and communities of interest and support*: Social accountability of public organizations—including universities and publicly traded[69] corporations—should take a socially and environmentally responsible position. It is important to make visible how the actions of organizations (i.e. their policies and initiatives) influence social and environmental outcomes.

Such standards emphasize closing the loop of information with a focus on building trust. These standards differ fundamentally from the overly simplistic notions of public accountability used for the past three decades. One of my aims in this chapter is to build an understanding of the roles of a culture of trust and of information to close the loop between action and outcomes as they relate to professional development and organizational change.

Moral Dimension

Open discourse can ease tensions around critical social and critical environmental issues, especially if organizations have strong policies promoting fairness and discouraging abuse. At the same time, there are potential risks involved with taking an open stance about assumptions and actions within organizations. To close the loop by building and using information on the linkages between actions and outcomes, it is necessary to build a culture of trust. Openness about action and outcomes, as contrasted to the rationalizing of actions, involves acknowledging failure as well as success. An organizational culture of information and trust among professionals represents a challenge for organizations and the communities of practice within these organizations.

Since strategic action is goal-oriented by definition, it can be difficult to raise critical issues that seem outside of formal codes and plans. Further, if habitual practices create dissent, these practices can seem false to those who are aware of injustice and careless action. Given the need to integrate concepts of care and justice into professional reasoning and organizational development—an overarching theme of this book—we need to consider the moral aspect of collective action within organizations in relation to the communities they serve. The debates on moral philosophy, human rights, and the public good are central to defining how and whether it is possible to build a culture of trust that values information. Relative to the role of trust, it is crucial to reconsider how we view collective and individual rights.

One vantage on the problem is offered by the communitarian view of policy, rights, and responsibility (Etzioni, 1988, 1993). Etzioni, the leading spokesperson for this view, argues for a new progressive movement:

> The public's current loss of control over our political institutions calls for a new progressive movement, a major social effort to energize a package of reforms that will reduce the role of special interests in the government of our local and national communities (1993, p. 234).

The recommended reforms are mainly political, emphasizing financing of elections by the public, enforcing rules, enhancing political parties, and restoring public debate (pp. 234–238). Etzioni argues that moral voices are stored in our memory and are threatened by unabashed pursuit of power:

> Moral voices achieve their effect mainly through education and persuasion, rather than through coercion. Originating in communities, and sometimes embodied in the law, they extort, admonish, and appeal to what Lincoln called the better angels of nature. They speak to our capacity for reasoned judgment and virtuous action. It is precisely because this important moral realm, which is neither one of random individual choice nor government control, has been neglected that we see an urgent need for a Communitarian social movement to accord these voices their essential place (p. 254).

While I agree that social progressive values have largely been lost over the past three decades (St. John & Parsons, 2004), the idea that a political movement is the solution or that government action is the locus of change seems inadequate. My argument for integrating moral reasoning into professional practice, organizational change, and professional development is predicated on the assumption that the moral ethos of social justice and environmental sustainability must be embedded in action, not just manifest in public policy.

An alternative view of the rights and responsibilities of global citizenship is offered by Martha Nussbaum. In *Hiding from Humanity: Disgust, Shame and the Law*, Nussbaum (2004) undertakes a rethinking of the role of the law in shaming people and promoting social equity. She asserts that arguments in the communitarian frame are so general as to have no value. For example, relative to Etzioni's arguments about individual rights and dissemination of information about bad acts, she concludes, "Etzioni is so unclear about what he is actually proposing that we really do not yet have a position to assess" (p. 246). In the end, she returns to her concept of human capabilities as the basis for rethinking policy and human action aimed at promoting justice. She argues for a capabilities approach to liberalism and social justice:

> Capabilities have an *inner* aspect: the person herself has to be prepared to engage in the form of functioning in question (by education, health care, emotional support, and so forth). They also have an *external* aspect: even someone who is all prepared, inwardly, to speak or think freely can be impeded from doing so by bad social and institutional arrangements (emphasis in original, p. 344).

Previously, I have argued that this approach can be used as a basis for rethinking educational policy (St. John, 2006). More recently, in collaboration with research teams from two other universities, along with researchers at the University of Michigan, I completed a study of Indiana's Twenty-first Century Scholars Program, a state program that provides aid guarantees to pay for college and support services to middle school students and their parents who make a pledge to prepare for college. It is evident, both from multivariate analyses (factor analyses and regression) and interviews with parents, students, and service providers that the program enables families to build academic capital (the knowledge of college expectation and the will to prepare), a process that increases the enrollment and degree attainment rates for low-income students (St. John, Fisher, Lee, Daun-Barrett, & Williams, 2008). This research illustrates a practical application of the human capabilities concept in policy and educational practice. As the expectation rises for college enrollment, families who have not previously had these opportunities (i.e. first-generation college families) may need supplemental support to attain the capabilities considered necessary for economic citizenship.

The process of adapting action within professional organizations to take steps to increase opportunity is complex, involves collective actions, and requires critical reflection on past practice. Over a 15-year period, starting with the dreams of a few politicians in the late 1990s, Indiana's Twenty-first Century Scholars Program evolved an approach to reform that enabled more low-income students to prepare for college. The program provides opportunities for preparation, access, and degree attainment (St. John et al., 2009). This program involves professionals in regional centers, high school teachers and counselors, and faculty members, staff, and administrators in colleges to provide support to families. It changes practices to meet critical social needs to equalize opportunity.

Building the organizational capacity to respond to critical issues requires new forms of human action within communities of practice. Government subsidy can help. However, the aid guarantees in Indiana's Twenty-first Century Scholars program have worked so well because of the human network of support provided for in the program, in addition to the financial commitment. The interviews with students and their parents, along with factors analyses of patterns of engagement, revealed models of networking and adult support that were necessary for students to develop an inner self-image that college was possible: They became able to envision themselves in college and take the actions necessary to move toward that aim. Rethinking the use of public tax dollars is critical to social change, but redistribution alone does not solve the long standing challenges facing education and society.

Each generation faces new challenges in equity and justice. For nearly a century, there was broad progressive consensus that valued public investment and social change. The forces of governmental action and professional responsibility play a role in promoting justice and fairness at very basic levels of human action. The willingness to reflect and act on the moral aspects of professional responsibility seems necessary. Whether core values for such human action are centered in faith traditions or in other notions of justice and care, it is essential that these values be integrated with, not divorced from, professional action.

Frames of Mind

Artistry of practice (i.e. the ability to reflect on and adapt methods) is needed to engage fully in open discourse about collective strategic action. Professionals who have experience learning from adaptive practices can take a step toward openly communicating about strategy. People who act on beliefs and do not reflect on action cannot communicate or think openly about experiences into which they have no insight. Yet the ability to reflect on practice does not guarantee an ability to reflect openly. Individuals cannot learn how to engage in these discourses unless they are trained. Graduate programs can be redesigned to encourage and enable this type of skill development. Being exposed to open reflection-on-practice in graduate education and/or in communities of practice can hasten learning to reflect openly. Further, neither artistry of practice nor ability to engage in open reflective discourse guarantees moral reasoning that is consonant with ethical standards. The fact that each of these abilities—to reflect on practice (artistry of practice), to reflect openly on action in relation to outcomes, and to reason morally in problematic situations—are somewhat independent, complicates organizational change, professional development, and graduate education.

The relationships between open-strategic action and moral reasoning are hypothesized in Table 7.1. The behavioral elements of open-strategic reflection include engaging with colleagues in (a) setting situational goals and designing strategies and (b) testing new strategies. They are consonant with the original Model II (see Chapter 3). These actions can take three forms with respect to implicit moral reasoning:

- preconventional (collaborating within communities of practice on strategies that use persuasion and other practices prone to power abuse);
- conventional (attempting to align analyses and action strategies with ethical and moral codes);
- postconventional (explicitly considering social and environmental consequences of action as part of the design and evaluation of action strategies).

While all three approaches use open reflection and even critiques of strategies informed by empirical evidence and reflection within the community of practice, the three frames are dramatically different with respect to their social consequences. The preconventional mode would intentionally overlook injustice and environmental decline, a pattern that seems to be pervasive in many professional communities.[70] In the conventional mode of reasoning, we would expect compliance with normal codes, but little action aimed at transforming underlying problems. The postconventional frame would be oriented to returning to a progressive attitude in professional action.

I conclude that Argyris and Schön (1978, 1996) were correct when they argued that there was a need for congruence between organizational change strategies and

Table 7.1 Open-Strategic Behaviors in Relation to Frame of Action and Types of Moral Reasoning

Moral Reasoning/ Frames of Action	Preconventional	Conventional	Postconventional
Open-Strategic Frames Focus	Collaborates on strategies that use power and persuasion to achieve aims with little regard for consequences.	Collaboratively develops goals and adapts strategies to achieve mission; reconciles strategies with ethical standards.	Collectively considers strategies for adapting of mission to address client concerns, diversity, and issues of justice.
Engages with colleagues in setting (situational) goals and design of strategies	• Coanalyzes strategies for improving profit or achieving other aims • Overlooks environmental and/or social consequences of action	• Balances social and environmental responsibility (as compliant action) in strategic analyses • Openly considers evidence of consequences of actions	• Treats issues of environment and social justice as part of criteria for decisions about actions and action strategies • Considers social equity in the design of action strategies
Engages with colleagues in projects to test new organizational strategies	• Cocrafts strategies to appeal to various interests • Rationalizes abuse of power	• Openly discusses strategies and actions • Openly reflects on actions in public sphere	• Voices social and environmental concerns • Encourages interventions aimed at improving justice

open discourse. Generally, professional action is constructed as being aligned with organizational mission, at least at an espoused level. Typically, professionals (e.g. faculty members, lawyers, doctors, etc.) rationalize their actions related to their professional expertise and rules along with their organization's aims. If Tierney's arguments about a culture of trust are valid, open reflection may be possible in professional settings where there is an orientation toward learning, even if there is not central control of action. In other words, it should be possible to have autonomous professional action that supports organizational aims without central control. Otherwise, the whole concept of professionalism would seem misconstrued. Thus, while it is reasonable to assume an alignment of mission and professional action in normal circumstances, it is not necessary to assume that professional action should be subject to central authority. Specifically, it should be possible to build communities of practice that have open, critical reflection even when change processes are not top down, a claim that deviates from the intervention method of Arygris and Schön (1996; Arygris, 1993).

PROFESSIONAL LEARNING IN ACTION

The issues of central control complicate efforts to intervene within organizations. Since most organizations exert strategic control through formal regulator systems, it is difficult for even experienced administrators to design interventions that address systemic problems.

During two decades of teaching action science as an integral part of courses on leadership and professional development, I have worked with some students who practiced open testing of assumptions and undertaking interventions in problematic situations.[71] Several students developed case statements that demonstrated engagement in interventions that focused on improving organizational outcomes using open testing of assumptions within organizations that were tightly regulated. Two cases are examined below: the case of university royalties provides an example of aligning practice with new regulations using open discourse, while the case of coaching in an elementary school illustrates an approach to leadership aimed at supporting teachers engaged in a school reform process.

University Royalties

Martha Turner managed an understaffed Technology Transfer office in an urban university. Her portfolio included managing development of a research park with a private corporation—a major initiative that required lobbying at the state and the federal levels—along with the day-to-day administration of new technology policies, including the royalties policy of the university. In the case statement (see Text Box 7.1), she reviewed her experience with the implementation of a new policy. In this case, a professor had inadvertently given permission to a student in her class to record and market an event conducted in her classroom (a workshop provided by an external guest). Since the production involved the university media center, the incident came to Martha's attention in an exchange with Professor Mathai (M1). After some difficulty, Martha arranged a meeting with the professor, her department chair, and the graduate student. After waiting for some time for the student to arrive, Martha started the meeting with the professor and department chair.

At the outset of the meeting, the department chair, Professor Kern, asserted that the student did not show up for self-defensive reasons (K1). At this point, Martha had the option of rescheduling, but instead overlooked the absence and decided to move ahead with the meeting. She started by restating the rule, which had been overlooked in the department (T2). At that point, she laid out the goal for an agreement that would spilt the royalties, providing a starting point for negotiations.

In stating the policy and opening up the conversation (T2), Ms. Turner created an opening for exchange on the problem. At this point, the department chair shared information about the circumstances of the recording (K1), then Ms. Turner asked for further information about university costs (T3). In response, Professor Mathai noted the expenses for the university (M2). Ms. Turner inquired about the visiting professor's expectations and rights (T3). The chair responded, proposing a straight forward approach (K3). Ms. Turner agreed and indicated she would move ahead (T5).

This exchange among the three people present at the meeting was open and based on evidence. They were applying a university rule in a way thought to be fair for all. However, problems ensued. The visiting professor was receptive to the agreement, but the student resisted. Ms. Turner's comments on the case indicate that a legal challenge did arise, causing problems for the student. However, eventually a deal was made along the lines of what had been proposed initially.

Text Box 7.1 Case Statement: University Royalties

Context: The Director of Technology Transfer, Ms. Turner, at a public university was contacted by Assistant Professor Mathai in Counseling regarding royalties for distribution and sales of a training tape prepared by a graduate student for a class project. The former graduate student who participated in filming, Mr. Weber, had made a claim of ownership. A meeting was set up to discuss the issue.

Situation: Ms. Turner described the situation:

> According to the university system by-laws any product made with university controlled facilities, or resources, belongs to the university. The director of the Office of Technology Transfer has the first responsibility to secure the title to the videotape for the institution by filing a copyright application in the U.S. Office on Patents and Copyrights. The conflict exists between Mr. Weber and the university.

Participants scheduled to attend:

Ms. Martha Turner (T), Director, Office of Technology Transfer

Mr. Randy Weber (W), a former graduate student who assisted with the project

Dr. Sri Mathai (M), a professor of Counseling

Dr. Patricia Kern (K), Chairperson of Counseling

Reflection	Dialogue
Dr. M. is being guarded with the details but is trying to deal with the problem rationally.	*Phone call* (M1) "Ms. Turner, we need your assistance with a student who has produced a videotape for a class project and now wants to distribute the tape commercially. He is being quite difficult about it. Could you possibly meet with Dr. Kern, the student and me to discuss the issues?" (T1) "Certainly, I will be there anytime convenient to the rest of you."
Mr. W. is possibly trying to avoid a threatening situation.	*At the meeting, Dr. Kern, Dr. Mathai, and Ms. Turner are present. Thirty minutes pass and the student does not come.*
Dr. K. attributes defensive behavior on the part of the student.	(K1) "Mr. Weber has not shown up because he believes we are ganging up on him."
Dr. M. echoes negative feelings about the student, protecting her own point of view.	(M2) "He is a very difficult person to deal with and has caused trouble in the department in the past."

Ms. T. is rational, invokes standard organizational behavior, tries to manage the environment, and takes a must-win stance.

(T2) "OK, let's use this time to decide what the department wants to do with this. I understand from Dr. Kern, Dr. Mathai, that you informed Randy that the university did not have any interest in the tape. Actually, that is not necessarily true. The university system by-laws, Chapter VII, concerning Intellectual Property specifies that any product created with university controlled resources or facilities belongs to the university. I have brought along copies of all legal documents necessary to show Randy what the university's rights and obligations are.

"If we decided to negotiate the royalty distribution with Randy we should be prepared with a 'bottom line' on the division between Randy, the supervising faculty member, and the department."

Ms. T. is being open to negotiation, risk-taking, but only to limited extent, within the limits of organizational rules.

Dr. K. introduces additional information, which may threaten the outcome.

(K2) "The problem is compounded by the fact that Randy used an instruction model created by Professor X [from an elite private university]."

Ms. T. continues to invoke standard regulations of her office, looks for information that may enforce her position.

(T3) "Is the model copyrighted? If so, we will have to have [Elite University Professor]'s permission to distribute the tape based on his model. Who paid for [Professor] to come here? And what is his attitude toward the project?"

Dr. M. adds information reinforcing university claim to title. Also suggests Randy has been deceptive, thereby polarizing attitudes.

(M3) "The department paid his air fare; he stayed at my house during his visit. He was most cooperative, and has given Randy suggestions where he might distribute the tape. The whole intent behind the project was to create an instructional tape that might be marketed for the benefit of the department.

"As for me, I don't want anything personally out of the project. My share would go to the department."

Ms. T. continues to advocate rule, as common practice in the institution.

(T4) "Well, we should include [Professor] in a proposed royalty distribution split. Patricia, what do you want out of this for the department?"

Dr. K. advocates her position, in accord with organizational regulations.	(K3) Well, I think we should do a 1/3 split all around: department, [Professor], and Randy.
Ms. T. tries to anticipate the threat of being in nonnegotiable position with Randy.	(T5) OK, I suggest we start offering Randy 1/5 to 1/4 tops. I will call him and also call [Professor] to find out where he stands on the project. We need his permission no matter what happens.

An extensive set of subsequent exchanges were included in the full case, including a call with Mr. Weber who argued on the phone,

> I don't care about university by-laws and regulations. When I was in law school I learned that the most important part of the law is intent. I don't care if Dr. Mathai does not speak for the university. She did, so she should have known better.

The external professor was amenable to any arrangement and seems somewhat amused by the situation. After legal costs to the student, an agreement was reached that reflected the original parameters discussed.

This case is complex because it illustrates the multiple levels of discourses. The three professionals from the urban university spoke openly, a pattern that was also evident in the followup exchange with the visiting professor (not included here). The student's resistance was problematic (noted in the closing comment in Text Box 7.1). However, having structured an agreement openly with the other parties, Ms. Turner was able to work her way through the problem. In a very basic sense, this case illustrates openness and adaptive behavior on the part of the professionals involved.

There is an obvious unresolved, problematic issue in this case: the process seems unfair from the perspective of the student. He had been told he could have the rights by the professor, who was unaware of the university by-laws. Martha Turner used conventional moral reasoning (i.e. treating the rules as such) to work her way through the problem. There was not a legal basis for the student's claims of rights, but this does not mean he was morally wrong. The advantage of continuing the initial meeting with the professor and department chair, without the student, was that common understanding within the group taking action was reached and attempts were made to resolve the issue fairly. We can speculate about whether: (1) the whole event might have gone differently had the student showed up for the meeting; and (2) the same openness would have been evident had the student been present. However, the case illustrates that being open within a group does not mean backing down from difficult circumstances but rather using information—facts of the case assessed in relation to the rules of the organization—to make judgments about how best to proceed in difficult circumstances.

Coaching in an Elementary School

Georgia Lazarus had a decade of leadership experience as a principal in her New Orleans school, Rutherford Elementary, which had won national attention as a model school in a comprehensive school reform process. The school case study (see Text Box 7.2) is properly understood within the context of the political school reform process in the city.

It is important that we situate this case—an incident of coaching and mentorship within a reforming school—within this politically charged climate of urban education. A few years prior, Rutherford Elementary had successfully undergone a major reform through implementation of the Accelerated Schools Project (ASP). Teachers and parents had been engaged in a process of taking stock of the school, developing a shared vision statement, identifying challenges, and initiating projects to address the challenges. In spite of the strong emphasis on standards, testing, and curriculum alignment, the school community decided to undertake a multicultural approach to reform that was compatible with community values. They emphasized improvement and high standards, but adapted curriculum and methods to address the learning needs of students as they had come to understand them through their own research on students and community. Georgia's conversation with Nanette, a new teacher, was a coaching process aimed at enabling the teacher to learn to adapt to the culture, vision, and practice of the school.

Text Box 7.2 Case Statement: Coaching in an Elementary School

Context: Rutherford Elementary School was a highly regarded urban school. For the prior five years the school had been engaged in a collaborative reform model that emphasized student centered learned. The school had modest improvement on test scores during this period. It also received some recognition in the city, especially for parental and university involvement.

Situation: Nanette Baker, a teacher, scheduled an appointment with the principal to discuss her dissatisfaction with her classroom management strategies. The principal has had one previous conference with Nanette on classroom management strategies following the first formal observations.

Participants:

Georgia Lazarus (G), Principal

Nanette Baker (N), fourth grade teacher

Reflection	Dialogue
Nanette is apprehensive about her teaching performance.	(N1) I'm glad we finally got a chance to talk. Your schedule has been real hectic lately and I've really wanted to see you before my next observation. I'm still having the same problems we talked about earlier this year.

Reflection	Dialogue
I'm feeling guilty about the times that I'm required to be away from the school and the fact that I'm not always there when the faculty needs me.	(G1) I understand Nanette. I'm glad that we finally took the time to talk. The number of meetings called for principals in this district is not to be believed. I'm sorry that I'm not always here when the faculty needs me.
Nanette knows she has some real serious problems.	(N2) As you know, I have been having trouble with discipline all year. No matter what I do, it seems as if I can't get control of the class. I've tried everything, including the suggestions you gave me. Nothing works.
I'm trying to get all of the information I can to make sure that Nanette and I can successfully address the problem.	(G2) I remember Nanette that we agreed that you had to find classroom management strategies which worked for you and your children and which relied on mutual respect between you and the students. Could you be more specific and tell me what you have tried and what you think went wrong.
Nanette appears frustrated by her unsuccessful efforts; she also wants to justify her unsuccessful attempt at classroom management.	(N3) Well, for two weeks I tried using the system we worked out where the first rule infraction resulted in the child's name on the board and further violations resulted in check marks next to the names. The children knew the consequences if they got three checkmarks. Well, almost every day just about everybody's name was on the board with marks and I found that it was too hard to do this all day and teach too.
Here, I'm trying to get information.	(G3) How were the rules set up Nanette?
Nanette knows this is not the way that we agreed the classroom rules would be formulated.	(N4) Well, I made up the rules and posted them on a chart in front of the class.
Again, I'm probing for information.	(G4) Did the children have any input to making the rules?
Nanette is again falling upon justifications and excuses for the problems in her class.	(N5) I know you have suggested that the students help make up the class rules but by that time I felt that I needed to get control of the class and the children needed firm discipline immediately.

I'm trying to place the issue squarely on the table so that there aren't any misunderstandings.

(G5) It's not going to work Nanette if the children don't have input and if they don't have a part in deciding how they are going to live in that room for six and a half hours a day, five days a week.

Nannette admits error.

(N6) I know that now. They really didn't care if their name went on the board or how many check marks there were.

I'm trying to encourage Nanette to keep talking.

(G6) Well, I'm glad you learned from the experience. What else have you tried?

Nanette understands that the problems in her classroom are serious and that quick action is called for. However, she does not know how to proceed.

(N7) I really like cooperative learning but the groups are not working well and the children are still not disciplined even though they like working in groups. I've had parent conferences and after-school detentions. Nothing works and I'm really getting tired.

I'm trying to focus on the real issue.

(G7) Nanette, it appears that you have been jumping from one method to the other to maintain discipline in your class. I feel the classroom management problems you are having are the real result of something else.

(N8) What do you mean?

(G8) Have you been reading the comments and suggestions I've been writing on your lesson plans?

Yet again, Nanette tries to justify her actions and avoid the real issues.

(N9) Yes, but I'm so busy in the class trying to keep order that I really can't do all of the things that you want me to do.

I'm trying to get Nanette to see the real problem once and for all by stating it bluntly so that she can't avoid it with justifications of her actions.

(G9) The first step is to plan good, interesting lessons which match the needs of the children. Your weekly plans skip from one concept to another; the activities are not challenging or motivating. The students are not interested so they find other ways to entertain themselves during class time. I feel that this is the real problem.

Nanette once again tries to justify her actions and avoid the problem.

(N10) I'm trying to cover all of the skills that the children will be tested on in April.

I again try to tackle the real problem in a straight-forward manner.

(G10) I realize that, but are the children learning any of this?

| Partial acceptance of the real problem is made by Nanette. | (N11) I guess not; their weekly tests are not so good. |
| | (G11) What do you think we should do? |

Georgia concludes: "The conference ends with Nanette and me working out the series of strategies upon which her weekly lessons are planned and executed. We also set a date for a second formal observation."

Nanette opened the conversation by expressing appreciation for the time to work on her problems (N1) and Georgia responded cordially (G1). Nanette explained her perception of the classroom problems she faced (N2). Contextually, it is important to note that before the reforms this school, like many others in the area, relied on sending students to the principal's office for discipline as a means of maintaining control. Rutherford School had implemented an alternative approach. In her response, Georgia reframed "discipline" as "classroom management" and requested more information (G2). In response, Nanette indicated she had tried the classroom management method they had previously discussed and indicated it had not worked; she seemed to deny personal responsibility (N3). Georgia responded with a question to gain more information about the actual methods Nanette had used (G3). Nanette elaborated with a statement about "posting the rules" (N4). Georgia reflected this was not what they had previously discussed, so she asked whether the students had input on the rules, which was more consistent with the engaged learning environment the school community had envisioned (i.e. a more empowering approach than the old disciplinary model). At this point, Nanette made an excuse for not involving the students in the process, indicating she had set the rules to gain control (N5). Georgia responded with her opinion that this control-oriented approach would not work (G5) and Nanette essentially confirmed this claim (N6). Georgia acknowledged the lesson learned.

It is evident the exchange is about two visions of classroom management: one that is control oriented and another that is empowering. The new vision of the school placed an expectation on teachers that they would engage in practices consistent with this vision. On reflection, Georgia could have stated her claim that "It's not going to work" as a question (i.e. "How did this work?"). This might have been less critical, but since evidence was given in the next statement it appears that the conversation continued to be based on evidence.

At this point, Nanette jumped to a statement about cooperative learning and other methods she was using, all of which related to the vision of the school (N7). This could be viewed as seeking positive feedback, given the frustration over classroom management. Georgia indicated the conversation was jumping around (G7). Nanette asked for more information (N8) and Georgia asked whether Nanette looked at the feedback she was given on the lesson plans (G8). Nanette said she had read the comments but had been too busy to make the changes recommended (N9). Georgia indicated a need for coherent planning (G9), and the conversation continued on this topic. In her comments, Georgia indicates they worked together on lesson plans for the rest of the meeting.

Analysis

These cases are similar to the prior ones with respect to the apparent alignment of strategic aims and personal action decisions. In the royalties case, the conversation centered on methods of complying with a policy about which the two faculty members had previously been unaware. In the case of coaching in a reforming school, the intention of the principal was to encourage and enable the new teacher to align her classroom management and lesson plans with the vision of the school.

However, these cases differ from those in prior chapters with respect to open discussion of the problem, including involving participants in the conversation. Increasing openness in communication provides the opportunity to address new challenges and raise critical issues related to clashes between different rules governing action, such as the strategic aims of an organization and the ethical codes of practice. Both of these cases illustrate the role of open inquiry within the dialogue: in the royalties case, the administrator, chair, and professor discuss how the problem came about and develop a plan for resolving it; in the elementary school coaching case, the principal engages the teacher in discussion of the classroom problems. In both case, the conversation was open to and engaging of the others, which contrasts them to the prior two cases. Such practices enable professionals to resolve problems as they emerge and improve organizational effectiveness (i.e. achievement of the mission and goals of the organization).

Further, in both of these cases the participants were engaged in the codesign of strategy, a behavior not evident in prior cases. After discussion, allowing participants to build a shared understanding of the problem, they collaborated on the design of a new action. In the royalties case it involved reaching an agreement to try a three-way split of royalties as a first position in the negotiations to follow. This was a simple, straightforward agreement based on discussion of the facts of the case. After encountering some resistance and defensiveness, the principal in the coaching case requested information before the two participants collaborated on the design of new curriculum plans.

Finally, there was evidence-based decision making in both cases. Rules were stated in the first case and reminders were given of the school vision in the second. But in neither case did the central decision maker—the administrator in the first case, and the principal in the second case—make a unilateral decision. Rather, in both cases the person in authority made an effort to collaborate in the decision-making process, inviting and using others' suggestions as a basis for planning. This codesign behavior differs fundamentally from the cases previously discussed.

There was also a striking difference between these two cases with respect to the critical social aspect. In the first case, a corporate (board) decision had been made about the policy on royalties and the administrator used her discretion to work with the two faculty members (the chair and the professor of the course) to craft an agreement on how to respond. Contrastingly, the second case, about school reform process, involved an organizational response to a critical social problem. The drop-out rates in urban schools have risen as schools have followed the tightly structured, centrally administered reform policies of the excellence movement. This principal and this school had departed from this path by developing a unique vision and engaging in local, situated reform strategies. In the Rutherford School case, the strategy involved aligning instruction and classroom management strategies with a vision that emphasized empowerment.

ACTION INQUIRY AND ORGANIZATIONAL CHANGE

Action inquiry can be used to allow communities of practitioners—professionals within functional units or cross-unit teams—to implement research-based change that promotes organizational learning along with achievement of organizational aims. It provides a method of collective engagement in defining problems, codesigning interventions, and using evaluation to determine if the intent of interventions was achieved. The Single Campus Community College (SCCC) case (see Text Box 7.3) provides an example of using this approach in a local campus of a state system that relied heavily on instrumental approaches to decisions and implementation.

Text Box 7.3 Action Inquiry at a Single Campus Community College (SCCC)

The Single Campus Community College (SCCC) provides the most complete example of going through the entire process of identifying a challenge through assessment and addressing it through the action inquiry process. The process was coordinated by the IPAS scholar, a professor who received a course reduction (i.e. one less course to teach) from the college for his involvement. He described the persistence analyses presented at the first meeting: "IPAS and the ICHE compiled persistence data for us and we noticed . . . challenge areas that seemed to be salient." He described the process:

> I think what IPAS allowed us to do was to look at the three challenge areas we had: first generation, financial aid, and academic support. They came to us with a more formalized structure that could essentially address those challenge areas.

Another SCCC interviewee described the inquiry process from the perspective of one working group:

> So we developed sub-committees. And . . . my assessments came through working with IPAS on financial aid. We worked with them to base the questions for focus groups . . . So we worked closely on that—I worked very closely on leading a group of other individuals . . . on the financial aid sub-committee, developing the focus group question.

Subcommittees on financial aid, academic support and first generation students converged on the need for a better orientation process. They decided to pilot test a new orientation process and to use pre- and postintervention surveys to assess changes in knowledge. The core component of the intervention was to change the registration process to require orientation first for new students:

> We required nothing [to register], really, at this campus. So going out of that paradigm, and requiring orientation is a big step for this campus. And not allowing them to register, because we are actually headcount driven, unless they go through orientation if you are a degree-seeking student, you cannot register. And they took a strong stance, very few exceptions, and I think we

are starting to see the benefits of that. So, that has been done without additional cost . . . It takes a lot of resources and a lot of time, and so we're trying to work on that.

The SCCC team coordinator described the overall results of the initial pilot test, both from personal and organizational perspectives:

> I cannot imagine what my work would be like here without my involvement. This has been truly rewarding. I have helped with retention and enrollment. The orientation program did not compromise enrollment [i.e., requiring orientation before registration] the way some people had feared. It had the opposite effect. Not only have students increased their enrollment but they also seem to be staying. I know when I go into the classroom, I see my students and they have much better questions for me. They will ask questions about the online grade book, where before they would not have known to ask about that.

The results of the pilot test were partially confirmatory of intent, but the coordinator for the student financial aid subcommittee indicated limitations:

> Our first evaluation, for example, when students pre-tested and post-tested . . . they weren't getting the information we wanted them to glean for the financial aid component. We immediately went to financial aid. If this student information is important enough for you to test it, you need to present it in a way so that they retain it. And they changed . . .

These comments illustrate a capacity to reflect critically on evaluative information, an open-minded attitude about the strategic decisions that had been made. The dean indicated that the IPAS process had changed the culture among administrators and faculty. She indicated that their pilot test of the registration system required them to think differently about systemwide policies:

> You had to have someone that was responsible for whatever . . . That became of course, my role because I sit on the cabinet. . . . The biggest help was . . . being able to give support to people to participate in the action inquiry stage and in helping those determine what our critical needs were. And then once we did, and we came up with the orientation program idea, in order for it to happen, there had to be some buy in by the chancellor [i.e., senior campus administrator] and the academic dean . . . It wouldn't have flown at all . . . In implementing the orientation, we changed our process. I had to convince them that we weren't changing policy, we were just changing our procedure for how we do things [chuckle] . . . because what we changed is that students are now, and this is recent, not allowed to register unless they have participated in the orientation program.

The SCCC dean also described how the action inquiry process itself helped them change the ways they thought about challenges at the campus:

At the time IPAS had come around and they had the ability to help us focus and structure ourselves and stay on task with the process. We kept jumping ahead to the solution and their words would echo in our head and we would say, "stop, stop, stop." We had to go back and look and make sure. We had to force ourselves not to jump to a solution. I really do think that something had to happen with orientation.

She indicated the process enabled them to openly communicate about problems embedded in the formal structure of their campus organization:

Instead of them being in their silos, we now have them participate in this group format and talk about financial aid. . . . The registrar is getting much more involved, and counselors can totally change their ways because people can choose to stay here.

Source: abstracted, shortened, and revised, St. John, 2009, pp. 202–206.

During the early part of the case, interviewees described how participants used the analyses of persistence—their campus had high drop-out rates across all groups—as a basis for reflection on challenges. They also used support from the IPAS staff to conduct focus group interviews, discovering the importance of student financial aid. Their team members attended many of the statewide meetings and were actively engaged in workshops that provided the opportunity to reflect on data analyses and initiate inquiry into critical challenge areas. During the inquiry, they discovered that the process of registering for courses could undermine persistence. New students simply did not have information on requirements, what to expect in courses, or how to apply for student financial aid. In fact, members of the three planning groups converged on the importance of providing information to students before they registered.

As their inquiry process proceeded, they realized that the state system regulations on registration precluded them from preventing student registration before orientation. They did not want to undermine open admission, which had been the intent of open registration, but they realized that most new students needed more information if they were to realize their degree goals. A campus dean was a member of the team, and she worked with the planning group to remove the blocks for pilot testing a new orientation procedure for newly admitted students. They implemented the experiment for one term and had pre- and post-tests to measure knowledge of the college, its procedures, requirements, and student aid. They found an improved retention rate, so they could rationalize continuing their intervention.

However, this group also reflected on the results to see which areas had shown improved understanding. As the interviews indicate, they realized that information on student aid was still incomplete even after the orientation, so they made refinements in their intervention, indicating a learning process. In the interview comments, members of these campus action groups praised the IPAS technical support staff for encouraging them to slow down and think through the problems rather than jump directly to solutions.

Contrasting the approaches of SCCC and RCC (see Chapter 5) illustrates the differences between jumping right to solutions and taking time to reflect. The SCCC group not only took more time to think about the problem, they also took the evaluation seriously and learned from it, as they continued efforts to improve learning opportunities on their campus. The SCCC team had coaches who encouraged them to follow the process and team members willing to engage in and learn from the process. In addition to engaging in an experiment, the SCCC team became a catalyst for change within the community college system. By taking the time to secure approval up the line for the experiment, testing the intervention, and sharing the results, they captured system interest in this method of information dissemination.

CONCLUSIONS

Collective action is complicated by a number of factors. Professional communities function within organizations that have central control of strategic initiatives and finances. Alignment of action strategies with the core mission of organizations is thought to be necessary in public corporations for profitability (i.e. the public expectations within organizations held accountable with the use of quantitative measures of success). Private non-profit organizations, including independent universities, can have greater freedom to initiate change and encourage innovation from within, but even these organizations function in competitive environments and have boards that maintain central control and internal accountability. These control mechanisms may be needed because, in theory, they protect the public good (even in corporations with public investors). It is a challenge for strategic organizations to create the openness necessary to enable communities of practice to respond to initiatives and create new pathways to success. The lack of a capacity for openness to change is most problematic when there are critical social issues being created by the practice.

Organizations and Communities of Practice

A communicative capacity among practitioners seems critical to the ability to adapt to new conditions. However, due to the organizational constraints implicit with central control of organizations, the process of learning to reflect openly is not natural for most people. In fact, the process of learning the rules of practice often makes it difficult to maintain openness. Placing these processes in a sequence of skill development (i.e. recognizing the need to learn the rules of a professional practice before expecting adaptation and artistry of practice) recognizes the role of learning in the professional development process. It also illuminates the role supporting and enabling professional development can play in the organizational change process.

The complexity of open-strategic action should not be overlooked. It requires openness, including communication about critical issues and acknowledgement of problems in practice, and alignment with central authority. A climate of trust is necessary for the alignment of decentralized strategic action within complex organizations, as was noted in prior cases, but openness requires additional organizational conditions. That is, to realize an environment that supports communicative action, professionals require discursive space to make and share judgments, acknowledge mistakes without fear of retribution, and engage in the codesign and testing of alternative strategies. This means that simple guides for action are insufficient; there must be space to discuss the limitations of the guides and the rules that are in place. This does not mean working around the rules, but rather bringing information about problems, alternatives, and findings into the discourse. Working around the rules can create system problems, adding to the possibilities of breakdowns and resistance, while working through the rules to fix problems can create a learning environment.

These requirements, evident in both the professional dialogue and the case studies, generally confirm the propositions of Argyris and Schön (1978, 1996) in their arguments about organizational and professional effectives. The problem is that open-strategic action, as a form of organizational action, is entirely dependent on the willingness of senior officials to learn about and correct problems that may have been created by current policies. This differs fundamentally from the strong notions of success embedded in closed-strategic action, where strategies and abundance of resources are used to steer action toward a central vision or goal. Open-strategic action, as an organizational form, assumes near simultaneous learning at the system and unit levels, or at least open communication between the two levels.

It is important to distinguish open-strategic action as a form of professional practice from open-strategic forms of organizations. The cases examined in this chapter illustrate the role of actions by professionals and do not include evidence of organizational openness per se. In only one of the instances (the coaching dialogue between the principal and the teacher) was there evidence of organizational and practitioner learning. In this instance it seemed necessary to have a principal willing to confront central administration in order to maintain the freedom to move toward a vision openly chosen within the school. In the case of the single campus community college, a cross-unit team of professionals used their collective understanding of the problem and the system to craft an open climate for the intervention. In all three cases there was abundant evidence of responsible professional action along with openness to other voices and points of view related to the evidence.

Professional Learning

Our primary aim is to learn more about the integration of reflective practice and moral reasoning into professional action. Below, I reconsider the theory and evidence from this chapter in relation to the aims set out in Chapter 4.

Aim 1: Encourage learning that enables practitioners to achieve their aims as professionals, as well as the dreams that motivated their choice profession. Perhaps the most rewarding aspect of coaching graduate students, interventionists, and practitioners in schools and colleges has been learning lessons of personal importance. Most people choose their professions based on an inner yearning or a dream to make a difference. The hard lessons professionals learn, tacitly, from their experiences in organizations often expose them to the compromises of professional life. As practitioners learn the common tactical behavior of subjugating their beliefs to the central aims of an organization, they feel compromised. What the pedagogy of professional practice (i.e. the use of reflective dialogues) enables students to learn is how to reflect in action and intervene in ways that create opportunities for the codesign of alternative courses of action. Similarly, the process of intervening in organizations using AIM provides opportunities for learning about openness within the strategic norms of organizations. The cases discussed above illustrate these learning patterns.

Aim 2: Enable reflection on assumptions, actions, and outcomes in ways that promote learning about improving practice and developing and refining skills, along with reflection

Table 7.2 Lessons Learned About Alignment of Strategic Orientations of Organizations with Norms and Practices within Communities of Practice: Open-Strategic Action

Frame	Hypothesized	Lessons Learned
Organization Strategic Orientation	Openness to adaptations of strategic initiatives	*Lesson 1: Openness to adaptation within organizations is dependent on the communicative capacities of practitioners.* Evidence: • Technology transfer officer creates conditions of open exchange of information with faculty member and department chair, minimizing defensiveness. • Principal coaches teacher to adapt classroom management practices and course planning to align with new mission.
System Relation to Lifeworld	Discursive openness creates room to adapt strategic initiatives via critical issue in lifeworld	*Lesson 2: Open, evidence-based discourse among practitioners builds their capacity to address social-critical problems (lifeworld issues).* Evidence: • Teams of professionals in single campus community college (SCC) think through underlying problems influencing early drop-out and communicate with central authorities to gain approval to pilot test alternative.
Communities of Practice Norms within Communities of Practice	Adapting practice to address new challenges	*Lesson 3: Creating new norms to work through problem, rather than to work around constraints, requires learning in practice.* Evidence: • Principal uses evidence in efforts to change norms in school district and in coaching of teacher. • Teams in single campus community college respond to coaching in efforts to dig deeper into potential causes for early drop-out.
Congruent Practice	Engaging in open-critical reflection on practice and in evidence-based reforms	*Lesson 4: Learning the skills of open-critical reflection requires overcoming fear of control implicitly in most organizational (and family) structures.* Evidence: • Faculty member's admission of misunderstanding policy enables development of base agreement in royalties case. • Ability of principal and teacher to communicate based on evidence from classroom enabled communication about alternative practices.

on the moral aspects of practice. The forms of reflection-on-action differ for closed- and open-strategic action. In open-strategic action reflections are shared in a process with implied risks for the individual. This means that the culture of trust must be extended from guidelines indicating acceptable patterns of practice used to encourage and enable open critical reflection. This represents a higher standard of professional behavior—one evident in the basic and espoused standards of ethical practices (e.g. the Hippocratic Oath and the ACPA standards in Chapter 5). However, the instrumental and closed-strategic values-in-action that dominate in many organizations can inhibit this type of moral practice. Therefore, professionals, including the central officials who monitor and control action, must pay attention to the moral aspects of practice. If organizations are to realize their missions and professionals within their organizations are to have the opportunity to act in consonant with the moral and ethical codes of their professions, then a higher standard is needed. The sad reality is that the organizational theories and practices of graduate programs essentially leave out moral reasoning, treating it as ancillary material for ethics courses. Consequently, administrators learn that overlooking the moral aspect, including critical social issues, is normal practice. Using open-strategic methods may create an opening to address these challenges, but a more specific orientation toward justice may be needed.

Aim 3: Promote organizational development that enables professional development and encourages learning. In the cases in this chapter there were two examples of organizational strategies for promoting professional development. One example was evident in the coaching of the principal in Rutherford School. The school community had developed a new vision for the school and the principal provided coaching to enable the teacher to change practice to move toward the vision. In the second example, a team at the Single Campus Community College used an action inquiry process to analyze problems related to retention, codesign a strategy for improving retention through improved orientation, and test pilot the new strategy through an action experiment. In combination, these cases illustrate that inquiry-based methods, including coaching, can improve openness within organizations that maintain strategic orientations.

Aim 4: Improve services provided by professional organizations that promote justice and sustainability. The two examples noted above—the coaching by a principal in a school moving toward a vision and the team of practitioners in a community college testing a new approach to orientation—also illustrate organizational transitions that improved justice for students and their families. I base this claim on the understanding from prior research in K–12 and higher education that more engaged learning (the underlying aim of these two interventions) promotes improvement in educational outcomes including increased rates of high school graduation, improvements in enrollment, and retention rates in college. Interventions in schools and colleges that improve engagement for diverse or underrepresented students should improve equity in educational opportunity. Both of these interventions took steps in the direction of improved educational opportunity.

REFLECTIVE EXERCISE

The rubrics for instrumental, closed-strategic, and open-strategic frames provide distinctively different frameworks for analyzing and reflecting on behavior in organizations. Using these frameworks, assessing their own practices can help beginning and experienced practitioners reflect on and inquire into changes of practice in relation to the recurrent challenges they face.

Text Box 7.4 *Reflective Exercise: Orientation Toward Professional Learning*

A four-step reflective exercise is encouraged. If this exercise is done in class, students should take about 15 minutes to reflect on their own case (Steps 1 and 2). Small groups should have about 20 minutes to discuss each case, with the author holding his or her own interpretation (Step 3) while listening to others.

1. Analyze your own case statement on learning rules of practice in your profession. In sequence, consider which behaviors from the three frames are evident in the dialogue.

2. If you have the opportunity to discuss your case with another person or small group, ask for their feedback using evidence from the dialogue. Your peer or mentor should conduct a review independent of your own. When discussing your case, answer questions but don't engage in the interpretation. Listen.

3. In addition, in small group or pairs review another dialogue using these same frameworks. Ask questions about the incident as needed for clarification. Provide feedback using your analysis of behaviors.

4. Reflect on the feedback in relation to your analysis of the case in relation to the feedback. Reconsider the issues as you think about strategies for moving toward your vision (referring back to your vision statement).

8

CRITICAL SOCIAL CHALLENGES

Most theories of organization and professional action make positivist assumptions about progress, which is an implicit assumption regarding the notions of effectiveness in organization theory[72] and economics. Such theories promote the belief that by following the rules of practice (e.g. the organizational missions, ethical codes, and standards of practice) the world will become a better place. However, if we are open to a post-progressive view of balancing democratic social justice values with a realistic view of the public policy consequences and human action, then these overarching assumptions about the rules of practice and social progress should be subject to critique and doubt. It is possible, at least in some instances, that habitual actions governed by the rules of professionals and legal codes are sources of injustice. This postconventional, post-progressive moral dilemma should not be overlooked by aspiring or experienced professionals.

UNDERSTANDING CRITICAL SOCIAL PROBLEMS

Postconventional moral reasoning focusing on the ways action impedes justice is outside of normal organizational practice, a point illustrated in the cases in prior chapters. It is possible for individuals to take the heroic action of confronting moral problems, but this is often not a viable mode of operation. Openness within communities of practice and a willingness to reflect on habitual action, including strategies consonant with generally accepted moral codes, may be necessary to confront the underlying causes of problems in practice. When organization members are aware of critical social problems in practice, however, they may be constrained by limited personal skills in addressing these challenges (see Text Box 3.1).

Expertise Dimension
Contending with critical social challenges within communities of practice requires organization members who are able to reflect critically and/or spiritually on problematic situations, and a collective capacity to examine empirical and experiential evidence

with respect to such challenges. These qualities and conditions, more unusual than they should be in professional settings, can be fostered with organizational support. Critical analyses, including Marxist analyses, often provide the most penetrating insight into the critical social problems at work. Most frequently, these analyses consider the role of workers, but give less attention to the clients of professionals. Consider the following example from research on universities as organizations.

In *Academic Capitalism and the New Economy: Markets, State, and Higher Education*, Sheila Slaughter and Gary Rhoades (2004) argue that a new model of organization and academic work has emerged as a consequence of university–industry partnerships. They argue that the notion of public good in scientific knowledge production has been replaced by organizational forms that interlink academic departments and corporations. Their underlying theory shifts from an argument about revenue substitution, a notion embedded in resource dependency theory, to a postmodern critique of the emergence of capitalist behaviors within universities in response to the new economy. This decision to situate their theory of academic capitalism (especially their review of public policy) as building on postmodern critiques by Foucault (1980), rather than on critical or economic theory, explains both the illuminating nature of this critique and the authors' failure to explain the causes of some of the inequalities they ponder. The strength of this volume is the discussion of the impact of academic capitalism on academic work.

Slaughter and Rhoades's (2004) treatment of patents and the new organizational partnerships that have been created to facilitate marketing is not particularly new. The topic was covered in the earlier book on academic capitalism as well as by others who treat it as a revenue problem (Bok, 2003; Powers, 2006; Priest, Becker, Hossler, & St. John, 2002). What emerges from this literature is that while there has been a change in patent behavior, the revenue from this behavior remains limited (Bok, 2003; Powers, 2006). What is new in the Slaughter and Rhoades book is the claim that there has been a loss to the public good as a consequence of the behavior. They argue that new organizational arrangements interact with the timing of publications in ways that erode the general public's ability to benefit from scientific discoveries. These arrangements concentrate the ability to profit in the hands of the corporations that invest in the research; the authors pay relatively little attention to the massive federal investment in health sciences.

One original and compelling aspect of Slaughter and Rhoades's analysis is their insight into the intrusion of universities into copyright on academic work. They carefully examine how the development of e-learning has been paralleled by universities claiming ownership and co-ownership of academic materials. Their thoughtful analysis of labor contracts and other documentary forms of legal constraints on copyright provides a compelling portrayal of changes in faculty rights. This is a fascinating look at the role of academic work and the rights of faculty to their intellectual contributions. It reinforces the image of faculty as managed professionals (Rhoades, 1998). This topic certainly merits the attention of faculty members engaged in union negotiations as well as faculty engaged in governance and budgetary affairs within their universities.

From a critical social perspective on universities, the most disappointing part of Slaughter and Rhoades's analyses is their discussion of federal student financial aid. While they note the shift from grants to loans in the 1980s, they rest their critique on the idea that the new policy shifted from giving money to colleges, as was the case in the early campus-based aid programs, to the practice of funding students. They fail to consider how the initial implementation of the Pell Grant program, which gives grants directly to students, helped equalize enrollment rates for whites and minorities in the mid- and late 1970s (see Chapter 3). The decline in the purchasing power of Pell Grants after 1978 contributed to the growing inequalities. Loans enabled a larger percentage of high school graduates to enroll in spite of rising prices, expanding opportunity for middle-income students and widening the enrollment gap. In sum, Slaughter and Rhoades provide insight into the ways contemporary organizations infringe on the rights of professionals, but overlook the vast inequalities among students created by these new policies.

Certainly workers' rights is an issue that should concern professionals. However, in my view there is a greater risk of harming clients (e.g. students in colleges, patients in hospitals, and clients of lawyers and insurance agents) if we focus on the rights and incomes of professionals without considering the rights of those we are supposed to serve. Building understanding of the ways professional actions can influence equality and inequality is critical to the quality and future of human life on the planet. While this statement may seem dramatic, to understand the problem one only need consider the perspectives of people who cannot afford to pay for college, are denied access to necessary care, or are mistreated or killed because of their race or faith tradition.

The links between the political and organizational constraints placed on professionals through strategic and managerial means, and their perceived freedom to address critical social issues as part of their professional practice, should not be overlooked. These complexities were evident in prior chapters, especially in the discussion of cases in Chapter 7. While the discussions below shift the focus to the moral aspect necessary for facing critical social challenges of communicative action and social justice, I return to practical issues in the second half of this chapter.

Moral Dimension

Even in communities of practice in which communicative framing of action is evident, there are times during which ideology constrains postconventional moral discourse on critical social problems. For example, in a period during which universities are forced to defend affirmative action, they may not be as open to considering alternative ways of measuring merit in admissions because of habitual patterns (e.g. use of merit tests without considering school contexts) and perceived constraints (e.g. national rankings based on test scores). In communicative environments, the problems may be known, but clashes may persist and goals may not be realized.

Postconventional moral reasoning about critical social issues involves serious consideration of both equal rights and human capabilities. While true equality of opportunity may be impossible to realize, there are certain basic opportunities that should not be denied under any conditions. The history of humankind, unfortunately, is a history of inequality, injustice, and contradictions between espoused values and action. The text of the U.S. Constitution emphasizes the God-given rights of all people at a time when the new nation allowed slavery. The Christian crusaders had a faith which emphasized social justice, yet they made claims of religious rights over a region that was the home of the Jewish and Islamic traditions.[73] Over the centuries, Great Britain developed a set of tenets about human rights that were not extended to colonial subjects—at least not without protest (e.g. the American Revolution).

Issues related to human rights are complicated because, within most systems of justice, legal authority rests with those in control of the system. The power to write and enforce laws—including legal constraints on citizenship and the right to vote—is often used to constrain human rights and deny opportunity. Global citizens and their legal representatives have the opportunity to argue their case in conventional legal systems whether or not their claims are true in a moral sense. In fact, legal systems in the US and other nations have been—and still are—used to deny rights to education and other services. The idea of a basic capabilities standard (Nussbaum, 1999, 2000, 2004) provides a lens for understanding when the denial of rights within a legal, religious, or political system is intolerable. Professionals of all types share responsibility for ensuring human rights are a basic standard of their profession.

My argument is that when there are critical social issues of inequality within the conventional system, professionals have the responsibility to act in ways that ensure a human capabilities standard is realized.[74] It is important to discern those capabilities (e.g. basic human rights to health care, education, etc.) that indeed should be inalienable. If they are the rights of all, then professionals, as privileged members of society, share an obligation to ensure these rights—a condition of service often recognized in ethical codes (see Chapter 5). Taking this position toward human capabilities can also help illuminate both the nature of injustice and avenues for action.

When we have visibility into injustices that create conditions which deny access to education, health care, and other services, what are our obligations to act? This is a complex question. As noted in prior chapters, the norms of professional action often reinforce the status quo and the convention of organizations. Acting in ways that initiate change in convention requires some risk, especially when it confronts the will of leaders or the codes of an unjust legal system. Two historical examples can illustrate the issue of human rights as a postconventional moral problem.

Mahatma Gandhi

Mahatma Gandhi is, of course, well known as the originator of nonviolence (see Chapter 2). His revolutionary actions in South Africa and India were a major source of inspiration for Dr. Martin Luther King and other civil rights leaders in the US during the 1950s and 1960s. With reference to his vision, it is important to consider Gandhi's background, his sources of inspiration, and how he reframed justice within a system that perpetuated racial injustice.

Assassinated in his native India in 1948, after nationhood, Gandhi was born in 1869, received his legal education in England, and started his career in South Africa. His protests for the rights of people of color began in 1893 in South Africa, when, after purchasing a first-class train ticket, he was denied his accommodation. After protesting, he was taken off the train. Reflecting on the incident, he realized an injustice had occurred, and he began a gradual process of learning nonviolent methods of protest. After mass protests and after Gandhi served time in prison, South Africa passed laws protecting the rights of Indians. Soon thereafter, Gandhi and his family left for India and began decades of reflection and nonviolent protests that transformed a nation.

Gandhi's introspection of faith was the inspiration for his conception of nonviolence. In his autobiography (2002), he wrote of his work as experiments that were open for the world to see: "I have believed all along that what is possible for one is possible for all, my experiments have not been conducted in the closet, but in the open, and I do not think this detracts from their spiritual value" (p. 51). The source of this inspiration began with introspection on and study of both Hindu and Christian texts while a student in England: "My young mind tried to unify the teaching of the Gita and the Sermon on the Mount" (p. 54). In particular, it is noteworthy that he derived the notion of nonviolent protest of "evil" from the Sermon on the Mount, the part of the New Testament he found most inspirational. Upon being taken off the train in South Africa, he writes,

> I began to reflect on my duty. Should I fight for my rights or go back to India, or should I go on Pretoria without minding the insults, and return to India after the case [he had gone there as a young professional]? It would be cowardice to run back to India without fulfilling my obligation. The hardship to which I had been subjected was superficial—only a symptom of a deeper disease of color prejudice. I should try, if possible, to root out the disease and suffer hardships in the process. Redress to wrongs I should seek only to the extent that would be necessary for removal of the color prejudice. So I decided to take the next available train to Pretoria (Gandhi, 2002, p. 55).

This postconventional moral reasoning shows deep reflection on responsibility and the issue of human rights. Having achieved this new vision of the possible in South Africa, Gandhi returned to India in 1915 as a middle-aged man. By 1920, Gandhi had persuaded the Indian National Congress to follow his strategy of "satyagraha to achieve freedom" (Dear, 2006, p. 25). He called for national nonviolent protests, which grew through 1921, but called off the protests after the deaths of police offers. This action was difficult for his followers, who felt they would lose momentum by delaying protests.

For Gandhi, the issue was always seeking truth in action. In one of the early incidents, before the national strike, he was put on trial for his protest. However, in his postconventional moral logic, it was the government that was on trial: "According to the law, I was put on trial, but truly speaking, the government was to be on trial. The Commissioner only succeeded in trapping the government in the net which had been spread for me" (Gandhi, 2002, p. 63).

For Gandhi, in both cases, the answer was to take true and just action. His reframing of justice also included a reconstruction of both religion and politics as they relate to seeking truth:

> To see the universal and all-pervading Spirit of Truth face to face one must be able to love the meanest of creation as oneself. A person who aspires to that cannot keep out of the field of life. That is why my devotion to Truth has drawn me into the field of politics; and I can say without the slightest hesitation, and yet in all humility, that those who say that religion has nothing to do with politics do not know what religion means (Gandhi, 2002, p. 67).

For Gandhi, postconventional moral reasoning was action based on pursuit of the truth, using a definition of truth that assumed justice for all. This set a high standard that he used to judge his own actions, as well as the actions of both his allies and his adversaries. He approached both adversaries and allies with respect and love. This is a standard of justice that merits our aspiration but is difficult to realize in action.

Earl Warren

The 1954 decision in *Brown v. The Board of Education* represents a landmark departure from the history of racism in American education. It remains an important reference point for postconventional moral reasoning, especially if we view this decision within the life history of Earl Warren, the Supreme Court Justice who crafted the decision. The case actually combined five cases from Kansas, Delaware, South Carolina, Virginia, and the District of Columbia that had been argued in the years preceding Warren's appointment in 1953. Warren engaged in a process of reframing the problem that is best understood in the context of decisions of the period.[75]

At the time of the decision, the NAACP had a history of litigating cases of race discrimination in education. The Court's decisions had been situated in the reinterpretation of the concept of "separate but equal" legitimized by *Plessy v. Ferguson*. While the Fourteenth Amendment had promised full rights of citizenship and equal protection to former slaves, there was a series of Supreme Court decisions in the late nineteenth century allowing segregation, culminating with *Plessy* in 1896: "As the century drew to a close, the Court read into the amendment segregation itself, a finding it explicated in one of the most intellectually dishonest rulings in history, *Plessy v. Ferguson*" (Newton, 2006, p. 293). The court decided equal treatment could be maintained without commingling the races, legalizing segregation. A form of judicial activism, this decision overturned the intent of the Fourteenth Amendment. Thus, decisions on school desegregation were being interpreted by the court through a narrow view of the Fourteenth Amendment curtailed by *Plessy*. The former Supreme Court Justice, Fred Vinson, and the majority of the Court agreed with this interpretation, treating *Plessy* as law. They used conventional moral reasoning to uphold injustices and violate the Fourteenth Amendment and the Bill of Rights.

Born in California in 1891, Earl Warren was raised in Bakersfield, educated at University of California-Berkeley, and joined the District Attorney's office in Alameda County upon graduation. Elected California attorney general in 1939 and governor in 1942, an office he held until 1953 when he became chief justice, Warren was influenced by Republican progressiveness in California during the early twentieth century, a period when the governor, Johnson, imposed controls on railroads and ushered in a period of reform and progress in the state. As attorney general of California, Warren played a central role in the internment of the Japanese during World War II. As governor and a presidential candidate in the post-World War II period, he took strong stances against communism, as was expected of politicians during the period. On the other hand, Warren voted against the Loyalty Oath as a member of the Board of Regents for the University of California and signed a bill dismantling separate schooling for Mexican-Americans. President Eisenhower lobbied Warren, encouraging him to favor this legal precedent, a tactic that contradicted Department of Justice which argued for segregation (Newton, 2006). As a centrist progressive, Warren had been supportive of education, but based on his background there only two decisions—his vote on the Loyalty Oath and the prior decision on desegregation for Mexican-Americans—that suggested he would break with then conventional legal reasoning about segregation.

The central issue in Warren's reframing of the case was the implicit belief in the racial superiority of whites necessary to uphold *Plessy*. His biographer describes his reasoning as follows:

Warren simply stated what others knew but would not say: Segregation was not equally good for blacks and whites. It was created by whites and imposed on blacks, intended to protect whites from blacks and thus to extend their power over blacks. Given that, Warren said, he had come to believe that for the Court to endorse school segregation, it would have to embrace the notion of racial superiority. That, Warren added, he would not do (Newton, 2006, p. 311).

This was postconventional reasoning for the time, breaking with the precedent of treating *Plessy* as law by questioning the underlying moral logic. With Chief Justice Vinson's death, Warren was appointed chief justice and voted as part of the five justice majority in favor of desegregation. He set about meeting with justices and crafting an implementation strategy. Elements of his reasoning in the case were quoted by Newton (2006) from handwritten notes on a legal pad. The series of notes follows:

Warren . . . relied most heavily on the presentation of the government: "It [the government] concluded that the Legislative history and the contemporary statements of . . . the Amendment as applied to the case were . . . inconclusive . . . This is not surprising . . . because neither the Constitution itself nor any of its amendments have been adopted under circumstances comparable to those in 1868 surrounding the adoption of the Fourteenth Amendment" (Newton, 2006, citation of Warren in quotes, p. 317).

Warren accused the 1896 Court of "attempting to serve two masters: 1, the master of equality under the law and 2, the master of the racial concept that existed in the Southern states of the union . . . It endeavored to retain both the philosophy of the Dred Scott case and the principle of the Fourteenth Amendment . . ." (Newton, 2006, citation of Warren in quotes p. 317).

No child can reasonably be expected to succeed in life today if deprived on the opportunity of an education (Warren cited in Newton, 2006, p. 318).

Does the segregation [and here Warren added three words, emphasis added] *of school children* solely on the basis of color, even though physical facilities may be equal, deprive the minority group of equal opportunities in the educational system? We believe it does (Warren cited in Newton, 2006, p. 318).

These four notes established a new legal principle in four steps: (1) it accepted the government argument based on the Fourteenth Amendment; (2) it argued that the 1886 Court had been misguided and prejudiced based on the ideological bias of the day; (3) it stated a standard of human capabilities being linked to education; and (4) it indicated that minority children were denied this basic standard as a result of "separate but equal." In its historical context, this was a profound restatement of the case that extended substantially beyond conventional legal reasoning at the time.

These two examples of postconventional moral reasoning illustrate frames of action that are just and caring, that radically alter conventional assumptions, and that set high standards for action. For Gandhi, the belief in the pursuit of truth through nonviolent action was centered in faith, while for Warren it was centered in progressive reasoning about social systems. The reasoning of both of these moral lawyers changed the conventions in their nations.

Frames of Mind

The diversity of methods of framing action and patterns of moral reasoning complicate efforts to change organizations. Having mature practitioners within the organization who are willing to voice problems and mentor colleagues is crucial, as is the capacity to support changes in response to critical challenges. The distinctions between different types of moral reasoning as frames of communication action are depicted in Table 8.1. The potential for communicative action aimed at building common understanding can be illustrated through the legal process, but is also possible in everyday action of professionals of all types. The Supreme Court's ruling in *Plessy v. Ferguson* illustrates a form of preconventional moral reasoning reached through discourse aimed at building understanding. It is possible to make appeals regarding human rights, as Gandhi did in the case cited and as Warren did in *Brown v. Education*. In contrast, conventional moral reasoning involves working within a consensus that may or may not be moral. Consider the decisions of the Supreme Court leading up to *Brown v. Board of Education*. Since the Supreme Court and lower courts across the land used *Plessy* as a legal standard in cases on segregation, discrimination could be maintained through enforcement of the law. The case of separate rail cars for people of color in South Africa, the event that triggered Gandhi's deep critical spiritual reflection on his responsibility as a professional, did not differ fundamentally from the *Brown* case decades later. In both cases, race was the basis of segregation.

The behaviors depicted in Table 8.1 are consonant with the discussed cases of Gandhi and Warren. My argument is that this same behavioral artifact of decision framing may also be evident in everyday human action, and that all professionals share a moral obligation to reflect on their own actions. In both Gandhi and Warren's cases, their reasoning and action was open to the public. Gandhi considered his actions as open experiments, using moral action and nonviolence to build a nation. In contrast, as the swing vote on the Supreme Court, Chief Justice Warren had the opportunity to reshape the legal standards of a nation, using postconventional moral reasoning to take a step beyond the legal arguments of plaintiffs, defendants, and the government. These same forms of open public reasoning can be created and used within an organizational context and other types of open, public discursive space.

CREATING DISCURSIVE SPACE

Creating discursive space for the discussion of critical social issues is necessary if practitioners are to build a practical and actionable understanding of morally problematic issues. Individual practitioners may face choices in case-specific situations, but dealing with critical problems that contradict the policies of organizations and the laws of society can place these professionals at risk. When individual practitioners work around critical problems (e.g. providing pain relief for patients who choose to end treatment), they are at risk professionally (if they break organizational rules and laws to provide the service). Creating discursive space to address the challenge provides room to envision methods of working through problems and changing systems, as illustrated by the case of the Single Campus Community College (see Chapter 7).

On her daily program on National Public Radio (NPR), Diane Rehm addresses complex social and moral issues with a range of practitioners. The case examined in two parts below uses excerpts from one of her shows. The show on October 18, 2005 focused

Table 8.1 Communicative Behaviors in Relation to Frame of Action and Types of Moral Reasoning

Levels of Moral Reasoning/ *Frames of Action*	Preconventional	Conventional	Postconventional
Communicative Frames Focus	Reaches false consensus within professional groups; uses beliefs to construct rationales that reinforce problems in practice; fails to consider diverse voices and dissent.	Focuses on action consistent with ethical standards; considers ambiguities between ethical codes and organizational strategies; may emphasize resolving moral ambiguities.	Openly reconstructs rules (i.e. practices and methods) to address moral challenges; focuses on including diverse views and evidence of effects of action; is willing to reconstruct theories of action.
Identifying morally problematic practices (for organizations or clients)	• Openly constructs agendas within communities of practice/advocacy groups • Engages in power tactics to promote agendas (prone to power abuse)	• Openly discusses problems in practice • Takes responsibility for actions • Collaborates on design of alternative practices	• Reflects openly on patterns of action causing inequality and injustice • Acts with justice and care with colleagues and clients
Designing solutions that encourage staff development and improve justice (within organization)	• Promotes external client rationales for collective action • Enables clients to overlook social and environmental consequences	• Reflects only on codes of ethics in relation to practice • Leads by example within communities of practice to encourage quality performance and ethical action	• Enacts practices to support development of communities of practice • Mentors colleagues and clients to ponder critical issues and act with justice and care

on Supreme Court consideration of Oregon's law on physician-assisted suicide, which was opposed by the federal government as a policy that could set a precedent for other states. At the time of the show, more than 200 terminally ill people had ended their lives with a doctor's help under the terms of Oregon's Death with Dignity law, implemented in 1998.

Specifically, most of the conversation focused on the prescription of Schedule 2 drugs, which are tightly regulated under federal law. A physician and pharmacist in Oregon were being challenged in a federal case, a situation created by the incongruence between federal and state law. While most of the show focused on the Oregon law, the excerpts discussed below consider a call from a New York physician who had faced legal challenges for his practice and a subsequent discussion of this case based on a call to the program.

Physician-Assisted Suicide

As part of the show on the Oregon case, Diane Rehm talked with Tim Quill, a Professor of Medicine Psychiatry and Medical Humanities at the University of Rochester Medical Center (see Text Box 8.1). She started with a question to the guest about how he was involved with the issue (DR1). Quill responded by describing a generic situation of a "tough conversation" with a patient about options regarding ending physician support (TQ1). Rehm asked whether this differed from the legal case, which related to providing Schedule 2 medications (DR1). Quill described a specific case in which he did prescribe a Schedule 2 drug, and later he wrote about in an article (TQ2). As a followup, Rehm asked if there was a legal consequence of taking this step (DR3). Quill responded that the case was investigated (TQ3), and he faced questions from the New York Grand Jury and the Medical Review Board. The conclusion of the review was that he had exemplified good medical practice and it led to further discussion in the State of New York. In response to the next question (DR4), Quill explained that nothing had changed in the state (TQ4), speculating that thousands of families have "underground" conversations with physicians about assisted suicide. This raised a complex issue about the moral reasoning of individual practitioners at risk of legal prosecution if they cross a boundary with the prescription of drugs.

Text Box 8.1 Tim Quill (TQ) Conversation with Diane Rehm (DR)

DR1:   And joining us now is Dr. Tim Quill (TQ). He's Professor of Medicine Psychiatry and Medical Humanities at the University of Rochester Medical Center. He's director of the Center for Palliative Care and Clinical Ethics at the University of Rochester. Please explain about how you got involved in speaking out on this issue.

TQ1:   Well, I had cared for a wide range of patients in hospice and in palliative care throughout my career. I had encountered many patients in fact who reached a point where they were ready to die and had entertained serious discussions with them. The easiest example to think of this is in a patient that's on life-sustaining therapy, say dialysis. People sometimes go on these therapies with the goal of living longer which they do, but then their condition changes and they decide that they want to stop such therapies.

And we agree by law and by medical ethics that people have a right to stop these treatments. So you have a tough conversation with them about whether it's the right timing, whether there's suffering that can be relieved. But ultimately you listen to the patient and you stop treatment if that's what they really decide they need to do.

DR2: But isn't stopping treatment very different from applying one of these Schedule 2 drugs?

TQ2: It's different from the point of view of public policy and ethics, perhaps, but from the patient's perspective and from the clinical analysis perspective it's very similar. Now I then encountered a patient in 1990 who didn't have a life support to stop, similarly situated, and that put me in a position where I had to try to that patient. And I did respond ultimately after meeting with her family, getting second opinions, by providing Schedule 2 medications that she could take at a time of her choosing. She subsequently went on to live for three months in a hospice program and only took her life when her suffering for her became unacceptable. Now there would have been nothing unusual about this case as long as I didn't talk about it, didn't document anything. That's what happens outside of Oregon. But I chose to write about the case and that put me in the middle of this discussion in the public arena.

DR3: What were the legal consequences of writing that article?

TQ3: Well the long and short of it is that after several months of exploration about whether I made up the story or not it was discovered that she had died as I said. And I had to testify before a Grand Jury which chose not to prosecute. And then I had to be evaluated by a professional review board which also said that what I had written about exemplified good medical care, but one of them asks New York State to take a look at this whole question.

DR4: So did this at all change the way you continued the way you practice medicine?

TQ4: I don't think it's changed anything. You know, it's interesting, I've become, because I've written out about this, a secure person for patients to talk to, to get a second opinion when they're thinking about these things. In Oregon under the Death with Dignity Act, this really accounts for about 1 in 1,000 deaths. But 1 in 50 patients in Oregon talk to their doctors about this and 1 in 6 talk to their families about it. In the rest of the country, the whole conversation is much more underground. And in fact the conversation usually leads to better ways to address suffering. People want to know that there could be this kind of escape, but very few patients actually need to use it.

DR5: How do you think it would affect both the doctors and the patients you know if the Supreme Court finds in favor of the Department of Justice?

TQ5: At the most superficial level, it would take Oregon, which is I think a leader in end of life care in so many ways. Not only do you have this choice but you have a high number of deaths at home where people want to die, you have high levels of hospice referral, you have excellent pain prescribing practices compared to the rest of the country, and I think it will put them back with the rest of the country. But even more worrisome to me is the impact in Oregon and the rest of the country of getting the DEA involved in end of life decision making. This is very serious business. It's nuanced. We use a lot of very large doses of medication to prevent suffering, to help people live a little bit longer. And the DEA, these agents who are used to going after criminals, are suddenly going to be going after caring doctors who are trying to take care of the sickest patients and potentially second guessing their prescribing practices, analyzing them. They have no experience doing this. And I do think the chilling effect is very real and very worrisome.

DR6:   So you're saying that a doctor's application of morphine, for example, to a patient who's experiencing a great deal of pain and increasing that dosage to help the patient help the pain go away could, in fact, draw the attention of the DEA.

TQ6:   Oh, it sure could. And let's say some of the time we have to use very large doses and accelerate them at the end because pain picks up at the end, you want doctors to feel secure enough to do this. And let's even say that a patient might at this very tender stage express some statement like, "Gee, I'm ready. I think I'm ready to meet my Maker," those kinds of things. Might that then be interpreted as some statement toward death? And might the doctor then be second guessed as trying to facilitate that death. These kinds of scenarios are not very far fetched because we have these very serious conversations all the time in palliative care.

Source: WAMU 88.5. *The Diane Rehm Show.* October 18, 2005.

The conversation then turned specifically to the Drug Enforcement Agency's (DEA) efforts to persecute "caring" physicians and medical practitioners who attempt to assist families through these life and death transitions with pain easing medication (TQ5), the core issue in Oregon and other states. The DEA imposes federal law in these cases regardless of state laws. Quill questioned this priority for the DEA on moral grounds. However, the question is complex, as the discussion of the evolution of the Hippocratic Oath (see Chapter 5) illustrated. As ethical codes of practice change—over millennia in the case of the Hippocratic Oath—there are shifts in reasoning. Further, as the Oregon case illustrates, it is possible that legal systems can be out of sync with professional codes.

Quill's story about the investigation of his actions as a physician indicates that practitioners can find a legal path through these complex moral issues with reflection and action. Open conversation about these cases seems a critical component of medical education and professional development for practicing professionals. Quill's actions illustrate the work through process, a set of ethical actions that can be achieved by individuals within the current conventional conception of the law regarding Schedule 2 drugs. If we assume that the law is correct—an assumption I am not questioning here and that I lack the expertise to judge—then it is important to understand that there are ways through this complex puzzle. It is possible that there will eventually be better defined case law, reducing the risk to caring practitioners. Until that time, medical practitioners who seek to reduce suffering are likely to be confronted by legal challenges.

Lawyers Discuss Ethics of Assisted Suicide

The legal aspect of the contemporary challenge to caring medical practitioners is illustrated by a subsequent exchange between Rehm and the lawyers on the program, sparked by a question from a caller (Mike). This exchange (see Text Box 8.2) illustrates that this complex, postconventional moral issue is framed within the legal discourses among lawyers representing different interests in the Oregon case. Joining Rehm were Walter Weber (WW), the senior litigation council for the American Center for Law and Justice arguing the government's case before the Supreme Court and Eli Stutsman (ES), an attorney representing a doctor and a pharmacist who would be vulnerable to prosecution if the law was struck down. Stutsman was also one of the drafters of Oregon's Death with Dignity Law.

Text Box 8.2 Dialogue Among Diane Rehm, a Caller, and Two Lawyers

Participants: Diane Rhem (DR), a caller (Mike), Walter Weber (WW), senior litigation council for the American Center for Law and Justice, and Eli Stutsmen (ES), attorney representing a doctor and a pharmacist who would be vulnerable to prosecution if the law was passed.

Mike: Well, the second question is, I just wonder how doctors get around the Hippocratic Oath which was do no harm. I think it's going to be terrible if elderly patients or the infirm really can't trust their doctor because of all sorts of fiduciary reasons or whatever. We're really allowing, if this goes on, to open up the gates to get rid of the people who can protest the least.

ES1:   With respect to the slippery slope, that's an argument that opponents of the Oregon law raise often, and I think it's a very telling argument. The slippery slope argument doesn't challenge what's happening today but it speculates about what might happen in the years to come and then it criticizes that activity. Well, that activity is not happening in Oregon. And, in fact, those of us who are responsible for the drafting of the Oregon law oppose euthanasia the way it's practiced in the Netherlands and the way it's practiced generally. We oppose the antics of Jack Kevorkian even though he has widespread support in this country. And we drafted a narrow law that prohibits that type of conduct. And anybody that engages in that type of conduct will face criminal sanctions here in Oregon and, unlike the case in Michigan where they tried repeatedly to prosecute and convict Jack Kevorkian, we would do it the first time because this is a narrow law. We supported a narrow law and we expressly prohibit the kind of conduct the caller is expressing might happen in the future.

DR2.1: What about the issue of doctors and the trust between doctors and patients. Do you think that the Oregon law might cause that trust to deteriorate?

ES2: In fact it works in just the opposite fashion. As you heard Dr. Quill explain this is a medical issue that is vibrant across the country, and patients and families want to talk about it. This is like any other end of life issue, advanced directives, whether to treat, whether not to treat, whether to hasten death, can I do it, how do you do it. It's happening everywhere. In Oregon it happens lawfully under narrow circumstances. 30,000 people die annually in Oregon; less than 30 use the law to provide some perspective. And none of the claimed abuses and fears are happening here in Oregon.

WW1: I think in the Oregon program they're trying to put their best foot forward. My view is it's a foot in the door, but not just that it was going to lead to problems but that in itself it's a problem. What you need to keep in mind is that when you go to a doctor, I mean I guess there are some patients who are so cantankerous they don't care what the doctor says, but most people are going to weigh very heavily when a doctor says, "You know, you can do this." and take that as a signal that it's therefore okay for them to do.

DR2.2: Well, now, I'd like to get a response to that. ES, is this something that doctors suggest or is it that it comes first from the patient?

ES3: It always comes first from the patient. Patients raise this question all the time across the country. It happens secretly in 49 states. It can happen openly in Oregon. But these are kitchen conversations throughout America and it's driven by the fact that all the evidence, all the public opinion research demonstrates this is something that they want to be able to talk about, they want to be able to talk to their physicians and other health care providers about. It's true in every state in this country that there's a large majority that feels there should be open discussions and it shouldn't be secret or criminal to have such a conversation.

Source: WAMU 88.5. *The Diane Rehm Show.* October 18, 2005.

Mike questioned how physicians get around the Hippocratic Oath, assuming the oath precluded the use of drugs in this action (an assumption consistent with the classical version of the oath). Stutsman responded by drawing the distinction between euthanasia and pain relief, noting differences between the Oregon law and laws in the Netherlands, where physicians have greater discretion (ES1). He invoked the image of "convict Jack Kevorkian" as an illustration of the moral and legal boundaries in this country.

At this point, Rehm (DR2.1) raised a question about the trust between physicians and patients. The exchange that followed illustrates the discursive process between lawyers on a conventional legal question. Stutsman responded by arguing trust increased after the law was enacted, evidenced by the small percentage of patients who actually use the law (ES2). Weber, the lawyer representing the government, pointed to the potential for distrust and abuse (WW1).

Rehm's final question focused on the core issue of whether the request for Schedule 2 drugs, and ultimately death, must come from the patient or can be initiated by the doctor (DR2.2). Stutsman responded by refocusing on the role of openness, comparing Oregon to the other 49 states. Openness creates freedom for patients to make choices as well as opportunities for physicians to learn about legal and moral pathways through these dilemmas. This conversation placed the issue in the context of family choices, which is an appropriate orientation. However, in a practical sense this issue is complicated by questions related to health care costs. Within the current health care system, it is possible to sustain life at a high cost to families, insurers, and the government.

Reflections

Voicing critical social concerns is a complex process, even within organizations that appear committed to social justice as part of their mission statement and codes of practice. The discursive space created by Diane Rehm illustrates that it is possible to have an exchange on topics usually treated as "underground" conversations. The Quill case illustrates that even in states that do not have legislation protecting the physicians who engage in open discussion with families, it is possible to act in caring ways toward families and patients facing death. There are many instances in which practitioners face choices about action that is moral and just but potentially beyond the boundaries of conventional practice. In most cases, these critical social problems are not about legal boundaries, but relate to the strategies of organizations. If it is possible to create discursive space in settings where there are legal boundaries that discourage openness, then it should also be possible to raise these questions in settings where organizational control, rather than legal boundaries, are the issue.

CASE STUDY OF ORGANIZATIONAL CHANGE

As the cases in prior chapters illustrated, the strategic initiatives of the campuses largely circumscribed choice on projects by campuses involved in the Indiana Project on Academic Success (IPAS). The most notable exception to this pattern was the emergence of a regional collaboration (see Text Box 8.3) among two four-year campuses and a regional community college. Through the process of reviewing research results on persistence, administrators and faculty members at the three campuses realized they shared a clientele of working students. The regional four-year campuses had high drop-out rates for new students, and the community college was in a position to compete for these students. However, rather than adopt a competitive frame, participants from the three campuses took a step back to build an understanding of their shared challenges.

Text Box 8.3 Regional Collaboration on Working Students

The three regional institutions—Regional Community College (RCC), Regional Comprehensive University (RCU), and Regional Technical University (RTU)— initiated a collaborative project as part of their involvement in the Indiana Project on Academic Success (IPAS). The campus-level persistence studies conducted as part of the IPAS assessment process had clearly shown that most of the new students entering the two public universities departed before the end of their second year. Yet the two campuses had success at graduating older students who had entered their colleges as juniors or seniors. Neither of the four-year campuses exhibited particular concern about this finding, at least initially, perhaps because they had a captive clientele in the city, and fairly stable enrollment and revenue generation as a consequence. Upon discussion, however, the administrators realized that the emergence of the new community college system put this traditional pattern at risk. The RCC could enroll many of the first-time students in the region, reducing first-year enrollment; the RCC could, on the other hand, generate more transfers. Being involved in the same training sessions where persistence studies were reviewed provided them the opportunity to reflect together on shared problems. The decision to focus on working students as a central aim of their collaboration represented an attempt to address a morally problematic issue outside the strategic initiatives underway at the three campuses.

A workgroup of administrators and faculty members from the three public campuses was formed to address the challenges facing working students. As part of their inquiry process, the team reviewed all of the research provided by IPAS, requested supplemental studies and reviews, and conducted a regional conference on working students. Through this process a range of issues emerged, from economic development to student aid. A member of the team described how the shared understanding of the critical importance of working students evolved:

> One of the strategic goals at this campus is to be involved in and support economic development in (the region) and another significant value of this campus is experiential learning involving students in real life experiences through internships, through all sorts of relationships with employers locally. So it wasn't hard to have those kinds of conversations led by IPAS folks and then evolve that into, well, let's find out about our working students.

An early symbol of the collaboration, the regional conferences focused on working students and student aid. In a focus group interview with individuals from the three institutions, a member of the cross-campus team described the conference:

> These chancellors [on the three campuses] wanted to do some sort of project, so decided to do it on financial aid . . . What [IPAS person] did was get [a well know person] here as a keynote speaker. That was a big deal. It was a great, standard, big picture lecture on the whole Midwest region . . . Then there were contributions from each of the three campuses in various offices—financial aid, career services—so anyway, we made a presentation about our project, that was last April.

Another interviewee from RCC observed:

> But it was all in context as [keynote speaker] pointed out that these are rust belt economies and no one has figured out what to do. Ohio, Michigan, Indiana, Buffalo had not figured out what to do and neither have the people

> who live here. So you can be turning out college educated students and there
> are not good jobs out here for them. Sometimes I think they could spend a
> lot of money on college and then never find a job. That is a problem.
>
> These comments illustrate that the collaboration among the three campuses used
> the conference, literature reviews, and other means to build a shared understanding
> of the challenges they faced in the region.
>
> *Source:* Abstracted from St. John, 2009, pp. 196–198.

As they discussed the research findings, the study teams realized they were all serving working students and that incongruities in schedules could make retention across terms difficult. They shared observations that students would run from class to their cars to go to work, then dash back for additional classes. They concluded that they shared the challenge of providing educational programs for working students in the region. The decision to form a collaborative group provided freedom for administrators from the three campuses to reflect on and address the challenge.

Their first step was to arrange a conference in the region about working students and student aid. The keynote speaker for the meeting referenced regional economic conditions related to the transition from smokestack industries to the newer service economy. Students who stayed in the region to work often found they needed more education for advancement. However, working students generally lacked knowledge of, if not access to, student financial aid and support services normally given to traditional students transitioning into college. Following the conference, the teams secured funding from their campuses to initiate a study of student working patterns, along with subsequent funding for a project to address these challenges.

Unlike the IPAS cases discussed in prior chapters, this collaboration took a step beyond the strategic initiatives of their colleges and the competitive boundaries of the three campuses. Collaboration to build understanding of the challenges facing the local student population could lead to a new generation of collaborative strategies, including easier joint registration and joint programs. The team members also hoped to generate collaborative projects with employers in the region.

This case illustrates a form of *postinstitutional* thinking that involves thinking outside of the normal institutional frameworks. As an artifact of creating discursive space within the training process, representatives of the three campuses had the opportunity to think and reflect together on common challenges, a perspective that enabled them to frame a critical social problem: Many of their students did not fit into the traditional student mold. They could step outside of their competitive positions to reflect together on the challenges facing students.

CONCLUSIONS
Organizational Change

While institutional strategies can change relatively quickly—in a matter of years in the cases examined in the prior chapters—adapting organizations and laws to address critical social problems can take decades (see Lesson 4, Table 8.2). The two examples of

Table 8.2 Lessons Learned About Alignment of Strategic Orientations of Organizations with Norms and Practices within Communities of Practice: Communicative Action

Frame	Communicative
Organization	
Strategic Orientation	Encourages new initiatives from within
	Lesson 1: Creating discursive and reflective space for practitioners is necessary to inform new courses of action. Evidence:
	• Medical professor writes an article opening up dialogue about the responses of caring medical practitioners regarding issues of life and death.
	• Administrators and faculty from different campuses find discursive space in workshops to identify new challenges.
System Relation to Lifeworld	Dialectic between system and lifeworld views of experience; change possible
	Lesson 2: The system logic constrains discourse, so practitioners must take extraordinary steps to create discursive space. Examples:
	• Challenges identified by the three campuses are aligned with strategic initiatives, going beyond the generally accepted boundaries for action.
	• Oregon law generates discursive space for families and medical practitioners to openly discuss issues normally treated in "underground" fashion.
Communities of Practice	
Norms within Communities of Practice	Crafts practices to reduce social injustice
	Lesson 3: When practitioners create discursive space, their actions may be a catalyst for organizational change. Evidence:
	• Gandhi and Warren reframe problems in ways that enable change within nations.
	• Collaborating practitioners take steps to introduce new issues at their campuses, potentially creating programs, in order to better serve working students.
Congruent Practice	Interventions that surface critical issues and test alternative practices
	Lesson 4: It takes time to generate change in institutions that addresses critical social problems. Evidence:
	• It took decades for Gandhi to facilitate changes in laws in South African and India.
	• The NAACP took decades to accumulate cases to provide a basis for case law to reframe legal challenges.

moral reflection—Gandhi and Warren—are illustrative of remarkable people using their moral consciousness to reframe crucial social problems. However, as their cases illustrate, having a critical understanding of a challenge does not provide an answer but it does illuminate the problem.

Some reflection on the aftermath of *Brown* may be necessary to illustrate the role of time as well as timing. The timing of Warren's appointment, along with his ability to reflect openly and act politically, enabled the Court to overcome a moral hurdle. However, in spite of this good timing, the problem of racism in education is far from resolved. It gook the federal government more than a decade to undertake initiatives that addressed the underlying problem: the 1965 Elementary Secondary Education Act (ESEA). I was introduced as compensatory education to address the educational inequalities; ESEA followed that by providing student aid that created a period of equalized college enrollment between 1965 and 1978 (St. John, 2003). However, neither of these remedies lasted long enough to address the underlying problem of unequal access inhibiting equal education. The ESEA reform was undermined by the publication of *A Nation at Risk* and subsequent federal efforts to redirect programs from compensating for prior injustice to subsidizing students based on merit, increasing inequality once again.

Problems of equity in higher education were not solved by *Brown*, which did not apply to higher education. In addition, the federal government did not actively promote federal enforcement of *Brown* until after the Supreme Court's *Adams* decisions in the 1970s. By 1978, the Middle Income Student Assistance Act (MISAA) had undermined need-based aid, shifting the focus to middle-income students (St. John & Byce, 1982). Further complicating the issue is workforce change and the rise in the human capabilities standard (i.e. the level of education needed to support a family) to having at least some college education. During the last two decades of the twentieth century, inequalities in college access grew as a consequence of the failure of K–12 reform and the decline of federal investment in student aid (St. John, 2006).

Critical analysis and reflection are essential to build understandings of critical social problems, a pattern not only evident in the examples above regarding South Africa and India, but also evident in the U.S. government's response to both physician discretion in patient care for their terminally-ill patients and the educational needs of students. Normative reasoning creates conventional and common understanding of problems. When critical problems surface it may take decades to respond. Discursive space for practitioners to reflect on real life challenges, along with a critical attitude toward moral challenges, is necessary to identify, reflect on, and address critical social challenges. Professional education should be altered to better prepare students to face critical social challenges as part of practice.

Professional Learning

The review of theory, research, and cases helps illuminate the professional learning process and provides a basis for suggesting strategies for integrating moral reasoning into professional education. With this background of communicative action coupled with critical moral reflection, we can return to the topic of professional learning.

Aim 1: Encourage learning that enables practitioners to achieve their aims as professionals, as well as realize the dreams that motivated their choice of profession. Practitioners learn about moral challenges as a consequence of practice. When personally affronted by being taken off a train in South Africa, Gandhi reflected on his faith and his responsibility, envisioning a strategy that evolved through a lifetime. Earl Warren learned about issues of justice by reflecting on the treatment of the Japanese during World War II and the Loyalty Oath, creating a keen moral predisposition to reflect on the limitations of *Plessy*. Tim Quill reflected on private conversations with patients about matters of life and death and faced a legal challenge. Faculty members and administrators in three colleges reflected on common challenges and found space to rethink strategies, a step that could lead not only to change in the three colleges, but also to increased opportunity for working students.

Thus, if the aim is to prepare aspiring practitioners to face to critical challenges, studying legal and ethical codes is necessary but not sufficient. It is crucial to include foundations—with moral and philosophical content, possibly coupled with case studies—to enable students to reflect on challenges and envision how they might act. In my experience, critical challenges are seldom chosen in advance, but encountered through reflection on the circumstances in which we find ourselves. It is important to provide the space for open critical reflection in graduate education to help students build the skills needed to reflect, collaborate, and act with justice and care.

Aim 2: Enable reflection on assumptions, actions, and outcomes in ways that promote learning about improving practice and developing and refining skills, along with reflection of moral aspects of practice. While the development and implementation of new ethical codes present challenges for practitioners (see Chapters 5 and 6), the process of reframing problems using a postconventional framework is extremely complicated. Critical reflection on moral challenges can lead to professional risk if practitioners leap to action regarding moral issues without reflecting on the systemic issues.

The systemic forces within organizations and society can impede moral action. Laws and policies can be crafted to penalize the just. The just and caring who work through legal problems are easier to find than criminals who hide from the law. Thus, it may be easier for DEA officials to go after moral medical doctors (e.g. Quill in New York or the defendants in the Oregon case) than to uncover serious transgressors. However, the tendency to work around problems, to go "underground" with moral decisions, creates a problem of a different sort. This form of closed action limits reflection on assumptions and is prone to violations of public trust and the social good. The alternative of emphasizing open critical reflection within graduate programs and communities of practice merits consideration in difficult circumstances.

Aim 3: Promote organizational development that enables professional development and encourages learning. IPAS was an attempt to introduce action inquiry as a method of reform. There is evidence the method creates discursive space. Practitioners engaged in the process made choices about how to work within their institutions to move ahead with the process. The overwhelming conclusion was that most action projects were chosen because they were aligned with organizational strategies. This major lesson from the project was that organizational initiatives constrain the ability of practitioners to address critical social problems uncovered by research. Specifically, the assessment research found inequalities of persistence opportunities across racial groups (St. John et al., 2004), but it was difficult for campuses to address these challenges. There were exceptions to this pattern: the initiative of a work group at a Single Campus Community College (Chapter 7), the regional collaborative (above), and efforts in an urban university to organize and support teaching innovations (a case that was not discussed). In these instances, groups of practitioners took action based on their own reflection. They found the space to reflect and act.

Aim 4: Improve services provided by professional organizations that promote justice and sustainability. For most of the challenges discussed in this chapter there was clarity about the problem. The most difficult issue related to physician assistance of death through prescription of drugs. The use of drugs to ease pain is legal and moral, and can be coupled with decisions by patients to stop treatment in terminal cases. Unexpectedly, I took part in my family's decision-making process regarding honoring my father's wishes to decline cancer treatment and go into hospice care. During a visit to his doctor, I was asked to join a conversation about options. It was difficult to deal with my own fear of loss in the context of his wishes for self-respect and the limitations of medical science. Such decisions are complicated because families share a wish for their members to survive.

The other issues addressed in this chapter seem clearer because they deal with questions of freedom, education, and equal opportunity. These issues, for which there should be a general consensus, are no less complex because, while justice remains an espoused value, legal systems can be used by the majority to undermine equal opportunity. With historical hindsight it is difficult to disagree with Earl Warren's reinterpretation of *Plessy*, but at the time most legal opinion attempted to balance the Fourteenth Amendment with this case as common law. For decades the NAACP had litigated to prove that "separate but equal" was too costly (e.g. in the remedy to *Garnes*, the State of Missouri built a "law school" for one qualified African-American student). It took postconventional moral reasoning by a new Chief Justice to speak of the immorality of separation. Even if resources were equal, he argued, education opportunity was not equal, and the equity standard of resources was not being met as the litany of NAACP cases demonstrated.

Providing equal service is not simple because it does not involve distributing equal resources for all. The flaw in the federal education reform strategies since 1983 has been that the movement toward services for all, a middle-class strategy, could only be equitable if the base opportunities provided by state and local agencies were equal, a condition that has never been met. Piling services on top of unequal systems can increase inequality. Need-based programs for health care and education have had the potential to reduce inequality and provide equal treatment for people in similar circumstances, but there is substantial resistance to these strategies. Even critical analysts of the political left can overlook equitable policies based on their beliefs. For example, Slaughter and Leslie (1997) provide a compelling analysis of the problems with the financing of national systems of education. However, their discussion of remedies for the US made arguments for campus-based programs based on beliefs (Leslie & Brinkman, 1988), rather than decades of evidence of the efficacy of portable need-based student aid (National Commission on the Financing of Postsecondary Education, 1973; Manski & Wise, 1983; Curs, Singell, & Waddle, 2006). It is difficult for all of us to overcome our biases, but if we are to engage in critical social discourses to remedy morally problematic situations, we are compelled to do so in the pursuit of just alternatives to injustices within the political and social systems.[76]

REFLECTIVE EXERCISE

I encourage readers to reflect on critical social situations from their own experience. Possible action strategies include the use of action inquiry. Organizational commitment is necessary for action inquiry to provide a workable approach in most professional settings. The assignment is for readers to reflect on their case analyses in relation to their career aims (from the first reflective assignment) and the issues of social justice that are of concern to them (see Text Box 8.4).

Text Box 8.4 Reflective Exercise: Critical Social Issues

Reflect on the following questions:

- What are the most problematic social situations you recall from your experiences in educational, professional, and community life?
- Did you take steps to intervene or were you silent? If you acted, what were the reactions from others in the situation? If you did not act, do you think that an intervention on your part might have changed the situation?
- Are there current circumstances that merit your attention and action? What are they? How might you prepare yourself to engage in addressing critical social problems as a professional in practice?

Readers are encouraged to reflect on these questions individually, writing down reflections as notes. When you have an opportunity in a situation that is safe for such conversation (e.g. with a mentor or a small group of trusted peers), engage in a conversation about these questions.

9

TRANSFORMATIONAL PRACTICE

Advancing caring and justice as part of professional practice represents a challenge rarely undertaken as an integral part of organizational practice. While there are many critical social issues that merit the attention of practitioners across professions, the diversity challenge cuts across all issues. The arguments made on behalf of the University of Michigan in the *Gratz* (2000) and *Grutter* (2003) cases provide compelling rationales for increasing diversity in leadership of the military, industry, and education (Cheng, Altbach, & Lomotey, 2006). Yet the public resistance to the use of race as a criterion for college admission or employment has led to banning affirmative action in California, Washington, and Michigan. The passage of Proposal 2, eliminating affirmative action in Michigan, is particularly ironic, given the Supreme Court's discussions in these cases, which confirmed the need for continued use of affirmative action. These conditions— the compelling need for diversity at a time of public resistance to Constitutional methods to achieve this end—create a paradoxical situation for educators, employers, and professionals of all types. The diversity challenge is related to racial justice, but it also relates to tolerance of differences in faith traditions, socioeconomic status, and sexual orientation. Given the critical nature of these issues, my discussion of transformational practices focuses on action with care and justice, but the underlying issue of transformation probably has broader applicability.

CARE AND JUSTICE IN TRANSFORMATIONAL PRACTICE

An orientation toward transformation of professional practice, at least according to stances taken in this book, involves a commitment to both justice and caring in practice. The rules of systems—the policies, procedures, and strategic initiatives that regulate action—can constrain activities in ways that complicate organizational action that is just and caring. Critical theory as an analysis method provides means of illuminating critical social problems, as discussed in Chapter 8. There is also a tradition within critical theory which involves developing *guides for action*[77] that define steps in a transformational process (Macey, 2000). This process generally includes reflecting on the causes of problems, envisioning a new state of society and alternative forms of action, and taking steps to move toward the new vision. This approach to change is compatible with liberation theology (Guterriez, 1988) and should not be marginalized as antireligious.[78]

A post-progressive vantage is particularly important to understanding the necessity of engaging in transformational strategies in education, health care, and other services. Even if the policy barriers to access were removed through universal access to education and health care, it would still be necessary to intervene in most organizations to enable the type of diverse dialogue essential for just action. Guides can improve action but they do not guarantee the intended change will occur. The chances that meaningful change will not occur are greater if the steps in a change process are followed without critical reflection or organizational support, as was evident in cases examined in previous chapters.

Habermas (1987) argues that communicative action oriented toward building understanding differs from strategic action aimed at specific goals. When a change process is used to build understanding of problems before envisioning new conditions and analyzing strategies, it is possible that an unintended outcome will emerge. The moral aspect involves considering why problems exist in the first place (Habermas, 1990). This is an orientation that, again in theory, enables thought about actions that could increase justice, fairness, and care. However, there is an implicit shift back to strategic action within this type of methodology. The notion that meaningful change can happen and moral problems can be addressed assumes that the new strategy will address the problem. At the very least, evaluative processes that reflect back on the problem are needed to assess whether the new action achieved its intent. Thus openness to new understandings of problems is essential within a process aimed at transforming practice in order to address critical social problems.

Using a guide for action runs the risk of returning to instrumental action. Whether guides are derived from religious codes or more radical concepts of social change, there is a risk that beliefs will constrain openness to building new understanding, either through fundamentalism or ideological action. The AIM examined in this book provides a means of creating pathways to morally conscious action, but does not guarantee such action will occur. Recurrent patterns of practice—the tacit behaviors inherent in professional action and faith traditions—complicate efforts to integrate postconventional moral reasoning into professional practice.

An orientation toward moral learning as an integral part of professional practice is a rare but necessary requisite for creating environments that support just, caring, and actionable transformational change. In the real world of practice, this may be an idealized state for organizations, but ideals are important in action settings. The behaviors associated with transformational action are differentiated by the three forms of moral reasoning illustrated in Table 9.1. The central tasks are redesigning action strategies and integrating justice and caring into practice. My hypotheses about action and moral reasoning are:

- Uncritical advocacy for specific actions (i.e. specified practices or restrictive scripts of action) runs the greatest risk of both pursuing agendas that replicate problems by placing aims over means and becoming a new form of preconventional moral reasoning.

- Facilitation and collaboration on these tasks has the greatest likelihood of maintaining systems consistent with the operant justice and control systems, exhibiting conventional moral reasoning.
- Openness to testing diverse claims in inquiry—a critical-empirical approach—has the greatest chance of addressing critical social problems. This involves testing assumptions that may differ from one's own preferences, exhibiting potential for postconventional moral reasoning.

Advocacy, facilitation, and a critical-empirical approach all provide possible means to pursing transformation, but advocacy runs the greatest moral risk. At the very least, it is important to recognize that a commitment to transformational action does not necessarily guarantee moral action. It is possible to inadvertently transform from action that is just to action that is unjust and creates inequalities, as has been illustrated by the history of educational reform in the late twentieth century (St. John, 2006). In fact, this

Table 9.1 Transformational Behaviors in Relation to Frame of Action and Types of Moral Reasoning

Levels of Moral Reasoning/ *Frames of Action*	Preconventional	Conventional	Postconventional
Transformational frames	Emphasize advocacy of agendas; follow the rules rather than reflecting on critical issues; overlook moral ambiguities; contest opposing views, except to advocate agenda. (Risks looping back to instrumental frame.)	Facilitate change strategies; collaborate on changing agendas of agencies; collectively construct action strategies with allies; consider opposing views in relation to ethical standards; collective dissent/ resistance.	Develop and test action guides to enable communicative discourse on moral challenges; be willing to reconstruct based on testing opposing views; reconstruct action theories based on testing assumptions.
Redesign structures and practices to encourage justice, reduce inequality, and empower others	• Collective assumptions about rightness of action • Believes that the process, openly chosen, will enable all participates to address challenges	• Justice and care are integral to and evident in practice • Generates and uses evidence to reflect on justice and caring practices	• Examines divergent claims about problems • Facilitates building of shared understanding of challenges and alternative actions
Engage in practices that integrate justice and caring	• Values reform agenda over conventional action (extreme example is suicide bombing)	• Encourages principled action • Encourages common practices that address social injustices and environmental challenges	• Initiates process that aims to engage others in communicative actions to address injustices

condition of society is the reason why a post-progressive stance and an orientation to transformation are needed.

The cases in this chapter focus on the use of a change process resulting in changes that appear just and meaningful. First, I examine a case study of a law school at a private university on the East Coast, where faculty engaged in a process of change in their admissions practices (and related student aid and support services) with the intent of improving robust dialogue in classrooms in ways consonant with the intent of the Supreme Court's decisions in the *Gratz* and *Grutter* cases. Second, I critically review evidence from the IPAS studies to discern lessons about the potential for interventions in higher education that are intended to facilitate transformation of practice.

LAW SCHOOL CASE

The *Gratz* and *Grutter* decisions did not settle issues related to the legality of race-conscious strategies for outreach and student aid (Banks, 2006; Ancheta, 2007). If applications, acceptance rates, or enrollment rates by admitted applicants are lower than thought desirable to maintain a robust dialogue about the law, then a law school could decide to use outreach strategies to increase minority applications, and student financial aid to improve the rate of enrollment by admitted students. In law schools that seek to raise admission standards, the challenge is to compete for more high achieving students of color. However, if race-conscious aid strategies remain of uncertain legality, especially if they are not narrowly tailored, then questions linger about the use of student aid in ensuring diversity.

The Private University Law School[79] implemented a new race-conscious approach to student financial aid to maintain a critical mass of students of color, while raising educational standards. A minority merit program was implemented in 2003, referred to as a Partnership in Diversity (PID) program. The PID program provided merit awards to students along with other support, including a mentoring program. Minority students with high LSAT scores who showed an interest in the law school (i.e. attended meetings at the school and responded to a supplemental aid application) were offered a PID fellowship, which amounted to the equivalent of a tuition subsidy. Other majority and minority applicants were offered merit aid based strictly on their LSAT scores.

Historically, there had been more emphasis on need-based student aid than merit aid at the law school, especially for students admitted through the legal educational opportunity program (EOP). The EOP provided a method of reviewing applications for students who indicated special circumstances, including those related to learning issues, financial status, and other factors. Students who were admitted to the EOP were usually required to take supplemental courses during the summer prior to enrollment. Before PID, most of the students of color enrolling at the law school had been admitted through EOP.

Intent of the Partnership in Diversity (PID) Program

In interviews with members of faculty committees on EOP and admissions it became evident that faculty critiques of the current system were the impetus for change. In particular, members of the admissions committee engaged in the review of cases felt the need to be more competitive in attracting high-achieving students of color. The vision for the PID program grew out of dual concerns about: (1) the nature of the discourse and apparent racism in the classroom; and (2) the desire to attract more high achieving students of color as a means of transforming the dialogue in classrooms, thus changing predispositions toward students of color held by many majority students in the classes.

Implemented in 2003 in response to a decline in enrollment rate by admitted minority applicants, the PID program provided merit scholarships for a small number of admitted applicants. The targeted grant program gave higher grants to minority students than they might have received through the law school's generally available merit program. Analyses of enrollment by admitted applicants using admission and student records for the law school found that financial aid was positively associated with enrollment for the entire population of admitted students and the population of admitted minority students (St. John, Affolter-Caine, & Chung, 2007). In combination, these analyses confirmed that the grant strategies being used at the law school were competitive enough to attract many of the high achieving majority and minority students who received these aid offers.

Studying the law comprises unique challenges given the nature of practicing the law postgraduation, and therefore demands a certain level of engagement in the learning process by students. Their engagement is shown through their level of preparedness, class participation, and ability to argue all sides of various issues according to the merits of the law rather than their opinion. Faculty indicated having a robust dialogue in the classroom is a critical component of this unique learning process (see Text Box. 9.1). Some described a negative predisposition within the law school toward students of color when they spoke and an assumption that students of color were there because of the EOP. Most students of color did not speak unless called upon. Most faculty members thought these conditions were problematic, given the use of the Socratic method of instruction, which involves active engagement in learning. As is evident from the faculty interviews, the PID not only increased the number of high achieving students of color in the law school, but it also increased their engagement in dialogue, enhancing learning for all students.

Text Box 9.1 Summary of Faculty and Student Interviews

Faculty and students describe the necessity of having a robust dialogue and reasoning for the Partnership in Diversity (PID) Program.

It is "absolutely necessary" to have "a robust dialogue in class" in order to teach the students "a way of thinking—maybe a shallow way, but thinking nonetheless." (Junior faculty member)

"Classroom engagement is very important to the learning process," particularly when learning the law, which is "a process, not a thing . . . and the doctrine is complicated." (Senior faculty member)

"People bring different perspectives to the table . . . being able to listen to different people and opinions . . . see things from all sides." (PID student, second year)

"A big part of it [Socratic method] is being prepared everyday . . . You don't have the same level of understanding when you aren't prepared . . . People who participate a lot have an advantage when it comes to exams." (PID student, second year)

Before PID, the visibility of EOP students was high, and it "stigmatized all minorities whether or not they were EOP participants or not, and clamped down on their participation in class." The part-time day program and the introduction of the PID program both worked to "mask" EOP students to "remove any stigma associated by race or the program," which was "intentional" in the creation of both new programs.

"Stereotyping [by students or faculty] is more difficult with EOP students as they are too small a sample of students of color" compared to other students of color admitted unconditionally or participate in merit scholarship programs like PID.

Faculty Comments on Effects

The faculty focus group unanimously (N=10) acknowledged that the introduction of the PID program alleviated the stigma associated with EOP students and students of color both among the faculty and the students.

In a focus group of ten faculty members, the consensus was that the qualifying objectives for PID students are related to "their potential to lead, and thus their ability to raise the robustness of classroom dialogue."

While faculty could not regularly identify which students participated in the PID program, those who did noted the value each student brought to the classroom dialogue through "these students' willingness to be academically engaged."

The faculty in the focus group who could identify PID students expressed their appreciation for these students' "ability to articulate diverse perspectives in class dialogues."

One junior faculty member said that some of the "best students" in her classes belonged to the PID program, and that she found these students to be a "Godsend" in their ability to "articulate issues" in class.

A senior faculty member said he had witnessed that "even the presence of a few merit students has achieved critical mass to change the classroom environment."

Change in the Learning Environment

A powerful portrait of a transformation in the student learning environment emerged from the interviews with students. The interviews with students of color revealed: (1) The features of the PID Program, including the opportunities for internships with major law firms and the supportive attitude at the campus, had influenced enrollment decisions; (2) Students who had a longer history at the school and who had been admitted under the EOP indicated a change in the stigma of being a person of color in the school after the PID was implemented; and (3) Both EOP and PID students in recent classes indicated they experienced respect in the classroom and in study groups. However, third year students (the group that entered before PID) commented on the lack of a robust dialogue.

The interviews with white students confirmed that some of them resented affirmative action in admission (see Text Box 9.2). However, interviews also revealed a relatively consistent attitude that students of color made substantial contributions in the class-room, and most students communicated a respect for diversity as a consequence. In sum, the student interviews indicate that the learning environment improved for all students.

Text Box 9.2 Student Comments on the Learning Environment

Students described a pattern of preparation and participation that involved all students in a robust dialogue within first-year classes.

Students in the focus group agreed that a robust dialogue is "especially helpful in Constitutional Law."

"The Socratic method gives knowledge, but the robust dialogue is achieved when people express opinions." (Student in focus group)

"I would put it [participation] about the same level, maybe slightly better than Princeton [where he had been an undergraduate] . . . In my class session all minority students felt they could participate." (PID student male, second year)

In general, "quality students" were defined by individual personal attributes, such as being prepared for class, being intelligent, engaging in discussion of the law (not just personal opinions), and offering diverse points of view.

"In retrospect, a diverse environment would be better educationally . . . [because] experience is everything." This white third year student added that as a homogenous group, interest in robust dialogue on issues, "particularly social issues" was limited.

Another third year white male student spoke at length about his desire for more "quality students," and when pressed defined these individuals as those who come to class prepared and ready to participate by arguing all sides of an issue from its legal merits. "I want to get a 360 degree view of an issue and be able to argue any side."

A graduate of the law school commented in the focus group that all students benefit from getting this 360 degree view of issues because at any point in their careers they will need to be able to advocate for clients with perspectives that are different from their own.

"Being engaged helps your understanding of the law, but when others are not, it stagnates the discussion," reported one white third year male student, and added that hearing alternate views on issues was "helpful."

One white male third year student who participated in the law review reported that he preferred engaged students to those who use law school as a non-academic extension of college life—a "place to kill time." This sentiment was also recognized by a white female third year student.

Students in the focus group articulated a preference for students who were engaged, and warned of the "myth of the 'A' grade" with respect to disengaged students.

Students acknowledged the value of having "qualified" students of color, as in the PID program, to remove any stigma or stereotyping associated with race or ethnicity.

"I am not even sure faculty knew I was in PID." (A female PID student)

"When we [PID students] go to the distinguished lecturers series . . . we go like everyone else . . . if you compared people in the PID program to other students [with merit scholarships] there would not be much difference." (A male PID student)

None of the white students knew the specifics of the PID program, the controversy surrounding it (N=5), nor who participated in it. None of these students were familiar with the EOP program either, even though this is not a race-specific program and is described in the application for admission.

In addition, the data from the Law School Survey of Student Engagement (LSSSE) indicated that students in the freshman cohort had more positive ratings of dialogue about diversity than was evident among third-year students. The specific LSSSE survey question asks about diverse perspectives (different races, religions, political beliefs, etc.) in class discussions or writing assignments, to which students responded by rating their experience on a four-point scale: 1=never, 2=sometimes, 3=often, and 4=very often. The first-year law students at the Private University had an average response of 2.64 to this question, compared to 2.48 for second-year students and 2.1 for third-year students. This is a strong indicator that PID made a difference across cohorts. Nationally, the scores on this question were also higher for first-year students than for comparison groups. The first-year score (2.64) was significantly higher for the Private University Law School, using LSSSE-reported effect size analysis method, compared to first-year students in law schools with more than 900 students (2.22), other private religious colleges (2.34), and all law schools responding to LSSSE (2.44).[80]

Creating a Robust Dialogue

The Private University Law School case illustrates an example of a faculty-initiated intervention in admissions, use of student aid, and partnerships with law firms. The transition was motivated by a desire for a robust dialogue within the classroom. The intervention improved the recruitment of diverse students with high LSAT scores. Interviews with faculty and students indicated that the aims of creating a diverse dialogue were achieved, at least for first-year students. The Private Law School intervention transformed a critical social problem, as confirmed by the national survey data.

CHANGING COLLEGE ORGANIZATIONS

The Indiana Project on Academic Success (IPAS) was an intervention using action inquiry at multiple campuses (St. John, 2009; St. John & Wilkerson, 2006). In theory, the process provided a guide for action that could facilitate transformational change in order to addresss critical social issues. In fact, the assessment (St. John, Carter, & Musoba, 2006) identified challenges with respect to differences in persistence by whites and students of color that could have been a source of information for reform, but new initiatives addressing racial inequality were limited. In most cases, IPAS provided a form of technical support to change processes already underway at campuses, a phenomena examined below. In addition, one of the colleges had a major reform underway that had potential for application at other colleges, a change process also examined below.

Managing Change

While the design of IPAS was theorized as a critical methodology improvement based on prior experience with school reform (St. John, 2009) and review of higher education research (St. John & Wilkerson, 2006), the process ended up providing support for initiatives already underway at most campuses. In fact, campuses able to align IPAS with existing strategic initiatives were most likely to continue engagement in the process after the first year. The evidence of change at five campuses examined in the qualitative study (St. John, 2009) is summarized in Table 9.2.

Five campuses were visited in the qualitative study and one multicampus project was also reviewed. In four of the cases, the initiatives undertaken with the support of IPAS were related to initiatives already underway. In fact, evaluation support, including focus group interviews and persistence studies evaluating the impact of interventions, was the most widely used service. In a very real sense, IPAS added to the resources these campuses could use to pursue their aims, a situation something like Cameron and Lavine's (2006) concept of positive organizational strategy.

In addition, it was apparent that having central initiatives provided administrators and faculty members with opportunities to engage in change at their campuses. At each of the five campuses there were faculty members and administrators who found advantages for themselves and their campuses from collaboration with Indiana University on

Table 9.2 Indiana Project on Academic Success (IPAS): Reform Initiatives and Evidence of Organizational Change from Case Studies

Campus	Initiative	Evidence
Regional Community College	Implemented linked courses for first-year students (see Chapter 5)	Faculty expressed positive attitudes toward the reform.
Regional Comprehensive College	Evaluated reform initiatives related to remedial instruction (St. John, 2009)	Mixed results in interviews and persistence studies.
Regional Technological University	Evaluated supplemental instruction involving upper division students (see Chapter 6)	Qualitative and quantitative evidence supported impacts on achievement and persistence.
Single Campus Community College	Test piloted orientation for newly admitted students (see Chapter 7)	Evidence of learning from pre- and post-tests; improved first-year retention.
Private Christian University	Evaluated the Life Calling Center (see below)	External evaluation provided evidence of positive effects of first-year program on retention.
Regional Collaboration	Collaborated on project related to working students (see Chapter 8)	Used research to learn more about working students; interventions not yet developed.

IPAS. Not only did the collaboration strengthen projects by providing evidence that could be used to refine and alter strategies, but the involvement provided visibility and prestige. Many administrators and faculty members had opportunities to go to statewide meetings and present their work. Several attended national meetings and participated on panels.

There were two cases in which initiatives were undertaken that were new projects: the Single Campus Community College undertook an initiative that deviated from system-wide policies when they test piloted a program requiring orientation prior to registration (see Chapter 7), and three regional institutions—each in a different state-wide system—collaborated on a new initiative to study working students (see Chapter 8). The SCCC initiative followed the entire inquiry process. The regional collaboration could go through the full cycle, but it was still in the process of building an understanding of the problem when the project ended.

This experience provides information about the alignment of reform initiatives with institutional change strategies. As part of IPAS, adaptations were made to align inquiry with campus initiatives (Musoba, 2006; St. John, McKinney, & Tuttle, 2006), an adaptation of the AIM that improved the ease of working with campuses interested in organizational change. This revised model was presented in Chapter 4 and has most recently been used to work with graduate students and administrative units at the University of Michigan where action inquiry is proving to be a workable approach to intervention.[81] This refinement of the method is both more modest in intent—shifting from the lofty aim of facilitating transformation to the more strategic aim of supporting ongoing reform initiatives—and more workable. In fact, I suggest that integrating research with change initiatives can be a workable strategy for reform in higher education, and perhaps in other professional fields.

Potential for Transformation

The Private Christian University (PCU) had confronted a major challenge in the years immediately preceding their involvement with IPAS. It was a small college with a high drop-out rate, especially for students who had not declared majors. In fact, drop out of first-year students was a critical issue for private colleges in Indiana and was apparently linked to not having an appropriate major. In addition to diagnosing a critical internal problem, PCU looked at a range of intervention strategies (see Text Box 9.3) using elements of action inquiry.

Text Box 9.3 Private Christian University (PCU)

Prior to their involvement in IPAS, PCU developed a Life Calling Center that was rooted in the theories of student development and used the notion of "calling" from the Christian tradition to support students through four years of college and with transitions to the work place after graduation. An administrator described the planning process:

> We looked at a lot of models. We looked at the area of developmental models . . . we can lay them all out and say: "The bottom line is there seems to be something about attaching to someone's purpose . . ." . . . So what we are

doing here is saying this [the major] is still important, but somehow we need to move into this area of the student's . . . [list of] what's the right purpose. We started this six year ago.

The PCU center provides courses that enable students to think about their life purposes, choose courses and majors that enable them to move toward those purposes, and engage in social, civic, and employment opportunities that connect to those purposes as well. The center provides life coaching, service learning, and leadership opportunities on and off campus.

The program as delivered to students on the campus was centered in the Christian tradition, a feature that made it difficult to transfer, in its current form, to many other colleges and universities. One of the professors teaching the core courses in the program observed:

> I think in one of the first Powerpoints that I even show Jesus and the disciples. I have to really speak to them in regards to the opportunity to look at the potential there: understand that people have gifts, understand what you are called to do. I'm in the ministry of mentoring—that's what we're doing. So when I say . . . "Understand the possibilities. Understand what God sees in you. And understand you could be an instrument of change." So they begin to look at the difference. So they begin to make a difference, not just work on a project.

At the core, the program offered at PCU asks students to reflect on their inner sense of calling from within their Christian values, an approach congruent with the Christian mission of the university.

When the IPAS project team began to work with PCU, the leadership was interested in evaluating the effects of the current program and exploring how the model could be transformed to a more universal centering of the method so it could be tried out more broadly. The director of the Life Calling Center commented on the origins of the center, calling attention to the founding ideals. One was:

> Higher education followed a career development model which is find some area of interest, choose a major, and then find a job with the major. That will help you get based upon the job availability, salary and job growth. The career model is very much a self-centered model. . . . It is hedonistic. . . . Well we come at it with a world changing theme . . . I am sure you have heard that many times today in your discussions . . . where the purpose of education is not just to get a job, but to make a significant positive impact on the world, to make it a better place. Right there you have a big difference.

In addition to focusing on making the world a better place, the aim was to enable people to engage in change making from being centered in their own sense of calling. The director also commented: "You enable them to develop an overriding purpose for life decisions, based on that purpose and . . . empower them to carry out that purpose in world changing leadership."

The director of the program also described how the university had modified the life changing model to work with adults and other groups that did not fit the Christian worldview of the original model. There were also plans to disseminate the model to other religiously affiliated colleges and universities. When asked about this plan, the center director commented:

> You have the [foundation name] investing a quarter of a billion dollars in 88 colleges and universities across the nation . . . [with] a wide range of religious arrangements . . . What they call the program for the theological exploration of vocations . . . so you have all this money and books and now it is fascinating for me to see . . . One of things that I have seen a whole lot of, and I think we do uniquely, is the fact that I have gone with a conceptual model and a developmental model. So we feel we have a logical, structural approach.

There was growing awareness at PCU that their life calling model has not only enabled the university to transform opportunities for undergraduates who enter with uncertainty about their future, but the method they have used to facilitate this process has potentially broad application. They have also been careful to reflect on the Christian origins of their model, as they engage in a broader, national discourse about dissemination.

Source: Adapted from St. John, 2009, pp. 210–212.

PCU implemented a Life Calling Center to provide services for students. A central feature of the intervention was a course for freshman students who had not declared a major or who had doubts about their major. The IPAS team conducted an evaluation using institutional data. In the years preceding implementation of the course, undeclared students were more likely to drop out than other students. After implementation, students who were undeclared had substantially higher odds of persisting through the first two years. Thus, IPAS provided empirical evidence to support the argument that the intervention had its intended effect.

In addition to supporting the reform initiative by providing an evaluation service, the project team provided support for efforts to test the intervention methods through workshops at other campuses in the state. In addition, opportunities for moving toward planned experiments were discussed.[82]

Making Sense of Change

IPAS provided an experiment with assisted change. In most cases, the changes undertaken as part of the reform process were modest and aligned with initiatives already underway. In many instances the strategic initiatives had not been created based on research, but had been generated from hunches shared in the planning process. Given the strong emphasis on strategic planning and market competition in higher education (Altbach, Berdhal, & Gumport, 2006), this should not be a surprise.

There were some cases of campuses that undertook efforts to address challenges discovered as part of the IPAS assessment. The Single Campus Community College tested a new orientation model to address the problem of high first-year drop-out rates, and the regional campuses collaborated on a working students project because of a shared understanding that their common departure patterns were attributable to the work environments facing their students. PCU had undergone its own inquiry process to address a critical drop-out problem.

The IPAS experiences illustrate that research can inform change in higher education. My guidance to professors in applied fields is to engage in research projects that support organizational change, especially if you are interested in topics related to practice. It is more interesting to engage in change and to test theories in action situations than merely to theorize and observe. Quantitative and qualitative methods are easily adapted to real life problems and engagement in change processes.

CONCLUSIONS

Looking across reform initiatives (e.g. IPAS and the law school case discussed above), it is becoming evident that practitioners can initiate reforms with *transformation potential* (the potential to improve the quality of learning experiences in ways that address critical social challenges). Another lesson from this experience is that the best mode of action for the interventionist is as facilitator. As noted above (see Table 9.1), the role of the facilitator, theoretically, is to use the method, not advocate nor necessarily expect transformational changes. This lesson is important because it relates to managing expectations of interventions. Many of us get into the process of facilitating change with hopes of making a big difference. The reality of managing change as an interventionist is not unrelated to managing one's own expectations. What is important is the intent of the practitioners in the organizations involved, not the aims of the interveners, because the practitioners will both make and have to live with the changes in practice.

Organizational Transformation

In this book, a distinction has become evident between: (1) strategic initiatives that follow hunches and are based on notions of best practice; and (2) change initiatives that address critical social challenges uncovered through open discourse and review of research, including institutional research. The contrast between the two forms of change is striking. The surprise in the IPAS project was that so few campuses actually engaged in the new initiatives that were uncovered by the assessment research. Instead, strategic, prestige-seeking behavior[83] predominated. However, their evidence of transformation with respect to the challenge of changing practice to address critical social issues included:

- the development of new orientation programs at a Single Campus Community College (Chapter 7);
- the development of a collaborative project to examine the learning needs of working students (Chapter 8);
- the development of new approaches to recruitment at Private University Law School (this chapter);
- the development of a new center to promote introspection on life purpose at Private Christian University (this chapter).

In these cases, evidence of critical social problems was used to reframe action strategies. The two examples in this chapter were classified as transformational practice because these changes had organizationwide implications. These examples illustrate that major changes can result from collective action within organizations. The cases considered in Chapters 7 and 8 illustrate the use of new initiatives within institutions to address critical social challenges. These examples illustrate it is possible to address critical social challenges even in organizations that maintain strategic control. The difference is that in the cases classified as transformational, the organization's central strategy was altered, at least somewhat, as a result of the new practice.

Based on these examples, we can derive lessons related to transformational changes that address critical social issues (see Table 9.3). These lessons further illuminate the central role communities of practice play in addressing critical social challenges, a phenomenon that is evident in strategic settings when there is evidence of organizationwide transformation. Central support of major changes is necessary for organizationwide change of practice.

Professional Development

These examples illustrate the central role reflective practice, coupled with postconventional moral reasoning, can play in organizational changes that address critical social challenges. It is crucial that graduate programs and interventions focus on the encouragement and development of these skills, along with the more prevalent focus on strategic action and conventional moral reasoning.

Aim 1: Encourage learning that enables practitioners to achieve their aims as professionals, as well as realize the dreams that motivated their choice of profession. The findings on organizational changes addressing critical social issues illustrate the importance of morally responsible professional action. The concerns people hold about social problems are often related to choice of profession. The professional training they receive, along with assimilating to organizational norms, may silence their voices related to these inner concerns. While there is risk in voicing concerns about social problems in practice, opportunities are created from a collaborative change process. Building skills in voicing concerns by initiating discussion of challenges in strategic settings is important. Trying different approaches to voicing concerns provides a starting point for developing skills. This foundation of personal skills seems critical to having the ability to engage in communicative discourse within communities of practice.

Aim 2: Enable reflection on assumptions, actions, and outcomes in ways that promote learning about improving practice and developing and refining skills, along with reflection on the moral aspects of practice. The testing of assumptions with evidence seems crucial to identifying the root causes of critical social problems. In the Private University Law School and Private Christian University, the voicing of concerns about troubling issues (i.e. the silence of students of color in the law school and the drop out of students lacking a focus in PCU) were locally situated. These were not raised as universal issues, but were local problems that could be addressed locally. It is possible to gain consensus about action on local problems even in environments where there are divergent views about larger social and political issues.[84] Graduate programs should focus on the skills of discerning claims, reviewing claims in relation to evidence, and designing interventions that test claims about remedies to critical social problems.

Table 9.3 Lessons Learned About Alignment of Strategic Orientations of Organizations with Norms and Practices within Communities of Practice: Transformational Action

Frame	Transformational	Lessons Learned
Organization		
Strategic Orientation	Emphasizes response to critical social issues as integral to aims	*Lesson 1: It is possible for practitioners to initiate reforms that address critical challenges.* Evidence: • Faculty members at Private University Law School initiate change in admissions and student aid to recruit high-achieving students of color and create a robust dialogue. • Administrators at Private Christian University undertake interventions to support student choice of major based on life purpose.
System Relation to Lifeworld	Balances adaptations to address critical issues with systemic strategies; equity and justice emphasized	*Lesson 2: Concerned professionals have knowledge that can be used to address critical social problems.* Evidence: • Substantial quantitative and qualitative evidence supports claims of change in robust dialogue at Private University Law School. • Private Christian University substantially improves persistence during the first two years, addressing the problem that was the reason for the intervention.
Communities of Practice		
Norms within Communities of Practice	Balances expert practice with care and justice	*Lesson 3: Teamwork and sharing credit is critical to transformational changes that address critical social challenges.* Evidence: • Open, collaborative environments are evident in universities that initiated major changes (e.g. SCCC, Regional collaborative, PCU, and Private University Law School).
Congruent Practice	Designs and tests methodologies to facilitate change within communities of practice	*Lesson 4: Research can inform reform in both the assessment and evaluation process.* Evidence: • There is extensive use of evaluation services to support strategic initiatives in IPAS. • Campuses undertaking critical social reforms used empirical evidence from assessment in designing interventions.

Aim 3: Promote organizational development that enables professional development and encourages learning. What is striking from a personal perspective is that so little transformational change was evident as a result of IPAS support. The examples of the Private Law School and the Private Christian University show changes that took place independent of external research support. There were however, more changes resulting from initiatives that addressed specific challenges. The interventionists who were most successful at facilitating change had received training in reflection in graduate courses and seminars, and had the time to provide support. In a few instances, graduate students

undertook major interventions using action science methods as part of their dissertations (Cadray, 1995; Kline, 2003) after becoming engaged with these methods in graduate courses. Thus, learning occurs through both courses and building upon teaching by experiencing the outcomes from initiating interventions. The overall outcome from these efforts is encouraging: Well-designed graduate courses and training within organizations can enable organizational changes that address critical social problems in practice. However, addressing these serious problems is the responsibility of practitioners, not professors or interventionists. In my view, facilitating learning and professional development should be the aim, rather than change per se. If specific changes are the aim then we run greater risk of returning to instrumental action and creating resistance.[85]

Aim 4: Improve services provided by professional organizations that promote justice and sustainability. The interventions examined in these chapters have addressed critical social problems and, thus, were aimed at promoting justice. There is evidence here and elsewhere that professionals can take responsibility for fair and just action through education and alteration of service. The evidence of action that promotes environmental sustainability is not as clear in Part II, but environmental sustainability is not the focus of this text. It may be that the methods discussed in this book could be applicable to engineering firms and other organizations in which ensuring environmental sustainability can be part of their mission. However, this remains hypothetical. At the very least, there is evidence that professional education and organizational interventions can enable change that addresses critical social problems in practice.

REFLECTIVE EXERCISE

As a final reflective assignment, I encourage readers to reflect on their own statements of personal values and philosophy (see Chapter 2), along with the analyses of cases, to derive lessons from their own experiences and generate their own list of lessons learned. As a final step in this process, I encourage readers to reflect on whether the action steps they proposed in their initial statement are still the ones most important to them as they pursue their careers. The process of reconstructing plans based on experience is central to learning and moral reasoning. Do not hesitate to revise your plans.

Part III

Conclusions

10

CONCLUSIONS

Each generation—and indeed each person—can bring new ideals into professional practice. The most visible signs of transformation in recent decades, at least for the veterans of professional practice, are the dramatic changes in technology. These are the phenomenon of the "flat world" described so eloquently by Thomas Friedman (2005). People can go nearly anywhere in the world and see similar eating establishments and businesses. Dig a little deeper (for example, walking into the door of a corporate office), and one can find the same technology, software, and information systems. Internet cafes put new communications capabilities, along with readily accessible information on any topic, within reach of almost everyone. Globalization has stimulated massive, rapid, and extensive structural and technological changes. These changes simultaneously put more resources in the hands of people and accelerate inequalities of access to basic goods and services with rapidly modernizing societies, but also hasten environmental decline.

Clearly there is a need for rapid and substantive change in culture and moral values within the world's rapidly changing societies. Since these readily visible changes are distributed, locally accessible and adaptable, and integral to the new forms of professional and personal life now emerging, it is not possible for any group to control social change and adaptation. The notion of social control now seems less critical than it was when college students at the University of California-Berkeley started the Freedom and Speech Movement (FSM) (Cohen, & Zelnik, 2002). But while the technology no longer makes people feel like a "computer card" as claimed by protestors in the FSM, technology is more pervasive and has a greater potential for influencing life experience. In addition, there is a very real prospect that politics has turned into a perpetual campaign of propaganda, as Scott McClellan (2008) argued in his memoir of the Bush administration. Public information, advertising, and instant messaging pervade lived experiences through computers, televisions, telephones, and other forms of telecommunications. Strategic manipulation of media and messages does not always have its intended consequences because all people have free choice in their ability to interpret, adapt, and change.

The new challenges facing aspiring and beginning professionals differ radically from those that faced experienced practitioners and professors who now teach in professional education. As seasoned professionals, we have a responsibility to enable aspiring and beginning professionals to prepare themselves for this new, changing, and challenging world of professional practice. We cannot always tell aspiring professionals how to act or what to do because the rules of practice change as rapidly as the technology. We can introduce ways to use new methods to analyze problems as preparation for the future. We can also provide opportunities for students to learn about themselves, their values and dreams, strengths and limitations, and strategies for development both personally and professionally. The process of self-development is crucial to new generations of professionals.

Aspiring and beginning professionals are faced with the challenge to codevelop professional know-how (i.e. the knowledge and skills of practice) with moral reasoning and a sense of personal and professional responsibility. I hope readers who persevered through this book and engaged in completing the reflective assignments and projects outlined in the reflective arguments, have an enhanced sense of self, culture, and social responsibility. My argument is that human communities must adapt and change to provide access to education, health care, and other services in order to ensure quality of life for all (or at least for more of those who are currently denied access). Social responsibility was integral to life in early tribal societies, just as it is to the religious traditions that accelerated the development of civil societies, and the humanist values that informed the evolution of modern societies. The religious and humanist values that were central to social cohesion in prior centuries (Durkheim, 1951; Taylor, 2007) are no less important now than they were in the past. Yet the process of integrating moral values with professional action and community life is more complicated now than in past centuries. The global news networks interject the vast diversity of belief traditions and value systems into everyday discourse.

Not only is social transformation necessary, it is pervasive and ongoing. Social transformations simultaneously evolve with technology and the globalization of products and professions. However, social transformation is not a worldwide, one-time process, and not all social transformations move us toward social justice and environmental sustainability. They are part of the massive systemic changes now underway. The challenges for all of us, including the young and the experienced, is to make sense of the social transformations around us and to create new forms of social good and environmental restoration from the challenges we face in our day-to-day lives. As people learn to reconcile their values and beliefs with the changing society and culture they experience, they have a chance of making meaningful social changes. This requires new frameworks and constructs—new ways of viewing the problems and challenges that are part of everyday life.

REFRAMING IN PROFESSIONAL PRACTICE

Three new ways of viewing the developmental processes of professional practice have been introduced in this book. In combination, these rubrics provide a new framework for teaching and learning about social action and change as an integral part of professional education.

- *Moral reasoning in action:* Rather than assuming maturation from childhood to adulthood as a basis for moral reasoning, as is the case with Kohlberg's theory, the reconstructed theory of moral reasoning in action focuses on situated behavior within professional practice, an orientation more applicable to adulthood than the earlier theory.

- *Professional development:* The foundational assumptions of reflective practice were reconstructed in relation to moral reasoning, providing a new basis for examining the development of professional judgment and reflection. The earlier literature on reflective practice largely overlooked the role of moral reasoning, adding to the conceptual distance between the rules governing professional action and moral responsibility. Integrating an emphasis on moral reasoning with reflective practice provides a more complete basis for understanding learning in practice than did the prior concept of reflective practice.

- *Organizational development:* A new perspective on organizational development was also introduced as a means of illuminating the ways professional discourse on problematic issues can be addressed within organizations. An action inquiry model (AIM) was also proposed as a method for integrating organizational change with efforts to address critical issues in organizational life.

Reconstructed understandings of these processes were needed because of breakdowns in professional responsibility. There are two major reasons why older assumptions about social and economic progress no longer hold up, increasing the need for integrating moral reasoning and reflection into professional practice across fields of practice: inequality and environmental decline. In the US, there has been growing inequality of educational opportunity since the early 1980s, undermining the progressive developments in the quarter century following the 1954 Supreme Court's decision in *Brown v. Board of Education* (St. John, 2006). There have also been greater inequalities of income and access to health care and other services (Fogel, 2000; B. M. Friedman, 2005). This growing inequality is exacerbated by long-standing discord about religion, race, gender, social class, and transgender identity in modern societies. The potential for remedying these regressive social inequalities is further complicated by decline in the environment and natural resources. Adjusting to the new global conditions may require living with less (Meadows, Randers, & Meadows, 2004). One of the major arguments in this book has been that in regressive periods (e.g. 1980 to present), professionals have even greater responsibility to act with justice and to address critical issues.

While ethical codes and best practices are often the focus in professional education, these foundations are only the starting point for professional development. It is indeed critical that professionals understand the standards and rule of their professions. However, rules can be misused and inappropriately applied, and can likewise become tools for undermining environmental and social justice. Therefore, new professionals should be prepared to confront two critical challenges as part of their professional growth: critical reflection-in-action and transforming practice (see Chapter 1). First, new professionals are challenged to seek truth in critical situations, rather than rely on beliefs and past practices rationalized by the rules of the profession. Second, they are challenged to engage communities affected by practice in discourse to seek inclusive understandings of problematic situations.

This standard of seeking truth is required for thinking-in-action and confronting conventional interpretations, as the case studies of Mahatma Gandhi and Earl Warren illustrated (see Chapter 8). As a conclusion, I reconsider the new conceptions of moral reasoning in action, reflective practice as a developmental process, and organizational development as methods for addressing critical social challenges. My aim in this chapter is to reconfirm the importance of understanding these two critical challenges (i.e. critical reflection and transforming practice) as integral to professional education and practice.

MORAL REASONING IN ACTION

Too often moral reasoning is treated as distinct from action. Professional education often treats moral and ethical issues as ancillary to core theories and foundations of practice (the knowledge and skills emphasized in profession education). The new theory of moral reasoning departs from the notion of psychological development as a foundation for action in adulthood. By early adulthood, most aspiring professionals have attained the psychological capacity for conventional moral reasoning; there is substantial research on college students to support this interpretation (Pascarella & Terenzini, 2005; Small, 2007). The challenge for professionals is to use sound moral reasoning in practice. My argument is that moral education starts with reflection on beliefs and values, but also requires reflection in action, minimizing gaps between espoused beliefs and behavior.

Reducing the Gap Between Values and Action

The process of centering oneself involves reflection on values and beliefs. The process of reducing the gap between values and action involves reflection on values in critical situations. To build understanding of critical issues, we should also seek to understand the values others hold rather than assume the superiority of a particular belief, argument, or rationale. My assertion is that the tensions among religion, humanism, and science are artifacts of instrumental and strategic reasoning. If we reflect collectively on values in actual situations, the divisions are not as great as is often assumed.

Having deeply held personal values should not stop us from engaging in discursive action aimed at improving justice, caring for others in troubling situations, and reducing the carbon footprint of our families and communities. These are universal aims with merit for all. If we approach these aims by encouraging open discourse, we can reduce the risk of damage and injustice being created by closed-strategic action that does not include open reflection on framing assumptions, a challenge facing adults in modern societies.

Most of the faith traditions originated with a concern for the underclass, and they provide a basis for reflection on critical issues. Moses, as founding father of Judaism, led his people from slavery to freedom in the ultimate liberationist act. Seeking freedom and justice through inner reflection and acknowledging God within others are integral aspects of the Jewish tradition. Christianity originated in the teachings of Jesus, a roving rabbi who encouraged Jews and Gentiles to reflect on the word as lived tradition inclusive of all. His actions, documented in the Synoptic Gospels of the New Testament, confronted the narrow interpretations of Priests and Pharisees alike. He challenged both authorities (Priests) and local leaders among people in revolt (Pharisees) to reflect on the word of God and act with justice for all (including, and especially, for the poor). The Prophet Mohammad, a leader of political and faith communities that originated Islam, was also fundamentally concerned about social justice and charity. Buddha reframed the Eastern notions of consciousness to argue that all people could reach nirvana; the ultimate state of consciousness was not a privilege of the Brahman caste. Hinduism started with a classicist notion of social caste, amended through the critical reflections of leaders in India, including Gandhi. The challenge peoples of all faiths face is to continue to reflect on the social aspects of their faith as they help illuminate inequality and enable just action.

Tensions about interpretations of doctrines across Christian traditions, and between Christians and Muslims, fueled the transitions to deism and humanism among faith-based nation states (Taylor, 2007). The moral philosophies of human rights, from Adam Smith to John Rawls, have provided frameworks for the democratization of nation states and the development of constitutions that guarantee equality. While these guarantees of rights have been hard to realize, given the instinctive prejudices and fears that we all must contend with, the humanist tradition also values equality and care for all. It is incumbent on all of us to avoid letting disagreements about specific traditions and the existence of God deny these commonalities. When individuals disagree about the source of values and the role of traditions, they should not be blinded to the ways their traditions value justice and care in critical situations. Differences in beliefs and values are not an excuse for injustice or cruelty. Reflecting on the spiritual foundations of our faith traditions provides one a means of building understanding of critical challenges.

Critical theory, originating with critiques of society by Karl Marx, provides another means of illuminating inequality in modern societies and communities. While an alternative workers' democracy did not materialize in ways consonant with Marx's original vision, we should not ignore the fact that critical analysis—whether centered in faith, humanism, or critical theory—can illuminate seriously problematic situations. In fact, the process of salvaging critical analysis from Marxism—a method I have adapted from Habermas (1985, 1987, 1991) in this and other books (St. John, 1994, 2003, 2006, 2009)—provides means of illuminating problematic situations. My argument is that once we illuminate critically problematic situations, we can reflect together to build shared understandings of the origins of the problem and possible solutions. Taking this step provides a means for working with people who are willing to share responsibility for solving the problem. It is possible to share responsibility for just social action among people with diverse beliefs, values, and ideologies. This practice can provide a way to reduce the gap between espoused beliefs and actions in professional practice.

Another step in reducing this gap involves making wise, well reasoned use of scientific and technical knowledge to promote justice and to reduce the exploitation of global resources. In the nineteenth and twentieth centuries, science prevailed over reason in economic development. The demise of global resources was not a major public concern until the 1970s; the environmental crisis has accelerated since that time (Meadows, Randers, & Meadows, 2004). While historic attempts at instrumental control of scientific reason and progress, exemplified by the Catholic Church's treatment of Galileo, illustrate the problems with efforts to interpret through the framing assumptions of faith as doctrine, there is little reason to doubt that the tenets of faith provide a basis for moral reasoning about the meaning of scientific discovery (Collins, 2006). When faith-based or humanistic values are treated as lists of rules, it is difficult to address social and environment challenges.

During a progressive period, it is possible for most people to improve their quality of life, just as it is during periods of rapid economic development in industrializing nations (B. M. Friedman, 2005). Now, however, the resource constraints on the planet must necessarily limit this type of growth. With global warming as an indicator of the boundaries of excessive development, it will be more difficult to realize across-the-board gains in the quality of life in the future. Tax reductions for all and a private market—the neoliberal platitudes that have dominated U.S. politics for two decades (Harvey, 2005)—do not provide the basis for resolving inequality or environmental decline. New forms of collective and individual action are clearly needed, and value-centered reflection and open discourse are crucial. Public policies that recognize basic human capabilities (Nussbaum, 2004) in education, health care, and legal rights may provide a framework for redistributing resources through taxation and incentives, ensuring families can support themselves while societies attempt to find pathways toward environmental sustainability.

Moral Reasoning in Action

The reconstructed theory of moral reasoning presented in this book provides a way of viewing the problems facing individuals as they pursue professional careers in this challenging context for action. Of course, devious human action is always possible and forms of preconventional moral reasoning will be evident in all human communities, including families, communities of professional practice, church communities, and other social organizations. Truly just societies are extraordinarily difficult to realize, even for brief periods within generations of peoples. If and when such states do eventuate, we need methods of addressing challenges as they emerge. It is important to consider the process of facing critical perspectives from the three frames of moral reasoning in action (Table 10.1): (1) preconventional, which includes working around the rules of systems to address critical challenges; (2) conventional, which includes working within the rules and strategic initiatives of systems to address critical challenges; and (3) postconventional, which includes critical reflection on ways the system contributes to problems and strategies to transform systems to address these challenges.

Preconventional Moral Reasoning in Action

Making the distinction between espoused beliefs and action illuminates how people who are concerned about critical challenges can use preconventional means of achieving their aims. Seeking understanding of truth-in-action situations is absolutely critical in avoiding preconventional moral responses to critical problems. Some of the simplistic questions in Kohlberg's early survey, such as the problem of a husband stealing drugs for a sick wife discussed by Gilligan (1982), illustrate the complexity of assuming that espoused values, including noble goals, justify breaking the rules. Instead, it is essential that responsible adults reflect on the likely consequences of action. Gilligan argues that if a husband goes to jail because of stealing drugs to delay the death of his wife, there is greater risk of having children bereft of both parents, which is an unintended, negative outcome.

Gilligan's (1982) reframing of this question illustrates the problem with assuming ends justify means. It is important to think problems through, seeking remedies within the system, or methods of changing the system. The difficult path of civil disobedience chosen by Martin Luther King, Jr. (1967) in the civil rights protests illustrates the

Table 10.1 Reflections on Critical Challenges in Relation to Modes of Moral Reasoning

	Challenge 1: Seek truth in critical situations, rather than rely on beliefs and past practices rationalized based on the rules of the profession.	*Challenge 2:* Engage communities affected by practice in discourse to seek inclusive understandings of problematic situations.
Preconventional Moral Reasoning	*Avoid:* • using critical issues to rationalize strategies that perpetuate problems (i.e. deceptive practices); • working around organizational problems to address critical challenges.	*Avoid:* • rationalizing abuse of peers using the language of justice and caring; • building alliances only with people of similar background and beliefs; • valuing expert judgments over voiced concerns of citizens.
Conventional Moral Reasoning	*Seek to:* • reflect on reasons for recurrent social and environmental problems; • share reflections and explore alternative scenarios with peers; • generate evidence of effects of current and alternative strategies.	*Seek to:* • construct understanding of problems that consider divergent views; • build communities of practice that value growth of others; • engage community on introspect on challenges.
Postconventional Moral Reasoning	*Seek to:* • understand personal values in relation to critical social and environmental issues; • engage in initiatives that seek to address critical challenges.	*Seek to:* • create learning environments engaging peers and citizens served; • transform practices to act with justice and caring.

complexity of changing the system and defying the law for reasons of justice. In fact, King must be considered a postconventional moral practitioner, along with Gandhi and Warren. One has to be willing to face the consequences of action (e.g. going to jail), a condition that is difficult in the life of a family in crisis. The decision of a husband to steal drugs for his dying wife could, as Gilligan argues, cause great harm to his family's continued well-being. Viewed from this perspective, actions rationalized on the basis of noble reasoning can contribute to injustice and inequality. The boundary between preconventional and postconventional moral reasoning is far more complex than previously assumed, even when the intent is pure.

It is also crucial to use critical reflection to resist using one's own expertise to create inequalities in the name of remedying them. Habermas (1990) argues that quid pro quo and asymmetry of power are the major forms of preconventional moral reasoning. While conceptually this distinction makes sense, I propose three forms of preconventional moral reasoning in action:

• *errors in practice*, a part of the learning process that may exhibit misuse of power or breaking of moral codes, possible through good intentions;

- *nefarious practice*, which involves intentional breaking of ethical codes to achieve goals or aims;
- *deceptive practice*, a process of acting within conventional codes but engaging in practices (e.g. not reporting errors in statistics) that support a desired point of view rather than pursuing the truth.

Errors in practice are part of the learning process and should be expected, especially among new professionals. My arguments are that new professionals should be mentored in their learning process and that discursive space is needed within professional organizations to create room for change in practice to address critical social issues.

Nefarious practice is, of course, a pervasive form of preconventional moral reasoning in human societies. Replicating patterns of nefarious action are evidenced in sexual harassment in professional settings (see Chapter 6), child abuse by clergy, systemic racism, and recurrent problems. These sorts of actions are clearly problematic, and it is not particularly difficult to understand them as such.

There are also many examples of deceptive practice in public memory, including misreporting evidence on the threat of weapons of mass destruction before the U.S. war of choice in Iraq and misreporting evidence on links between smoking and cancer by researchers working for cigarette companies. Reporting of false or error-prone statistics is particularly troubling because it can be due to the misuse of power (e.g. requiring misreporting to keep funding), ideological belief (e.g. using statistics to support beliefs), quid pro quo (e.g. misshaping research and misreporting evidence for pay), or errors in action. This problem has been evident for several decades in research on college access and persistence (Becker, 2004; Heller, 2004), and it is not always easy to discern the reasons. Most of the government reports on access and attainment over the past decades have made serious statistical errors. These errors are a common feature of reports that advance false academic arguments and intentionally obfuscate financial inequality (Heller, 2004).

In my experience, situations that involve deceptive practice,[86] including misreporting of statistics, are extremely complicated. As a principal in a private firm in the 1980s, I helped bring a study of the racial inequality of college enrollment into the firm. Going into the study, we had long known there were inequalities in schools serving different racial groups—a fact evident in *Brown* and addressed by the *Elementary and Secondary Education Act* before 1980.[87] Nearly equal college enrollment rates had been realized in the 1970s as a result of education reforms and need-based student aid for low-income students (St. John, 2003). The U.S. Department of Education asked us to do this study to address potential causes for the opening of the gap in college enrollment rates beginning in the early 1980s. The final report for the minority enrollment study did not consider the possibility that the new inequality of college enrollment could have resulted because of the decline in Pell Grants during the 1980s. Instead, it was reported that the underlying cause of inequality was differences in preparation, especially access to algebra in the eighth grade (Pelavin & Kane, 1988, 1990). Making the argument that school inequality had caused the opening of the gap was deceptive at the time. It has become more problematic since because it has been used to rationalize the shift to the movement toward excellence for all in education. The original report overlooked the inequalities being created by the shift in public funds from programs for low-income students to middle-income students.[88]

In my efforts to reconcile my beliefs in social justice with the problems created by the report for the minority enrollments study, I published the research I had conducted on the role of student aid in enrollment (e.g. St. John, 1991). I had originally completed this work for a related project as a means of informing the public discourse. From this experience, I concluded that as educators working with aspiring professionals (future academics as well as practitioners in professional fields) we have an obligation to provide learning opportunities that help illuminate moral challenges in practice.

I also learned it was possible for people who espoused the best of intents, and perhaps even believed in social justice, to pursue immoral pathways out of false beliefs, pursuit of pay, or failure to resist power.[89] Based on more than three decades of experience as a policy analyst and professor, I am convinced that professional education has an obligation to prepare aspiring practitioners for future dealings with the influence of power on action, and encourage students to take responsibility for addressing critical challenges.

Conventional Moral Reasoning in Action

It is appropriate to consider the process of learning conventional moral reasoning in action as part of the professional development process. Professional education can introduce students, who are aspiring professionals, to ethical codes and other rules of practice. However, as illustrated in Part II, learning to practice as moral citizens in professional organizations serving a diverse society is not an easy task. The process of learning to act morally in practice only begins in professional schools. Experience, including the opportunity to reflect, is also necessary. During the course of a career, it is rare to never encounter a compromising situation in which one's own values are confronted by being asked to undertake tasks that do not seem right. It is important to manage one's way through these problems. In the best case scenario, one's work organization provides avenues for corrective action. Prior chapters presented examples of individuals and organizations that made adaptations within the system to address critical challenges. When one has the chance to engage in collaborations for problem solving, there are greater possibilities for personal growth and development as a professional.

The moral codes of the professions are not easy to understand in practice because professional judgment plays a crucial role in building understanding. Faith traditions provide methods of reconciling with people who we may have harmed and seeking forgiveness. Professions also need methods of promoting moral learning. The tendencies to rationalize actions, cover up bad practices, and conspire to achieve aims are widely practiced norms. It is in this regard that the practice of open reflection is so critical to but precarious within organizations. Creating the discursive space for learning is not only crucial to creating cultures of justice and care within organizations that serve the public, but also to developing organizations capable of responding to new challenges.

As noted in Table 10.1, there are several ways practitioners can work together in teams to address critical challenges that emerge in organizations. It is important to reflect on the reasons for the problem and generate evidence related to it. This requires openness to discuss the critical nature of challenges and alternative explanations. Sometimes there are organizational barriers to this type of introspection and few rewards for taking these steps. For example, the administrator in the medical school found it difficult to raise issues about alternative groups being invited to training workshops (see Chapter 6). However, there are also instances in which teams can work together to solve problems, as in the technology transfer case and the orientation program (see Chapter 7). In these cases it was possible for practitioners to align organizational strategy with efforts to address critical challenges.

When confronted by deceptive practices, it is important to reason one's own way through the problem. For example, in the case of the federal research on inequality in college enrollment discussed above, I did not follow the lead of some peers who left the firm over the issue because I lacked employment alternatives at the time. Instead, I later completed studies that provided a more complete explanation for the decline in the enrollment rates, and published the research (e.g. St. John, 1989, 1991; St. John & Noell, 1989) that was overlooked in the deceptive report. I hoped these actions would help set the record straight. Personally, I learned to confront critical challenges and avoid collusion in situations that result in public deception, an attitude toward practice that has since been central to my career. Reflecting on these early career challenges helped me to mature in my perceptions of moral responsibility in action. I used this case from my own experience to illustrate the importance of reflecting on values as one makes career choices and engages in responsible practices. It represents a strategy for working within the system to address a critical problem.

Postconventional Moral Reasoning in Action

The idea of engaging in collective and individual efforts to change systems as a means of improving justice and sustainability seems appealing. Certainly many student protestors against the Vietnam War and segregation in the South demonstrated this idealism (Cohen & Zelnik, 2002), but acting on a belief is different from struggling with the challenges of truth in action. In this book, I have argued that postconventional moral reasoning in action is closely aligned with the concept of truth-in-action, a stage of reasoning that can happen as a result of struggles with critical challenges.

This stage of reasoning in action was illustrated in the cases of Mahatma Gandhi and Earl Warren (see Chapter 8). While both undertook action that changed nations, moving them toward justice and fairness, neither of these inspirational leaders led perfect lives with respect to acting with justice and fairness. As young professionals, both were enmeshed in systemic injustice. Gandhi was born into an elite caste in a discriminatory, classist society, as was the nature of Hinduism in India. As he commented in his autobiography, it was only when he reflected on his personal sense of being offended by being moved from a first-class train car in South Africa that he began to reflect deeply on the meanings of injustice, truth, and social action. Earl Warren had been instrumental in the detention of Japanese citizens of the US during World War II as attorney general of California. After serving as governor and pursing the presidency of the United States for nearly a decade, he was named chief justice of the Supreme Court. He pondered prior judicial activism in the Supreme Court (i.e. *Plessy v. Ferguson*) as he rethought the legal arguments in *Brown v. Board of Education*. He realized that the legal arguments about "separate but equal" had denied basic rights and was inconsistent with the Constitution. This was a reframing that advanced equality and social justice. Both men had matured through their careers, reflecting, analyzing, and building moral consciousness, ultimately enabling new forms of action.

It is difficult to prepare aspiring professionals to take these sorts of bold steps in their lives. Certainly the life histories of Mahatma Gandhi and Martin Luther King, Jr.

illustrate activists who exemplify seeking truth in action. Using conscious resistance of the law to illuminate how it denies justice represents an exceptional form of postconventional moral reasoning in action. In addition, Earl Warren's history illustrates how postconventional moral reasoning can be used within the system to make changes. It is possible to emerge from critical circumstances with a new moral vision of what is possible. These are rare and distinctive people who provide role models for us to consider when we reflect on moral reasoning.

PROFESSIONAL DEVELOPMENT

This book refines a developmental view of professional reflection in action and uses case studies of reflective practice and organizational change to illustrate the challenges. The cases studies show that it is possible to address critical challenges within organizations that maintain a strategic orientation, especially if they foster and encourage open discourse. My argument about professional development was predicated on the assumption that individual practitioners were responsible for their own development, a proposition that is reexamined before returning to the developmental schema.

Professional Responsibility

Reflective practice is essential both to develop moral reasoning in practice and become an effective professional. A professional can become highly skilled and effective in technical matters but overlook critical issues in practice. In fact, some artful practitioners are highly skilled at advising their clients on getting around the law. The demise of Andersen Consulting and the bankruptcy of Enron illustrate how highly skilled professionals can systematically engage in deceptive practices.[90] Reflection on strategy and consequences helps build technical skills. In addition, reflection on actions in relation to their consequences and outcomes is necessary to build skills in seeking truth-in-action through reflection on problematic situations, building understanding of causes, designing and testing alternative solutions, and refining and adapting solutions that do not work as intended. Educators can design curricula to encourage the development of reflective skills and moral reasoning, and colleges, corporations, and public agencies can support professional development, but only individual practitioners can take charge of steering their own paths toward moral and responsible action.

For two decades, especially since publication of *Educating the Reflective Practitioner* (Schön, 1987), many professors in professional programs have recognized the need to integrate an emphasis on reflective practice along with the basic knowledge and skills of the profession. Based on the lessons learned in this book, I offer the following agenda for enhancement and reform:

- *Learn the instrumental (basic) foundations of the profession.* These foundations include the knowledge and skills associated with the profession (e.g. counseling, teaching, or nursing), along with a basic orientation to issues of justice and care (i.e. learning the moral codes of practice). Most professional programs meet this challenge.
- *Learn to adapt practices to meet diverse client needs and build new skills.* The artistry of professional practice involves reflection on practice with a focus on improving service, including being more just and caring in practice. Teachings regarding the

adaptation of practice are evident in most professional programs, but the process of encouraging critical reflection is often overlooked and/or optional.

- *Learn to engage in setting goals and designing strategies in a community of practice.* Students should be given opportunities to work in teams on action projects that provide opportunities to engage collectively in setting goals (a process that differs fundamentally from giving and receiving directions, even when done in a friendly manner) and carrying through on projects.
- *Learn to recognize critical, and possibly recurrent, challenges and to envision practices that address these challenges.* After being engaged in a community practice over a period of time, it is possible to approach problems in new ways. If the professional education programs encourage action inquiry, it should be possible for students to build skills in collaborative processes of addressing the challenges. Action inquiry is not emphasized in most professional programs, including the study of higher education.
- *Learn to envision and enact interventions that enable communities of practice to develop communicative skills.* Most organizations need senior practitioners who care about mentoring and the design of more caring and just communities of practice. To achieve this type of pedagogy as an integral part of professional education, it would be necessary to have faculty members actively engaged in action inquiry projects and to involve their students in them.

Organizations that employ professionals, including colleges and universities, face a range of professional development challenges. In colleges and universities, faculty members are motivated to gain tenure during their early careers; often their performance patterns are set when this stage of career development is achieved. Colleges need senior faculty members who are capable of mentoring assistant professors and initiating organizational change. In Chapter 3, I hypothesized the forms of support that were needed, and the cases in Part II illustrate the need for these forms of support:

- *support for development of basic professional knowledge and skills:* an organizational environment with support for best practices, including mentoring and professional support;
- *support for development of strategic skills/artistry:* incentives for professional development within the system including encouragement and support for innovation and ongoing improvement;
- *support for development of open-strategic skills:* professional development support for senior managers, encouraging communicative skills and the integration of just and caring practices into the organization;
- *support for development of communicative skills:* research support for action inquiry, including quantitative and qualitative operational analyses and support for evaluations of collaborative experiments that address injustices and inequalities within the system;
- *support for development of transformational skills:* build a culture and tradition of caring and justice, integrate justice and caring into the mission, and establish support structures for systemic innovations.

In most professional organizations, the first two forms of support are commonly understood and practiced. Some organizations also invest in training leadership. For example, there are numerous workshops available in universities and professional associations, and there are institutes for deans. Support for action inquiry aimed at organizational improvement and changing the culture of organizations to value these qualities is less common, as the case studies in Part II illustrated.

Developmental View

This book refines the sequence of professional development frames—instrumental, closed-strategic, open-strategic, communicative, and transformational frames—as a cycle for learning to reflect on critical problems. The case analyses in Part II support the hypothesis that this skill development process has a sequential aspect: new skills; adaptation and artistry and open communication of using skills to address new challenges; taking responsibility for raising critical issues in organizations, possibly pertaining to the service of clients; and development of methodologies for transforming practice. Engagement in working groups addressing critical challenges is also beneficial, which is why it is important, especially for mid-career professionals, to expand professional education to include an emphasis on these skills.

The critical challenges of seeking truth in action and working to resolve problematic situations face professionals across the framing sequence. Table 10.2 considers the relationships between critical challenges and this sequence of professional frames. These relationships are hypothesized based on the case analyses. Beginning professionals can engage in critical inquiry by reflecting on the needs of clients. Learning the skills of listening to and engaging in dialogue with people from different backgrounds is essential to building these skills. Early-career professionals can try out new approaches in practice as means of meeting the needs of diverse clients. Overly restrictive standards can undermine the development of these skills.[91] Experienced professionals have responsibilities, as senior members of their communities of practice, to provide leadership in reform initiatives and mentor beginning and early career practitioners. Professionals and the clients they serve share responsibility for voicing critical issues and engaging in discourse on resolving challenges when opportunities arise.

These relationships help distinguish the career cycle (i.e the stages of learning and using expertise) from the obligations for the social good among professionals and the citizens they serve. The discursive space for reflection on the social good is frequently overlooked and deemphasized. In many organizations, practitioners feel at risk professionally if they raise critical issues or attempt to voice issues on behalf of consumers served by their organizations. Professionals frequently devalue the everyday knowledge of consumers, making it difficult for them to voice concerns.

In my practice as a professor, I test piloted new approaches to using action inquiry projects within graduate courses as means of enabling students to build skills in using research to support organizational change. My hope is that this type of pedagogy will build skills in creating, honoring, and valuing discursive space to voice critical issues in practice. It is important that faculty members who engage in this type of teaching and action in higher education programs and other professional fields also write about and publish their work. Action scholarship has the potential of broadening the professional literature to include an emphasis on the social good in practice. There is a potential for transformational action by educators, college professors, and professionals of all types. I speculate that this form of action involves working with global citizens and

Table 10.2 Reflections on Critical Challenges in Relation to Sequence of Professional Development

	Challenge 1: **Seek truth in critical situations, rather than rely on beliefs and past practices rationalized based on the rules of the profession.**	*Challenge 2:* **Engage communities affected by practice in discourse to seek inclusive understandings of problematic situations.**
Instrumental: Focus on	learning best practices and reflecting on their strengths and limitations.	routinely considering client needs regarding services and the outcomes of practice.
Closed Strategic: Add	reflection on opportunities to adapt practice to improve success with critical problems.	consideration of diverse perspective on social and environmental challenges in practice.
Open Strategic: Add	engagement in initiatives that enable use and development of reconstructed understandings of challenges and solutions to problems.	generation of evidence from observations, listening, and researching social and environmental challenges.
Communicative: Add	reflection on underlying causes of challenges, including systemic constraints.	consideration of actions that work through systemic constraints to moral action. Break rules only when it is the best moral option.
Transformational: Add	collaboration with allies to envision new forms of practice and new systemic strategies.	working with citizens and peers to transform systems and practices to build cultures of justice and caring.

professionals on action projects using action inquiry and other guides to address critical challenges. My experience with teaching courses on professional development and guiding organizational interventions with graduate students has raised my hopes about this possibility. However, evidence of success, of facilitating individual and organization transformation, is sparse. The big lesson is that there is not a script for teachers or students to follow. Having guides for action helps. Following all the steps, especially those for using evidence to examine assumptions, is essential. At the same time, preconceived frameworks require adaptation to become workable in many settings. For example, I have often found it necessary to move from assessment of challenges (quantitative studies) to evaluations of existing practices as a means of engaging in inquiry before jumping into the process of building an understanding of challenges. Interventionists, like other professionals, must adapt methods to ensure they meet the needs of those with whom they work.

ORGANIZATIONAL DEVELOPMENT

Another framework involves the stages of organizational development: instrumental, closed strategic, open strategic, communicative and transformational. The intervention processes observed within organizations had a common intent of improving the capacity of professionals to address critical challenges, but the intervention methods that worked for practitioners within organizations varied across the states of organizational development. Organization theories too often focus on structural strategies for improvement, including the use of human relations to support organizational missions. My argument has been that organizational support for professional development, with an emphasis on skills in moral reasoning and action inquiry, is integral to organizational development. Before concluding with practical guidance for leaders in professional organizations who seek to address critical challenges, I reconsider the role of strategy in organizational development.

Strategy and Development

It is critical to distinguish strategy that promotes organization control and growth (i.e, the system aspect of organization) from patterns of practice that provide the context for moral judgment and wise professional action among professionals (i.e. the lifeworld of organizations). The two aspects differ, but are integrally related in the organizational development process. It is appropriate for leaders to seek balance between these two aspects of organizations as they pursue and encourage professional development, and create a climate for change and innovation. Table 10.3 summarizes understandings reached in the analyses of Part II about the natural alignments of the system and lifeworld aspects, with intervention strategies practitioners used to engage in reform

Table 10.3 Stages of Organizational Development in Relation to System, Lifeworld, and Intervention Methods

Stage/Sphere	System	Lifeworld	Intervention
Instrumental	• Central control of policy and practice • Regulated procedures for common practice	• Compliance with policy and regulations • Resistance possible • Workaround problem possible	• Alignment with procedures. *Example:* RCC • Seek permission to deviate from practice/pilot test. *Example:* SCCC
Closed Strategic Add	• Strategic initiatives	• Ability to adapt practices related to initiatives	• Integrate innovations with initiatives. *Example:* RTU
Open Strategic Add	• Openness to critical feedback	• Discursive space to collaborate on strategic choices	• Openly chosen strategies and coaching for professionals. *Example:* Principal in reforming school
Communicative Add	• Ability to adapt strategic initiatives to address critical issues that emerge	• Discursive space to change systems and strategies based on the discovery of challenges	• Collaborate to foster system transformation. *Examples:* Regional collaborative and Private Law School
Transformational Add	• Capacity to export change strategies as guides and models	• Reflection on implications of new discoveries and models	• Generate action guides for other reformers. *Example:* PCU

initiatives. The stages of organizational development appear sequential and to build on each other, a discovery reflected in the discussion of cases below.

There were examples of organizations that maintained tight control over policy and strategy, most notably the community colleges in Indiana. The lifeworld experience of practitioners within tightly regulated systems was an apparent choice between compliance and resistance. There was also evidence from student case statements that illustrated the difficulties of practitioners who were treated instrumentally. It is important to distinguish instrumental systemic controls, like the central regulation of course content and enrollment procedures in Indiana's community colleges, from instrumental treatment of practitioners. In the case statement written by the staff member in international student services, the practitioner was treated instrumentally in a situation where there were options for discretion in specific cases. Making this distinction helps clarify two forms of intervention within organizations with instru-mental systemic approaches. It may be easiest to limit interventions to experimentation within the system rules (e.g. RCC), but it is also possible to test pilot new practices that involve altering system rules. In the SCCC case, open-strategic discourse was used by an action team, which enabled them to reframe issues so they could gain approval for the experiments.

If it is possible to have open discourse in action teams formed within instrumental organizations, it should also be possible in other types of organizational settings. While this type of intervention can be difficult to arrange, it is more functional and has greater potential for resolving systemic problems than does resistance or workarounds (i.e. breaking rules to solve critical problems). The role of open discourse by teams of practitioners in organizations with instrumental control merits study. Examination of these questions can help inform a new generation of strategies for organizational changes that can be included in professional education.

Closed-strategic systems provide opportunities for practitioners to align their own interventions with change strategies underway. Thus, adaptive organizations provide more room for innovation and more potential for engagement of practitioners in the improvement of practice. Encouraging practitioners to use their discretion to make adaptive changes not only promotes artistry of practice, it also enables flexibility and change within organizations. The case for the RTU efforts utilizing evaluation services in support of efforts to improve supplemental instruction illustrates this type of adaptive behavior. Individual practitioners can also intervene to encourage action within closed-strategic organizations (e.g. Kim Kline's intervention in planning a student event).

Practitioners can also take steps to encourage strategic adaptation in problematic situations. The case statement by the technology transfer administrator illustrates the transitional behaviors associated with developing adaptive skills: She engaged the department chair and professors in a process of setting shared goals for addressing a new policy. Through this process, she gained support within the organization for dealing with a problematic issue raised by a student making legal claims that were based on a misunderstanding created by policy changes that were not well known.

When organizations or joint ventures between organizations maintain an open-strategic orientation, there is greater opportunity for practitioners to raise issues of concern related to the quality of services. In fact, when discursive space can be created for practitioners to raise new challenges and think through ways they might be addressed, there is great potential for organizational change. In Part II, the case of the working group from the three regional campuses illustrates how a communicative process within a work group can create an opening for change within organizations that maintain strategic control. One dealt with change instrumentally (RCC) and two through closed-strategic methods (RTU and RCC). The communicative process within the collaboration had the potential of creating more room for open discourse within the three colleges. This case of the regional collaboration illustrates that open discourse can be a positive force for change with respect to increasing social justice (i.e. the potential for outcomes like adapting programs to meet the learning needs of new students as a positive change).

Communicative action as an orientation within organizations may be rare and only periodically evident. In the case of the Private University Law School, faculty members raised issues about changing admissions and student aid awards as means of attracting high achieving students of color. The underlying goal was to improve the quality of the dialogue on critical legal issues that involved race and justice. Judging from the interviews with faculty and students, the atmosphere of discourse changed, which was the reason for classifying this case as transformational. In fact, when communicative interventions have their intended outcomes, transformations in the quality of services for consumers are possible. The distinction being made between strategic and communicative action is that through discourse about problematic situations, practitioners can build understanding of problems and try out new initiatives that influence deep organizational change that will be widely accepted.

There is also a possibility for transformational action (i.e. the development of guides for action that other organizations can use for change) to emerge from communicative practices that change cultures and practices within organizations. I used the case study of the Private Christian University to illustrate this potential. PCU undertook a change in services for undeclared students that became a transformational force on the campus, leading to an engaging four-year cocurriculum open to all students. Over the four years, students had opportunities to explore their own interests, designing a learning plan, gaining leadership and community-service experiences, and engaging in a job search. The academic cocurriculum provided a model other campuses could use to inform their efforts to develop new programs.

This book has distinguished change strategies that are guides and have a potential for transformation from change models that are thought to be best practices for replication. Efforts to replicate tend to be implemented instrumentally, without critical reflection, while guides for transformation (e.g. the Action Inquiry Model [AIM]) have the potential for enabling change through critical reflection and local adaptations to address local challenges. This type of change strategy—focusing on transformational changes in practices to address critical challenges—is relatively rare.

Facing Critical Challenges in Organizations

With this background, we can refocus on the challenge of addressing critical problems within organizations. The relationship between the critical challenges and strategies for addressing critical issues is depicted in Table 10.4. In organizations that maintain an instrumental approach, it is crucial to recognize the ways the mission—along with policy and procedures designed to carry out the mission—enables practitioners to address critical challenges. In theory, a small, single-purpose organization can maintain

Table 10.4 Reflections on Critical Challenges in Relation to Sequence of Organizational Development

	Challenge 1: **Seek truth in critical situations, rather than rely on beliefs and past practices rationalized based on the rules of the profession.**	*Challenge 2:* **Engage communities affected by practice in discourse to seek inclusive understandings of problematic situations.**
Instrumental Focus on	Core mission and practices that have evidence of success	Build practices that support professional development and community engagement
Closed Strategic Add	Capacity to generate strategic initiatives that address critical challenges	Emphasize mentoring with reflective exchange as central to organizational development
Open Strategic Add	Capacity to adapt strategies to address critical challenges	Use research on effects of actions with evaluative feedback loop
Communicative Add	Commitment to try out new strategies that address emergent critical social and environmental challenges	Foster open, critical discourse of social and environmental challenges as common practice
Transformation Add	Commitment to balance mission and strategic initiatives with highest values of profession and society	Engagement with community and citizen groups in collaborative problem solving and project initiatives

a capacity to address critical issues related to their core missions. However, as the community college cases and some of the case statements by graduate students reflect, instrumental treatment of practitioners undermines innovations. The challenge is to define procedures that are inclusive of the discretion needed to address critical changes related to core practices.

When organizations begin to use strategic initiatives to alter core practices, there is increased potential to address new critical challenges when, or soon after, they emerge. Strategic plans identify directions for action and programs to move toward new goals. In this environment, there should be more room for practitioners to adapt their practices. Coaching and other forms of mentoring can be particularly helpful in this stage of organizational development.

Open-strategic change encourages open reflection about whether strategies are achieving their intent. Using evidence of effects (i.e. the ways practices relate to outcomes) helps practitioners think through change strategies. Thus, when an open-strategic approach is used, it should be possible to alter strategic initiatives to adapt and alter organizational strategy. Projects started as part of new strategic initiatives might provide a chance to better address problems that emerge. Such an environment could become chaotic if there was not a commitment to using information to inform decisions about altering practice.

When a communicative orientation is evident in practice, the priority of adaptation to address challenges can be central in the organization and culture of practice. From the perspective of 1960s social reform, this could be considered an ideal form of organization. Using organizational resources of personnel and funding to address critical challenges would be central, possibly even an integral part of the organizational mission. From my own perspective, this seems like an approach to organizing that is ideal for the creative environment desired in some academic programs in colleges and universities, as well as in other professions. As the case statements illustrate, this form of organization is possible but is difficult to create and maintain.

The notion of a transformational culture and practice is ethereal. The problem is that any guide for practice and change can become routine rather than innovative; creative energies are easily expended in organizations. Therefore, it is appropriate to envision episodes of transformation between stable periods. Stable organizations capable of addressing critical problems are probably more desirable for most practitioners than organizations oriented toward transformation as a constant state of affairs. An appealing notion is that transformational strategies can be used by organizations to encourage and enable major transitions by the organization, both as a whole and within its subunits. Thus, we can develop and use guides for action to facilitate transformational processes in organizations that have apparent need for rapid change as a result of critical challenges.

CONCLUDING REFLECTIONS

Rather than promoting social transformation as a goal, I have argued that critical social challenges face all professionals as part of their daily practices. It is possible that a deeper integration of moral reasoning into professional action will improve justice, but an emphasis on just practice is critical whether one aims for true social transformation or simply a just and caring practice. While the idea that we generate new policies that will transform society may have intuitive appeal, our common history shows how difficult it is to realize social justice. In this book, I have argued that the progressive period of the late nineteenth and early twentieth centuries culminated in the 1970s, and that since then we have been in a period of adjustment to limited resources, environmental decline, and growing social and economic inequality. The economic progress of the last three decades has increased economic inequities within nation states rather than decreased them (Fogel, 2000; B. M. Friedman, 2005; Harvey, 2005). It will be even more difficult to address inequality in the period ahead because of the limited access to natural resources like oil in the ground and fish in the sea, along with the high cost of overusing these resources.

Even if public policies change to address these big challenges of social inequality and environmental decline, professionals will face critical challenges in their daily practices. Building the capacity to educate aspiring professionals as reflective practitioners who are conscious of the moral dimensions of professional action is critical as a starting point moving toward this aim. Continuing to build a body of research and case studies specific to professions is also crucial. This book introduced new frameworks for moral reasoning in action, professional development, and organizational development that can be used to facilitate reform in professional organizations.

The reconstructed theory of moral reasoning in action shifts the focus from maturation of children to the professional practice of adults. Within Kohlberg's theory, abstracted conceptions of postconventional and conventional moral reasoning rest on the foundation of childhood development. My reconstructed framework assumes adults face new challenges. I have illustrated the importance of avoiding deceptive practices and coaching beginning professionals who aim to work on problems in practices as means of reducing critical social problems. Open discourse can foster conventional moral action that aligns organizational strategies with new practices that confront social and environmental problems. Further, critically analyzing the causes of recurrent problems provides a basis for transforming conventions to promote justice within organizations. Critical analysis is a practical approach to postconventional moral reasoning and problem solving.

Reconstructing concepts of reflective practice to include an emphasis on professional maturation and moral reasoning provides a new framework for professional development. Obtaining the knowledge and skills that comprise the rules and ethical standards for professions provides a foundational point of departure for professional practice. However, using expertise in problem solving can easily lead to overlooking the ways in which established practices contribute to inequality and injustice, subsequently leading to the denial of access to basic services, including education. The alternative is to encourage critical reflection on problems that emerge in practice, testing new techniques that build artistry of practice and engaging teams of professionals in reconstructing organizational strategies. Encouraging reflection on the reasons for problems, including openly discussing the intended consequences of current practices, is critical to reflective and just practice within professional organizations.

The reconstructed approach to organizational development provides practical approaches to integrating action inquiry—using quantitative and qualitative methods of analysis—into the organizational reform process. While the common strategy of emphasizing best practices is a point of departure for quick fixes, it is crucial to have systematic processes that examine the effects of those practices and encourage open conversation among practitioners about strategies for improving practice. Improvement of techniques is part of the process, but encouraging changes in practice to address inequalities and encourage responsible action by, and service to, consumers is no less important.

NOTES

1. In the U.S. system, opportunity can expand while racial isolation persists, an artifact of deep racism that has been hard to remedy. While segregation and equal opportunity are related issues, it is possible to make progress on one and not the other. Different policies affect integration and diversity than those that affect opportunity for low-income students.
2. There was, of course, greater inequality of opportunity based on gender and race in the late 1800s, when colleges and universities held to religious values, than in the twentieth century (Marsden, 1994; Thelin, 2004). Therefore, we should not idealize the historical relationship between faith and education.
3. I undertook this interpretive introspection on the Synoptic Gospels as a "Christian Catholic" teaching in a secular university. This was an exploration of the role of faith and moral reasoning in practice. I wanted to explore how faith provides a foundation for critical and spiritual introspection. My argument is that critical and/or spiritual introspection is a necessary component of postconventional moral reasoning, which is a more inclusive perspective on moral learning than either enlightenment-situated theories of justice (e.g. Habermas, 1991; Kohlberg, 1981; Nussbaum, 1999; Rawls, 1971) or the religious traditions.
4. In this book I refer to a *critical challenge* as a recurrent problem that requires recognition, inquiry, and understanding before it can be addressed. This book is primarily concerned with *critical social challenges*, which are recurrent problems of social injustice that challenge practitioners to assess their own practices, identify and test alternative practices, and build understanding of the ways critical social problems can be addressed. I also recognize that there are many *critical environmental challenges* that also require change in practice and that complicate efforts to reduce inequality and other injustices, but that are nonetheless important issues for all professionals to concern themselves with as they make efforts to improve their professional practice.
5. Habermas (2003) argues communicative action is oriented toward both moral development and *social integration*. He provides a distinct discussion of human rights as part of social integration. Regarding professional action, I argue it is appropriate to think of action as being oriented toward the social good rather than merely relying on the overused term of social integration.
6. In this book, I view graduate education of future professors as a form of professional education.
7. Weber wrote during an earlier period and had a historical perspective of the transition to nation states. He was among the first to observe the emergence of bureaucracy and to conceptualize its implications. In contrast, Parsons worked during the modern period and sought universal explanations of organization and society.
8. I use the term *frames* to denote linked sets of assumptions as patterns of reflection and action that are commonly used in professional practice. The cases in Part II illustrate frames of practitioner reflection.
9. This theory was originally conceptualized in the 1960s when access to business was largely through undergraduate education. Recipients of MBA degrees from elite institutions are among the highest earning groups. In the sense of wealth accumulation, business may no longer be considered a middle-class

profession, especially for recipients of advanced degrees. However, business degrees are among the most common undergraduate degrees and have replaced liberal arts as the certificate for entry into beginning professional work.

10. The ABA and AMA have different roles in regulating entry into their professions than the AAUP. The AAUP standards have a stronger influence on the tenure process in research universities than in the typical U.S. college or university.

11. While it may seem ideal to have a society in which neither race nor income are considered, this is not an attainable standard at present, given the impact of income on access to quality elementary and secondary education. The methods used in selection for admission to graduate and undergraduate programs are among the contested issues professionals need to address.

12. Ability measures are difficult to discuss at the same time as issues of social justice are being considered. However, prior grades and test scores (ACT or SAT for undergraduates in the US, or GRE or other specialized tests for applicants to graduate school) are used in admissions. There are alternative measures (e.g. Sedlacek, 2004), but they are not widely used and there are concerns about their validity (King & Bowman, 2006). Thus, it is crucial to openly discuss achievement and ability measures as part of the discourse on professional action and education.

13. In most universities, the fields of arts, science, and humanities or literature form the core academic subjects. Consistent with the liberal arts tradition (Thelin, 2004), undergraduate students are required to take some courses in each area—sometimes they are required to take common courses or to choose from a common list of courses. In addition, when students choose a major, they have common basic courses in the major, as well as specialization courses. Within this basic structure, universities typically have professional schools (or programs in smaller colleges) that offer courses in undergraduate fields with professional content (e.g. nursing, education, engineering, agriculture, and so forth).

14. In most colleges and universities, much of the content specialization is acquired in courses in the core disciplines.

15. Students who graduate from diverse fields can also apply to doctoral programs in higher education, history of education, counseling, and some other specializations in education that do not require teaching certificates.

16. Different theories are used to explain career choice. For example, there is a great deal of research on personality types in relation to vocation (e.g. Smart, Feldman, & Ethington, 2000), but such methods of codification may not fully capture the diversity of learning styles and habits of practice that go into these individual decisions. Nevertheless, developmental theories provide another way of viewing patterns of educational choices.

17. Andersen Consulting, once a "big five" firm, went out of business after malpractice in the Enron case (see http://en.wikipedia.org/wiki/Arthur_Andersen). For background on Enron, see http://en.wikipedia.org/wiki/Enron.

18. I make this observation based on my own experience with finding competent medical help for myself and family members. Veterans of health care have many stories of this sort of malpractice, which is a relatively common pattern of patient treatment when high cost procedures could result from alternative diagnoses.

19. The class action suits against the tobacco industry document a consistent pattern of deception (see www.smokershistory.com/lawsuits.htm).

20. For reviews of research by the National Center for Education Statistics (NCES) on the educational pipeline see Advisory Committee on Student Financial Assistance (2002), Becker (2004), Fitzgerald (2004), and Lee (2004).

21. In this book I use the terms *social good* and *economic development*, rather than using the term *public good*, which is often interpreted to emphasize economic development and economic returns to individuals (Pasque, 2007). Using the two terms presents a more specific and appropriate emphasis.

22. The book uses *she* and *her* for individuals rather than he/she or him/her. The choice is influenced by the history of use of the latter and out of respect for the fact that the majority of high school graduates and college students are women.

23. As a student of an earlier era, I started journaling as an undergraduate. My preference was to use text journals and I continued this method for decades. Periodic reflections, along with meditations during some periods of transition, provided means of steering a professional path that I could live with, as I struggled with the development of my own moral consciousness as an adult and a professional researcher and educator.

24. Deism was thought of as a belief in God, but it was not centered in any particular religion or sect.

25. The statement of rights guaranteed in the U.S. Constitution as originally ratified by the states.

26. Native American and other older religious traditions also merit study and, in many instances, preservation.

Indeed, understanding one's own cultural and religious heritage is critical, and it is important that we all act respectfully to diverse traditions.

27. It is important we do not forget that a substantial portion of the Indian subcontinent gained freedom through the nonviolent revolution led, at least in spirit and deed, by Mahatma Gandhi. The states of Pakistan, India, and Bangladesh (originally East Pakistan) eventually formed after much conflict, turmoil, and violence. This standard of human action set in the revolutionary period was not retained in the reformation of the three nations.

28. While the Hindu and Buddhist traditions situated moral authority in tradition, the Jewish tradition set forward laws as moral codes.

29. Historically, the land known both as Israel and Palestine has been claimed as sacred by the Jewish, Islamic, and Christian traditions. For centuries, wars have been fought in the region over religious claims of rights to the land. Since my focus is images of development and social justice, I do not emphasize the issues related to the claims of nation states about regional dominance in this book.

30. The recorded history of Jesus was reinterpreted over time by scribes who added their own interpretations as they translated and copied the texts. In my study of biblical text, I have used the King James Bible, as republished by Sharman (1917), because it places the three Synoptic Gospels side by side in tracing events in a common order.

31. Matthew, Mark, and Luke were the earliest books of the Bible handed down and copied by scribes in different languages (Ehrman, 2005). The scribes sometimes editorialized and reinterpreted texts. Consequently, the original source material of the life of Jesus is not retained, but there is strong evidence to support the argument that he lived in the region (Crossan, 1992).

32. As a Christian and Catholic who studies the Gospels, I approach this tradition more directly than I can for the other traditions. My comments convey my own interpretation of the Gospels (adapted from St. John, 2009) rather than focusing on the interpretations of others.

33. Conversely, social engagement without critical self reflection can create, instead of solve, critical problems. See the discussion of preconventional moral reasoning in the next chapter.

34. I used the term *global citizens* to address the limits of legal citizenship with different nations. In my view all people are citizens of the world and have rights as such.

35. The Pell Grant maximum award actually declined in the late 1980s (as discussed in reference to Figure 2.2).

36. People denied legal citizenship also have human rights to global citizenships, and as such they should have access to the education they need for economic survival and wellbeing. In fact, much of the illegal migration is attributable to the desire for economic wellbeing.

37. Bolman and Deal (1991) use four frames (see Chapter 5): political (akin to a critical view of justice), structural (akin to technical-scientific), human resources (akin to social), and culture (akin to interpretive). Cameron and Lavine (2006) also propose four similar frames to differential role in organizations (see Chapter 6). I am using the terminology of critical, interpretive, social, and technical-scientific as appropriate ways of differentiating ways to view problems with social and, possibly, environmental justice.

38. In Chapter 5 these frames' differences are further explored in relation to organizational frames and professional expertise.

39. Argyris and Schön's discussion of Model II also identified two consequences for the quality of life: (1) "quality of life will become more positive than negative"; and (2) "effectiveness of problem solving and decision making will be great, especially for difficult problems" (1974, p. 87). With the broader questions of moral reasoning and the social good, these rubrics were of little value.

40. While Argyris and Schön's implicit assumptions about organizational effectiveness were problematic with respect to moral action, ET and TIU are independent of assumptions about efficacy. Whether one focuses on achieving an aim or building a collective understanding of action situations, these two mechanisms can accurately depict the role of action theories.

41. In colleges and universities, for example, annual pay increases for faculty are usually tied to research production, teaching evaluations, and other performance indicators.

42. I encourage readers to take a step beyond the instrumental application of the methods introduced and to try these processes with a focus on building their reflective skills and an awareness of critical social issues.

43. Habermas (1984) makes this distinction, as do others. The distinction is important when thinking about theory in action, including the assumptions people hold about action situations. In addition, it should be noted that Argyris and Schön (1974) focus on situated reasoning (see Chapter 3).

44. The use of indicators of statistical significance when examining associations between variables can be misleading if we do not fully consider their meaning. For example, a high correlation (on a scale of 0 to 1) is considered to be 0.5, but that means that only 50 percent of the cases are correlated. Further, a correlation does not mean causality. Two factors thought to be linked could both be caused by some other variable

outside the statistical model. This point is that researchers frequently use statistics, especially the cumulative body of research from multiple studies, to make claims about universal patterns of relationship. It is important to be more circumspect about causality, especially in circumstances that involve situated human action. A strong pattern of relationships reported in the research literature may not hold in many individual cases. For example, the correlation between high parental education and enrollment in college by children is often reported, but many individuals who enroll in college do not have college-educated parents. In other words, there is a universal pattern of a relationship between parents' education and the educational attainment of children, but it does not hold in all cases. There can be circumstances in which universal claims have little meaning.

45. I examined persistence (i.e. whether a student maintained continuous enrollment) rather than intent to persist. People may have the intent to persist but may not be able to do so for academic reasons.

46. The complexity of the organization needs to be considered in the design of an assessment process that involves professionals in the organization. Ideally, the process would take place at the level of practice as well as at an aggregate level which combines data and collective reflections, creating opportunities to gain insight into patterns of practice as they relate to recurrent problems. In IPAS, the state student information system (SIS) and other databases in Indiana were used to develop a baseline assessment, and supplemental studies were conducted for specific campuses. Statewide groups met to discuss shared challenges and campus teams focused on identifying local problems.

47. Computer simulation of alternatives works in cases where there is historical data (e.g. student price response), but many critical challenges lack this type of historical data because the alternatives generally have not been previously tried.

48. An action hypothesis can be treated as testable in practice. However, if people actually believe in a form of practice, their attention shifts to making the method work rather than focusing on testing whether it really works or fits the specific situations in which it is used.

49. While there are several decades of research on organizational frame (Bolman & Deal, 1991; Smart and St. John, 1996), the relationship between frames and content within different professional fields has not been previously studied.

50. The Pareto Principle, a pseudo science widely used in management sciences, assumes 20 percent of the cases cause 80 percent of the problems.

51. As a professor in the field of higher education, I had not reviewed these standards before starting this chapter. I made assumptions about the profession based on experience. Since my specialization is not student affairs per se, and I have not been professionally affiliated with ACPA, I did not even think about reviewing these standards before one of my students wrote about them. I had realized it was important for professors to have an understanding of the ethical codes in their fields, but I had not acted on this assumption. I am glad I took this step and encourage other seasoned professionals to make sure they review the ethical standards for their field of practice.

52. These statements are personal reflections. The first three probably apply to most faculty members in this and other universities. The last statement refers to the content of my research and the obligation I feel toward just action. Each professional can probably make their own statement about social responsibility.

53. The cases presented in Part II were originally drawn, with permission, from student papers. The cases have been modified as appropriate to disguise specific circumstances.

54. This case was previously presented and discussed by Kim Kline (2003) and is reproduced with her permission.

55. Rather than creating themes across courses to attract students, the apparent strategy in this case was to intervene and assign a group of students to the same classes.

56. Post-hoc reflections, such as the discussion of the case statements (which were written and analyzed by students), encourage individual learning, but this retrospective form of learning does not change organizations.

57. While The Reflective Practitioner (Schön, 1983) followed earlier work on professional effectiveness (Argyris & Schön, 1974), in my view reflective practice fills a missing link in structural and process-oriented theories of organizational change. I argue that reflective skills are needed to engage in open discourse, based on an understanding of the underlying sequence of skill development and actionable knowledge (St. John, 2008).

58. The concept of abundance implies having the resources to address problems, a condition that may not be present in many organizations.

59. The importance of trust is explored further in Chapter 7.

60. This is the most troubling aspect of the theory of professional effectiveness. It treats problem solving as central, but overlooks critical social contexts for professional action (St. John, 2009). The same problem could apply to individual professional action.

61. Films can provide a window on behaviors, like sexual harassment, that are not normally discussed even in interviews. They show patterns illustrative of human experience. These and other scenes were discussed by Patricia First (1993), myself, and others in a meeting of the American Educational Research Association.

62. The behaviors outlined in Table 6.1 are similar to those in Arygris and Schön's Model I. In my view, the closed-strategic frame is developmentally more advanced than the instrumental behavior of applying rules. This reconstruction is consonant with Schön's concepts in *Educating the Reflective Practitioner* (1987), as previously discussed. These earlier conceptions of reflective behavior did not explicitly consider the problem of power abuse.

63. While the SAE had been part of the process for eight years, Margaret had been the administrator of the office for only about four years, long enough to observe the pattern.

64. This case is discussed in Chapter 9 in the discussion of transformational change. PCU's adaptation used IPAS support for evaluation of an existing program which illustrates closed-strategic action. At the same time, the intervention itself, along with efforts to use the model as a framework for reform in other colleges, illustrates features of transformational change (as discussed in Chapter 9). There are other examples of individuals being engaged in projects illustrating different forms of reasoning (e.g. members of RCC who were instrumental in implementing linked courses [Chapter 5] were involved in communicative multicollege projects [discussed in Chapter 9]). These examples further illustrate the situational nature of problem framing and analysis.

65. As noted in the Introduction, I agree with Habermas's argument that professionals should equally value the lifeworld experience and system intent. I have doubts about the notion of effectiveness as a meaningful concept, given the implicit alignment with central aims. I think a greater specificity of outcomes that is implicit in the concept of effectiveness is needed. With this caveat, I address the complex issue of using reflective learning in the organizational improvement process.

66. Even Arygris and Schön's Model II is prone to this problem because of the emphasis on effectiveness and an intent tied to an organization's mission, aims, and strategies.

67. Tierney's one reference to inequality is in relation to Bourdieu's (1977) concept of social capital: "Bourdieu focuses on the function and production of inequality and power" (2006, p. 28). In my view, we need to understand the reproduction of inequality before we can formulate new hypotheses about how to intervene to reduce injustice. Tierney (2006) emphasizes building trust and does not delve into strategies for reducing inequality, a topic he has addressed elsewhere (e.g. Tierney & Venegas, 2007).

68. In my view, paying taxes is a right and responsibility of global citizenship, but not all people have sufficient income to pay taxes. Access to services should not be determined by payment of taxes or ability to pay. All global citizens have rights to education and health care, although public laws may change access in some states.

69. My argument in this book is that private corporations have a moral obligation to society as well as to the people who hold ownership through stocks. Constructing a practical understanding of this responsibility is crucial, but is beyond the aims of this text.

70. In my own experience in consulting firms I have observed this tendency as a form of collusion between consultants and clients. I do not know how pervasive these practices are, but the conditions of contemporary society suggest that a post-progressive stance is appropriate.

71. Several students did go on and practice methods of intervention that exhibited these qualities, including Joseph Cadray, a case discussed previously (Cadray, 1997; St. John, 2008; St. John & Cadray, 2004), and Cleveland Hill (1995).

72. After reviewing Arygris and Schön's theory of professional effectiveness in relation to Habermas's critical theory, I concluded that their positivist assumptions about effectiveness limited the applicability of their theory in social change, along with their assumption of top–down control (St. John, 2009).

73. Historically, Jesus was a Jewish rabbi. While he preached a doctrine that differed from contemporary interpretations by Temple Priests, his references were to the holy texts of the Jewish faith. The Roman Empire created the Christian faith as it is known, situating its locus along the north Mediterranean, not the Middle East. The notion of Christian domination of the region in the Middle Ages was hegemonic.

74. As noted earlier (see Chapter 7), there is room to debate some items of Nussbaum's list of capabilities. For example, women's right to health can be constrained by laws on abortion, and moral arguments about allowing women's right to choose, even in the third trimester, are still subject to moral debate across faith traditions.

75. This discussion draws primarily from Jim Newton's *Justice for All: Earl Warren and the Nation He Made* (2006).

76. In St. John (2007) I discuss cases in which I have changed my position based on evidence. I have done this many times over the years, so I am not holding colleagues to a standard that I do not value. Rather, we all

must engage in a discourse that seeks to find better pathways to economic, social, and educational justice, even when this involves altering our views.

77. Critical theories (Geuss, 1981; Argyris, Putnam, & Smith, 1985) assume it is possible to design intervention strategies that include introspection of the state of affairs and envisioning and implementing new practices. These guides for action create opportunities for transformational change, but do not guarantee it will happen, even if the elements of the action steps are implemented (St. John, 2009).

78. While Marxism was often criticized as being atheist, the underlying concepts have been widely adapted and are consonant with biblical texts (Gutierrez, 1998) and other faith traditions.

79. The research for this case was conducted for the NAACP Legal Defense fund (LDF) with the assistance of Britany Affolter-Caine. This support is gratefully acknowledged. The opinions expressed are the author's and do not reflect policies or positions of the LDF.

80. LSSSE survey results are provided to law schools based on their participation in the survey. The results are campus specific and not otherwise published. This case study is presented with permission of the law school and references the actual report provided by the campus. No specific reference can be provided: the report is not in the public domain; providing the specific identifiers would reveal the campus name, which would be inappropriate.

81. At the University of Michigan, I am working with groups on projects that involve partnerships with public schools, the evaluation of interventions in undergraduate engineering and science programs, and the development of new projects to support improvements in diversity.

82. I resigned leadership of the IPAS project when I moved to the University of Michigan. There is some evidence that planning process for replication has proceeded. In their volume of *Readings on Equal Education*, Hossler, Ziskin, and Gross (in press), observe that action research is difficult, but their volume illustrates a continuation of the process.

83. I am using the term "prestige-seeking behavior" here to denote efforts to replicate best practice without critical thought about local circumstances. This implies taking action that looks good to external groups is a priority in the organization.

84. For example, in interviews with faculty members differences of opinion were expressed about how the law school should respond to legal challenges, but there was agreement about the value of PID among faculty members with divergent opinions about defense of the university in the case. In contrast, at PCU the commitment to the Christian tradition created a commonality of values in the college.

85. This is a personal opinion derived from decades of experience. I am more than happy to review evidence to the contrary. However, there is a serious problem with researcher or interventionist bias. When a facilitative approach is used, it is easier for participants to reflect on their own aims and values in relation to the problems they see. When we act as advocates, we encourage what is important to us, and those we are working with may end up acting instrumentally. Consider the RCC case in Chapter 5 as an example.

86. I am using the term deceptive practice here to illustrate complicated moral problems in practice. There are many personal pathological reasons for making problematic choices. In this section, I am open about a situation that troubled me for decades.

87. The *Education Consolidation and Improvement Act* of 1980, legislated during President Jimmy Carter's administration, removed requirements from laws, gave more discretion, and started the country down the path of lower funding.

88. The *Middle Income Student Assistance Act* of 1978 started this shift and the budget agreements over the next three decades carried forward public finance polices favoring the middle-income population over equal access for the poor (St. John, 2006).

89. As I have discussed elsewhere (St. John, 1994, 2003), I was involved as a researcher in the study of minority enrollment that generated the now infamous Algebra finding (Pelavin & Kane, 1988). At the time, many researchers exposed the problem with the conclusions in the report. In fact, several researchers quit the firm over the issue. My own reflection of this personal moral challenge has been part of my own decision to take the academic path, rather than remain a consultant, and address questions of social justice and moral responsibility in my research.

90. For background on Enron, see: http://en.wikipedia.org/wiki/Enron.

91. Standards are used to guide professional practice. Unfortunately, in K–12 education, overly restrictive standards run the risk of suppressing the creativity of teachers (Mirón & St. John, 2007).

REFERENCES

Adelman, C. (2004). *Principle indicators of student academic histories in postsecondary education, 1972–2000*. Washington, DC: U.S. Department of Education, Institute of Education Sciences.

Advisory Committee on Student Financial Assistance (2001). *Access denied: Restoring the nation's commitment to equal educational opportunity*. Washington, DC: Advisory Committee on Student Financial Assistance.

Advisory Committee on Student Financial Assistance (2002). *Empty promises: The myth of college access in America*. Washington, DC: Advisory Committee on Student Financial Assistance.

Alejandro, R. (1998). *The limits of Rawlsian justice*. Baltimore: Johns Hopkins University Press.

Alexander, K. L., & Eckland, B. K. (1974). Sex differences in the educational attainment process. *American Sociological Review, 39*(5), 668–682.

Alexander, K. L., & Eckland, B. K. (1978). Basic attainment processes: A replication and extension, 1999. *Sociology of Education, 48*(4), 457–495.

Allen, W. R., Harris, A., & Dinwiddie, G. (2008). Saving grace: Comparison of African American Gates Millennium Scholarship recipients and non-recipients. In W. T. Trent & E. P. St. John (Eds.), *Resources, assets, strengths among diverse students: Understanding the contributions of the Gates Millennium Scholars Program*. Readings on Equal Education (Vol. 23 pp. 20–48). New York: AMS Press.

Altbach, P., Berdahl, R., & Gumport, P. (2005). *American higher education in the twenty-first century: Social, political, and economic challenges*. Baltimore: Johns Hopkins University Press.

Ancheta, A. N. (2007). Antidiscrimination law and race-conscious recruitment, retention, and financial aid policies in higher education. In G. Orfield, P. Marin, S. M. Flores, & L. M. Garces (Eds.), *Charting the future of college affirmative action: Legal victories, continuing attacks, and new research* (pp. 15–34). Los Angeles: Civil Rights Project, UCLA School of Education.

Argyris, C. (1993). *Knowledge for action: A guide to overcoming barriers to organizational change*. San Francisco: Jossey-Bass.

Argyris, C., Putnam, R., & Smith, D. M. (1985). *Action science: Concepts, methods, and skills for research and intervention*. San Francisco: Jossey-Bass.

Argyris, C., & Schön, D. A. (1974). *Theory in practice: Increasing professional effectiveness*. San Francisco: Jossey-Bass.

Argyris, C., & Schon, D. A. (1978). *Organizational learning: A theory of action perspective*. Reading, MA: Addison-Wesley.

Argyris, C., & Schön, D. A. (1996). *Organizational learning II: Theory, method, and practice*. Reading, MA: Addison-Wesley.

Armstrong, K. (1993). *A history of God: The 4,000-year quest of Judaism, Christianity, and Islam*. New York: Random House.

Bair, D. (2003). *Jung: A biography*. New York: Bay Back Books.

Banks, R. R. (2007). Race-conscious affirmative action and race-neutral policies in the aftermath of the Michigan Cases. In G. Orfield, P. Marin, S. M. Flores, & L. M. Garces (Eds.), *Charting the future of college affirmative action: Legal victories, continuing attacks, and new research* (pp. 35–56). Los Angeles: Civil Rights Project, UCLA School of Education.

Bastedo, M. N. (2006). Curriculum in higher education: The historical roots of contemporary problems. In P. G. Altbach, R. O. Berdahl, & P. J. Gumport (Eds.), *Higher education and the twenty-first century: Social, political, and economic challenges,* Second edition, (pp. 425–461). Baltimore: Johns Hopkins University Press.

Becker, G. S. (1964). *Human capital: A theoretical and empirical analysis with special reference to education.* New York: Columbia University Press.

Becker, W. E. (2004). Omitted variables and sample selection in studies of college-going decisions. In E. P. St. John (Ed.), *Public policy and college access: Investigating the federal and state roles in equalizing postsecondary opportunity.* Readings on Equal Education (Vol. 19, pp. 65–86). New York: AMS Press.

Blau, P. M., & Duncan, O. D. (1967). *The American occupational structure.* New York: Wiley.

Bok, D. (2003). *Universities in the marketplace: The commercialization of higher education.* Princeton, NJ: Princeton University Press.

Bolman, L. G., & Deal, T. E. (1991 & 1996). *Reframing organizations: Artistry, choice, and leadership.* San Francisco: Jossey-Bass.

Bolman, L. G., & Deal, T. E. (1995). *Leading with soul: An uncommon journey of spirit.* San Francisco: Jossey-Bass.

Bourdieu, P. (1974). The school as a conservative force: Scholastic and cultural inequalities. In J. Eggleston (Ed.), *Contemporary research in the sociology of education* (pp. 32–46). London: Metheun.

Bourdieu, P. (1977). *Outline of a theory of practice* (R. Nice, Trans.). New York: Cambridge University Press.

Bourdieu, P. (1990). *Reproduction in education, society, and culture.* London: Sage.

Braxton, J. M. (Ed.). (2000). *Reworking the student departure puzzle.* Nashville, TN: Vanderbilt University Press.

Braxton, J. M., Sullivan, A. S., & Johnson, R. M. (1997). Appraising Tinto's theory of college student departure. In J. C. Smart (Ed.), *Higher education: A handbook of theory and research,* (Vol. 12, pp. 107–164). New York: Agathon Press.

Brown v. Board of Education, 347 U.S. 483 (1954).

Brown, R. E. (1994). *An introduction to New Testament christology.* New York: Paulist.

Bstan-ʾdzin rgya, mtsho, Dalai Lama XIV, (2005). *The universe in a single atom: The convergence of science and spirituality.* New York: Morgan Road Books.

Bstan-ʾdzin rgya, mtsho, Dalai Lama XIV, (2007). *Mind in comfort and ease: The vision of enlightenment in the great perfection.* Somerville, MA: Wisdom Publications.

Cadray, J. P. (1995). *Enhancing multiculturalism in a teacher preparation program: A reflective analysis of a practitioner's intervention.* University Microfilms No. 9701563. *Dissertation Abstracts International, 57*(8).

Cameron, K., & Lavine, M. (2006). *Making the impossible possible: Leading extraordinary performance—the Rocky Flats story.* San Francisco: Barrett-Koehler.

Carter, D. F. (2001). *A dream deferred? Examining the degree aspirations of African American and white college students.* New York: Garland Publishing.

Ceric, M. (2004). Judaism, Christianity, and Islam: Hope or fear of our times. In J. L. Heft (Ed.), *Beyond violence: Religious sources of social transformation in Judaism, Christianity, and Islam* (pp. 43–56). New York: Fordham University Press.

Chaffee, E. E. (1983). Role of rationality in university budgeting. *Research in Higher Education, 19*(4), 387–406.

Cheng, M. J., Altbach, P. G., & Lomotey, K. (2006). Race in higher education: Making meaning of an elusive moving target. In P. G. Altbach, R. O. Berdahl, & P. J. Gumport (Eds.), *American higher education in the twenty-first century: Social, political, and economic challenges,* Second edition (pp. 517–536). Baltimore: Johns Hopkins University Press.

Cohen, R., & Zelnik, R. E. (Eds.) (2002). *The free speech movement: Reflections on Berkely in the 1960s.* Berkeley, CA: University of California Press.

Collins, F. S. (2006). *The language of God: A scientist presents evidence of belief.* New York: Free Press.

Commission on the Skills of the American Workforce, (2007). *Tough choices, tough times: The report of the new commission on skills of the American workforce.* Washington, DC: National Center on Education and the Economy.

Conklin, K. D, & Curran, B. K. (2005). *Action agenda for improving America's high schools.* (Retrieved November 14, 2008.) Sponsored by Achieve, Inc., and the National Governors Association. http://www.nga.org/Files/pdf/0502ACTIONAGENDA.pdf/.

Connell, R. (2007). Poverty and education. In C. D. da Silva, J. P. Huguley, Z. Kakli, & R. Rao (Eds.), *The opportunity gap: Achievement and inequality in education. Harvard Educational Review.* Reprint Series (No. 43, pp. 13–36). Cambridge, MA: Harvard Education Press.

Connerly, W. (2000). A vision for America, beyond race. *Intellectual ammunition.* (Retrieved October 2, 2002.) www.heartland.org/ia/novdec00/connerly.htm.

Cox, H. (1977). *Turning east: Why Americans look to the orient and what the search can mean to the west.* New York: Simon & Schuster.

Creswell, J. W. (2003). *Research design: Qualitative, quantitative, and mixed methods approaches,* Second edition. Thousand Oaks, CA: Sage Publications.

Crossan, J. D. (1992). *The historical Jesus: The life of a Mediterranean peasant.* San Francisco: HarperCollins.

Curs, B. R., Singell, L. D., & Waddell, G. R. (2006). The Pell program at thirty years. In J. C. Smart (Ed.), *Higher education: Handbook of theory and research* (pp. 228–261). Dordrecht, Netherlands: Springer.

Daun-Barrett, N. (2008). *Preparation and access: A multi-level analysis of state policy influences on the academic antecedents to college enrollment.* Ph.D. Dissertation: Ann Arbor, MI: University of Michigan.

David, L., Bender, L., & Burns, S. Z. (Producers), & Guggenheim, D. (Director) (2006). *An inconvenient truth.* [Film]. United States: Paramount.

Dear, J. (2006). Introduction. In M. Gandhi, *Mohandas Gandhi essential writings* (pp. 17–48). Maryknoll, NY: Obris.

Dewey, J. (1927 & 1988). *The public and its problems.* Athens, OH: Swallow Press.

Dobel, J. P. (1999). *Public integrity.* Baltimore: Johns Hopkins University Press.

Durkheim, É. (1951). *Suicide* (J.A. Spaulding & G. Simpson, Trans.). Glencoe, IL: The Free Press.

Edelstein, L. (1943) *The Hippocratic oath: Text, translation, and interpretation.* Baltimore: Johns Hopkins Press. (http://www.pbs.org/wgbh/nova/doctors/oath_classical.html).

Ehrenberg, R. G. (2002). *Tuition rising: Why college costs so much.* Cambridge, MA: Harvard University Press.

Ehrman, B. D. (2005). *Misquoting Jesus: The story behind who change the Bible and why.* San Francisco: HarperCollins.

Elementary and Secondary Education Act (ESEA) (Pub.L. 89–10, 79 Stat. 27, 20 U.S.C.)

Erickson, E. H. (1969). *Gandhi's truth: On the origins of militant nonviolence.* New York: W. W. Norton and Company.

Etzioni, A. (1988). *The moral dimension: Toward a new economics.* New York: Free Press.

Etzioni, A. (1993). *The community spirit: Rights, responsibility, and the communitarian agenda.* New York: Crown.

Fields, F. (Producer), & Brooks, R. (Director). (1977). *Looking for Mr. Goodbar.* [Film]. United States: Paramount.

Finn, C. (1990). Why we need choice. In W. L. Boyd & H. J. Walberg (Eds.), *Choice in education: Potential and problems* (pp. 3–20). Berkeley, CA: McCutchan Publishing Corporation.

Finnan, C. R., St. John, E. P., McCarthy, J., & Slovacek, S. P. (Eds.). (1995). *Accelerated schools in action: Lessons from the field.* Thousand Oaks, CA: Corwin Press.

Firestone, R. (2004). Judaism on violence and reconciliation: An examination of key sources. In J. L. Heft (Ed.), *Beyond violence: Religious sources of social transformation in Judaism, Christianity, and Islam* (pp. 43–56). New York: Fordham University Press.

First, P. F. (1993). *Exploring the dark side of academic culture: Film as a window on sexual harassment in higher education.* Paper presented October 21–22 at American Educational Research Association Annual Meeting, Atlanta, GA.

Fitzgerald, B. K. (2004). Federal financial aid and college access. In E. P. St. John (Ed.), *Public policy and college access: Investigating the federal and state roles in equalizing postsecondary opportunity.* Readings on Equal Education (Vol. 19, pp. 1–28). New York: AMS Press.

Fogel, R. W. (2000). *The fourth great awakening and the future of egalitarianism.* Chicago: Chicago University Press.

Foucault, M. (1980). *Power/knowledge.* Brighton, UK: Harvester Press.

Fowler, J. W. (1981). *Stages of faith: The psychology of human development and the quest for meaning.* San Francisco: HarperCollins.

Friedman, B. M. (2005). *The moral consequences of economic growth.* New York: Vintage.

Friedman, T. L. (2005). *The world is flat: A brief history of the twenty-first century.* New York: Farrar, Straus, and Giroux.

Garnes v. McCann, 21 Ohio St. 198, 210, State ex rel.

Geuss, R. (1981). *The idea of a critical theory: Habermas and the Frankfurt School.* New York: Cambridge University Press.

Ghandi, Mahatma (2002). *Ghandi (in my own words).* London: Hodder & Stoughton.

Gilligan, C. (1982). *In a different voice: Psychological theory and women's development.* Cambridge, MA: Harvard University Press.

Gilpin, R. (2001). *Global political economy: Understanding the international economic order.* Princeton, NJ: Princeton University Press.

Globus, Y., & Golan, M. (Producers), & Ross, H. (Director). (1987). *Dancers.* [Film]. United States: Golan-Globus Productions.

Gordon, E. B. (1999). *Education and justice: View from the back of the bus.* Albany, NY: SUNY Press.

Gratz v. Bollinger, 539 U.S. 244 (2003).

Greenberg, I. (2004). Religion as a force for reconciliation and peace: A Jewish analysis. In J. L. Heft (Ed.), *Beyond violence: Religious sources of social transformation in Judaism, Christianity, and Islam* (pp. 88–112). New York: Fordham University Press.

Grutter v. Bollinger, 539 U.S. 306 (2003).

Guggenbuhl-Craig, A. (1971 & 1982). *Power in the helping professions.* Dallas, TX: Spring Books.

Gumport, P. J. (2001). Divided we govern? *Peer Review, 3*(3).

Gumport, P. J. (2006). Graduate education and research: Interdependence and strain. In P. G. Altbach, R. O. Berdahl, & P. J. Gumport (Eds.), *Higher education and the twenty-first century: Social, political, and economic challenges,* Second edition (pp. 425–461). Baltimore: Johns Hopkins University Press.

Gumport, P. J. (2007). *Organizational studies in higher education: Insights for a changing enterprise.,* Presented December 4, 2006, "CSHPE 50th Celebration," Center for the Study of Higher and Postsecondary Education. Ann Arbor, MI: University of Michigan, Revised January 2007.

Gutierrez, G. (1988). *A theology of liberation: History, politics and salvation.* Maryknoll, NY: Orbus Books.

Habermas, J. (1985). *Reason and the rationalization of society. The theory of communicative action* (Vol. 1). Boston: Beacon Press.

Habermas, J. (1987). *Lifeworld and system: A critique of functionalist reasoning* (T. McCarthy, Trans.). *The theory of communicative action* (Vol. 2). Boston: Beacon Press.

Habermas, J. (1990). *Moral consciousness and communicative action.* Cambridge, MA: MIT Press.

Habermas, J. (1991). *The structural transformation of the public sphere: An inquiry into a category of bourgeois society.* Cambridge, MA: MIT Press.

Habermas, J. (1996). *Postmetaphysical thinking: Philosophical essays* (W. M. Hohengarten, Trans.). Cambridge, MA: MIT Press.

Habermas, J. (2003). *Truth and justification.* Edited and translated by B. Fulmer. Cambridge, MA: MIT Press.

Hartle, T. W., Simmons, C. A. M., & Timmons, B. H. (2005). *What every student should know about federal financial aid.* Washington, DC: American Council on Education.

Harvey, D. (2005). *A brief history of neoliberalism.* New York: Oxford University Press.

Hearn, J. C. (2001). Access to postsecondary education: Financing equity in an evolving context. In M. B. Paulsen & J. C. Smart (Eds.), *The finance of higher education: Theory, research, policy, and practice* (pp. 439–460). New York: Agathon Press.

Heft, J. L. (Ed.) (2004). *Beyond violence: Religious sources for social transformation,* Second edition. New York: Fordham University Press.

Heller, D. E. (2004). NCES research on college participation: A critical analysis. In E. P. St. John (Ed.), *Public policy and college access: Investigating the federal and state roles in equalizing postsecondary opportunity.* Readings on Equal Education (Vol. 19, pp. 29–64). New York: AMS Press.

Henry, M., Lingard, B., Rizvi, F., & Taylor, S. (2001). *The OECD, globalization and education policy.* Amsterdam: Pergamon Press.

Hill, O. C. (1995). *Implementing a process of inquiry to improve a dropout prevention program.* Ed. D. Dissertation, University of New Orleans.

Hoeller, S. A. (1989). *Jung and the lost gospels: Insights into the Dead Sea scrolls and the Nag Hammadi library.* Wheaton, IL: Quest.

Hossler, D., Ziskin, M., & Gross, J. (Eds.) (in press). *Enhancing institutional and state initiatives to increase student success: Studies of the Indiana Project on Academic Success.* Readings on Equal Education (Vol. 24). New York: AMS Press.

Huber, E., & Stephens, J. D. (2001). *Development and crisis of the welfare state: Parties and policies in global markets.* Chicago: University of Chicago Press.

Hurtado, S., Saenz, V. B. & Dar, L. (2008). Low-income students of color in higher education and the Gates Millennium Scholars Program. In W. T. Trent & E. P. St. John (Eds.), *Resources, assets, strengths among diverse students: Understanding the contributions of the Gates Millennium Scholars Program.* Readings on Equal Education (Vol. 23, pp. 229–252). New York: AMS Press.

Jung, C. G. (1968). *The archetypes and the collective unconscious,* Second edition. Princeton, NJ: Princeton University Press.

Jung, C. G. (1971). *Psychological types.* (Revision by R. F. C. Hull of the translation by H. G. Baynes.) Princeton, NJ: Princeton University Press.

Jung, C. G. (1984). *Psychology and western religion.* Princeton, NJ: Princeton University Press.

Katz, M. B. (2001). *The irony of early school reform: Educational innovation in mid-nineteenth century Massachusetts.* New York: Teachers College Press.

Kaufmann, W. (1992). *Freud, Adler, and Jung.* (Reprint Edition). New Brunswick, NJ: Transaction Publishers.

Keller, G. (1983). *Academic strategy: The management revolution in American higher education.* Baltimore: Johns Hopkins University Press.

Khadduri, M. (1966). *Islamic law of nations: Shaybani's Siyar.* Baltimore: Johns Hopkins University Press.

Khadduri, M. (1969). *Republican Iraq: A study in Iraqi politics since the revolution of 1958.* London and New York: Oxford University Press.

King, M. L., Jr. (1967). *Where do we go from here: Chaos or community?* New York: Harper & Row.

King, P. M. & Bowman, N. A. (2006). Review of *Beyond the big test: Noncognitive assessment in higher education* by William E. Sedlacek, *Journal of Higher Education 77*(6), 1104–1110.

Kline, K. (2003). *The use of action theories, social justice issues and reflection in a student affairs masters' course.* PhD Dissertation, Indiana University.

Kline, K. (2007). Professional development in student affairs: From learning about diversity to building just communities. In E. P. St. John (Ed.), *Confronting educational inequality: Reframing, building understanding, and making change.* Readings on Equal Education (Vol. 22, pp. 314–348). New York: AMS Press.

Knott, K. (1998). *Hinduism: A very short introduction.* Oxford: Oxford University Press.

Kohlberg, L. (1981). *The philosophy of moral development: Moral stages and the idea of justice.* San Francisco: HarperCollins.

Kohlberg, L. (1984). *The psychology of moral development: The nature and validity of moral stages.* San Francisco: Harper & Row.

Lasagna, L. (1964). *Hippocratic Oath—Modern Version.* (Retrieved December 7, 2007.) http://www.pbs.org/wgbh/nova/doctors/oath_modern.html.

Lee, J. B. (2004). Access revisited: A preliminary reanalysis of NELS. In E. P. St. John (Ed.), *Public policy and college access: Investigating the federal and state roles in equalizing postsecondary opportunity.* Readings on Equal Education (Vol. 19, pp. 87–96). New York: AMS Press.

Leslie, L. L., & Brinkman, P. T. (1988). *The economic value of higher education.* New York: Macmillan.

Levinson, D. J. (1978). *The seasons of a man's life.* New York: Knopf.

Lewin, K. (1952). *Field theory in social science.* London: Tavistock Publications.

Macey, D. (2000). *The Penguin dictionary of critical theory.* New York: Penguin.

Manski, C. F., & Wise, D. A. (1983). *College choice in America.* Cambridge, MA: Harvard University Press.

Marsden, G. M. (1994). *The soul of the American university: From Protestant establishment to established nonbelief.* New York: Oxford University Press.

Marx, K., & Engels, F. (1848 and 2002). *The communist manifesto.* London: Penguin Classics.

McDonough, P. M. (1997). *Choosing colleges: How social class and schools structure opportunity.* Albany, NY: SUNY Press.

McClellan, S. (2008). *What happened: Inside the Bush White House and Washington's culture of deception.* New York: Public Affairs.

McLendon, M. K., Heller, D. E., & Young, S. P. (2005). State postsecondary policy innovation: Politics, competition, and the interstate migration of policy ideas. *Journal of Higher Education, 76*(4), 363–400.

Meadows, D. H., Meadows, D. L., Radners, J., & Beherns. W. W. (1972). *Limits to growth.* New York: Universe Books.

Meadows, D. H., Randers, J., & Meadows, D. L. (2004). *The limits of growth: The 30-year update.* White River Junction, VT: Chelsea Green Publishing.

Mirón, L. F., & St. John, E. P. (2003). Implications of the new global context for urban reform. In L. F. Mirón & E. P. St. John (Eds.), *Reinterpreting urban school reform: Have urban schools failed, or has the reform movement failed urban schools?* (pp. 299–326). Albany, NY: SUNY Press.

Moore, R. (Producer, Director). (2007). *Sicko.* [Film]. United States: The Weinstein Company.

Musoba, G. D. (2006). Using evaluation to close the inquiry loop. In E. P. St. John & M. Wilkerson (Eds.), *Reframing persistence research to support academic success. New Directions for Institutional Research.* (Vol. 130, pp. 77–94) San Francisco: Jossey-Bass.

National Center for Education Statistics (1997). *The condition of education 1997.* NCES 97-388. Washington, DC: National Center for Education Statistics.

National Center for Education Statistics (2001). *Digest of education statistics 2000.* NCES 2001-34. By T. D. Snyder. Production Manager C. M. Hoffman. Program Analyst C. M. Geddes. Washington, DC: National Center for Education Statistics.

National Commission on the Financing of Postsecondary Education (1973). *Financing postsecondary education in the United States.* Washington, DC: Government Printing Office.

Newton, J. (2006). *Justice for all: Earl Warren and the nation he made.* New York: Riverhead Books.

Noll, R. (1994). *The Jung cult: Origins of a charismatic movement.* Princeton, NJ: Princeton University Press.

Nussbaum, M. C. (1999). *Sex and social justice.* Oxford: Oxford University Press.

Nussbaum, M. C. (2000). *Women and human development: The capabilities approach.* New York: Cambridge University Press.

Nussbaum, M. C. (2001). *Upheavels of thought.* Cambridge: Cambridge University Press.

Nussbaum, M. C. (2004). *Hiding from humanity: Disgust, shame, and the law.* Princeton, NJ: Princeton University Press.

Orfield, G., & Eaton, S. E. (1997). *Dismantling desegregation: The quiet reversal of Brown v. Board of Education.* New York: Free Press.

Osman, G. (2006). Identity and community in a new generation: The Muslim community in the early seventh century and today. In J. L. Heft (Ed.), *Passing on the faith: The transforming tradtions for the next generation of Jews, Christians, and Muslims* (pp. 187–203). New York: Fordham University Press.

Ouspensky, P. D. (1971). *The fourth way.* New York: Random House.

Pagels, E. (1981). *The gnostic gospels.* New York: Vintage.

Parsons, T. (1960). *Structure and process in modern societies.* New York: Free Press.

Patton, L. D., Morelon, C., Whitehead, D. M., & Hossler, D. (2006). Campus-based retention initiatives: Does the emperor have clothes? In E. P. St. John & M. Wilkerson (Eds.), *Reframing persistence research to support academic success. New Directions for Institutional Research* (Vol. 130, pp. 9–24). San Francisco: Jossey-Bass.

Pascarella, E. T., & Terenzini, P. T. (1991). *How college affects students: Vol. 1. Findings and insights from twenty years of research.* San Francisco: Jossey-Bass.

Pascarella, E. T., & Terenzini, P. T. (2005). *How college affects students: A third decade of research* (Vol. 2). San Francisco: Jossey-Bass.

Pasque, P. A. (2007). Seeing more of the educational inequalities around us: Visions toward strengthening relationships between higher education and society. In E. P. St. John (Ed.), *Confronting educational inequality: Reframing, building understanding, and making change. Readings on Equal Education* (Vol. 22, pp. 37–84). New York: AMS Press.

Pathways to College Network. (2004). *A shared agenda: A leadership challenge to improve college access and success.* (Retrieved November 14, 2008.) www.pathwaystocollege.net/agenda/index.html.

Paul, R., & Thompson, R. C. (Producers), & Bridges, J. (Director). (1973). *The paper chase.* United States: 20th Century Fox.

Pelavin, S. H., & Kane, M. B. (1988). *Minority participation in higher education.* Prepared for the U.S. Department of Education, Office of Planning, Budget and Evaluation. Washington, DC: Pelavin Associates.

Pelavin, S. H., & Kane, M. B. (1990). *Changing the odds: Factors increasing access to college.* New York: College Board.

Perna, L. W., Cooper, M. A., Li, C. (2007). Improving educational opportunities for college students who work. In E. P. St. John (Ed.), *Confronting educational inequality: Reframing, building understandings, and making change. Readings on Equal Education* (Vol. 22, pp. 11–12). New York: AMS Press.

Piaget, J. (1971). *Biology and knowledge: An essay on the relations between organic regulations and cognitive processes.* Chicago: University of Chicago Press.

Platt, G. M., & Parsons, T. (1970). Decision-making in the academic system: Influence and power exchange. In C. E. Kruytbosch & S. L. Messinger (Eds.), *The state of the university: Authority and change* (pp. 133–180). Beverly Hills: Sage Publications.

Plessy v. Ferguson, 163 U.S. 537 (1896).

Porter, M. (1980). *Competitive strategy.* New York: Free Press.

Powers, J. B. (2006). Patents and royalties. In D. Priest & E. P. St. John (Eds.), *Privatization and public universities* (pp. 129–150). Bloomington: Indiana University Press.

Priest, D. M., Becker, W. E., Hossler, D., & St. John, E. P. (Eds.) (2002). *Incentive-based budgeting systems in public universities.* Northhampton, MA: Edward Elgar.

Priest, D., & St. John, E. P. (Eds.) (2006). *Privatization and public universities.* Bloomington: Indiana University Press.

Rawls, J. (1971). *A theory of justice.* Cambridge, MA: Belknap Press of Harvard University Press.

Rawls, J. (1999). *A theory of justice* (Revised Edition). Cambridge, MA: Harvard University Press.

Rawls, J. (2001). *Justice as fairness: A restatement.* Cambridge, MA: Belknap Press of Harvard University Press.

Reese, W. J. (2005). *America's public schools: From the common school to no child left behind.* Baltimore: Johns Hopkins University Press.

Revell, P. (2006) Parishioners shocked by allegations of Priest misconduct. *Midford Daily News.* (November 29) http://www.bishop-accountability.org/news2006/11_12/2006_11_29_Reuell_ParishionersShocked.htm.

Reynolds, P. J., & Hossler, D. (in press). The IPAS paper trail: An analysis of documents and reflections of the IPAS staff. In D. Hossler, M. Ziskin, & J. Gross (Eds.), *Enhancing institutional and state initiatives to increase student success: Studies of the Indiana Project on Academic Success.* Readings on Equal Education (Vol. 24). New York: AMS Press.

Rhoades, G. (1998). *Managed professionals: Unionized faculty and restructuring academic labor.* Albany, NY: SUNY Press.

Riggs, R. O., Murrell, P. H., & Cutting, J C. (1993). *Sexual harassment in higher education from conflict to community.* ASHE-ERIC Monograph No. 2. Washington, DC: George Washington University.

Rosovsky, H. (1990). *The university: An owner's manual.* New York: Norton.

Ruthven, M. (2007). *Fundamentalism: A very short introduction.* New York: Oxford University Press.

Rutter, P. (1991). *Sex in the forbidden zone.* New York: Facell Crest.

Salk, J. (1983). *Anatomy of reality: Merging intuition and reason.* New York: Columbia University Press.

Schön, D. A. (1983). *The reflective practitioner: How professionals think in action.* New York: Basic Books.

Schön, D. A. (1987). *Educating the reflective practitioner: Toward a new design for teaching and learning in the professions.* San Francisco: Jossey-Bass.

Sen, A. (1999). *Development as freedom.* New York: Anchor Press.

Sharman, H. B. (1917). *Records in the life of Jesus.* New York: Duran.

Sheehy, G. (1977). *Passages: Predictable crises of adult life.* New York: Bantam.

Sedlacek, W. E. (2004). *Beyond the big test: Noncognitive assessment in higher education.* San Francisco: Jossey-Bass.

Sharman, H. B. (1917). *Records in the life of Jesus.* New York: Duran.

Sheehy, G. (1977). *Passages: Predictable crises of adult life.* New York: Bantam.

Siddle Walker, V. (1996). *Their highest potential: An African American school community in the segregated south.* Chapel Hill: The University of North Carolina Press.

Siddle Walker, V., & Snarey, J. (Eds.) (2004). *Race-ing moral formation: African American perspectives on care and justice.* New York: Teachers College Press.

Slaughter, S. E., & Leslie, L. L. (1997). *Academic capitalism: Politics, policies, and the entrepreneurial university.* Baltimore: Johns Hopkins University Press.

Slaughter, S. E., & Rhoades, G. (2004). *Academic capitalism and the new economy: Markets, state, and higher education.* Baltimore: Johns Hopkins University Press.

Small, J. L. (2006). *Faith development theory for non-Christians: New conceptualizations.* Unpublished manuscript.

Small, J. L. (2007). Do you buy into the whole idea of God, the father: How college students talk about spiritual transformation. *Journal of Religion and Education, 34*(1), 1–27.

Smart, J. C. (1985). Holland environments as reinforcement systems. *Research in Higher Education, 23,* 279–292.

Smart, J. C. (1988). College influences on graduates' income levels. *Research in Higher Education, 29,* 41–59.

Smart, J. C. (1989). Life history influences on Holland vocational type development. *Journal of Vocational Behavior, 34,* 69–87.

Smart, J. C., Feldman, K. A., & Ethington, C. A. (2000). *Academic disciples: Holland's theory and the study of college students and faculty.* Nashville, TN: Vanderbilt University Press.

Smart, J. C., & St. John, E. P. (1996). Organizational culture and effectiveness in higher education: A test of the "culture type" and "strong culture" hypotheses. *Educational Evaluation and Policy Analysis, 18*(3): 219–242.

Snarey, J. R., & Siddle Walker, V. (2004). Conclusions. In V. Siddle Walker & J. Snarey. (Eds.), *Race-ing moral formation: African American perspectives on care and justice* (pp. 130–146). New York: Teachers College Press.

Spong, J. S. (1997). *Liberating the Gospels: Reading the Bible with Jewish Eyes.* New York: HarperCollins.

Stage, F. K. (2007). *Using quantitative data to answer critical questions,* New Directions for Institutional Research. San Francisco: Jossey-Bass.

Stern, C. S. (2003, March 10). Colleges must be careful not to write bad policies on sexual harassment. *Chronicle of Higher Education,* Section 2, pp. B–B2.

Stiglitz, J. E. (2002). *Globalization and its discontents.* New York: W. W. Norton.

St. John, E. P. (1989). The influence of student aid on persistence. *Journal of Student Financial Aid, 19*(3), 52–68.

St. John. E. P. (1991). The impact of student financial aid: A review of recent research. *Journal of Student Financial Aid, 21*(1), 18–32.

St. John, E. P. (1994). *Prices, productivity, and investment.* ASHE/ERIC Monograph No. 3. San Francisco: Jossey-Bass.

St. John, E. P. (1997). Desegregation at a crossroads: Critical reflections on possible new directions. In *Special issue: Rethinking college desegregation,* D. Hossler & E. P. St. John (Issue Eds.), *Journal for a Just and Caring Education, 3*(1), 127–134.

St. John, E. P. (2002). Workforce development. In J. Forest & K. Kinser (Eds.), *Higher education in the United States: An encyclopedia,* Vol. 2 (pp. 715–717). Santa Barbara, CA: ABC-CLIO.

St. John, E. P. (2003). *Refinancing the college dream: Access, equal opportunity, and justice for taxpayers*. Baltimore: Johns Hopkins University Press.

St. John, E. P. (Ed.). (2004). *Improving access and college success for diverse students: Studies of the Gates Millennium Scholars Program*. Readings on Equal Education (Vol. 20). New York: AMS Press.

St. John, E. P. (2006). *Education and the public interest: School reform, public finance, and access to higher education*. Dordrecht, Netherlands: Springer.

St. John, E. P. (2007). Finding social justice in education policy: The critical-empirical approach, with a case study of college access. In F. K. Stage (Ed.), *Using quantitative data to answer critical questions*. New Directions in Institutional Research (Vol. 133, pp. 67–80). San Francisco: Jossey-Bass.

St. John, E. P. (2008). Financial inequality and academic success: Rethinking the foundations of research on college students. In W. Trent & E. P. St. John, *Resources, assets, and strengths among successful diverse students: Understanding the contributions of the Gates Millennium Scholars Program*. Readings on Equal Education (Vol. 23). New York: AMS Press.

St. John, E. P. (2009). *Action, reflection and social justice: Integrating moral reasoning into professional education*. Cresskill, NJ: Hampton Press.

St. John, E. P., Affolter-Caine, B., & Chung, A. S. (2006) *The impact of student financial aid on enrollment at a private university's school of law*. Prepared for the NAACP Legal Defense Fund, New York.

St. John, E. P., & Byce, C. (1982). The changing federal role in student financial aid. In M. Kramer (Ed.), *Meeting student aid needs in a period of retrenchment* (pp. 21–40). New Directions for Higher Education, No. 40. San Francisco: Jossey-Bass.

St. John, E. P., & Cadray, J. P. (2004). Justice and care in post-desegregation urban schools: Rethinking the role of teacher education programs. In V. Siddle Walker & J. R. Snarey (Eds.), *Race-ing moral formation: African American perspectives on care and justice* (pp. 93–110). New York: Teachers College Press.

St. John, E. P., Carter, D. F., Chung, C. G., & Musoba, G. D. (2006). Diversity and persistence in Indiana higher education: The impact of preparation, major choices, and student aid. In E. P. St. John (Ed.), *Public policy and educational opportunity: School reforms, postsecondary encouragement, and state policies on higher education*. Readings on Equal Education (Vol. 21, pp. 341–386). New York: AMS Press.

St. John, E. P., Fisher, A. S., Lee, M., Daun-Barnett, N., & Williams, K. (2008). *Educational opportunity in Indiana: Studies of the Twenty-first Century Scholars Program using state student unit Record data systems*. Report prepared for the Lumina Foundation (to be available on the Internet).

St. John, E. P., McKinney, J., & Tuttle, T. (2006). Using action inquiry to address critical challenges. In E. P. St. John & M. Wilkerson (Eds.), *Reframing persistence research to support academic success*. New Directions for Institutional Research (Vol. 130, pp. 63–76). San Francisco: Jossey-Bass.

St. John, E. P., Musoba, G. D., & Chung, C. G. (2004). Academic access: The impact of state education policies. In E. P. St. John (Ed.), *Public policy and college access: Investigating the federal and state roles in equalizing postsecondary opportunity*. Readings on Equal Education (Vol. 19, pp. 131–151). New York: AMS Press.

St. John, E. P., & Noell, J. (1989). The effects of student financial aid on access to higher education: An analysis of progress with special consideration of minority enrollments. *Review of Educational Research, 64*, 531–555.

St. John, E. P., & Parsons, M. D. (Eds.). (2004). *Public funding of higher education: Changing contexts and new rationales*. Baltimore: Johns Hopkins University Press.

St. John, E. P., & Wilkerson, M. (2006). Editors' Notes. In E. P. St. John & M. Wilkerson (Eds.), *Reframing persistence research to support academic success*. New Directions for Institutional Research (Vol. 130, pp. 1–8). San Francisco: Jossey-Bass.

Smith, A. (1759 & 2000). *The theory of moral sentiments*. Amherst, NY: Prometheus Books.

Tabb, W. K. (2002). *Unequal partners: A primer on globalization*. New York: The New Press.

Taylor, C. (2007). *A secular age*. Boston: Harvard University Press.

Thelin, J. R. (2004). *A history of American higher education*. Baltimore: Johns Hopkins University Press.

Tierney, W. G. (2006). Trust and the public good. *Counterpoints: Studies in the Postmodern Theory of Education*, Vol. 308. New York, NY: Peter Lang Publishing.

Tierney, W. G., & Venegas, K. (2007). The cultural ecology of financial aid decision making. In E. P. St. John (Ed.), *Confronting educational inequality: Reframing, building understanding, and making change*. Readings on Equal Education (Vol. 22, pp. 1–36). New York: AMS Press.

Tinto, V. (1987). *Leaving college: Rethinking the causes and cures of student attrition* (First edition). Chicago: University of Chicago Press.

Trent, W. T., & St. John, E. P. (Eds.) (2008). *Resources, assets, and strengths among successful diverse students: Understanding the contributions of the Gates Millennium Scholars Program*. Readings on Equal Education (Vol. 23). New York: AMS Press.

U.S. Congress (1978). *Middle Income Student Assistance Act* (H.R. 15 and S. 2539).

U.S. Congress (1981). *Education Consolidation and Improvement Act* 20 U.S.C. 2711. (Pub. L. 97–35).

U.S. Congress (2001). *No Child Left Behind Act of 2001* (Public Law 107–110).

U.S. Department of Education (1983). *A Nation at Risk.* Washington, DC: U.S. Department of Education.

U.S. Department of Education (2006) *A Test of Leadership: Changing the Future of U.S. Higher Education.* Washington, DC: U.S. Department of Education.

Unknown. *Hippocratic Oath.* (Retrieved November 11, 2007.) http://en.wikipedia.org/wiki/Hippocratic_Oath.

Walzer, M. (1983). *Spheres of justice: A defense of pluralism and equality.* New York: Basic Books.

Wangyal, G. (1995). *The door of liberation: Essential teachings of the Thebetan Buddist tradition* (G. Wangyal, Trans.). Boston: Wisdom Publications.

Weber, M. (1948). *The theory of social and economic organization* (A. M. Henderson & T. Parsons, Trans.). New York: Oxford University Press.

Wells, A. S., & Serna, I. (2007). The politics of culture: Understanding local political resistance to detracking in racially mixed schools. In C. D. da Silva, J. P. Huguley, Z. Kakli, & R. Rao (Eds.), *The opportunity gap: Achievement and inequality in education. Harvard Educational Review* (Reprint Series No. 43, pp. 133–158). Cambridge, MA: Harvard Education Press.

INDEX